Days of the Lord

THE LITURGICAL YEAR

Days of the Lord

THE LITURGICAL YEAR

Volume 5.

Ordinary Time, Year B

THE LITURGICAL PRESS
Collegeville, Minnesota

The English translation of Volume 5 of this series is by Madeleine Beaumont. The original French text of *Days of the Lord (Jours du Seigneur*, Brepols: Publications de Saint-André, 1988) was written by the authors of the *Missel dominical de l'assemblée* and *Missel de l'assemblée pour la semaine* under the direction of Robert Gantoy and Romain Swaeles, Benedictines of Saint-André de Clerlande.

ACKNOWLEDGMENTS
Excerpts from the English translation of *Lectionary for Mass* © 1969, International Committee on English in the Liturgy, Inc. (ICEL); excerpts from the English translation of *The Roman Missal* © 1973, ICEL; excerpts from the English translation of *The Liturgy of the Hours* © 1974, ICEL. All rights reserved.

Scripture selections are taken from the New American Bible *Lectionary for Mass*, © 1970 by the Confraternity of Christian Doctrine, Washington, D.C., and are used by license of said copyright owner. All rights reserved. No part of the New American Bible *Lectionary for Mass* may be reproduced in any form without written permission from the copyright owner.

Scripture quotations are from the *New American Bible with Revised New Testament*, © 1986 Confraternity of Christian Doctrine. The text of the Old Testament in *The New American Bible with Revised New Testament* was published in *The New American Bible*, © 1970 Confraternity of Christian Doctrine. Other quotations, as indicated, are from *The Jerusalem Bible*, © 1966 by Darton, Longman & Todd, Ltd. and Doubleday & Company, Inc.

Cover design by Monica Bokinskie.

LIBRARY OF CONGRESS CATALOGING-IN-PUBLICATION DATA

(Revised for vol. 5)

Days of the Lord.

Translation of: Jours du Seigneur.
Includes bibliographical references.
Contents: v. 1. Season of Advent. Season of Christmas/Epiphany —   — v. 4. Ordinary time, Year A — v. 5. Ordinary time, Year B — [etc.]
1. Church year. 2. Catholic Church—Liturgy.
BX1970.J67313 1990   263'.9   90-22253
ISBN 0-8146-1899-5 (v. 1)   ISBN 0-8146-1902-9 (v. 4)
ISBN 0-8146-1900-2 (v. 2)   ISBN 0-8146-1903-7 (v. 5)
ISBN 0-8146-1901-0 (v. 3)   ISBN 0-8146-1904-5 (v. 6)

Contents

Ordinary Time Year B

Each year of the three-year liturgical cycle is dedicated to one of the Synoptic Gospels: It is Mark in Year B.[1] Most of the Gospel is read from the beginning of Jesus' ministry (Mark 1:14-20) through the discourse on the coming of the Son of Man (Mark 13:24-32).[2]

However, Mark's Gospel is noticeably shorter than Matthew's or Luke's.[3] As a consequence, it would have been difficult to find enough material for all the Sundays unless one used texts rigorously parallel to those of the preceding year (Year A, Matthew). This is why the reading of Mark is interrupted at the multiplication of the loaves, Jesus' walking on the water, and the cures wrought in Gennesaret (Mark 6:35-56). For five Sundays—from the Seventeenth to the Twenty-first—we read the Discourse on the Bread of Life from John's Gospel (John 6:1-69). We resume the reading of Mark on the Twenty-second Sunday (Mark 7:1-8, 14-15, 21-23).

The first lessons, chosen in correlation with the Gospel readings, are taken from nineteen of the forty-eight books of the Old Testament: Genesis, Exodus, Leviticus, Numbers, Deuteronomy, Joshua, 1 Samuel, 1 Kings, 2 Kings, Job, Proverbs, Wisdom, Isaiah, Jeremiah, Ezekiel, Daniel, Hosea, Amos, Jonah. The second lessons are taken from three of Paul's letters—1 Corinthians, Second to Sixth Sunday; 2 Corinthians, Seventh to Fourteenth Sunday; Ephesians, Fifteenth to Twenty-first Sunday—and from the Letter to the Hebrews, Twenty-seventh to Thirty-third Sunday.

Every year on the Second Sunday in Ordinary Time we read a passage from John's Gospel. In Year B, it is the call of the first disciples—John, Andrew, and his brother Simon Peter (John 1:35-42).[4]

Such is the structure of Ordinary Time, Year B. As we go along, we shall see that it is driven by a forceful dynamism, owing to Mark's vigorous style and his manner of organizing his subject matter. He shows Jesus always on the go, unceasingly moving elsewhere, farther, and urging his disciples to follow him without ever stopping and getting settled. There

1

is not the slightest lull in the drama that rapidly unfolds.[5] Mark holds his readers breathless, not by suspenseful narrative (for the issue of the confrontation between Jesus and those who from the outset plot against him has been known all along: there is not the slightest surprise in the denouement), but by continually prodding his readers to make up their minds. He speaks, and in fact his style is that of conversation, as preachers who vehemently challenge their hearers: "This is no longer the time to remain neutral, to shilly-shally. You must choose sides—for or against Jesus. He is not shut up in his tomb. Throw your lot with him, the Living One, the Son of God."

Furthermore, Ordinary Time, Year B, offers an opportunity not for rest but for meditation, by having us read, from the Seventeenth through the Twenty-first Sunday, the Discourse on the Bread of Life.[6] By then, the time of year is July-August,[7] vacation time for many. The liturgy furnishes the opportunity to join the Lord in the synagogue at Capernaum in order to renew and deepen, in faith, our understanding of the mystery of the Eucharist, in which Christ gives his body and blood as food for eternal life.

Maybe more than other Ordinary times, that of Year B appears as a journey of initiation to be undertaken anew every third year. The option for Christ must indeed be repeatedly ratified, because it is counteracted by unceasing contradictions outside and inside ourselves.

Practical Plan
of the Gospel of Mark

Contrary to the custom that prevailed later, the evangelists did not give us the plan of their exposition of Jesus' life, words, and actions,[1] whether by a table of contents or an introduction. An attentive reading of their writings, however, reveals that their work is much more elaborate than at first appears, albeit according to principles very different from ours. We are used to divisions into chapters, setting forth the facts, their concatenation, their consequences, in strictly chronological and geographical order, so that they can be presented in clear charts. When we treat of doctrinal matters, we proceed in an analytical manner, successively dealing with each particular point before eventually attempting a synthesis. Chronological and geographical landmarks are present in the Gospels.[2] Luke, for instance, places his Gospel in a significant geographical framework;[3] Matthew, for his part, organizes his in large segments or units, with alternating narratives and discourses.[4] In spite of what is sometimes said, Mark's Gospel is subtly and skillfully composed. When we begin reading it, we are overtaken by its dynamism and find it difficult to set the book down before finishing it. If we ask ourselves why we feel this way, we realize that this Gospel is built as a drama that culminates in Jesus' death and the discovery of the empty tomb (Mark 16:8). This abrupt conclusion is gripping. It leaves the readers alone and faced with the mystery and their decision to believe or not to believe[5] and invites us to reread the Gospel with closer attention to the great drama presented according to subtle but rigorously defined principles of rhetorical composition.[6] On the basis of these remarks, we may establish a practical plan of Mark's Gospel. No doubt, it contains a part of conjecture and remains open to discussion since it is based on hindsight and relies upon internal criteria.[7] But it is based upon modern exegetes' work.[8] It has the advantage of emphasizing the internal dynamism of a narrative manifestly structured to urge its readers to take sides in the action Mark recounts. He wrote it to incite them to recognize, along with the centurion who witnessed Jesus' death, that "Truly this man was the Son of God" (Mark 15:39) and to receive the good news with joy and faith before the empty tomb: "Do not be amazed! You seek Jesus of Nazareth, the crucified. He has been raised; he is not here" (Mark 16:6).

Prologue: "The beginning of the gospel of Jesus Christ [the Son of God]" announced by John the Baptist, baptized in the Jordan, tempted in the desert.   Mark 1:13

1. Signs of the Impending Drama   Mark 1:14–6:13

    Statement of Jesus' preaching   1:14-15
    Call of the first four disciples   1:16-20

    A. First confrontations   Mark 1:21–3:6

    Inaugural day in Capernaum   1:21-39
    Transitional account: cure of a leper   1:40-45
    Five controversies with scribes   2:1–3:6
    Jesus and the crowds   3:7-12
    Call and mission of the Twelve   3:13-19

    B. First reactions to Jesus' behavior,
       teaching, and miracles   Mark 3:20–6:13

    Incomprehension of Jesus' family and calumnies by
       certain scribes   3:20-35
    Discourse in parables   4:1-34
    Transitional account: the tempest calmed   4:35-41
    Three accounts of miracles   5:1-43
    Who is Jesus of Nazareth?   6:1-6
    The Twelve sent on mission   6:7-13

2. At the Heart of the Drama   Mark 6:14–10:52

    The question of Jesus' identity   Mark 6:14-16
    Transitional account: death of John the Baptist   6:17-29
    "Section of the breads"   6:30–8:12
    Transitional account: cure of a blind man   8:22-26
    Peter's confession of faith   8:27-30
    First prediction of the passion   8:31-33
    Conditions of discipleship   8:34-38
    Mystery of the Transfiguration   9:1-13
    Transitional account: cure of a possessed boy   9:14-29
    Second prediction of the passion   9:30-32

Teaching on entry into the kingdom   9:33–10:31
Third prediction of the passion   10:32-34
The Son of Man has come to serve and give his
    life for the multitude   10:35-45
Transitional account: cure of a blind man   10:46-52

3.   Denouement of the Drama   Mark 11:1–15:47

   A. Encounter with the city and the Temple   Mark 11:1–12:40

Messianic entry into Jerusalem   11:1-11
Parable of the barren fig tree   11:12-14, 20-25
Merchants expelled from the Temple   11:15-19, 27-33
Parable of the homicidal tenants   12:1-12
Controversy over the tax to Caesar and the
    resurrection of the dead   12:13-27
Jesus' last teachings   12:28-40
Transitional account: the widow's small coins   12:41-44

   B. Discourse on the end times and the coming
     of the Son of Man   Mark 13:1-37

   C. The Passion   Mark 14:1–15:47

Introduction: the plot against Jesus, the anointing
    at Bethany, the betrayal of Judas   14:1-11
The last supper with the disciples   14:12-50
Transitional account: at Gethsemane, flight of the
    naked young man   14:51-52
Trial and sentence   14:53–15:20a
Execution of the sentence   15:20b-41
Transitional account: burial of Jesus   15:42-47

Epilogue: "He has been raised; . . . he is going before you": The good news announced by the angel,
preached by the apostles   Mark 16:1-8
    Appendix: The risen Christ's appearances   16:9-20

The Texts of the Lectionary

Sunday	1st Reading	Psalm	2nd Reading	Gospel
2nd	1 Sam 3:3b-10, 19	40	1 Cor 6:13b-15a, 17-20	John 1:35-42
3rd	Jonah 3:1-5, 10	25	1 Cor 7:29-31	Mark 1:14-20
4th	Deut 18:15-20	95	1 Cor 7:32-35	Mark 1:21-28
5th	Job 7:1-4, 6-7	147	1 Cor 9:16-19, 22-23	Mark 1:29-39
6th	Lev 13:1-2, 45-46	102	1 Cor 10:31–11:1	Mark 1:40-45
7th	Isa 43:18-19, 21-22 24c-25	41	2 Cor 1:18-22	Mark 2:1-12
8th	Hos 2:16, 17b, 21-22	103	2 Cor 3:1b-6	Mark 2:18-22
9th	Deut 5:12-15	81	2 Cor 4:6-11	Mark 2:23–3:6
10th	Gen 3:9-15	130	2 Cor 4:13–5:1	Mark 3:20-35
11th	Ezek 17:22-24	92	2 Cor 5:6-10	Mark 4:26-34
12th	Job 38:1, 8-11	107	2 Cor 5:14-17	Mark 4:35-41
13th	Wis 1:13-15; 2:23-24	30	2 Cor 8:7, 9, 13-15	Mark 5:21-43
14th	Ezek 2:2-5	123	2 Cor 12:7-10	Mark 6:1-6
15th	Amos 7:12-15	85	Eph 1:3-14	Mark 6:7-13
16th	Jer 23:1-6	23	Eph 2:13-18	Mark 6:30-34
17th	2 Kgs 4:42-44	145	Eph 4:1-6	John 6:1-15
18th	Exod 16:2-4, 12-15	78	Eph 4:17, 20-24	John 6:24-35
19th	1 Kgs 19:4-8	34	Eph 4:30–5:2	John 6:41-51
20th	Prov 9:1-6	34	Eph 5:15-20	John 6:51-58
21st	Josh 24:1-2a, 15-17, 18b	34	Eph 5:21-32	John 6:60-69
22nd	Deut 4:1-2, 6-8	15	Jas 1:17-18, 21b-22 27	Mark 7:1-8, 14-15, 21-23
23rd	Isa 35:4-7a	146	Jas 2:1-5	Mark 7:31-37
24th	Isa 50:5-9a	115	Jas 2:14-18	Mark 8:27-35
25th	Wis 2:12, 17-20	54	Jas 3:16–4:3	Mark 9:30-37
26th	Num 11:25-29	19	Jas 5:1-6	Mark 9:38-43, 45, 47-48
27th	Gen 2:18-24	128	Heb 2:9-11	Mark 10:2-16
28th	Wis 7:7-11	90	Heb 4:12-13	Mark 10:17-30
29th	Isa 53:10-11	33	Heb 4:14-16	Mark 10:35-45
30th	Jer 31:7-9	126	Heb 5:1-6	Mark 10:46b-52
31st	Deut 6:2-6	119	Heb 7:23-28	Mark 12:28b-34
32nd	1 Kgs 17:10-16	146	Heb 9:24-28	Mark 12:38-44
33rd	Dan 12:1-3	16	Heb 10:11-14, 18	Mark 13:24-32
34th (Christ the King)	Dan 7:13-14	93	Rev 1:5-8	John 18:33b-37

The Division of Sundays into "Sequences"

Ordinary Time, Year B

This division is determined by the Gospel readings that form the framework of the Liturgy of the Word on each Sunday. It does not pretend to exclude any other division, but it has its foundation in the "plan" of the Gospel of Mark and the selection of texts given in the Lectionary.

2nd and 3rd Sundays

1 Sam 3:3b-10, 19	1 Cor 6:13b-15a, 17-20	John 1:35-42
Jonah 3:1-5, 10	1 Cor 7:29-31	Mark 1:14-20

4th, 5th, and 6th Sundays

Deut 18:15-20	1 Cor 7:32-35	Mark 1:21-28
Job 7:1-4, 6-7	1 Cor 9:16-19, 22-23	Mark 1:29-39
Lev 13:1-2, 45-46	1 Cor 10:31–11:1	Mark 1:40-45

7th, 8th, 9th, and 10th Sundays

Isa 43:18-19, 21-22, 24c-25	2 Cor 1:18-22	Mark 2:1-12
Hos 2:16, 17b, 21-22	2 Cor 3:1b-6	Mark 2:18-22
Deut 5:12-15	2 Cor 4:6-11	Mark 2:23–3:6
Gen 3:9-15	2 Cor 4:13–5:1	Mark 3:20-35

11th and 12th Sundays

Ezek 17:22-24	2 Cor 5:6-10	Mark 4:26-34
Job 38:1, 8-11	2 Cor 5:14-17	Mark 4:35-41

13th and 14th Sundays

Wis 1:13-15; 2:23-24	2 Cor 8:7, 9, 13-15	Mark 5:21-43
Ezek 2:2-5	2 Cor 12:7-10	Mark 6:1-6

15th and 16th Sundays

Amos 7:12-15	Eph 1:3-14	Mark 6:7-13
Jer 23:1-6	Eph 2:13-18	Mark 6:30-34

17th, 18th, 19th, 20th, and 21st Sundays

2 Kgs 4:42-44	Eph 4:1-6	John 6:1-15
Exod 16:2-4, 12-15	Eph 4:17, 20-24	John 6:24-35

---

1 Kgs 19:4-8	Eph 4:30–5:2	John 6:41-51
Prov 9:1-6	Eph 5:15-20	John 6:51-58
Josh 24:1-2a, 15-17, 18b	Eph 5:21-32	John 6:60-69

22nd and 23rd Sundays

| Deut 4:1-2, 6-8 | Jas 1:17-18, 21b-22, 27 | Mark 7:1-8, 14-15, 21-23 |
| Isa 35:4-7a | Jas 2:1-5 | Mark 7:31-37 |

24th, 25th, and 26th Sundays

Isa 50:5-9a	Jas 2:14-18	Mark 8:27-35
Wis 2:12, 17-20	Jas 3:16–4:3	Mark 9:30-37
Num 11:25-29	Jas 5:1-6	Mark 9:38-43, 45, 47-48

27th and 28th Sundays

| Gen 2:18-24 | Heb 2:9-11 | Mark 10:2-16 |
| Wis 7:7-11 | Heb 4:12-13 | Mark 10:17-30 |

29th and 30th Sundays

| Isa 53:10-11 | Heb 4:14-16 | Mark 10:35-45 |
| Jer 31:7-9 | Heb 5:1-6 | Mark 10:46b-52 |

31st and 32nd Sundays

| Deut 6:2-6 | Heb 7:23-28 | Mark 12:28b-34 |
| 1 Kgs 17:10-16 | Heb 9:24-28 | Mark 12:38-44 |

33rd Sunday

| Dan 12:1-3 | Heb 10:11-14, 18 | Mark 13:24-32 |

34th Sunday: Christ, King of the Universe

| Dan 7:13-14 | Rev 1:5-8 | John 18:33b-37 |

In this volume, when we refer to a Sunday without further qualification, we are speaking of a Sunday in Ordinary Time, Year B. When we refer to a Sunday in another part of the liturgical year without specifying Year A or Year C, we also are speaking of Year B.

The Second and Third Sunday in Ordinary Time

Every year, on the Second Sunday in Ordinary Time, the continuous reading of one of the three Synoptic Gospels is introduced by a passage from John. This year, John reminds us of the manner in which two disciples of John the Baptist are led to recognize "the Lamb of God," shown to them by the Precursor.[1] This text is especially appropriate for more than one reason, as we shall see. For Mark, "Jesus Christ [the Son of God]" is the good news (Mark 1:1). Therefore, he briefly mentions John the Baptist's preaching, Jesus' baptism in the waters of the Jordan, and his temptation in the desert (Mark 1:2-13). Indeed, everything begins with these events. But Mark cannot wait to come to Jesus' personal manifestation, when he starts to preach in Galilee and calls his first four disciples; this passage (Mark 1:14-20) is the Gospel of the Third Sunday. Moreover, Mark explicitly notes that the beginning of Jesus' ministry coincides with the Precursor's arrest (Mark 1:14). The first sequence[2] is therefore harmoniously constituted by two Gospels that fit perfectly together.

On each Sunday in Ordinary Time, the first reading is chosen in relation to the Gospel. The account of Samuel's vocation reminds us of the way in which Eli the priest leads his young disciple to enter the service of the God who calls him (1 Sam 3:3b-10, 19). In like manner, John the Baptist prompts Andrew and John to follow the new master whose way he has prepared (Second Sunday). At Jonah's preaching, all the inhabitants of Nineveh, the pagan city "enormously large . . . turn from their evil way" (Jonah 3:1-5, 10). When he begins to preach in Galilee, Jesus proclaims: "This is the time of fulfillment. The kingdom of God is at hand. Repent and believe in the gospel" (Mark 1:14-15). From now on, the message of salvation is addressed to the whole world (Third Sunday).

On the Second Sunday, we begin the reading of Paul's First Letter to the Corinthians,[3] which will continue until the Sixth Sunday. In all these passages Paul treats of important moral questions relating to sexual behavior. He does it in a remarkable way, and his teaching proves to be surprisingly appropriate to our times. On the one hand, Paul, as always, shows that moral conduct is the consequence of the Christian's belong-

9

ing to Christ. On the other hand, the problem is that of the relation between Christian life and the prevailing culture, a singularly important
problem today. Paul has an exemplary attitude. There are ways and doctrines totally irreconcilable to the gospel—for instance, an unrestrained
sexual freedom or, on the contrary, a contempt for the body that holds
as an absolute ideal the renunciation of marriage. A complete break, with
no compromise, is in order. Paul absolutely upholds the demands of
authentic Christian morality. But he no less boldly welcomes anything
which, in his correspondents' culture, proves to be compatible with the
newness of Christianity. In this, as in many other ways, Paul is really
the apostle of the nations.[4] "Without any doubt, the proposed solutions
are stamped by cultural conditions different from our own (see 1 Cor 11:2-
16); but the situation facing Paul has much in common with our own,
and the principles that guide his answers still can enlighten us."[5]

Second Sunday

When the Lord Calls Us

You Have Called Me, Here I Am: Your Servant Is Listening
The first reading tells a beautiful, simple, and moving story recorded in the First Book of Samuel. A young child, dedicated to the service of the sanctuary, is awakened three times by a call. Naturally, he thinks that Eli, the priest who is in charge of the sanctuary, called him. Immediately, the child rises: "Here I am. You called me." No, "I did not call you," the priest answers twice. The child must have had a dream in which he heard a voice; this commonly happens. The third time, Eli understands; it was not an ordinary dream, but one of those in which God speaks: "Go to sleep, and if you are called, reply, 'Speak, LORD, for your servant is listening.' " Samuel does as he is told. The Lord—for it *was* the Lord— "came and revealed his presence, calling out as before, 'Samuel, Samuel!' " And Samuel answers, "Speak, LORD, for your servant is listening." He grows up and becomes one of the most important persons in the Old Testament (1 Sam 3:3b-10, 19).[1]

The simplicity of this affecting story contains a profound religious meaning that the holy-card industry has unfortunately failed to recognize. It has popularized the image of a youngster in a luminous halo who, in the sanctuary shadows, listens, entranced, to the Lord's call.[2] The Bible has not understood and developed the account of Samuel's vocation in this manner. "At that time, Samuel was not familiar with the LORD." Of course, he knew in whose service he had been enlisted; he knew, too, the name of the God who was worshiped in the sanctuary. Eli the priest had taught him (we would say catechized him). But God's word had not been addressed to him personally to reveal his mission to him. Now, that night, God calls, "Samuel, Samuel!" This simple story is, from several viewpoints, an exemplar of the prophetic vocation and, beyond, of every vocation.

At the outset, we always find the initiative of God, who reveals himself and calls the one he has selected, set apart, with a sovereign freedom. This happened to Moses, Gideon, Samson, Amos, Jeremiah, the Virgin Mary, Paul, and many others, known or unknown throughout the ages.[3] Whatever its concrete form, this revelation is felt as a mysterious call perceived in the depths of the heart. It does not necessarily assert itself with an immediate evidence either to the ones called or to those they consult. Eli acts wisely. Surprised by what Samuel, perhaps deceived by an illusion, tells him, he first urges the boy to remain calm: "I did not call you . . . Go back to sleep." When he gets an inkling that this could be something other than an illusion, he humbly gives Samuel the obvious advice, "If you are called, reply, 'Speak, LORD, for your servant is listening.'" The lesson is a permanent one in two ways. All who are called to discern a vocation must first of all react so as not to interfere with the possibility of a divine initiative, but without shirking their responsibility because of a conflict of interest. Without playing God, without unduly trusting their own judgment, they must advise those who seek their guidance to remain totally and peacefully open. If the call truly comes from God, it will be confirmed and clarified. Haste would smack of presumption and would be gravely imprudent. Trustful openness is the proper attitude: "Speak, LORD, for your servant is listening."[4]

Another aspect of the story must hold our attention. When he hears the first call of God, Samuel is still a child. In this, too, the account of his vocation proves to be typical; it reminds us of the preference God has for the little ones, the poor, those whom most people do not see as predestined for great things. In any case, whatever the age of the one chosen, the Lord's call reaches for weak beings whom he entrusts with a task out of proportion to their strength. All those sent by God are aware of this and use their natural inability as an objection. Moses says, "If you please, LORD, I have never been eloquent, neither in the past, nor recently, nor now that you have spoken to your servant; but I am slow of speech and tongue" (Exod 4:10). Jeremiah cries, "Ah, Lord GOD! . . . I know not how to speak; I am too young" (Jer 1:6). Amos explains: "I was no prophet, nor have I belonged to a company of prophets; I was a shepherd and a dresser of sycamores. The LORD took me from following the flock, and said to me, Go, prophesy to my people Israel" (Amos 7:14-15).[5] All other reactions would be suspect. Only persons devoid of any insight or hypocrites would deem themselves up to a divine mission. Every human being remains an "infant," unable to utter a word of God.[6] The Lord knows it, but he gives to the weakest the power of working prodigies:

> But you, Bethlehem-Ephrathah,
>   too small to be among the clans of Judah,

From you shall come forth for me
> one who is to be ruler in Israel.
(Mic 5:1)

"God chose the foolish of the world to shame the wise, and God chose the weak of the world to shame the strong, and God chose the lowly and despised of the world, those who count for nothing, to reduce to nothing those who are something, so that no human being might boast before God" (1 Cor 1:27-29). Those whom he chooses must rely on him with all trust and humility, "Speak, LORD, for your servant is listening." "Behold, I am the handmaid of the Lord. May it be done to me according to your word" (Luke 1:38).

Samuel hears God's call in the sanctuary and in the silence of night. Of course, God's word can resound anywhere and at any hour. He does not limit his presence, his action, and his initiatives to sacred enclosures. But it is always in "peaceful silence" that "the all-powerful word . . . [leaps] down from heaven, from the royal throne."[7] In silence one can be more attentive to God's presence, and no distraction hinders the recollected listening to God's word. To listen: no activity is more important for those who divine something of God's mystery and want to remain open to his call. The place for this encounter is, par excellence, the sanctuary to which one goes to bow before God and pray to him; but the place can also be the desert or the sanctuary of a silent heart.

> When we face God, in our most intimate relations with him, is not a listening heart that better part which the Lord said would not be taken away from us? "Mary sat beside the Lord at his feet listening to him speak" (Luke 10:39). The word which old Eli teaches young Samuel, "Speak, LORD, for your servant is listening" (1 Sam 3:9), expresses a fundamental attitude of the soul which, through faith, knows that God wants to communicate with it. It remains thus, straining its ear to all calls from God, to all stirrings of the Spirit. "Blessed are those who hear the word of God and observe it" (Luke 11:28). But it is only when a deep silence surrounds everything that the Word speaks in us. Give me, O Lord, a listening heart— for the one Word does not multiply words (Matt 6:7). When the Lord, the uncreated Wisdom, takes possession of a soul, he does not cry out or shout (see Isa 42:2), but he is silent in his love (see Zeph 3:17).[8] Those who listen to him dwell in peace (see Prov 1:33). It is enough to listen in one's heart to God's silence until it refines our heart and until God gives it his wisdom (see Prov. 2:6)—Wisdom, a gift that transforms silence into taste and makes us able to taste the uncreated savor, the Spirit.[9]

We would really miss the meaning of the narrative of Samuel's call if we remembered only the affecting image of a child who falls asleep while saying his prayer, "a chubby little child, at once bold and timid, who says 'Good morning' twenty times and twenty times 'Good night' while jumping about . . . a kid who talks with God and gives the answers to his own questions (it is safer that way)."[10] God speaks to Samuel; the child says nothing beyond declaring himself ready to do what the Lord will ask, with a complete trust regarding the result, because God does not reveal this yet (one might be frightened). The future is God's. Those who trust his word can be assured of finding him always at their sides, in good days as well as in times of aridity and loneliness, of weariness and discouragement, when the task or the trial appears insurmountable.[11] In all this, Samuel is a model not only for those God chooses for a particular mission but for all disciples who remember Jesus' word, "Whoever does the will of God is my brother and sister and mother" (Mark 3:34).

> *Here am I, Lord;*
> *I come to do your will.*
>
> I have waited, waited for the LORD,
>   and he stooped toward me and heard my cry.
>
> ———
>
> And he put a new song into my mouth,
>   a hymn to our God.
>
> ———
>
> Sacrifice or oblation you wished not,
>   but ears open to obedience you gave me.
> Holocausts or sin-offerings you sought not;
> then said I, "Behold I come;
>   in the written scroll it is prescribed for me.
> To do your will, O my God, is my delight,
>   and your law is within my heart!"
> I announced your justice in the vast assembly;
>   I did not restrain my lips, as you, O LORD, know.
> (Ps 40:2, 4, 7-10)

Eminent Dignity of the Human Body

Paul's First Letter to the Corinthians is, from several points of view, the most timely of all the epistles. At the time, Corinth was a city newly rebuilt that had recovered its prosperity because of its two ports: Cenchreae on the Aegean Sea and Lechaeum on the Adriatic.[12] It was a cosmopolitan city where all races and religions existed side by side, an intellectual center where the most diverse currents of thought were represented. As always in large ports, the population was made up of a minority of well-to-do people who dwelt in the city permanently or temporarily for business, and a multitude of low-class persons, among whom were a considerable number of slaves.

Corinth was notorious as a city of pleasure and debauchery. Its dissoluteness was probably no worse than that of any other great city of the Greco-Roman world, but it had become proverbial. This reputation likely rested on travelers' stories concerning ill-famed neighborhoods where licentiousness was shamelessly displayed.[13] Nonetheless, the fame of Corinth was certainly well deserved; the prevailing climate was one of extreme license. Consequently, the Christian community Paul had founded there[14] was confronted with the problems and dangers—known all too well today—of their immersion in a singularly unwholesome environment.[15] The young Church of Corinth was not sheltered from the noxious influence of the general mentality and from the bad example of dissolute morals. There were scandals: a case of incest, another of blatant fornication. Paul writes to the community to remind it of Christian ethics. This reminder has lost nothing of its pertinence (1 Cor 6:13b-15a, 17-20).[16]

"The body has its needs. There is no difference between the need for food and the sexual appetite. The way we satisfy those urges has no moral connotation. Besides, my body belongs to me. I am the only judge of its needs and of what can hurt it, because this varies from person to person. And even if my lifestyle harms me, this is my business. I don't owe an account to anyone."

This way of speaking and of preaching sexual freedom is not the monopoly of our time. Paul already denounces its falsehood, "Food for the stomach and the stomach for food" (1 Cor 6:13a). It is absolutely impossible to say the same thing for sexual activity because it is not simply the satisfaction of a physical need like the need for food and drink, but involves the totality of the human being: body and spirit.[17] In no way can we dissociate these two. Human beings express themselves through their bodies; what they say with their bodies involves the whole of them. It is contrary to reality to say that we do not sin with our bodies. This is tantamount to disregarding or mocking the dignity of the body. This is the more curious in a time when a claim is made from other quarters for the rediscovery and rehabilitation of its value.[18]

But Paul does not stop here. Our body does not belong to us: "The body . . . is . . . for the Lord, and the Lord for the body." We are not robbed of our bodies, but from now on they are in league with the Lord.

Like him, through God's power, we shall rise and, with our bodies, we shall live forever. Even at present we are "members of Christ," forming with him "one Spirit." Lust—impurity—is doubly grievous. It is not simply an external and superficial defilement without importance or significance, because it is a sin against the body itself, an integral part of the person. Moreover, it injures the holiness of the body of Christ, of which our bodies are members[19] and to which we belong.[20]

Paul continues: "Do you not know that your body is a temple of the holy Spirit within you, whom you have from God, and that you are not your own? For you have been purchased at a price. Therefore glorify God in your body." The image of the temple to designate the Church in which God dwells among believers is dear to Paul.[21] It must have been a familiar theme of the apostolic catechesis since he writes, "Do you not know . . . ?" But usually believers were called "living stones" of this spiritual edifice (1 Pet 2:4-5), which entailed the demand for holiness of life.[22] Here, Paul says that the Christian's body is the temple of the Holy Spirit. As a consequence, impurity becomes a desecration of the dwelling dedicated to God, for whom the Lord bought it "at a price." Through their bodies, Christians must render to God a worship of praise and thanksgiving. "I urge you therefore, brothers, by the mercies of God, to offer your bodies as a living sacrifice, holy and pleasing to God, your spiritual worship" (Rom 12:1). "Clear out the old yeast, so that you may become a fresh batch of dough, inasmuch as you are unleavened" (1 Cor 5:7).[23]

Paul is really admirable. Faced with a concrete case of moral disorder, he does not react with a moralizing discourse against loose morals and against an intolerable scandal tainting the Christian community. This sort of speech does not hold hearers' attention and often gets on their nerves. Of course, we must unequivocally condemn what is insufferable. But to stop there limits the efficacy of the intervention and does not open perspectives for responsible conduct based on solid convictions and principles that are a constant norm. Starting from a particular fact, Paul recalls the eminent dignity of the human body, its vocation and its destiny, as seen by the light of faith. As a result, what he wrote one day to the Christians in Corinth has lost none of its value. On the contrary, this teaching, which was part and parcel of the ordinary apostolic catechesis,[24] proves to be quite relevant to our day.

> The Creator's hand
> While molding the body,
> Made it such

That it might sing its maker;
But, mute lyre,
It had no voice
Until the final instant
When he breathed into it a soul
Able to utter a song.
The strings now given sound,
The soul gained, in the body,
A language of wisdom.[25]

Witness of the Believers and Encounter with the Lord

The four evangelists attest that Jesus' ministry began quite simply after John the Baptist prepared the way by his preaching. However, the Fourth Gospel insists more than the others on the testimony given to Jesus by a deliberately self-effacing John.[26] Furthermore, the Fourth Gospel is the only one to note that Jesus' first disciples belonged to the entourage of the Baptist, who himself urged them to follow the one he had shown them (John 1:35-42).

As is often the case with John's Gospel, the scene is sparingly drawn: a brief exchange of words, not the slightest indication of the protagonists' feelings. The facts are precisely stated, but their meaning is what holds the attention. We have here, indeed, a decisive event for those who, first, are directly concerned. "It was about four in the afternoon." We remember the day and hour of an encounter that has turned our lives upside down. Such a precise description is like the signature of the persons recording facts in which they themselves are involved. However, it is not for personal reasons[27] that John places this narrative at the beginning of his Gospel. The first public appearance of Jesus—for the baptism is not mentioned—contains an important doctrinal and spiritual teaching about the Lord's person and on the faith of his followers.

"In Bethany across the Jordan where John was baptizing,"[28] he has received a delegation of priests and Levites from Jerusalem, come to question him. "I am not the Messiah," he openly declares. "I baptize with water, but there is one among you whom you do not recognize, the one who is coming after me, whose sandal strap I am not worthy to untie" (John 1:19-28).

"The next day John was there again with two of his disciples, and as he watched Jesus walk by, he said, 'Behold the Lamb of God.'" In the Book of Revelation, this appellation, familiar to Christians, is the proper name of Christ dead and risen, exalted at God's right hand.[29] It has its source in the Christian understanding of prophetic oracles and of the paschal sacrifice that announced the Lord's pasch.[30] Whatever the origin of this title, John intends for us to look at it with eyes enlightened by paschal faith, from the moment of Jesus' first public appearance. We must keep this in mind as we begin to read Mark's Gospel, which ends with the narrative of the discovery of the empty tomb by Mary Magdalene, Mary the mother of James, and Salome.[31]

The readers are thus confronted with the decision to believe or not to believe, a decision to which the whole of Mark's Gospel leads them by progressively unveiling the mystery of Jesus, who is, John the Baptist says from the beginning, the Lamb of God. Through the voice of the Baptist, who is the last of the prophets, it is the Old Testament that designates Jesus as the victim of the new Pasch. "John testified to him and cried out, saying, 'This was he of whom I said, ''The one who is coming after me ranks ahead of me because he existed before me'' ' '' (John 1:15). He behaves as an authentic ''friend of the bridegroom'': ''He stands and listens for him, rejoices greatly at the bridegroom's voice. So this joy of mine has been made complete. He must increase; I must decrease'' (John 3:29-30). John is not content with simply testifying to Jesus; he effaces himself before him, after showing him to two of his disciples in order that they might detach themselves from him and go to the Lamb of God.

> John rises and says again, ''Behold, the Lamb of God.'' Christ keeps silence. Only John speaks. Likewise, the groom says nothing to the bride: he stands there, silent. He is introduced; the bride is led to him and introduces herself; he receives her not from herself but from another's hand. Then, hardly has he received her, he becomes attached to her to the point of forgetting those who have given her to him. Here is what Christ does. Having come to earth to wed the Church, he says nothing; he simply appears. John, the bridegroom's friend, leads her to him and wins over human hearts to him by his words. Once John has given them over, he manages not to have them come back to him who has made known to them their heavenly spouse.[32]

''Jesus turned and saw them following him and said to them, 'What are you looking for?' '' He does not seek information; he gives a call; he arouses desire. ''Where are you?'' God says to Adam, who is hiding from him (Gen 3:9). ''All of human history as described in the Bible may be summarized in one phrase: *God in search of man*. Faith in God is a response to God's question. . . . The way to God is a way of God. Unless God asks the question, all our inquiries are in vain.''[33] ''Morning after morning he opens my ear that I may hear'' (Isa 50:4). ''The soul seeks the Word, but it does so because the Word has been seeking the soul.''[34] ''What are you looking for?'' The two disciples of John the Baptist have correctly understood this question. "Rabbi (which translated means Teacher), where are you staying?'' "Where is your school?'' "Where can we learn to know you?'' In the same way as they had become attached to John the Baptist, the two disciples speak their desire to follow the Lamb of God from now on.

"Come, and you will see.'' Jesus' reply means that he is ready to accept these two men's request. But they must, in total freedom, ratify it, so to speak, by a concrete action, by accompanying Jesus wherever he goes. "So they went and saw where he was staying, and they stayed with him that day.''

"To see,'' "to stay'': These verbs do not have a commonplace meaning in John's vocabulary. They are quasi-technical terms that refer to faith in the Lord and to the relation that it establishes with him. The apostles attest to what they have "seen,'' "heard,'' and even "touched'' of God's Word (1 John 1:1-3) so that we may believe in our turn (John 19:35).[35] The Father and the Son "remain'' in the believer.[36] "Come, and you will see'' is an invitation, addressed to all, to walk toward a personal meeting with the Lord. Although he has a vivid recollection of that day—"It was about four in the afternoon'' the day after the Baptist had said for the first time, "Behold the Lamb of God'' (John 1:39, 29)—John says nothing of the conversation, of Jesus' first teaching. But he uses a series of verbs that provoke reflection: The Baptist "watches'' Jesus, who "sees'' those who "follow'' him and invites them to come and "see'' where he "is staying,'' which they do, deciding further to "stay'' with him. These verbs evoke the acts which lead from one's initial discovery of the Lord to the resolute commitment to follow him in order to be near him and live in intimate association with him.

> This is gospel
> For all.
> Because we who have seen him
> Meet him everyday
> In all other persons.
> Let us witness to this:
> If we know how to contemplate,
> Every human brow is a dove
> with outstretched wings.
> And this happens forever
> On Jordan's bank
> Where John baptizes.[37]

Andrew and the other disciple join Jesus, who is walking by along the Jordan, because they have heard the Baptist's testimony. After spending one day at the Master's house, Andrew shares their discovery with his brother Simon Peter: "We have found the Messiah (which is translated Anointed)."[38] Jesus "looked at him and said, 'You are Simon, the son of John; you will be called Kephas' (which is translated Peter)."[39] It is thus with every call. It is the Lord who first marks us out, he who invites us and chooses us.[40]

> You stand before us
> As one of our own
> Whose names we know.
> But you look at us:
> In the same breath, you name and change
> Our names.
> You make of us stones
> Marking out the sea.
>
> And because it is impossible
> We believe you.[41]

Every encounter between two persons who become attached to one another in a shared movement of faith and trust is a story that is almost impossible to reconstitute in all its details. The question of knowing which one took the first step often remains open to discussion. However, one keeps the memory of privileged moments when for the first time there was mutual recognition, when everyday words suddenly took on a decisive meaning. One also remembers how others made the encounter possible. The encounter with the Lord usually follows a similar pattern, but we clearly realize that nothing would have happened if he had not, unbeknown to us, taken the initiative of calling us and making himself known. The first call is not always clear, as is shown by the story of Samuel's vocation and of many others after him. But it gains clarity when it finds a listening heart, thanks particularly to the mediation and testimony of those who have already met and recognized the Lord. They help us to advance, to progress toward him who is at the core of faith, and to follow him. Every believer has a responsibility toward others. Faith is not a treasure to be jealously guarded for ourselves; on the contrary, it grows in the measure in which it is shared, the measure in which we say with thanksgiving, not only by our words but by our lives, "Come and see; Jesus is Lord."

Where then is your dwelling,
Lamb of God who invites us?
Has the tenth hour come at last
for the disciple in search of you?
For no one knows the day or the hour
when you will come and say to us:
  Come and see!

The joy of encountering you
is the light that transfigures;
is it bright in the heart of the world
since your luminous Pasch?
Reveal yourself stronger than the darkness,
you of whom the Spirit whispers:
  Jesus is Lord!

Filled with your presence,
God who dwells in our dawns,
we announce the burning joy
to everyone alive looking for you.
Only you can say whence comes
your Apostles' cry:
  Blessed are those who believe![42]

Third Sunday

Everything Begins with the Good News

God's Forgiveness Always Offered

The Book of Jonah, one of the shortest in the Bible,[1] appears only once in the Sunday Lectionary.[2] Although placed with the prophetic books, it is clearly distinct from them, for it contains no oracle. It is a story, written with gusto and with a somewhat grating humor, which transmits an authentically biblical teaching of permanent value[3] in the playful manner of a popular account. The excerpt for this Sunday gives us the essentials (Jonah 3:1-5, 10).

"Set out for the great city of Nineveh,[4] and announce to it the message that I will tell you." This is the second time Jonah receives this order (Jonah 1:1). He cannot evade it any longer. His fantastic adventure is too recent for him to dream of attempting a new flight (Jonah 1:1–2:11). His feelings remain the same; but since there is no choice, he rises, sets out for Nineveh, and begins to cross the city proclaiming, "Forty days more and Nineveh shall be destroyed." As soon as they hear this threat, the inhabitants realize their sinfulness, and "all of them, great and small," do penance and ask God for forgiveness. Seeing their repentance, God renounces punishing them as he has threatened.

As it is told, the story of the people of Nineveh illustrates in its own way a teaching that runs through the entire Bible and is worth recalling at any time.[5] God does not want the death or the misery of sinners but that they be converted and live. The announcement of the punishment reveals the gravity of sin. It aims at arousing consciousness of the tragedy of obstinacy in evil. It is an expression of the divine mercy that does not resign itself to letting the sinners go blindly to their doom. God is always ready to intervene in order to stop the process that has begun. To repent of the evil he had planned,[6] to change his mind, is not, on God's part, to lose face but on the contrary to reveal his true nature and his power to master his righteous anger.

> Precious in the eyes of the LORD
> is the death of his faithful ones.
> (Ps 116:15)[7]

The conversion of one single sinner who renounces evil, the return home of a child gone astray, fill him with joy (Luke 15:3-32). He is "a gracious and merciful God, slow to anger, rich in clemency, loathe to punish" (Jonah 4:2). As a consequence, to be converted, to renounce one's bad conduct, is not to lose face either, but on the contrary to find again, through penance and God's grace, one's true face, one's status as son or daughter in the father's house (Luke 15:22-24).

The conversion of the inhabitants of Nineveh is exemplary because it is radical and general.[8] It is the more admirable as it involves pagans who listen to a stranger's words—a lesson for us. Recalling this example, Jesus indeed said one day, "At the judgment the men of Nineveh will arise with this generation and condemn it, because at the preaching of Jonah they repented, and there is something greater than Jonah here" (Luke 11:32).

The promptness of the conversion of the inhabitants of Nineveh ought to fill us with a salutary confusion, inciting us to resolutely turn to God without wasting one instant.

> Late have I loved Thee, O Beauty so ancient and so new; late have I loved Thee! For behold Thou wert within me, and I outside, and I sought Thee outside and in my unloveliness fell upon those lovely things that Thou hast made. Thou wert with me and I was not with Thee. I was kept from Thee by those things, yet had they not been in Thee, they would not have been at all. Thou didst call and cry to me and break open my deafness: and Thou didst send forth Thy beams and shine upon me and chase away my blindness: Thou didst breathe fragrance upon me, and I drew in my breath and do now pant for Thee: I tasted Thee, and now hunger and thirst for Thee: Thou didst touch me, and I have burned for Thy peace.[9]

Finally, this story shows in a concrete way that God is concerned with all human beings and offers his pardon to all: to the people of today's Nineveh as to those of yesterday's. Some might think that the Bible contains other pages, other examples that more vividly illustrate God's universal mercy. But the story of Jonah has a flavor akin to that of parables. It presents a person whose behavior the hearers spontaneously approve or reprove. The storyteller then says, "You are wrong, because you reason in a human manner, whereas you should recognize that God acts otherwise, according to a superior justice, with mercy, etc." "Are you envious because I am generous?" (Matt 20:15). Jonah is the portrait, almost the caricature, of the believer who sees in God a judge whose dominant trait is inflexibility. The prospect of a possible pardon for the corrupt big city seems unthinkable to him. By fleeing far from Nineveh, he is going to protect God himself from the temptation of weakness. Is God not in danger of giving himself the lie, of losing his credibility if he relents and forgives those sins instead of punishing them as they deserve? The misadventures that befall Jonah show him that God is determined to offer the inhabitants of Nineveh the opportunity to be saved.

In this genre of popular story, the characters are exaggerated so as to become caricatures, and the main person appears somewhat ridiculous. When Jonah realizes that God has been merciful, his vexation is so great that he wishes for death: all his ideas about God are jeopardized (Jonah 4:1-3). The Lord reprimands him by making fun of him. At this point we have the episode of the providential gourd vine in whose shadow Jonah is happy to rest. But by sunrise the plant has dried up, and here is Jonah overwhelmed by heat. Then God says to him: "You are concerned over the plant which cost you no labor and which you did not raise; it came up in one night and in one night it perished. And should I not be concerned over Nineveh, the great city, in which there are more than a hundred and twenty thousand persons who cannot distinguish their right hand from their left, not to mention the many cattle?" (Jonah 4:10-11). We have at the end of this spiritedly narrated tale the same lesson we have in the parable of the prodigal son—the tone of which is sterner—where the father addresses his angry elder son, saying, "We must celebrate and rejoice, because your brother was dead and has come to life again; he was lost and has been found" (Luke 15:32). Even though our own reactions lack the elder son's virulence, it is not easy for us to share the disconcerting views of God. "Look, all these years I served you and not once did I disobey your orders; yet you never gave me even a young goat to feast on with my friends. But when your son returns who swallowed up your property with prostitutes, for him you slaughter the fattened calf" (Luke 15:29-30).

> *Teach me your ways, O Lord.*
>
> Your ways, O LORD, make known to me;
>   teach me your paths,
> Guide me in your truth and teach me,
>   for you are God my savior. . . .
> Remember that your compassion, O LORD,
>   and your kindness are from of old.

> In your kindness remember me,
>   because of your goodness, O LORD.
> Good and upright is the LORD;
>   thus he shows sinners the way.
> He guides the humble to justice,
>   he teaches the humble his way.
> (Ps 25:4-6, 7-9)

Time Is Short and the World Is Passing Away

It is difficult to find a right norm of conduct when one lives in a society and at a time in which the most contradictory ideas and doctrines abound and intermingle, in which absolute permissiveness rules behavior and morals. This was the case in Corinth. Paul was obliged to step in because abuses were vitiating the Christian community and because diverse questions put to him demanded answers. He did this, on the one hand, by recalling what had already been taught the Corinthians;[10] on the other hand, by showing with concrete examples the practical conclusions to be drawn from a few well-understood principles.[11] The three verses from the First Letter to the Corinthians read on this Sunday are an example of this teaching (1 Cor 7:29-31).

"Time is running out," literally "it has furled—folded up—its sails": the journey is nearing its end. This may be an allusion to the end of the world, which was thought to be close at hand, and also to the shortness of individual existence, as when we say, "Life is short." At all times, people have drawn diverse conclusions from this statement. Paul alludes to this in the First Letter to the Corinthians; if there is nothing after this brief life . . .

> "If the dead are not raised:
>   'Let us eat and drink,
>   for tomorrow we die.' "
> (1 Cor 15:32)

This is indeed what is often said; "Since life is short, let's make the best of it, let's have a good time." Hence this frenzy of pleasure, of unbounded satisfaction of instincts and desires of all kinds which was rampant in Corinth and which we also know well today. But Paul does not stop at this conception of time as inexorably vanishing—something we all observe. He adds, "For the world in its present form is passing away." It is going elsewhere, toward another world, another shore. Time belongs to the history of salvation, which is "nearer now than when we first believed" (Rom 13:11). Defined by God's interventions and, decisively, by the pasch and the presence of Christ, time is not a mere succession of fleeting moments.[12] Definitively oriented toward its goal, it goes shiplike, steering for the haven already in view.[13] Knowing this, we are kept from panicking, from making ill-considered decisions—for example, changing our marital status or placing ourselves in impossible situations on account of useless problems of conscience. Likewise, taking into account the shortness of life justifies neither license nor contempt for and refusal of marriage (1 Cor 7:1-11, 25-40). Neither laxity nor rigor is in order, but rather a responsible behavior guided by the just appreciation of the present situation, its meaning and value, but also its ambiguities.

Salvation has already occurred but is not yet accomplished. Saved in hope, the present world and time still remain stamped by sin and precariousness because God is not yet "all in all" (1 Cor 15:28). We would go astray if we blindly trusted earthly realities, if we became ensnared by the prince of this world (2 Cor 4:4); we would go to our doom. But if we despised these realities, if we were radically distrustful of them and rejected them altogether, we would disregard the fact that the Son became incarnate to save the world, that we cannot be saved outside this world. We must, therefore, live the earthly realities with discernment, by appreciating them at their just value proportionate to their purpose. Paul gives four examples.

First, he considers marriage: "a great mystery"—a great sacrament— he says "in reference to Christ and the church" (Eph 5:32).[14] We must look at it not as an end in itself, but in the perspective of the search for God , who is above all. And this is why there are other ways to go to God, according to each one's vocation: celibacy in order to be undivided in the Lord's service, and the single life voluntarily assumed (1 Cor 7:1-16, 25-40). To live with one's spouse as if one did not have a spouse is to recognize the relative character of the married state in comparison to what is, in every state of life, the absolute: union with Christ.[15]

Second, the diverse situations in which we may find ourselves must be shouldered within the same perspective. When undergoing trial, we must not stiffen ourselves in an attitude of stoicism, indifference, lack of feeling. Jesus did not have a heart of stone; on the contrary, he keenly and painfully felt in his flesh and heart physical and moral suffering, sadness even to anguish when faced with his ordeal (Luke 22:44). He did not keep his tears back (Luke 19:41; John 11:35), nor did he conceal the inner turmoil that seized him when he thought of Judas' betrayal (John 13:21). But he also knew and showed joy (Luke 10:21) and feelings of admiration (Matt 8:10; Luke 7:9). Insensibility, impassibility cannot claim

Jesus' example or the manner in which the Bible presents God. Paul, for his part, was the opposite of a man inured by nature or by dint of virtue against the assaults of sensitivity, as is abundantly clear from his letters. The same is true of all saints, who are examples of humanity; their feelings were under control, of course, but by no means repressed.[16]

Sorrows and joys must be lived, as everything else, "in the Lord." God will not forget any tears entrusted to him; he will not erase any moment of happiness for which one can be thankful to him. "As if" does not proclaim unbending will power or dissembling that would lead us to appear joyful in order to repress or hide sadness or to look crestfallen in order to contain or conceal joy. What Paul wishes for all is not to be defeated by trials or to be wildly elated by a joy that does not lead us to God. He says this quite clearly and vigorously in his Letter to the Philippians: "Rejoice in the Lord always. I shall say it again: rejoice! Your kindness should be known to all. The Lord is near. Have no anxiety at all, but in everything, by prayer and petition, with thanksgiving, make your requests known to God. Then the peace of God that surpasses all understanding will guard your hearts and minds in Christ Jesus" (Phil 4:4-7).

Paul's last two examples concern the acquisition and the use of material goods ("those buying" and "those using the world"). There is no possible life in society without exchange of goods.[17] Economic self-sufficiency does not exist in a group after it reaches a certain size.[18] But Paul is not speaking of this. None must act as the absolute owners of what is in their possession. The right to use and abuse acquired goods at one's whim is not Christian. God said, "The land is mine" (Lev 25:23). Humans have received the world in trust for the good of all.[19] The acquisition of goods in order to become ever richer cannot be life's goal. " 'You fool, this night your life will be demanded of you; and the things you have prepared, to whom will they belong?' Thus will it be for the one who stores up treasure for himself but is not rich in what matters to God" (Luke 12:20-21). "You cannot serve God and mammon" (Matt 6:24; Luke 16:13). In order not to become entangled in material goods, we must handle them with detachment. However, the motive is not to keep our hands clean but to remember that the world—which passes away—does not deserve our true attachment. To be aware of its perishable nature helps us to consider seriously what its orientation is: toward that which does not pass away. Finally, Paul's teaching here allows us to understand that Christian asceticism is always linked to freedom in the use of earthly things.

The modalities of asceticism reflect the times as do the saints' faces. It is symptomatic that in a world tired and bent under the weight of worries, St. Therese speaks of spiritual childhood, marks out "the little way," and invites all to sit down "at the sinners' table." Depth psychology, for its part, underscores the transcendence of humility and the incarnations of spiritual realities in social life. Modern asceticism views itself as dedicated to the service of what is essentially human, that which the Incarnation has assumed; it is violently opposed to every diminution or abandonment of humankind.

"I no longer call you slaves. . . . I have called you friends." This word of the Lord announces the adult state of humankind where humankind moves beyond humankind. Spiritual life orients itself towards divine friendship. Asceticism loses its penitential mentality and becomes a preventive therapy. Almost everywhere, monasticism seems to be seeking, beyond the bodily and psychological asceticism of the Middle Ages, the eschatological asceticism of the first centuries, that act of faith which transformed the whole human being into a joyous expectation of the Parousia.[20]

The Time Is Fulfilled—Repent!

After briefly recalling John the Baptist's preaching, Jesus' baptism, and his temptation in the desert, Mark comes to the announcement of the good news. From this beginning, the characteristics of Mark's Gospel are given: brisk narratives; energetic style; more action than speech; presentation of a Jesus always on the go, who invites others to follow him in haste, farther, always farther. At the same time, there are significant landmarks and, at each turning point of the narrative, the pressing invitation to discover in Jesus "the Son of God" (Mark 1:14-20).

"The beginning of the gospel of Jesus Christ [the Son of God]" (Mark 1:1). Set at the opening of Mark's Gospel, this statement is equivalent to a postulate: Jesus is in himself, personally, the Good News. Everything that went before was preparing this manifestation which takes place "after John had been arrested,"[21] John the last of the prophets, whose preaching was brutally stopped, but who, through his martyrdom, gives supreme testimony to him whom he was announcing.[22]

In order to manifest himself, "Jesus came to Galilee." Nazareth, where he had lived, belonged to this province. But he had left it in order to receive John's baptism (Mark 1:19), then to remain in Judea "in the desert for forty days" (Mark 1:12-13). He is coming back to Galilee now; Mark does not indicate exactly where in this vast province. Throughout his Gospel, he frustrates our curiosity. We would like to be able to follow on a map Jesus' comings and goings, but such details are unimportant to Mark. He would rather focus his hearers' and readers' attention on the meaning of the hurry with which Jesus goes through this region and, later, other regions. And he does so here. Owing to its mixed population and its geographical location, which made it a crossroads for trade, Galilee was called "the District of the Gentiles" (Isa 8:23). To note that Jesus, the Good News, first goes to Galilee immediately suggests that, from the outset, his manifestation concerns all nations. Moreover, unlike John the Baptist, Jesus does not wait for people to come to him; he takes the initiative and goes to them in order to sow the word to the four winds.

As told by Mark, Jesus' inaugural message appears general, if not vague. But we must take a closer look. "This is the time of fulfillment. The kingdom of God is at hand." This proclamation reminds us of what the Book of Isaiah announced before:

> Go up onto a high mountain,
>   Zion, herald of glad tidings;
> Cry out at the top of your voice,
>   Jerusalem, herald of good news!
> Fear not to cry out
>   and say to the cities of Judah:
>   Here is your God!
> (Isa 40:9)

"He is near" (Isa 50:8; 51:5).[23] Such is the message of salvation proclaimed by Jesus, first in "the Galilee of the nations," then beyond, to human beings of the whole earth. But he adds, "Repent, and believe in the gospel." This is a call to turn to Jesus and believe in him. His activity, his miracles, the expulsions of demons will show that God's power is, in fact, acting in him, and Satan's reign is tottering. Hence the question posed with growing acuteness: "Who is He? John the Baptist? One of the prophets?" We shall be progressively led to decide among so many opinions and to renew our faith: "You are the Messiah" (Mark 8:29). Only then will Jesus be able to speak clearly of his death and resurrection, of the necessity for his disciples to follow him carrying their crosses (Mark 8:31-35). Such is the itinerary on which Mark guides us. By reporting at this point the call of the four first disciples, Mark completes the presentation of Jesus, Son of God.

Again, Mark omits details[24] and limits himself to an extremely streamlined account. "As he passed by the Sea of Galilee,"[25] Jesus first sees Simon and his brother Andrew, then "a little farther," James, the son of Zebedee, and his brother John. They are fishermen. Jesus finds them busy, Simon and Andrew casting their nets, James and John readying

them to go fishing. ''Come after me.'' ''Then they left their nets. . . .
they left their father Zebedee in the boat along with the hired men and
followed him.''

This episode demonstrates the extraordinary authority of Jesus' word,
which Mark will emphasize at every opportunity, showing that it works
on everyone, even demons.[26] The recognition of this authority and the
unhesitating response to Jesus' call are the earmarks of discipleship, whatever each one's vocation and in whatever manner it is first known. This
is the fundamental teaching of this narrative which Mark wants to give
us without delay. He streamlines it to the utmost to throw it into sharp
relief; he keeps only Jesus' call and the four disciples' immediate response.
Of course, we cannot conclude that, in reality, things happen—or ought
to happen—this way.

On the one hand, the Lord's call does not directly reach us, as in the
case of the four first apostles. Even when loud and clear to the recipient,
an inner call must be verified and tested by those who have received the
gift and the ministry of discernment. Prudence is the more in order since
no one is free of the risk of illusions whose consequences can be very
serious for oneself and others. ''Do not quench the Spirit. Do not despise prophetic utterances. Test everything; retain what is good'' (1 Thess
5:19-21). ''Beloved, do not trust every spirit but test the spirits to see
whether they belong to God'' (1 John 4:1). The spiritual tradition attests
to the necessity and the wisdom of this prudent course.[27] God's call does
not eliminate the human mediations he himself has willed.[28]

On the other hand, the Lord's call, even a sudden one, is always inserted within a history. As a rule, it is communicated in such a discreet
and hardly perceptible manner that people become conscious of it only
gradually, following the rhythm of divine preparations. But one thing
is certain: conversion is always a free response of the human being to
the initiative of a call coming from God.

> I call upon Thee, O my God, my Mercy, who didst create me and didst
> not forget me when I forgot thee. I call Thee into my soul, which Thou dost
> make ready to receive Thee by the desire that Thou dost inspire in it: do
> Thou not abandon me now when I call upon Thee, for it was by Thy aid
> going before me that I called upon Thee; and Thou hadst urged me over
> and over, in a great variety of ways, to hear Thee from afar off and be con-
> verted and call upon Thee who wert calling me.[29]

According to his custom of coming to us wherever we are and taking us
as we are, Jesus calls Simon, Andrew, James, and John when they are

at work near the shore of the Sea of Galilee.[30] Jesus speaks to these four men about what they are presently doing to express what he has in store for them. "I will make you fishers of men." We do not have here a kind of "by the way," a pun whose meaning could remain ambiguous. In current usage, people speak of nets as snares set for human beings as well as for birds and fish.[31] But Jesus does not refer to this meaning of the word when he says to Simon, Andrew, James, and John, as they are occupied with casting or mending their nets, "I will make you fishers of men." There is nothing in Jesus' ministry, nothing in the precepts he gives the disciples, nothing in the way in which the disciples will exercise their apostolate to suggest, even faintly, an attempt to entrap anyone. On the contrary, even though Jesus' and the Apostles' preaching urges people to be converted and believe, it always challenges them to face their personal responsibility and asks them for their free commitment: "Whatever place does not welcome you or listen to you, leave there and shake the dust off your feet in testimony against them" (Mark 6:11).[32]

In the Bible, the sea evokes a fearful place that strikes the imagination and on which it is dangerous to venture—a lair of monsters, a destructive force.[33] To pull people out of the sea is not to drag them in a net out of their natural element, but to snatch them from a bad world, to free them from the powers of evil, for the kingdom of heaven when, on Judgment Day, the sorting out will take place (Matt 13:47-50). By making them "fishers of men," Jesus calls the fishermen of the Sea of Galilee "that they might be with him and he might send them forth to preach" the kingdom of God at hand "and to have authority to drive out demons" (Mark 3:14-15). Thus this brief narrative delineates the mission of the Church, even with a discreet allusion to the role of Peter, already named first.[34]

> Everything begins as any other morning, but
>   that morning becomes its own tomorrow.
> The tomorrow of a common story which in an
>   instant will completely vanish.
> But for the moment, it is still yesterday and
>   all work at their usual tasks.
> The fishers are in their fishing boats and
>   the powerful at their momentous business.
> This is a workday, not a holiday; no one has
>   time for any heaven anywhere.
> (But no one looks for heaven on Sunday
>   either, so depressing is the idea.)

> The order of things is useful by definition;
>   to doubt it is to lose one's place in it.
> Therefore nothing must ever happen here
>   except what is needed for business as usual.
>
> But it is always on such a morning that
> Jesus, whether by chance or by design,
> decides to up and go.[35]

The itinerary on which the Church leads us, along the Sundays of Ordinary Time, has characteristics proper to each of the three years. Every Sunday we celebrate the Day of the Lord and the mystery of his pasch. At the heart of this liturgy there is always the Gospel of our Lord Jesus Christ, but successively announced by Matthew, Mark, and Luke. The road on which each one leads us has its peculiarities, though it does not totally differ from the other two. The three of them introduce us into the same mystery, make us follow the same Lord. But one tarries here and there while another willingly uses shortcuts; one gives more space to long discourses, while another is more interested in events. The result is that the itineraries, which year in year out have the same number of stages, are traveled at different rhythms.

At first glance, we realize that Mark, the guide for Year B, does not stop at details; he goes directly to what seems to him essential, more significant; and he highlights it by the way in which he structures his narratives rather than by explanations.

All the evangelists place the beginning of Jesus' ministry in direct relation to that of the Precursor, who disappears when the one he announced appears. The Fourth Gospel notes that the first disciples came to Jesus at the Baptist's urging. Mark goes directly to the call of Simon, Andrew, James, and John, whom Jesus recruits on the shore of the Sea of Galilee in order to make them fish for people. Mark wants to make it clear that from Jesus' first appearance, the time of mission has begun: we must hurry to recognize the Son of God and to follow him without hesitation or delay.

For his part, Paul reminds assembled Christians that during this limited time they must use the world and earthly realities, taking pains not to get ensnared in them.

This first sequence gives the pitch and rhythm that will be maintained throughout the series of Sundays in Ordinary Time, Year B.

From the Fourth to the Sixth Sunday in Ordinary Time

After having recorded the call of the first four "fishers of men," Mark shows how Jesus, accompanied by his disciples, exercised his ministry. In order to explain and illustrate the object and the style of this activity, the evangelist presents the activities of one day, the first, in Capernaum, on the sabbath in the synagogue. Jesus teaches and afterwards frees a man from an unclean spirit that is tormenting him (Mark 1:21-28—Fourth Sunday). After the service, he goes to the house of Simon and Andrew, where he cures Simon's mother-in-law, who is in bed with a fever. Then, "when it was evening, after sunset," therefore when the sabbath is over,[1] he cures many sick persons and expels many demons. On the following day, "rising very early before dawn," he goes to a deserted place to pray. After finding him, Simon and his companions want to bring him back to the people, who are looking for him. But Jesus leads them elsewhere, to the nearby villages that must also hear the good news. He walks "throughout the whole of Galilee," teaching in synagogues and driving out demons (Mark 1.29-39—Fifth Sunday). He then cures a leper (Mark 1:40-45—Sixth Sunday). Here we have a general presentation, a sort of summary of the activities that typically filled Jesus' days: prayer, teaching, and healing. The three Sundays on which we read this report constitute a unit, a sequence.

We also read three more excerpts from Paul's First Letter to the Corinthians (7:32-35; 9:16-19, 22-23; 10:31–11:1).

Fourth Sunday

A New Teaching, Proclaimed with Authority

God Will Raise Up Another Moses

Following the example of the Old Testament, Christian tradition gives a very important place to Moses.[2] Moses remains the prophet par excellence, the man chosen among all to transmit to the people God's words and law, with an authority received from above. Any prophet whom God will raise up after him will have a similar mission and must be similarly listened to.[3] This is the message of the first reading of this Sunday (Deut 18:15-20), chosen because the Gospel reading speaks of the "new teaching with authority."

The Bible preserves the memory of the terrifying manifestation on Mount Horeb and the request the people's delegates made to Moses, "Let us not again hear the voice of the LORD, our God, nor see this great fire any more, lest we die."[4] And God said, "This was well said." He wants to show his glory and his grandeur by this manifestation. He has proved that he can speak to human beings and that they can hear his voice without dying. But he does not intend to terrify them and obtain their obedience through terror. "Would that they might always be of such a mind, to fear me and to keep all my commandments! Then they and their descendants would prosper forever" (Deut 5:29). God has created everything that exists—heaven and earth—and has given it to human beings (Gen 1:28-30) so that, contemplating creation, they may recognize and adore the Creator.[5] A manifestation like that on Horeb will not be repeated. Elijah found this out when he reached this "mountain of God." There was a heavy wind, an earthquake, a fire; but the Lord was neither in the wind nor in the earthquake nor in the fire (1 Kgs 19:11-12). After Moses, God will address people through the intermediary of humans.

"I will raise up for them a prophet like you from among their kinsmen, and will put my words into his mouth; he shall tell them all that I command him." This statement expresses the originality of biblical prophetism, compared with that known throughout the ancient Middle

East, in Egypt, and in the neighboring regions. The initiative comes from God. Prophets do not claim to unveil God's secrets or his intentions. What they know and what they say comes from God. They have received the order of transmitting God's words, and they cannot shirk this mission, whatever the cost. Such is Moses; such are all true prophets: servants of God and his word. Others, who would presume to say, in the Lord's name, a word that does not come from him must not be listened to (Deut 18:20-22). People must treat them as they do soothsayers, charmers, diviners, those who cast spells and consult ghosts and spirits or seek oracles from the dead, for "anyone who does such things is an abomination to the LORD" (Deut 9:13). God will demand an account from those who would not listen to the words of prophets speaking in his name. As to those who dare speak without having been commissioned or speak in the name of other gods, they will die.

By tracing prophetism to Moses—one of the most characteristic institutions among the people of the Bible—this passage of Deuteronomy gives us a sure criterion for recognizing the true spokesperson of God.[6] At the same time, it promises that God will never abandon his own but will always remain present among them and will continue to make his will known to them. However, the lineage of the great prophets was interrupted:

> Deeds on our behalf we do not see; there is no prophet now,
>   and no one of us knows how long . . .
> (Ps 74:9)

This lament attests to the vigorous hope of seeing a prophet arise one day. Was this not what Moses announced? Was he not speaking of another than himself? Hence, what people said concerning Elijah's return, which would precede the Messiah,[7] the question put to John the Baptist,[8] and the questions concerning Jesus.[9]

The Christian rereading of Deuteronomy is explicit. Jesus, the Christ, is the prophet announced, the new Moses (Acts 3:22; 7:37), greater than the original Moses (John 1:17; Heb 3:1-6). This interpretation, going beyond the letter of Deuteronomy, expresses Christian faith. Jesus is the Father's emissary, who knows God's secrets because he comes from him and reveals him.[10] He is the prophet who, with an unheard-of authority (Mark 1:27) interprets the Law by fulfilling it (Matt 5:17). Moses reported God's words; Jesus proclaims: "You have heard that it was said . . . But I say to you. . ." (Matt 5:27-48). We can neither add to nor subtract from these decisive words transmitted to us by the apostles' preaching. Before leaving his own, Jesus declares, "The Advocate, the holy Spirit that the Father will send in my name—he will teach you everything and remind you of all that [I] told you" (John 14:26). The Spirit has been given to the Church that it might better understand the Lord's teaching and unfold the meaning of his words according to the signs of the times.[11] "To believe in the relevance of God is to believe in the presence of prophets among us who show the relevance of his word. To believe in the faithfulness of God and in his Church is to believe that he will not let it fall asleep, be overwhelmed, lose its vigor and the dynamism of its hope. And for that reason, Jesus Christ, "the" Prophet, is present through the intermediary of men and women prophets who, in their individual ways, in their places and times, actualize the Word that invigorates all those who believe in him."[12]

> *If today you hear his voice,*
> *harden not your hearts.*
>
> Come, let us sing joyfully to the Lord;
>   let us acclaim the Rock of our salvation.
> Let us greet him with thanksgiving;
>   let us joyfully sing psalms to him.
>
> ———
>
> Come, let us bow down in worship;
>   let us kneel before the Lord who made us.
> For he is our God,
>   and we are the people he shepherds, the flock he guides.
> Oh, that today you would hear his voice:
>   "Harden not your hearts as at Meribah,
>   as in the day of Massah in the desert,
> Where your fathers tempted me;
>   they tested me though they had seen my works."
> (Ps 95:1-2, 7-9)

Celibacy Freely Chosen for the Lord's Service

In the Church, the body of Christ, prophets rank immediately after apostles; among the Spirit's gifts, we must aspire to prophecy above all (1 Cor 14:1-5). For prophets play an essential role in the ecclesial community: under the Spirit's guidance they speak in God's name, unveil his mystery, interpret his will; they build up, exhort, encourage, discern good from evil.[13] Paul the Apostle remains one of the greatest prophets of the Church, as the First Letter to the Corinthians attests, especially when it broaches complex questions, such as those concerned with sexuality. The Spirit prevents Paul from yielding to the temptation of rigorism as a reaction against loose morals. But at the same time, it shows him the value of celibacy freely chosen or willingly accepted and its significance in the perspective of the kingdom (1 Cor 7:32-35).

Misconduct and license are to be strictly condemned, especially among Christians, who know themselves to be members of Christ's body (1 Cor 5:1-5; 6:12-19). But what about marriage? Should we banish it because "it is a good thing for a man not to touch a woman."[14] Certainly not. We must not impose or even advise continence for couples, unless they choose it by mutual consent, and only for a time, in order to devote themselves to prayer. Celibates may marry, and widowers and widows may remarry if they cannot live in continence (1 Cor 7:1-28). But there is a Christian way to live in the married state as there is a Christian way to be in joy or affliction or to possess and acquire goods. This Christian way is based on the conviction that "time is running out . . . the world in its present form is passing away" (1 Cor 7:29-31).[15] This being understood, Paul can now treat of celibacy.[16]

"I should like you to be free of anxieties. An unmarried man is anxious about the things of the Lord, how he may please the Lord." This first sentence is capital. First of all, it clarifies the scope of what Paul says and the way it should be understood. He writes, "Now in regard to virgins, I have no commandment from the Lord, but I give my opinion as one who by the Lord's mercy is trustworthy" (1 Cor 7:25). He does not want to deceive anyone; there is no innuendo in his words, there are no second thoughts in his statements. There is nothing in the world that would make him want to place those who trust him in an impossible situation. He wants only their well-being; this is why he proposes what seems good to him, without denying that marriage remains the normal way, willed by God.[17] Paul even says explicitly that "it is better to marry than to be on fire" (1 Cor 7:9). The celibacy Paul proposes to those who feel equal to assume it, is chosen for a higher motive, the undivided availability to "the things of the Lord."[18] Married people, he adds, are absorbed by the business and the cares of this life.

All of this must be correctly understood. First of all, we should note that Paul says nothing that suggests any disapproval of sexuality in general and of the sexual life of married persons in particular (1 Cor 7:34).[19] Besides, the will to devote oneself to "the things of the Lord" is the motive for celibacy as Paul presents it, not the desire for a life unencumbered by the care of a family or the fear of any responsibility of any kind.[20]

He knows from experience that a life entirely dedicated to the service of the gospel is no bed of roses. Not everyone will necessarily have to undergo all he has endured on account of his faithfulness to this radical choice (2 Cor 11:24-32). But whoever renounces marriage to "please the Lord" must do so joyfully, trustfully, unconditionally.

Now, what one thinks and says about celibacy necessarily implies a certain conception of marriage. The Book of Genesis relates that after having created man and woman, "God blessed them, saying: 'Be fertile and multiply; fill the earth and subdue it' " (Gen 1:28). For the author, a sage who is pondering the origin of everything, the union of man and woman, in view of procreation, has been willed by God, who gives life and fruitfulness to all living beings. Immediately afterward, the author tells us that "so it happened": the birth of Cain and Abel, then of Seth (Gen 4:1-5:32); after the Flood, the repopulation of the earth by Noah and his descendants (Gen 9:18-11:32). Such is the teaching of these first pages of the Bible. The origin and the propagation of life among human beings is due to God, who blessed Adam and Eve; the strength, the beauty, the dignity, and also the exigence of faithfulness to the conjugal bond come from the divine institution of marriage "from the beginning."[21]

This teaching has molded the mentality of the people of the Bible. Children are desired and welcomed as manifestations of divine benevolence, as blessings of God.[22] Consequently, to be childless is perceived as a suffering, a blemish, and if not a curse, at least a sign of abandonment by God, who has averted his eyes. If he grants a child to a couple long childless, the event, which shows God's power, is greeted with joy.[23] To marry in order to have children—many children—is to obey the creator's command, to perpetuate and increase the people of God.[24]

Paul knows all this and appreciates this just view of things. But for him, to marry and have children is not the only vocation of man and woman, the only way to fulfill God's plan. Natural parenthood is good; but the choice of celibacy by anyone "not under compulsion but [having] power over his own will" (1 Cor 7:37) for the Lord is better. For it is a sign of the expectation of the kingdom that Christ will inaugurate on his return at the end of time. The value of natural fatherhood and motherhood helps us to understand the price of spiritual fatherhood and motherhood. Despising marriage or belittling its dignity is incompatible with the just appreciation of celibacy for the Lord. Conversely, denigrating celibacy implies a faulty understanding, whether conscious or unconscious, of marriage as a state willed by God.[25] The reciprocal recognition of the high value, the demands, the merit, the grace of the two states of life, the two vocations, allows us to correctly appreciate marriage and celibacy in their originality and complementarity. In this case, the two kinds of life will stimulate each other in a friendly emulation to seek God and holiness.

> As to the correct understanding of the relationship between marriage and continence, as Christ spoke of it and the whole tradition has understood it, it is worthwhile to add that "superiority" and "inferiority" are contained within the limits of the very complementarity of marriage and continence embraced for the sake of the kingdom of God. Marriage and continence are not opposites and do not divide the human (and Christian) community into two camps—let us say: the camp of the "perfect" because of continence, and that of the "imperfect," or less perfect, because of the reality of conjugal life. But these two fundamental situations or, as was the customary expression in former days, these two "states," explain one another in a certain way and complement one another. They both point to the Christian life of this community, which as a whole and in all its members finds its realization in the dimension of the kingdom of God and possesses an eschatological orientation proper to this kingdom. Well now! In relation to this dimension and this orientation—common to all in the entire faith community, that is to all that belong to it—continence for the sake of the kingdom of God has a particular importance and a particular eloquence for those who live the conjugal life. We know of course that these constitute the majority.[26]

Jesus' Words and Actions Show His Authority

"This is the time of fulfillment. The kingdom of God is at hand. Repent and believe in the gospel." Such is, according to Mark, the fundamental content of the message proclaimed by Jesus as soon as he begins to preach in Galilee.[27] After this "summary," which expresses in a nutshell Jesus' mission and ministry, Mark continues by showing how Jesus manifests that he is the messenger of the good news, or rather that he himself is the Good News. Mark, as we notice throughout his Gospel, always proceeds in a concrete manner. His account is a succession of scenes, of tableaux traced with a few firm lines without the slightest unessential addition. We have here a sophisticated literary technique, apparently very simple but masterfully used.[28] Besides, it is an effective pedagogical device. For the readers find themselves not simply spectators but personally involved in what is happening; they receive the Lord's words at their full force; they cannot help take sides in the discussions and controversies. Thus Mark draws us to accompany Jesus; to enter the synagogue at Capernaum with him on the sabbath; and to follow him during the first day of his ministry, whose beginning today's Gospel reports (Mark 1:21-28).[29]

With his disciples—Peter and Andrew, James and John (Mark 1:16-20)— Jesus, faithful to the Law, goes to the synagogue, where the gathering of the community furnishes him with the opportunity for public speaking and teaching.[30] The presentation of Jesus' first manifestation contains some important lessons to keep in mind. First of all, the good news is placed within the continuity of Jewish tradition; Jesus' word comes, officially we might say, as a prolongation of God's word set down in the Law and proclaimed by the prophets.[31] But, as Mark insistently notes, Jesus teaches "as one having authority and not as the scribes." Mark does not offer any comment. He simply relates the fact, which arouses astonishment in everyone. In this, he prompts us to ask ourselves how we in turn receive this teaching.

> He was not saying, "The Lord says this," or "He who sent me says that"; he spoke in his own name, he who first of all had spoken through the prophets. There is a nuance of difference between the expressions "It is written" and "The Lord says this"; but there is a further difference in saying "In truth, I say to you." See, for instance, "You have heard that it was said 'You shall not kill' . . . 'You shall not commit adultery.' For whom was this written? For Moses, in God's commands. If this was written by God's hand, how dare you say—you—"But I say to you . . ." since you are not the first to have formulated the law? No one has the power to change the law, except the king himself. But is it the Father or the Son who promulgated this law? Answer, you heretic. Whatever your intentions, I am pleased to retort: for me, it is the same thing! If the Father has given this law, it is he who also alters it. Now the Son is equal to him, he who changes what the other has ordained. Whether it is he who gave the law or transformed it, an equal authority is necessary to promulgate and modify; no one may do this except the king.
>
> "The people were astonished at his teaching." What new teaching had he given? What unheard-of thing did he say? He was saying, he personally, what he previously had said through the prophets. And they were astonished because his teaching gave them the impression that he possessed the authority, contrary to the scribes. He was not speaking as a master, but as the Lord. His statements did not appeal to a higher authority; he was speaking in his own name. Furthermore, he himself declared that he who was speaking to them now was the same who had spoken through the prophets: ". . . it is I who have foretold it. Here I am!" (Isa 52:6).[32]

Mark adds to this presentation of Jesus speaking with authority the account of an exorcism, rather strange in some respects. Whereas the crowd heard this teaching with admiration, "an unclean spirit" violently confronts the preacher: "What have you to do with us, Jesus of Nazareth? Have you come to destroy us? I know who you are—the Holy One of God!" Usually, the sick or their relatives are the ones to cry their distress to Jesus, whose divine power they recognize and whose mystery they more or less clearly perceive.[33] Now in Mark's Gospel, the first one to publicly acknowledge Jesus' divine origin is a demon. In spite of the perfect accuracy of the declaration, we must not see it as a profession of faith that a sort of evidence would wrench out, against its will, from the "unclean spirit." Faith entails worship, praise, and thanksgiving. But we have here a cry of rage and despair.[34] This is perhaps the place in which to seek a key for the interpretation of this disconcerting scene. Mark wants to bring the readers beyond the astonishment provoked by the event to the understanding of what is at stake in the Lord's coming. The Spirit "drove him out into the desert, and he remained in the desert for forty days, tempted by Satan." Mark limits himself to a mere mention of this fact, saying nothing of this initial confrontation that had for its only witnesses the wild beasts and the angels who ministered to Jesus (Mark 1:12-13). But now he wants to show that the proclamation of the good news is the beginning of the overt, public, and decisive struggle between Jesus and Satan. "I know who you are." This is of no advantage to the unclean spirit.[35] On the contrary, it sees itself unmasked and, at the same time, lost in advance. As to Jesus, he is not yet known. "What is this?" However, thanks to his teaching and actions, he will be progressively recognized as emissary, as Son of God. His identity will clearly appear to believers' eyes when he is on the cross (Mark 15:39). For only at that moment will the affirmation "Jesus is the Son of God" be the expression of authentic faith. Unless we accept the cross, we cannot claim to fully and truthfully know who Jesus is.[36]

To recognize Jesus' sovereign power over the forces of evil is a first step. At Capernaum, Jesus demonstrates a striking authority over Satan: "Quiet! Come out of him!" He will speak in a similar manner to the raging sea, a symbol of the evil forces he has come to vanquish: "Quiet! Be still!" (Mark 4:39).[37] In both cases, the bystanders' reactions are identical: "What is this? . . . He commands even the unclean spirits and they obey him" (Mark 1:27); "Who then is this whom even wind and sea obey?" (Mark 4:41). Mark leaves us with this grave question; it is up to each one of us to give an answer.

The Eucharist is eminently the "sacrament of faith" in a double capacity. Participation in the liturgy is a profession of faith shown by an act: "I am here because I believe." At the same time, the liturgy does not cease challenging believers, driving them, as it were, to the last extremity: "You proclaim your faith and no one contests the sincerity and truth of your words. But do not stop here. In order to know the Lord, you must assiduously follow him, day after day, up to the cross on which the Son of God has conquered all the forces of evil."

Besides, the liturgical celebration invites all of us to examine the way in which, according to our own vocation, we give God the place that is his in our daily lives.

> Word of a self-revealing God,
> Surprising Word,
> Decisive Word,
> Jesus,
> fear seizes
> all who meet you:
>
> *Who are you, Lord,*
> *that we may believe in you?*
>
> I am the prophet,
> God's voice among you.
>
> I am the truth,
> God's strength that frees you.
>
> I am love beyond all fear,
> God's gift that transfigures.[38]

The Good News of Salvation Carried Ever Farther

The Intolerable Scandal of a Life of Unending Suffering

Suffering in general, undeserved suffering—of the innocent and just in particular—is one of the most agonizing problems to confront the human mind. It does not admit of simplistic and definite answers. For a believer, it is even more difficult, as it implicates God: "If he is not responsible for suffering, how can he allow it and leave the just in its clutches?" This is the topic of the Book of Job.[1] The source of the author's reflection is an ancient Middle Eastern tale. Job, a just man endowed with honor and riches, finds himself overwhelmed by all sorts of calamities: he loses his children and all of his possessions; he himself is stricken with a hideous disease and reduced to the state of a wretched beggar. Why? Those close to Job seem quick to give the usual explanations: "Either God has punished you for your sins, or else he has unjustly abandoned you. In the latter case, why not rebel and curse this God who so cruelly makes sport of you? Resignation is unworthy of a sensible man; it is degrading." If we want to know the way in which the Book of Job confronts the problem of suffering and what conclusion it reaches, we must read the story in its entirety. Isolated fragments of answers would be of no interest.[2] However, there are passages that deserve attention, even outside of their context. This is the case with the first reading of this Sunday's liturgy (Job 7:1-4, 6-7).

The author depicts the human condition in especially somber tones. Life is a "drudgery" endured without joy, its only purpose being to earn a daily wage for bare subsistence. Worse still, it is the life of slaves who long "for the shade," a short moment of respite in the course of their grueling workday. Even night is not without suffering. Hardly in bed at night, we all tend to think of the work awaiting us in the morning. Nightmares and anguish disturb sleep. And where does all this lead? To nothing: tomorrow the thread of life will be cut as that of the shuttle that weavers move back and forth on the piece of cloth they are making. When the shuttle is empty, it is refilled, and the movement resumes with another thread that will again be used up. God seems to look on from afar.

> Remember that my life is like the wind;
>   I shall not see happiness again.
> (Job 7:7)

However, this is not a cry of revolt, but rather a complaint of people who are poised between despair and hope, who hardly dare to turn to God to remind him of life's nothingness and suffering. We read similar messages—who could say whether they are addressed to God or human beings?—in the eyes of exhausted children, in the photographs of men and women subjected to slavery in death camps.

Job's pessimism will appear exaggerated to those whose lives, despite their difficulties and sorrows, are brightened by just enough glimpses of light or sunrays to rekindle their courage and hope against hope. They cannot make Job's heartrending laments their own. But we must let these lamentations resound within us because they echo to us the hopeless lives of innumerable brothers, sisters, sons, and daughters of Job who languish throughout the world, perhaps close by, just as Job languished at the city gates (Job 2:8).[3]

At the time the book was written, the concept of an afterlife was still indistinct. But even today we would be ill-advised to say, by way of consoling Job and encouraging him in his adversity: "Think of heaven, of the reward that today's intolerable suffering will earn you." "Patience, you will have a prosperous future." "All that we have observed is the truth. It remains for you to listen and benefit by hearing it." The poem attributes similar words to Job's friends.[4] These fine discourses, that seem to him to be delivered by rote, are unable to bring the slightest relief to Job's wounds, but only make them worse. On his hospital bed, Cardinal Pierre Veuillot said: "We know how to make beautiful speeches on suffering. I myself have spoken of it with enthusiasm. Tell the priests to say nothing about it; we don't know what suffering is. I weep to think of it."[5] An appeal to faith in the resurrection and to the certainty of a heavenly reward is not by itself a satisfactory answer to the problem of suffering that remains a scandal, especially when it strikes the innocent.

> [Ivan said] ". . . I hasten to protect myself and so I renounce the higher harmony altogether. It's not worth the tears of that one tortured child who beat itself on the breast with its little fist and prayed in its stinking outhouse, with its unexpiated tears to "dear, kind God"! It's not worth it,

because those tears are unatoned for. They must be atoned for, or there
can be no harmony. But how? How are you going to atone for them? Is
it possible? By their being avenged? But what do I care for avenging them?
What do I care for a hell for oppressors? What good can hell do, since those
children have already been tortured? And what becomes of harmony, if
there is hell? I want to forgive. I want to embrace. I don't want more suffering. And if the sufferings of children go to swell the sum of sufferings which
was necessary to pay for truth, then I protest that the truth is not worth
such a price. I don't want the mother to embrace the oppressor who threw
her son to the dogs! She dare not forgive him! Let her forgive him for herself, if she will, let her forgive the torturer for the immeasurable suffering
of her mother's heart. But the sufferings of her tortured child she has no
right to forgive; she dare not forgive the torturer, even if the child were
to forgive him! . . . Is there in the whole world a being who would have
the right to forgive and could forgive? . . .''

[Aloysha said] ''. . . [Y]ou said just now, is there a being in the whole
world who would have the right to forgive and could forgive? But there
is a Being and He can forgive everything, all *and for all*, because He gave
His innocent blood for all and everything. You have forgotten Him, and
on Him is built the edifice, and it is to Him they cry aloud, 'Thou art just,
O Lord, for Thy ways are revealed!' ''[6]

When we are faced with suffering—our own and, even more, that of
others—we must remain silent and raise our eyes to Christ. He, the Innocent One, the Just, who knows suffering, having assumed freely but
painfully the suffering of all humanity, forgave his tormentors. He can
address the Father, who allowed his Son to die so that ''by his stripes
we [might be] healed'' (Isa 53:5). It is he whom we bless, and not the
suffering whose ''lost weight''[7] he has assumed in his offering.

Praise the Lord who heals the brokenhearted.

Praise the LORD, for he is good;
  sing praise to our God, for he is gracious;
  it is fitting to praise him.
The LORD rebuilds Jerusalem;
  the dispersed of Israel he gathers.
He heals the brokenhearted
  and binds up their wounds.
He tells the number of the stars;
  he calls each by name.
Great is our Lord and mighty in power:
  to his wisdom there is no limit.
The LORD sustains the lowly;
  and the wicked he casts to the ground.
(Ps 147:1-6)

Free in Every Way in Order to Be All Things to All

Paul's First Letter to the Corinthians speaks a great deal about freedom. "Everything is lawful for me" must have been a formula often repeated in Paul's preaching. He does not deny coining it; on the contrary, he affirms that Christians live under a regime of freedom, but of responsible freedom. We are not authorized to do as we please: freedom is not license. It must take others into account, particularly the weakest, whom we must not scandalize. In a word, true freedom always focuses on the good, the better, charity.[8] By vocation, and because they have received the strength to do so, some choose to live as celibates in order to entirely devote themselves to "the things of the Lord." It is, in fact, not only permissible but good, for this higher motive, to free oneself from the general law of marriage and from the duty of procreation, both of which come from God, as well as from the prevailing idea that marriage is incumbent on all men and women. In any case, whether married, widowed, or celibate, the disciples must keep the freedom that the fate of this present world makes necessary.[9] Paul now comes to the choice he personally has made in order to exercise his ministry without any hindrance (1 Cor 9:16-19, 22-23).

No one can attribute to oneself the merit of apostleship. Whatever the way in which one has been led to exercise a ministry in the Church, and whatever the freedom with which one has accepted to devote one's life to this ministry, everyone must recognize that first of all there was a call from the Lord, in one form or another. Some responded immediately and without hesitation. Others at first turned a deaf ear and sought to evade the call, like Jonah (Jonah 1–2). But all must recognize that it was a "necessity" that was imposed on them.[10] The manner of his conversion and his mission has made Paul particularly conscious of this truth and made him realize how senseless, how absurd pride in his missionary work would be. Had he known it,[11] he could have quoted the Lord's words recorded in Luke's Gospel: "When you have done all you have been commanded, say, 'We are unprofitable servants; we have done what we were obliged to do'" (Luke 17:10). No, Paul really cannot boast of the fact he is doing the task imposed on him, "Woe to me if I do not preach [the Gospel]."

Paul not only labors as a good and faithful servant; he also has voluntarily renounced the rights legitimately associated with the exercise of the ministry, and to which there is a corresponding duty in Christian communities. It is indeed normal for apostles to live at the expense of the community that benefits from their services and therefore to "have the right not to work" (1 Cor 9:4-14).[12] Although they must be content with what they receive, servants of the gospel must not be ashamed to accept this salary (Luke 10:7). But Paul has made another choice; he wants to provide for his own needs by the work of his hands in order not to be a burden to anyone.[13] Why such a choice? To respond to his personal vocation, not to distinguish himself from others or lecture them, still less to yield to an obstinacy and compulsion and to adopt a mode of life rigidly controlled by will power. During a stay in Corinth, however, Paul will gratefully accept provisions from Macedonian disciples (2 Cor 11:9). Did the arduous beginnings of his apostolate influence Paul's decision to make his own way (Acts 9:26-31)?[14] It is possible. But it is safer to abide by what Paul himself says. The choice of material self-sufficiency seems to him personally preferable in order to be "free in regard to all" and to be "all things to all." Thus, he has acquired a total freedom of speech and action. He has shared the precarious condition of the "weak" without leaving himself open to the remonstrances of the "strong."

Thanks to his being absolutely disinterested, he gives free play to the gospel and to God's power. He never seeks to "seduce for himself in order to seduce for Jesus Christ."[15] All Christians, and in particular the ministers of the gospel, must protect this transparency and—taking into account the circumstances, the calls of grace, their own personal vocations—see to it that they do not place a screen between God, Christ, and others.

> Saints who really live, who are greater than life, who no longer look at themselves guide us to God, who is at the core of our life, who is the only real experience that reveals humans to humans. For as long as humans pretend to be virtuous, humble, there is nobody. What is marvelous about saints is that there is Someone in them, at last there is a human being, a spring, a freedom, and, at last, intimacy. There is really a mystery. . . . When there is no I, it is He: it is as simple, as daily, as obvious as that. We must therefore look in that direction: we shall find God, the true God, only by being liberated from ourselves. As long as it is I, it is not He. When it is He, then it is He.[16]

This is why everyone must remember Paul's example, even though his choice is not for all to make. Those whom the Lord calls to be similarly disinterested must follow their path with generosity, but also with humility, without boasting of their choice, and without pretending to best anyone. Others will see in their example a call to live with an equal generosity in the situation where God has placed them. All will act "for the sake of the gospel, so that [they] too may have a share in it."

After Capernaum, the Whole of Galilee

Everything began on a sabbath day in the synagogue with a session of teaching and then by an exorcism—events that revealed Jesus' extraordinary authority. "What is this?" Christians know the answer when they open the Gospels or hear the proclamation in the liturgical assembly they have joined. As soon as they hear "The gospel of Jesus Christ," they answer, "Glory to you, Lord." We have here a profession of faith: the Lord Jesus is the gospel, the good news, God's Word.[17] For his part, Mark knows full well that he is addressing brothers and sisters in the faith, as we can see in particular in the ending of his Gospel. Because he addresses believers, he leaves the readers in front of the cross on which Christ has just died.[18] In the way he structures his narrative and by his lively style, Mark, at every scene, goads his readers to test, make explicit, and renew their faith. He does this as early as his presentation of the first day of Jesus' ministry, which this Sunday's Gospel continues to record (Mark 1:29-39). "On leaving the synagogue he entered the house of Simon and Andrew with James and John. Simon's mother-in-law lay sick with a fever. They immediately told him about her. He approached, grasped her hand, and helped her up. Then the fever left her and she waited on them." The simplicity and shortness of this account, devoid of any frills, again accentuates Jesus' authority (Mark 1:22-27). However, if we pay attention, we understand that this is not just an intervention, normal after all, on Jesus' part. Since he has the necessary power, why would he not use it for the benefit of this woman who is receiving him in her house and must be embarrassed not to be able, because of her sickness, to render him the duties of hospitality?

At this point in his narrative, Mark has recorded only one cure, that of the demoniac at the synagogue. Jesus has just left in the company of his four disciples. Of course, we could explain the juxtaposition of these two cures by recalling the ancient conception of disease as always in some way linked to the action of an evil spirit. But it is also said that Jesus "helped her up." The expression is not ordinary; Mark employs a verb—*egeirein*—which usually means "to raise."[19] The same word is found in a text from the Letter to the Ephesians (5:14), which most interpreters believe to be a fragment of a paschal and baptismal hymn.

> Awake, O sleeper,
>   and arise from the dead,
> and Christ will give you light.[20]

Finally, we read that Simon's mother-in-law, freed from her fever, immediately resumed her duties as hostess and "waited on them." This last observation underscores the instantaneous and complete character of the cure. But does Mark want to suggest something more? Once standing, the baptized are constituted the servants of their brothers and sisters in the ecclesial community, after the example of Jesus, who came not "to be served but to serve" (Mark 10:45). We remember that after multiplying loaves and fishes, Jesus tells the disciples to serve this unexpected food to the people, who all eat to their hearts' content (Mark 6:41-42; 8:6-7).

Wishing to round out the presentation of Jesus' ministry, which this first day exemplifies, Mark shows him in the midst of the crowd. At sunset, the sabbath ends. People are free to come and go, to resume the activities interrupted by the sabbath rest. "They brought to him all who were ill or possessed by demons. The whole town was gathered at the door." All are cured. By this generalization, Mark shows us that nothing resists Jesus' power and authority. He has been "sent by the Father to heal and save human beings."[21] He came for the sick and the sinners (Mark 2:17).

Mark concludes the narrative of this first day by saying that Jesus did not permit the demons "to speak because they knew him." The devil, therefore, has been the first to know and broadcast the truth about the identity of Jesus, Son of God, who silenced this compromising testimony.[22] We must confess that Mark's exact intention escapes us. We could suggest that Mark wants to show how grave is the incomprehension of human beings: whereas Jesus multiplies benefits towards them, they do not recognize the Son of God in him, while the unclean spirits whom he strips of their power know right away who he is. In fact, this contrast gives us food for thought even today. For us Christians, who *really* is Jesus Christ? Is our profession of faith a formula learned merely by rote, or is it truly the expression of a deep conviction that changes our very lives because one day we met the Lord?

Every participation in the liturgical celebration inexorably poses these questions, not to arouse in us feelings of guilt but to encourage us to humbly and confidently progress in the way of faith. This faith is weak and sometimes wavering. However, we must dare to say, "Jesus, the Son of God, is the Good News," asking him to take our hand, to wake us up from this lethargy that unceasingly threatens us and often immobilizes us. "The Lord has come as the physician of those who are sick. He himself declares: 'Those who are well do not need a physician, but the sick do. I did not come to call the righteous but sinners.' How will the sick get well? How will the sinners repent? Is it by continuing in the same state? Is it not, on the contrary, by a great change that causes them to leave their diseased and sinful condition?''[23]

"Rising very early before dawn, he left and went off to a deserted place, where he prayed." For Mark, the general overview of Jesus' activity would be incomplete without the mention of Jesus' prayer. The time devoted to prayer is not taken at the expense of the care of the sick or the demands of teaching—"very early before dawn." Habitual intimacy with God—total and without break in Jesus' case—does not do away with those pauses in silence and solitude, those face-to-face encounters, without distraction from the divine presence. Mark gives no information on Jesus' prayer. No one can fathom its secret, because the relationship between Father and Son has no equivalent that could be used as a reference. But we do know that the whole of Jesus' life was an offering to the Father, whose will he perfectly accomplished in all things. His prayer must have been the expression of this offering and the renewal of his obedience.[24] If prayer was a necessity for Jesus, it is all the more so for us. "If we do not know how to reserve a place for recollection and silence in our life, we cannot reach a higher degree and become able to pray in public places. Prayer makes us realize that one part of our being is immersed in our immediate circumstances, is constantly worried and scattered, whereas another part of ourselves observes it with astonishment and compassion. The agitated person causes the angels to shake with laughter."[25]

Simon and his companions go looking for Jesus, who has left the house. They find him and urge him to go back to the crowd waiting for him. Jesus replies: "Let us go on to the nearby villages that I may preach there also. For this purpose have I come."[26] Is there a causal relation between Jesus' prayer and this decision? One thing is certain: Jesus has received from the Father the mission of announcing the gospel ever farther, without stopping on the way. One is reminded of the sower in the parable who also "went out" in order to cast seed by the handful, saving neither strength nor seed. One part of it will not fall on good soil. But in the good soil, the seed will yield thirty, sixty, and even a hundred-fold and will console the sower for what did not germinate for lack of favorable conditions (Mark 4:3-8). Then Jesus leads his disciples throughout the whole of Galilee. After the resurrection, Galilee will be the place where he instructs his disciples to meet him (Mark 16:7). He will tell them, "Go into

the whole world and proclaim the gospel to every creature" (Mark 16:15).
"They went forth and preached everywhere" (Mark 16:20).

The Church must likewise be missionary in order to always carry the
gospel elsewhere. An ecclesial community closed in upon itself forgets
the Lord's example and demonstrates a lack of trust in the Spirit. It will
soon become hardened. Every great period in the history of the Church
has, in fact, been characterized by a powerful missionary thrust. It is told
of Pope Pius XI (1922-1939) that he answered a bishop who was asking
for guidance, "Go farther." Mark no doubt remembers Paul and his great
missionary journeys. In any event, the reading of his Gospel throughout
the Sundays of this year's Ordinary Time ought to awaken, stimulate,
encourage the zeal and missionary boldness of Christian communities.

The life of each one of us, of all communities, of the Church is crossed
by trials that could produce moroseness, even pessimism. But instead
of letting ourselves fall prey to these, we must in a trustful prayer turn
to the Father. "Rightly is my hope strong in Him, who sits at Thy right
hand and intercedes for us; otherwise I should despair. For many and
great are my infirmities, many and great; but Thy medicine is of more
power."[27] The Lord raises us by the hand and makes us stand again. He
calls us to his service and drives us to follow him, to be the servants of
all, and to announce the gospel, as far as we can go.

> Evil gnaws at our life:
> you free us.
> You draw from the Father
> the strength that saves us.
> The whole world looks for you,
> straining towards the Good News:
>
> *Jesus Christ, Savior of the world!*
>
> When I cried to you, Lord,
> my God, you healed me.
>
> You drew me out of the abyss
> and revived me when I went down into the pit.
>
> Celebrate the Lord, you, his faithful ones,
> render thanks by recalling his holy name.[28]

"If You Wish, You Can Make Me Clean"

A Terrible Disease, Image of Sin

In all ages there have been diseases that inspire fear and strike the imagination because of the mysterious character of their appearance and spread and of our inability to find a remedy for them. If, moreover, they cause disfiguring lesions or noticeable deformities, they arouse revulsion. People dare not look at the persons stricken with such sickness, and still less they want no contact with them; they avoid them. Whether justified or not, the fear of contagion results in the isolation of the sick. Such was the case for leprosy[1] for a long time, singularly in the Near East. When religious concepts link health and holiness,[2] sickness and sin,[3] those who are stricken with a mysterious and incurable ailment are readily considered to be undergoing divine punishment. We do not have here a merely archaic conception of religion, of temporal retribution and, as a consequence, of the meaning of adversities that befall individuals and entire populations.[4] Whatever the degree of sophistication of religious thought, the problem of suffering—and death—remains. What meaning can misfortune and disease have? Where do calamities such as a disastrous epidemic, sudden or endemic, come from? Are they not always blamed in some way on sins, understood either in the strict personal sense or in the wide sense of faults committed, voluntarily or not, by human beings?[5] Leviticus does not ask these questions in so many words, but it promulgates laws of prophylaxis regarding leprosy. Today's first reading reminds us of these because the Gospel depicts the cure of a leper by Jesus, and because this cure is fully understood only in reference to the manner in which lepers were regarded and treated (Lev 13:1-2, 45-46).

Lepers were unclean, but not only by reason of their diseased skin. They were to dwell "apart . . . outside the camp," but not only for fear of contagion. Their lesions evoked memories of those festering boils that had afflicted the Egyptians and their cattle (9:8-12). These were punishments in retribution for Pharaoh's hardening his heart and opposing

God's will. The Israelites were spared. But recalling the evils befalling the Egyptians, Deuteronomy says that the same would strike God's people if they were unfaithful to the Lord's law (Deut 28:21, 27, 35). Moreover, the Book of Isaiah envisions the whole people as a single person seriously ill for having repeatedly broken the covenant (Isa 1:5-6). However, a mysterious Servant of God will arise, a Just One who will take upon himself the sins and the sufferings of the multitude. "By his stripes" all will be healed (Isa 53:1-12). God has heard him interceding for human beings stricken with the leprosy of sin, now assured that their cries of distress will be heard.

> I turn to you, Lord, in time of trouble,
> and you fill me with the joy of salvation.
>
> Happy is he whose fault is taken away,
>   whose sin is covered.
> Happy the man to whom the LORD imputes not guilt,
>   in whose spirit there is no guile.
>
> ———
>
> Then I acknowledged my sin to you,
>   my guilt I covered not.
> I said, "I confess my faults to the LORD,"
>   and you took away the guilt of my sin.
>
> ———
>
> Be glad in the LORD and rejoice, you just;
>   exult, all you upright of heart.
> (Ps 32:1-2, 5, 11)

For the Glory of God and in the Interest of All

When he is called to settle a question of morality, to determine what attitude is appropriate to such and such a concrete situation, Paul always rises to higher perspective. He obliges his correspondents to face their responsibilities as believers. He reminds them of the mystery of God and Christ, in which they participate; the condition to which they have been raised by faith and baptism; their belonging to the Church, the body of Christ. Put in this context and this perspective, Paul's moral teaching is truly theological and Christian: it has its origin and its motivation in God; it is the imitation of Christ. It is distinct from a moralistic theory characterized by a rigid, voluntaristic, and often formalistic adherence to objective norms of behavior. Even when it appeals to God's law, this moralistic attitude remains, in fact, at the level of a merely human morality. The standards can be very high. The strong thus feel called to unceasingly go beyond themselves, but the others, unable to keep themselves at these heights, are disheartened. On the other hand, the gospel calls all humans to perfection and to a joyous response to this vocation whose limitless demands go hand in hand with the assurance of God's grace. This is what Paul preaches at every occasion: the gospel morality. The way opened to all by Christ is arduous; it excludes any compromise with evil and worldly morals; but those who falter can count on mercy. Mercy helps them up again and gives them new strength to go on.

Paul always and precisely answers concrete questions. However, his way is not that of casuistry, which limits itself to solutions case by case. When Paul deals with a particular topic, his answer always goes beyond the case under examination. We thus have a point of reference helping us to determine the conduct that is necessary or appropriate in similar circumstances, albeit always original, if not unheard of.[6] This is why what Paul wrote long ago remains appropriate to our times. In other words, he enunciates principles that can be applied always, by all, and everywhere. It is thus in the brief excerpt from the First Letter to the Corinthians that we read on this Sunday (1 Cor 10:31–11:1).

This passage gives us the conclusion of the discussion of a problem that no longer concerns us. In Corinth, as well as in all Gentile cities, markets offered meat that had come from the slaughter of animals sacrificed to idols in temples. Might Christians buy and eat this meat? Was this not a kind of participation in the pagan worship they had renounced? The discussion was lively in the community, and opposite opinions gave rise to confrontations. Paul's answer is at once clear and full of nuances. Idols are nothing; therefore, the sacrifice of animals in the sanctuaries does not give the meat sold in the markets any particular qualification. Those who understand this can eat it without scruple. But they must renounce this freedom if it scandalizes some brothers and sisters (1 Cor 8:1-13; 10:23-29). The problem of *eidolothuta*—the term designating meat coming from sacrifices to idols—is utterly foreign to us. But the principle Paul appeals to in order to solve it has not lost its vigor: everything that is permissible is not always becoming or edifying. The renunciation of one's more enlightened conscience is sometimes a duty.

Everything we do—eating, drinking, whatever else—we must do ''for the glory of God,'' to which anything can contribute.[7] This is the supreme object. But we ought not forget that the concern for God's glory must make us careful to act in such a way that others, in particular the weakest, may be encouraged to also give glory to God. Otherwise, freedom becomes a lack of respect and an obstacle in the way of some people.[8] "Knowledge inflates with pride, but love builds up" (1 Cor 8:1). The immediate interest of others takes precedence over personal interest. We must seek the salvation of all, which entails humbly and patiently helping others to accede, in their turn, to the freedom of a well-formed conscience. In this, too, Christ is the model: he was never discouraged with his disciples, so slow to understand. And, fortunately, he behaves in the same way with each one of us.

> Lord,
> as a good soil that bears fruit,
> your Eucharist
> carries us in your love:
> May it be for us
> seed of love
> and sign of the joy
> of the children of God who
> already today
> live in freedom,
> waiting for its full manifestation
> for ever and ever.[9]

Jesus Cures a Leper

As a way of ending the general presentation of Jesus' ministry, Mark depicts for his readers a truly extraordinary scene of healing (Mark 1:40-45). For it has to do not with just any sort of disease, as feared as it might be, but with leprosy, which rendered those it affected unclean, excluded from society and from participation in worship. Jesus allows this leper to come to him. He cleanses him with a word, while touching him with his hand. He then gives a stern warning to the man he has just cured; this surprises us and we do not know what to make of it. The man, for his part, does exactly the opposite of what he is told: he broadcasts to all and sundry what has just happened to him. Jesus appears much annoyed by this. But he does not succeed in escaping the crowds that manage to find him and leave him no peace. Every one of the elements in this picture must hold our attention because they no doubt contain teachings that Mark wants us to discover. First of all, to alert us to this, he inserts such a narrative at this point; he abruptly launches into it without any historical or geographical context. All this throws the story into striking relief and suggests that it has a particular meaning in Mark's Gospel.

"A leper came to him." This action, which defies all the interdictions, is scarcely believable. We do not see how the leper was able to approach Jesus without being restrained by those who saw him coming; they should have shouted in order to chase him far away. But Mark says nothing about this; he does not even mention witnesses, as if Jesus' companions, present up to now, have vanished. "A leper came," was able to come, "to him." All barriers are down. All lepers must know this as well as those who keep them apart from everything and everyone. Whoever believes that Jesus, if he so wishes, can purify them, let them draw near and rely upon the Lord's kindness. From the beginning of his Gospel, Mark has shown that Jesus' teaching, his power over evil spirits and disease manifest his authority. This is precisely what attracts the attention of the multitudes to Jesus. By emphasizing this authority, Mark urges us to follow Jesus on the roads where he announces the good news. However, the way Jesus exercises this sovereign authority during the day at Capernaum may appear somewhat cold and remote. Jesus seems to put his power at the service of the sick, while remaining impassive. The cure of the leper convinces us to go beyond this first impression: Jesus is "moved with pity." In current usage, "pity" belongs to the realm of feeling; it is "sympathy with the grief or misery of another; compassion or fellow suffering";[10] there is a connotation of condescension.[11] The Bible does not give this meaning to pity or mercy, but speaks of them as powerful feelings, made of tenderness and love, gut-wrenching and producing acts that relieve and heal those who inspire them.[12] Such is Jesus' pity.

> Jesus' compassion is not skin-deep; it is an upheaval of the depths of his being. There is no true compassion without passion: those who are compassionate really suffer in their own persons. Compassion is a communion in suffering. It is impossible for the Father to remain impassive when the children suffer—and among them the eternal Son made a human being. The Father's suffering is a great mystery, and when we want to speak about it, we stammer miserably. However, it is urgent to reject from our mind the idea that the Father, because of the perfection of his nature, looks from afar on human suffering without himself being painfully involved and wounded. . . .
>
> The cure of the leper orients my meditation in this direction. I cannot believe that Jesus does not suffer as much as the poor sick man and that the Father does not suffer as much as Jesus.[13]

"I do will it. Be made clean." As the Roman centurion had proclaimed, "Only say the word and my servant will be healed" (Matt 8:8; Luke 7:7), these words of Jesus would be sufficient, as were the words, "Come out of him!'' to deliver the demoniac at Capernaum from the evil spirit (Mark 1:25-26). But the Lord ''stretched out his hand'' and touched the leper. This gesture, accompanying the word, concretely illustrates the pity of Jesus, whose compassion for the one who is imploring him with trust is not a remote sort of thing. Christians cannot help but evoke the laying on of hands, the unctions that, along with words and prayers, constitute sacramental rites.[14] When reading this account, we could even think of what happens in the sacramental encounter with the Lord. Faith impels us to ask that he use his healing power: ''If you wish, you can make me clean.'' The sacrament is the answer to this expectation and the seal that authenticates faith. ''Jesus confirms and corroborates what the leper had said; and, consequently, he does not merely answer, 'Be made clean.' By speaking in this manner, he verifies the truth glimpsed by the man and confirms the leper's own statement.''[15] What follows is the more surprising. ''Then, warning him sternly, he dismissed him at once. Then he said to him: 'See that you tell no one anything, but go, show yourself to the priest and offer for your cleansing what Moses prescribed; that will be proof for them.' '' We can understand the command to go and submit to the official examination by the priests charged with that duty, according to the manner prescribed by the Law (Lev 14:1-32). It was in the man's interest to have the cure verified in due form and thus to be officially reintegrated into the community.

If Jesus had been content with reminding him of this obligation, fearing that in his joy the man might forget to fulfill it, we could see in Jesus' command a mark of delicacy. But Jesus speaks in strongly threatening tones.[16] What is going on? Obviously Jesus wants the leper to leave as fast as possible, as if the man were an embarrassing witness whom Jesus wants to disappear and to melt into the anonymous crowd. For lack of an explanation on Mark's part, we can only refer to the fact that he mentions several times a similar command to keep silent.[17] At the time of Mark's writing, the good news, far from being kept a secret, is publicly proclaimed from the rooftops, according to the Lord's command. But Mark is keen on progressive pedagogy. We must respect the steps in Christian initiation lest the Lord's true identity and the meaning of his mission be misunderstood. He is not a healer or exorcist among others, even though endowed with unheard-of powers. He is the Savior, who gave his life to heal humankind from the disease of sin, evoked at that time by leprosy more than by any other illness. There would be a grave equivocation if we were mistaken about the meaning of the healings he performed. There was great risk of such ill-considered publicity in the lepers's cure. The lesson retains all its relevance. A catechesis that would hurry through the necessary steps could rapidly prove disastrous in its results.

But the healed leper cannot contain his joy. "The man went away and began to publicize the whole matter. He spread the report abroad. . . ." Jesus then tries to escape the crowds and their infatuation. He enters the towns on the sly; he even avoids inhabited places, but to no avail; people come to him from everywhere. His peacefully begun mission is going to take a completely different turn. He must now confront no longer the ambiguous enthusiasm of the crowds but overt opposition to his person and teaching from those who should have recognized his authority as Son of God from the testimonies of the leper and other sick persons made whole.

It is impossible to live in the world without being exposed to its chaotic and unyielding nature. There are no desert places to spare us its contact. Having assumed human nature in its totality, Jesus experiences this from the outset of his ministry. Since the crowds come to him, he goes to them, endeavoring with patience and without discouragement to make them understand that he is not the earthly Messiah they are dreaming of. By inopportunely proclaiming his title of Son of God, demons are seeking to discredit him and pretend he is their leader (Mark 3:22). Whenever demons raise their voices, Jesus silences them. But he will have to face their repeated assaults and will not escape this war of attrition. He will emerge victorious but only on the cross, when a pagan, seeing "how he breathed his last" will cry out in an act of wholehearted faith, "Truly this man was the Son of God!" (Mark 15:39).

Battling with the world, its weight, and its ever-recurring temptations, we can trustfully turn to the Lord and ask him without hesitation to say the word that will set us back on our feet so that we may continue to walk despite the obstacles on the way, saying with Paul, "My model is Christ."

> Lord, my God, what about the universe?
> Affirm you as I may, I am in its grip.
>
> It forcefully rules my heart,
> I am caught in its laws, in its chains.
>
> It drives me, I am going to yield to it,
> to it which has no future for me.

But you, you predestine your servants,
They take hold of their chains, they rise.

Turned toward you, they turn their chains around,
And around they turn the universe.

With its laws for pain or pleasure,
With its beat within which is a knell.

But you, you seized it back and already there is trust!
The feast is not yet here, but it is coming.

The feast echoes the universe that prolongs the feast,
And chains also sing in the concert.

One single word, and I shall be free!
Trust, and I am free![18]

In Mark's Gospel, the beginning of Jesus' ministry—his first day in Capernaum and the leper's cure—is presented in the manner of a neatly delineated sequence, introducing us to what follows As a result, the Fourth, Fifth, and Sixth Sunday in Ordinary Time, Year B, during which we read Mark 1:21-45, constitute a unit.

The authority manifested by his teaching, his power over disease and evil spirits, unceasingly pose the question of Jesus' identity. The Christians assembled for the liturgy certainly know that he is the Son of God, the Good News, the Savior, who on the cross took upon himself our sicknesses and sins: this is the mystery of faith celebrated in every Eucharist. But to celebrate it in spirit and in truth requires that we constantly allow ourselves to be purified by the word and touch of the Lord from every stain on our faith, that we accept to be driven ever farther by Christ and the liturgy. If we want to belong wholeheartedly to the Lord, we shall often have to make choices contradicting those of the world or those of our immediate small world. But then we set out on the way of freedom and, being all things to all, we share in the work of salvation for God's glory, with our eyes fixed on Christ, our model.

From the Seventh to the Tenth Sunday in Ordinary Time

For these four Sundays, the liturgy and Mark lead Christians in the footsteps of Jesus, who moves on at such a pace that it is impossible to follow his itinerary on a map. This new sequence begins "at home," probably Simon's home, in Capernaum. It concludes in another, unknown, house. We get the impression that Mark voluntarily omits details lest they divert our attention from the essential: what Jesus says and does, the ensuing reactions, his answers to the reproaches and accusations aimed at him. In any case, Mark manages his narrative in a way that makes it impossible for the readers to remain indifferent; they feel, as it were, forced to get involved in these debates, however out of date. People accuse Jesus of blasphemy (Mark 2:1-12—Seventh Sunday); they reproach him with making light of traditional practices like fasting (Mark 2:18-22—Eighth Sunday); they charge him with violating the Sabbath (Mark 2:23–3:6—Ninth Sunday); his own family thinks he has gone mad, and some scribes go so far as to say he is possessed by the prince of demons (Mark 3:20-35—Tenth Sunday). Therefore, all must decide for or against Jesus, recognize or deny his authority and, by the same token, his being the Son of God. Moreover, these disputes on the Law and religious observances, on how they are understood and kept, are revealing: "Show me your praxis and I will show you your God." This is the core of the debate between Jesus and his opponents. The principles he enunciates with authority and his behavior remain the norms applicable for all times, whatever the legitimate evolution of laws and customs might be.

It is particularly important for Christians to remember this when they are gathered for the liturgy. They are invited to question themselves about their manner of celebrating and on the connection—or lack thereof—between the worship they render to God and, in particular, their attitude toward their neighbor.

On the Seventh Sunday, we begin the reading of generous excerpts from Paul's Second Letter to the Corinthians, a reading that will continue until the Fourteenth Sunday.[1]

Seventh Sunday

Jesus Prosecuted

Forgiveness of Sin, A New Creation

The first faith experience attested by the Bible is that of a God who saves; it is rooted in the memory of the liberation from the slavery in Egypt.[1] From a mob of unsaved men and women and through Moses, to whom he revealed his plan, God formed a free people with which he made a covenant by giving them his Law and to whom he taught, along with his name, the manner of worship pleasing to him. By pondering this fundamental experience, the sages of Israel progressively understood that if God can act with such sovereignty, he must have created everything: the universe and all the things it contains, with humankind placed at its center.[2] As a consequence, every further intervention of God in the world is always referred to creation, which is the first manifestation of his initiative and of his plan for humankind and the chosen people. This is especially the case when he acts to free the people from sin and its consequences—loss of dominion over the earth and exile. Isaiah develops this theme when he announces to the exiles in Babylon their forthcoming liberation. However, the oracle has a much wider scope than the precise event the prophet deals with. In fact, like most other prophetic oracles, it was endlessly read and reread in order to shed light on the decoding of present events and "signs of the times." Today's liturgy proposes to us one of these readings (Isa 43:18-19, 21-22, 24c-25).[3]

"See, I am doing something new!" Each step of the history of salvation is a new creation at God's initiative. His intention continues in the direction of his original intention; God does not act by fits and starts. Nor is he capricious, like persons constantly hesitating, being unsure of the value of their work. But he never repeats himself; he always creates new things never seen before that arouse astonishment and admiration. He does not abolish the past, but he renews himself indefinitely. The prophet thinks of the return from exile. Signs that foretell it are occurring; the announced future "springs forth, do you not perceive it?" Once more, this liberation is glimpsed as a new Exodus, more beautiful than the first because, on their way, the people will no longer suffer from the aridity of the wilderness. Nor will they murmur as they so often did between leaving Egypt and entering the Promised Land. They will "announce [the Lord's] praise" by recognizing that every initiative comes from God. This ancient oracle sheds a surprising light on the mystery and the mission of Christ. Obviously Jesus was inspired by Isaiah's message when he proclaimed the good news and the prompt coming of the kingdom.[4] In Jesus people saw God's power at work. Paul speaks of "new creation" (2 Cor 5:17) when describing what the Lord has done. "The grace of God has sprung; it has refashioned and turned souls around; it changed them by transforming not their being but their will. Human reason is no longer allowed to contradict the true reality of things: grace has, in effect, removed the scales covering the eyes; now the eyes acutely perceive the monstrous ugliness of vice and the dazzling beauty of virtue."[5]

> It is I, I who wipe out,
>> for my own sake, your offenses;
>> your sins I remember no more.

This is the great novelty of the new creation: a forgiveness offered in a completely gratuitous manner, "for my own sake," God says.

> Yet you did not call upon me, O Jacob,
>> for you grew weary of me, O Israel.

> ———

> Instead, you burdened me with your sins,
>> and wearied me with your crimes.

When we hear this oracle today, how can we help but turn toward Christ, his arms outstretched on the cross, and confess both our sins and his infinite mercy that makes of us new creations in a new world in which "new things have come" (2 Cor 5:17)?

> *Lord, heal my soul,*
> *for I have sinned against you.*
> Happy is he who has regard for the lowly and the poor;
>> in the day of misfortune the LORD will deliver him.
> The LORD will keep and preserve him;
>> he will make him happy on the earth,
>> and not give him over to the will of his enemies.
> The LORD will help him on his sickbed,
>> he will take away all his ailment when he is ill.
> Once I said, "O LORD, have pity on me;
>> heal me, though I have sinned against you.

But because of my integrity you sustain me
and let me stand before you forever.

———

Blessed be the LORD, the God of Israel,
from all eternity and forever. Amen.
(Ps 41:1-5, 13-14)

Our Yes and Amen Like Christ's

Faith rests on the authenticity and the veracity of an uninterrupted line
of testimonies going back to Christ's unimpeachable testimony. God is
the guarantee of the preaching of the apostles and the Church, of the
authenticity of all Christians' testimonies. Everything must be judged by
this criterion. What Paul writes on this topic to the Corinthians, in response to some people who challenged his ministry, appears singularly
appropriate for a time in which there is an overabundance of messages
that—even in the religious domain—capture the attention and trust of
people by sometimes using slogans for publicity purposes (2 Cor 1:18-22).

Paul always seeks to be "all things to all" (1 Cor 9:22) but never at the
expense of the gospel, never by watering it down, even in a small way.
"For I resolved to know nothing while I was with you except Jesus Christ,
and him crucified . . . and my message and my proclamation were not
with persuasive [words of] wisdom, but with a demonstration of spirit
and power, so that your faith might rest not on human wisdom but on
the power of God" (1 Cor 2:2, 4-5). In this, he is aware of imitating the
Lord himself. ". . . I did not speak on my own, but the Father who sent
me commanded me what to say and speak. And I know that his commandment is eternal life. So what I say, I say as the Father told me" (John
12:49-50). In their turn, the Lord's disciples must be able to attest that
they do not speak of themselves but that they proclaim and announce
what they have learned and received (1 Cor 11:23): the gospel of our Lord
Jesus Christ. But it is not enough to mouth the words. One's whole life
must bear witness to one's exclusive attachment to the will of God and
of his Son, who gave us the example of such submission. When he came
into this world, he said, "Behold, I come to do your will" (Heb 10:9).
And Jesus never wavered from this "Yes," this "Amen," said to the Father, and he sealed it by his death on the cross. Such are, in the Lord's
footsteps, Christ's disciples.

> Christians are beings who take upon themselves . . . They commit them-
> selves. Not only here or there, but totally in every act, so that if they re-

spond to what God and the world expect of them, any one of their acts should be as the concentration of their whole lives, and their whole lives should tend to reproduce the thrust of any single individual act. Their "sincerity" is not that sentimental, blind, passive, changing assurance that led some of our contemporaries to mistake the gushing of their most superficial self-satisfaction for a deep source of life. It is a unity resulting from effort as well as from gifts not so much sought after as deserved by those who always say "I," thinking of their *ego* as little as possible. For the "I" that commits itself and asserts itself is so directly connected to the reality to which it gives itself that it effaces itself with a self-effacement superior to ordinary self-effacement, as a mediator, as one who answers and who would be entirely contained in the answer. What the "I" so transfigured receives from Christian life is the prize of a response ever more personal, different from the tyrannical motto of a collectivity or the dull reply of a logical argument, a principle foreign to personal anguish, but a unique word in a unique gift: "This drop of blood that I have poured out for you. . . ."[6]

At his first preaching in the synagogue at Nazareth, Jesus read in the Book of Isaiah that was handed to him,

> The Spirit of the Lord is upon me
> because he has anointed me
>   to bring glad tidings to the poor.

Rolling up the scroll and handing it back to the attendant, he said, "Today this scripture passage is fulfilled in your hearing" (Luke 4:18, 21). In their turn, the apostles were consecrated by the unction of the spirit that the Lord communicated to them in order that they might go to announce the gospel to the whole world. It is for the benefit of others that the gifts of the Spirit were poured into the hearts of the apostles; but they are also poured into the hearts of all baptized persons, who are called to be faithful witnesses of Christ and the good news.

In the course of the liturgy and in prayer, we often say "Amen." This simple word—that any translation would weaken—expresses an adherence that takes in the whole being of those who pronounce it.

> It is a wholehearted Yes, Father,
> Which you say upon us through Jesus Christ;
> And besides, through him you enable us
> To answer Amen to your call.
>
> In him your promises to human beings
> Have forever found their fulfillment;
> There is no hope, no expectation in the world
> That does not find its future in him.

In response to your gospel
May my Yes be an unconditional Yes,
And become in my mouth a hymn
Proclaiming the glory of your name.

Like a seal your love stamps
Its eternity on our lives;
You pour into our hearts the earnest
and the royal unction of the Spirit.[7]

Forgiveness of Sins for Those Who Believe

Mark shows that Jesus' ministry, begun in Capernaum, first aroused the enthusiasm of the crowds that came to him and were astounded by his authority when he preached, healed the sick, and expelled demons. It is also in that city, become Jesus' own in a certain way, and in that house where he feels at home, that his ministry takes a new turn. In fact, Mark wants to lead his readers to take a further step in the knowledge of the Lord and to examine their faith and the strength of their attachment to the one whose works they marvel at. The question, already asked at the beginning, is asked again and again with renewed intensity, "But who is this man?" Mark takes us within the circle around Jesus from which rise voices, shy at first—mere whispers—then louder and louder, saying, "Who does he think he is?" Faced with these ever more violent assaults, we must take a stand, declare ourselves unambiguously for or against Jesus. From the first confrontation, we perceive that a drama is in the making, albeit still covert (Mark 2:1-12).[8]

So Jesus "returned to Capernaum." The news immediately spreads and the house is soon invaded; even the door is blocked by people who cannot get in. Four men arrive, carrying a paralytic on a stretcher; they cannot get near. They do not give up. They have come to obtain the paralytic's cure; they must get him near Jesus. Climbing onto the roof by the outside staircase, they lower the stretcher down through an opening they have made.[9]

The scene is described so vividly that we have the impression we are a part of it. We even catch ourselves imagining the various feelings and remarks of the people within the house and those unable to get in. Filled with admiration, indignation, or resentment at such audacity, they certainly have their eyes on Jesus in order to watch his reaction; and this is precisely what Mark invites us to do without allowing ourselves to be distracted by the din of conversations. Jesus sees only one thing: these men's faith that motivates their action, showing a total trust in him.[10]

What is it to have faith? It is to break the roof open. It is to gamble one's life on the invisible, that is, on what one has never seen. It is to lean on God in order to create, to bring to birth what does not yet exist, what is unheard-of, unlikely, mad sometimes. To break the roof open.

What is it to have faith? It is to challenge Jesus to do the impossible. He will take up the challenge. He too breaks open a roof, thicker than that of the house. He is going to enter this crippled person, walled up by infirmity, and say the crazy words, "Your sins are forgiven."[11]

"Child, your sins are forgiven." These words surprise us. We would expect Jesus, as in other circumstances, to express his admiration for these men's faith and to dismiss the paralytic, saying to him for instance, "Your faith has made you whole. Go in peace and be cured of your illness."[12] For the paralytic was before him to obtain his cure. Why does Jesus make him wait? One single word and the happy man would know that he has not trusted Jesus in vain. Why not simply take him by the hand, helping him to rise? In this very house, Simon's mother-in-law, laid up with a fever, had been helped to her feet in an instant with this lovely gesture, full of delicacy and consideration (Mark 1:31). Certainly Mark foresaw all these questions. In this narrative, the words "Child, your sins are forgiven" are a sort of enigma, at any rate a sentence that could only appear intriguing and hold the attention: "Why does this man speak that way?" This is a perfectly reasonable question that does not surprise us coming from scribes, masters of the art of comprehending the meaning of words with the accuracy of professional exegetes and the exactness of lawyers.[13] They know that no one can forgive sins "but God alone." Sure of this, they could ask themselves whether Jesus is not empowered to speak with authority in God's name; instead, they yield to prejudice. They are familiar with Isaiah's oracle announcing a new world characterized by the forgiveness of sins.[14] They could wonder whether the prophetic oracle is not in the process of being fulfilled; instead, they pronounce in their hearts a categorical condemnation, "He is blaspheming."

We would misconstrue Mark's intention if we stopped at the scribes' murmurings in order to justify ourselves, saying, "How is such a reaction possible? We would never have reasoned as those people did. In any case, we do know that Jesus has the power to forgive sins, because we confess that he is the Son of God, whose coming fulfills prophecies." We had better continue reading. " 'Which is easier, to say to the paralytic, "Your sins are forgiven," or to say, "Rise, pick up your mat and

walk''? But that you may know that the Son of Man has authority to forgive sins on earth'—he said to the paralytic, 'I say to you, rise, pick up
your mat, and go home.' ''

''Which is easier . . . ?'' Jesus is not speaking, of course, of any difficulty in pronouncing such and such words, but of the verifiable efficacy
of the words pronounced. In this sense, it is easier to say, ''Your sins
are forgiven,'' than, ''Rise, pick up your mat and walk.'' On the one hand,
we could think of words said airily, since their results cannot be seen;
on the other hand, we shall see whether the words make anything happen or not. The paralytic's cure then becomes for the witnesses a sign—
or a pledge—that Jesus gives to prove that he can also forgive sins. Very
well. But what about us? How can this narrative—even a most truthful
one—of a cure worked long ago constitute for us a proof or a sign of Jesus'
power to forgive sins? The more so as, frankly, we find this power exor-
bitant and unimaginable.[15]

What is true of all other signs is true of this one also: it directs us to
a higher, invisible reality; it invites faith but does not impose it. Besides,
although it is possible to believe because of one single sign, this isolated
sign remains ambiguous or at least demands verification. Its authenticity
and therefore its potency and its value are in fact due to its similarity to
the other signs. Finally, in order to perceive what the sign means and
how it touches us, we must not only have our eyes open, but we must
have a keen desire to see and a mind that is prepared to welcome what
is new and unforeseen. Otherwise, whatever happens, we shall remain
uncomprehending spectators, unaware of the importance of the events
that are unfolding before us; we shall not even suspect that they might
have a meaning and concern us. At best, we shall remember for a while
their extraordinary character. At worst, we shall shrug our shoulders or,
not trying to see any farther, we shall turn away, rejecting the signs without having examined them.

''We have never seen anything like this,'' say the people, who seem
more impressed by the paralytic's cure than astonished by Jesus' words
on the forgiveness of sins. At least they give thanks to God. But others
speak of blasphemy, although they are professional exegetes. They
zealously scrutinize the Scriptures, but with their eyes so riveted on each
individual letter of the text that they end up believing that nothing exists
or can happen beyond what they read and what they have learned. The
lesson is severe. Scribes of this sort are present at all times, and we all
agree with them in our hearts, at least sometimes. But they also can and

must accept conversion and become "like the head of a household who brings from his storeroom both the new and the old" (Matt 13:52). They assiduously ponder the Scriptures, always looking for something. It is hoped that they do not lose sight of Jesus, of whom all Scriptures speak and who, by his person, his teaching, and his actions, reveals their ultimate meaning.

"Who therefore is this man?" The question recurs time and again in Mark's Gospel. It will be tragically asked once more in front of the Crucified One (Mark 15:39). We must, every time, bring our personal and thought-out answer, not the result of book knowledge, to which we give lip service and which we repeat without conviction. Such a personal answer matures through the persevering contact with the Lord revealed by Scripture and liturgy; then one is able to detect the Lord's actions and recognize the signs in everybody life. In Mark's account of the paralytic's cure, the mysterious title of Son of Man appears for the first time, harking back to Daniel's prophecies. The Son of Man receives power over everything (Dan 7:13-14), and he will come on the last day to judge the sinner and save the just (Mark 13:26-29).[16] Before the Sanhedrin, Jesus will openly declare himself "the Messiah, the son of the Blessed One" and say,

> "You will see the Son of Man
>   seated at the right hand of the Power
>   and coming with the clouds of heaven."
> (Mark 14:62)

Jesus will be accused of blasphemy by the tribunal and, for that, condemned to death (Mark 14:63-64). But "on earth," the power of the Son of Man is exercised in the forgiveness of sins. The suit against Jesus is initiated from the very first weeks of his ministry. It continues until the end of time, and the object of the debate is always the same: "Who is this man? Where does the power he arrogates to himself come from? By what right does he proclaim himself the Son of Man who can forgive sins and be the judge of good and evil?"

In our own situation we are both actors and subjects, not merely spectators able to detach ourselves from the debate. We are the actors because we must personally decide for or against the one who is accused of being an impostor and a blasphemer. We are the subjects because this prosecution is against the Church and Christians. If we recognize that the Lord has never been anything than Yes and that "however many are the

promises of God, their Yes is in him," we must say our Amen in front
of the world and our Yes "through him to God for glory."

> Inert before you, this man
> at your word takes his pallet
> in the very instant God forgives.
> Paralyzed by our fear
> we hope to see the sinner
> freed, walking in your footsteps.

> Come to us again on our roads,
> You, the Lord who can heal us!
> Say one word, stretch out your hand,
> Our wounded bodies will blossom anew.[17]

Jesus, the Bridegroom Who Came and Who Is Expected

I Will Espouse You in Fidelity and You Shall Know the Lord
The history of God and his people is a long love story involving serious crises, owing to the repeated infidelities that injure the Lord's honor and discredit his name before the nations. But this does not alter his love and does not cause him to cancel his irrevocable promise of faithfulness made once and for all.

In order to express this relationship initiated by God, who from among all peoples has chosen this one, the Old Testament first speaks of covenant. Proposed by God and submitted to the people's ratification, it is afterwards recalled in all circumstances: by the Lord to bring the people back to its promises; by the people to ask for God's help and protection, to entreat his mercy and his pardon. This mutual contract—the meaning of the term covenant—respects the hierarchy existing between the signatories; it even unambiguously affirms it. God remains the Most High, the Almighty. But through this covenant, he has taken the initiative of establishing between him and his people an intimate relationship, something without parallel in other religions.

We can even go so far as to say that in risking this sort of relationship, the God of the Bible shows himself to be the All-Other, since his transcendence has nothing to fear from a proximity, albeit a close one, with his creature, from his involvement in human history and its ups and downs. We could say that God knows the risks he takes and he assumes them knowingly, as a bridegroom who does not doubt for one instant that his love will always bring back the unfaithful one in the end.

So from the metaphor of covenant, we have gone to that of marriage, which is akin to it. It is especially developed in the Book of Hosea the prophet,[1] from which we read a passage on this Sunday (Hos 2:16, 17b, 21-22).

God is not a naive or lenient bridegroom; he does not make light of the infidelities of his people. They wound him, especially as he can be reproached with nothing, nothing at all. But his people forget him (Hos 2:15) and abandon themselves to the most egregious prostitution.[2]

> So I will allure her;
> I will lead her into the desert
> and speak to her heart. . . .
> She shall respond there as in the days of her youth . . .

This desert is that of the Exodus, the wandering in the desert, when God had revealed himself and had concluded a covenant with the people he had elected. This new sojourn in the desert will no longer be a time of trial, but one of a new betrothal, this time "forever."[3] The Lord himself will give his fiancée what she needs to live, a strong[4] relationship, happy and, from now on, without upheaval.

> . . . I will espouse you in right and in justice,
> in love and in mercy;
> I will espouse you in fidelity . . .

These are the marvelous and precious engagement gifts that only the Lord is able to offer.[5]

Finally, there will be a heart-to-heart relationship whose foundation is no longer fear but trustful love.

Hosea's image will be taken up in the New Testament and applied to Christ, the bridegroom, and to the Church, the bride.[6] The Fathers of the Church, spiritual writers, and great preachers will develop all its riches.

> The Church as Bride belongs to Jesus Christ through his choice; the Church as Body belongs to Jesus Christ through God's very intimate operation. The mystery of election through promises appears in the name of Bride; and the mysteries of the union consummated by the outpouring of the Spirit appear in the name of Body. The name of Body shows us how much the Church belongs to Jesus Christ; the title of Bride shows us that once she was a stranger whom he voluntarily sought. Thus, the name of Bride shows us unity by love and will; and the name of Body suggests to us a natural unity, so that something more intimate is present in the unity of the body and something fuller of feeling and tenderness is present in the unity of the Bride.[7]

The Bible does not demonstrate God's existence, does not elaborate on his attributes; it shows them at work.[8] Humans have learned to know him because he revealed himself through his action in the world, in particular his actions in favor of his people. Thus the Bible is a book that narrates the centuries-long experience of the people to whom God chose to reveal himself and whom he made his witness in the midst of the nations. Like the experience, this witness is concrete; for it is that of the history through which the chosen people discover who God is, why he chose them, and according to which principles and with what intentions and feelings he rules the world.

The function of sages and prophets consists precisely in opening human eyes and hearts to the understanding of this history; in encouraging humans to enter into its dynamic movement, to work like wise collaborators of God, who constantly keeps them abreast of his projects and teaches them how they should contribute, day after day, to the coming of the promised kingdom. In sum, we have here the relationship between God, always faithful and unceasingly bent on furthering his plan, and the people, regularly forgetful of the covenant, the pledge of their future.

Hosea speaks of the mystery of this unprecedented relationship—"For what great nation is there that has gods so close to it as the Lord, our God, is to us whenever we call upon him?" (Deut 4:7)—in the accents of a person who has known the heartrending experience of a flouted love, an unshakable love that nothing can weaken, a love that forgets the worst infidelities. Centuries later, John will write, "God is love" (1 John 4:8).

The Lord is kind and merciful.

Bless the LORD, O my soul;
  and all my being, bless his holy name.
Bless the LORD, O my soul,
  and forget not all his benefits;
He pardons all your iniquities,
  he heals all your ills.
He redeems your life from destruction,
  he crowns you with kindness and compassion . . .
Merciful and gracious is the LORD,
  slow to anger and abounding in kindness.
Not according to our sins does he deal with us,
  nor does he requite us according to our crimes.
As far as the east is from the west,
  so far has he put our transgressions from us.
As a father has compassion on his children,
  so the LORD has compassion on those who fear him . . .
(Ps 103:1-4, 8, 10, 12-13)

A New Covenant Imprinted in the Heart

In the course of his apostolate, Paul, like so many after him, has known trials that have not all come from outside the Church.[9] For a variety of reasons, some have contested his ministry, and even his title of apostle,[10] questioning his authority and comparing him to some other people judged more brilliant or less acerbic. Besides, there have been misunderstandings, faulty interpretations of what he has said or is supposed to have said, often taken out of context and twisted, whether willfully or not, into meanings he has not intended.[11] It has even happened that some have insidiously questioned the authenticity of his mission for lack of guarantees. All this worries Paul because the well-being and progress of the Christians of Corinth could suffer from these rumors (2 Cor 3:1b-6).

To be accepted as authentic apostles, "do we need, as some do, letters of recommendation to you or from you?" Paul addresses the faithful of a community he himself evangelized during the course of a mission entrusted to him by the Church of Jerusalem and its legitimate leaders (Acts 13:2-3). He does not mean that no mandate is necessary, no delegation in order to exercise a ministry; that one can, on one's own, declare oneself a legitimate apostle. To draw such a conclusion would be wrong.

It is sometime after their evangelization that some in the community question the legitimacy and value of his apostolic work at Corinth. Under these circumstances, the response he gives to this unlikely objection is understandable, "You are our letter, written on our hearts, known and read by all." Paul calls his dear Corinthians back to reason, and all those who would resemble them. It is vain to discuss the respective qualifications of the missionaries; this results only in creating damaging and scandalous divisions (1 Cor 10:17): "What is Apollos, after all, and what is Paul? Ministers through whom you became believers, just as the Lord assigned each one" (1 Cor 3:5). We must regard the apostles "as servants of Christ and stewards of the mysteries of God. Now it is of course required of stewards that they be found trustworthy. It does not concern me in the least that I be judged by you or any human tribunal; I do not even pass judgment on myself. I am not conscious of anything against me, but I do not thereby stand acquitted: the one who judges me is the Lord" (1 Cor 4:1-4).

The Corinthians must turn their eyes toward the Lord because he, and he alone, is the author of the admirable change that happened to them, a change evident to all who have eyes to see. As to the authenticity of the missionaries' call, it is proved by its fruits (Matt 7:16). Many controversies, as painful as they are useless, would be avoided in the Church at-large and in particular Christian communities if people would have recourse to these same principles of discernment, sure and simple, instead of wasting their energies on fruitless questions of personalities.

Now, as always, Paul takes the debate to a higher plane. Every good comes from Christ through the Spirit. Christ writes God's law in hearts as the prophets had foretold, "I will place my law within them, and write it upon their hearts" (Jer 31:33).[12] In a few words, Paul reminds his readers of his teaching on the superiority of the new covenant over the old (Rom 8:2-27). It is by God's grace, not by their own power, that Paul and all others after him have been able to obtain some results. Indeed, one plants, the other waters: only the one who causes the growth is important—God (1 Cor 3:6-7). Therefore, let none boast of their apostolic success or grow sad at the sight of others' success. But let all recognize the action of the Spirit wherever it happens and bless God for enabling human beings to be "ministers of a new covenant, not of letter but of spirit; for the letter brings death, but the Spirit gives life."

> Do not believe in me, in my word,
> believe in that within, which seeks the Lord.
> Listen to the tentative names I find for him,
> but remember them only if they arouse your cry.
>
> Except when you adore the Lord,
> do not keep your distance from him.
>
> Do not crush within you what trustfully whispers his name,
> he himself has sown it within your flesh and bone.
>
> It is a germ that needs his light to grow
> and become a response of blood.[13]

New Wineskins for New Wine

In order to bring his readers to discover for themselves Jesus' person—"Who is this man?"—Mark involves them in controversies during which the Lord is led to take revealing positions. The subjects of these discussions may appear marginal in themselves when compared to the gospel message (as when fasting is discussed), but it is worthwhile to take a closer look, as this Sunday's Gospel invites us (Mark 2:18-22).[14]

"Why do the disciples of John and the disciples of the Pharisees fast, but your disciples do not fast?" All great religions give an important place to fasting in their practice. This fact alone is worth noting. Judaism today still has a great fast, that of the Day of Atonement, Yom Kippur, yearly observed on the tenth day of Tishri in the Jewish calendar. It is strictly enjoined upon all who belong to God's people.[15] For a long time, fasting had been part of the rites of penance and mourning.[16] After the Exile, a four-day fast was instituted in memory of the calamities visited upon the nation.[17] Some, like the Pharisees and the disciples of John the Baptist, added still other fast days.[18] In certain circles, these fasts expressed the dissatisfaction with the present world because the Messiah had not come.

These practices were eminently praiseworthy in spite of the risk of formalism, already denounced by the prophets.[19] The fact that Jesus does not keep these observances can only surprise, even shock, the Pharisees and the disciples of John, the great faster who "fed on locusts and wild honey" (Mark 1:6), he who in the wilderness had announced the coming of one greater than he (Mark 1:7). Whatever his inquirers' intentions, Jesus cannot evade their question. His answer interests us because it is set on a plane different from that of the usual polemics between partisans of diverse observances. This sort of discussion leads nowhere. The arguments traded back and forth easily become ridiculous. The contest frequently turns into a free-for-all in which all blows are allowed. In the end, the protagonists leave full of resentment, all contentiously clinging to their positions. As to the witnesses of such debates, whether amused or passionately interested, they are content with keeping score, and the exchange of arguments does not make a dent in their own preferences.

"Can the wedding guests fast while the bridegroom is with them? As long as they have the bridegroom with them, they cannot fast." Unclouded by any polemical or aggressive spirit, this answer first shows that Jesus takes the question seriously; he even thinks that it is a very good question. But his answer surprises us. He is asked to explain, to justify his disciples' behavior, manifestly divergent from accepted conventions: How can he tolerate, if not encourage, such off-handedness that scandalizes pious persons whose example should be followed? We would expect Jesus to recognize the neglect of the virtuous practice that people have a right to remind him of. Such an admission would strengthen both the good opinion that the observant have of themselves and their admirers' esteem; it would also discredit the young master in the eyes of a good number of the bystanders. Others, and above all the implicated disciples, no doubt hope that Jesus will find a way of justifying the liberty they have taken with traditional observances not imposed by the Law.

Jesus satisfies neither the one group nor the other. But he speaks to us a most important word of revelation that cannot leave us indifferent. We must take a stand, give our own answer, get involved, not in a debate on observances between people interested in that sort of thing but with regard to Jesus.

John's disciples furnish the basic material of his answer. The Precursor had called himself "the best man, who stands and listens for him, [rejoicing] greatly at the bridegroom's voice." He said further, "So this joy of mine has been made complete. He must increase and I must decrease" (John 3:29-30). Jesus' answer is equivalent to a proclamation similar to that at the synagogue of Nazareth, "Today this scripture passage is fulfilled in your hearing" (Luke 4:21). Moreover, not only John's words but also the prophet's oracle from which John had borrowed have a bearing on Jesus' answer.

> Fear not, you shall not be put to shame;
>   you need not blush, for you shall not be disgraced.
> The shame of your youth you shall forget,
>   the reproach of your widowhood no longer remember.
> For he who has become your husband is your maker;
>   his name is the LORD of hosts;
> Your redeemer is the Holy One of Israel."
> (Isa 54:4-5).

John the Baptist has been sent before him to prepare the way. He preached "a baptism of repentance for the forgiveness of sins"; and he said, "I have baptized you with water; he will baptize you with the holy Spirit" (Mark 1:2-8). Here we have again, and with fresh insistence, the question put from the beginning: "But who is this man?" He has been seen to teach with authority, command even the demons, who obey him (Mark 1:21-28), heal all sorts of diseases (Mark 1:29-45), and forgive sins (Mark 2:1-12).[20] And now he is declaring himself to be the Bridegroom whose presence stops the fasts practiced by those who expect the Messiah. Therefore, he claims to be the expected one announced by the prophets.

But what of the question about fasting? Jesus does not forget it—on the contrary. He recognizes not only its value but also the suitability of the meaning given it. Furthermore, Jesus makes this meaning his own, amplifying it into a new dimension; he has not come to abolish the Law or the Prophets but to fulfill them (Matt 5:17). Since the Bridegroom is here among his own, we must not fast as if we still awaited the promised Savior. "But the days will come when the bridegroom is taken away from them, and then they will fast on that day." They will fast again, in the expectation of his return and of the wedding solemnly celebrated in the heavenly Jerusalem.

> "Alleluia!
> The Lord has established his reign,
>   [our] God, the almighty.
> Let us rejoice and be glad
>   and give him glory.

For the wedding day of the Lamb has come,
his bride has made herself ready.
She was allowed to wear
a bright, clean linen garment."
(The linen represents the righteous deeds of the holy ones.) . . . "Blessed
are those who have been called to the wedding feast of the Lamb."
(Rev 19:6-9)

Without ignoring its other meanings, Jesus favors the fast that expresses a faith aspiring to the full realization of the kingdom that he came to inaugurate on earth. All forms of fasting, all ascetical and penitential practices that the Church continues to observe, all states of life, the liturgy itself have in common this qualification, this fundamental dimension: the active expectation of the Lord who has come and is coming. None of these looks inward, has its value in itself. Fasting, penitential practices, states of life in which voluntary asceticism play a large place are evangelical and lived in an evangelical manner, inasmuch as they are animated by the joy born of an assured hope not to be disappointed.[21]

One cannot help but think here of the Eucharist and the Day of the Lord. The Eucharist is the great breaking of the fast, which must be interrupted on Sundays. The Eucharist is the sacrament that, under the appearance of bread and wine, announces and anticipates the banquet of the wedding of the Lamb. "We celebrate his death and resurrection and look for the coming of that day when he will return to give us the fullness of joy."[22] "Happy are those who are called to his supper." To fast on Sunday would be to forget—or in fact deny—that the Lord, on the day of his incarnation, truly united himself to human nature, forever.[23]

We have here a question that is not very interesting at first glance, one that is not put in the same terms today; then Jesus gives an unexpected answer that is delivered seriously, gravely even: the liturgy of this Sunday in Ordinary Time challenges our faith. The new covenant is "not of letter but of spirit" (2 Cor 3:6). This covenant is founded on the word and the promise of God, who chose a people for himself, wanting to attach it to himself as a bride whose lapses he forgives because he loves her with a love regarded as irrational to human eyes. This reconciliation is not like those we know—"We forget everything and we start again from square one." God never retraces his steps; he always creates new things:

What eye has not seen, and ear has not heard, and what has not entered the human heart.
(1 Cor 2:9)

He sent his own Son to earth, "and the Word became flesh" (John 1:14).

> Lord, Bridegroom of the Church,
> Speak to our hearts,
> We are listening to you;
> In the mirror of your Word
> You fill us with your image
> And we live by your light.
>
> Jesus, handed over for the Church,
> Show us the way,
> We are following you;
> On the way of suffering
> Your freedom renews us
> And our strength is in the Spirit.
>
> O Christ, you the portion of the Church,
> May your Day come,
> We are waiting for it;
> By longing to encounter you
> We are advancing in the mystery
> Where you unveil your face.[24]

Ninth Sunday

This Day of the Lord
We Celebrate

A Day of Sacred Rest in God's Honor

The sabbath, a completely original[1] Jewish institution, is the distinctive observance which manifests, in the eyes of all, one's belonging to the community,[2] and which must be observed most faithfully.[3] Among the prescriptions concerning the sabbath, that of the weekly rest remains the strictest and most dramatic.[4] But to celebrate the sabbath does not consist of abstaining from work only. A whole spirituality has progressively developed, expressing the religious meaning and scope of this weekly rest in God's honor.[5] On the one hand, the sabbath rest evokes the creator's;[6] on the other, its humanitarian motivations link it to the deliverance from slavery in Egypt.[7] Throughout the centuries, prescriptions multiplied. A meticulous casuistry came into existence, particularly concerned with what it was forbidden to do on the sabbath. Jesus strongly reacted against this burden of regulations. This Sunday's Gospel shows us Jesus debating with people who made much of these rules. And this is why we read a text from Deuteronomy indicative of the authentic spirit of the Law (Deut 5:12-15).[8]

"Take care to keep holy the sabbath day as the LORD, your God, commanded you. . . . the seventh day is the sabbath of the LORD, your God." In order to understand well these expressions, we must read them side by side. Taken by itself, the first one could reduce the sabbath rest to a mere precept, no doubt venerable by reason of its origin, but still a precept that could be obeyed in a purely external way. In this case, two perils threaten the observance of the day of rest. The first consists in submitting to the law for lack of possibility to do otherwise, but with ill will and mutterings against its tyranny. Prophets often vehemently denounced this attitude.

> 'When will the new moon be over,' you ask,
> 'that we may sell our grain,

and the sabbath, that we may display the wheat?'
(Amos 8:5)[9]

The second danger, threatening rather the overzealous, consists in multiplying the prohibitions, stretching them to include whatever could even remotely look like work—until, for instance, plucking a few ears of wheat while going through a field was equalled to the work of the harvest.[10] To start down this path leads to endless quibbling; for example, one determines how many steps may be taken on the sabbath. Such dangers always threaten when legalism and juridical propensities predominate in the way even the most sacred laws are understood and practiced, when the letter takes precedence over the spirit to the point of totally obscuring it.[11]

The sabbath is a holy day, a day of rest in honor of the Lord because its observance has the value of an act of faith in God the creator: ''Since on the seventh day God was finished with the work he had been doing, he rested on the seventh day from all the work he had undertaken'' (Gen 2:2).

God has given this universe with everything it contains to human beings for them to use properly (Gen 1:26-30). By abstaining from work on the seventh day, human beings not only imitate God; they render him homage. On the one hand, they recognize that everything comes from the creator without whom human work would remain vain. On the other, through the sabbath rest, they make an offering of their daily work to God by devoting the free time of this holy day to meditation on the Law and the Word of God announced by the prophets, to the memory of the marvelous deeds accomplished by God, to praise and adoration of the Most High, to intercession for the people and the coming of the kingdom.

Among all the events whose memory the sabbath recalls, Deuteronomy mentions the deliverance from slavery in Egypt.[12] Released by ''a mighty hand and an outstretched arm'' (Ps 136:12) from the taskmasters' implacable and unceasingly increased demands (Exod 5:7-8), led into the desert to worship the Lord (Exod 5:1), the people at last ceased to be slaves. On Sinai, God gave them a law of freedom and proposed a covenant, treating them as a partner capable of self-determination; he promised them a land where the people would be free from the domination of oppressing strangers who for so long had submitted them to harsh forced labor. We can understand that the sabbath rest, still colored by the memory of this painful experience, entailed a rather pessimistic view of work from which at least one day a week they were dispensed. Indeed, at that time, the conditions and the means of work made the discharge of daily tasks singularly strenuous. Even for free men and women this everyday work was not unlike slavery. And this is still true today, particularly for certain categories of workers.[13]

But the institution of weekly rest, freeing the people from the work of other days, also had another meaning: human beings were not to be dominated by material interests; they could and had to avoid being ruled by work, since God had delivered them from slavery.[14]

> In the biblical perspective, work is not an end in itself; the sabbath, day of rest, day on which people refrain from any work, does not have as its aim to allow men and women to recuperate their lost energies and to ready themselves, once rested, for fresh tasks. The sabbath is the day of life. Human beings are not beasts of burden whose productivity would be increased by the sabbath rest. "Last created but first intended," the sabbath is "the fulfillment of the creation of heaven and earth"[15]
>
> "A world without the sabbath would not realize that eternity has a window that opens onto time."[16]

This spirituality of the sabbath elaborated by the sages and rabbis of Israel, who meditated at length on the Law, is a precious asset of the biblical tradition, which sheds light on the meaning and the observance of the Sunday rest. When rightly understood, the sabbath rest and the Sunday rest imply an art of living, both human and spiritual, to which believers must witness today with greater conviction, as our world tends to lock us into new forms of slavery—in the name of profit—because "time is money."

The obligation of sabbath rest imposes on believers the duty to make sure that all share in it, male and female servants, immigrants, even beasts of burden. This last detail not only implies the respect we owe to animals that help humans in their work; it refers to the harmony of the universe and the solidarity of all creatures willed by God. Everything has been created by his wisdom (Ps 104:24). All creatures are invited to bless God (Dan 3:56-88). The sabbath rest—and the Sunday rest—gives them, once a week, a leisure time to praise the Lord.

Sing with joy to God our help.
Take up a melody, and sound the timbrel,
   the pleasant harp and the lyre.
Blow the trumpet at the new moon,
   at the full moon, on our solemn feast;

> For it is a statute in Israel,
>   and ordinance of the God of Jacob,
> Who made it a decree for Joseph
>   when he came forth from the land of Egypt.
> An unfamiliar speech I hear;
>   "I relieved his shoulder of the burden;
>   his hands were freed from the basket.
> In distress you called, and I rescued you . . .

———

> There shall be no strange god among you
>   nor shall you worship any alien god.
> I, the LORD, am your God
>   who led you forth from the land of Egypt . . ."
> (Ps 81:3-8a, 10-11b)

Power of the Risen Lord and Weakness of Humankind

Both the sabbath and Sunday recall the work of salvation and liberation that God pursues with power throughout history, and they announce it not in words but in acts. The apostles' life and ministry also proclaim this work, especially when the instruments chosen by the Lord are the weakest. Paul is conscious of being a good example of this, and he explains it to the Corinthians so that all disciples may profit by his experience (2 Cor 4:6-11).

With one word, God, in the beginning, caused the light to shine in darkness (Gen 1:3). We must go back to this first word of the creator in order to understand what happens in us. Faith in the risen Christ has shown us "the glory of God on the face of [Jesus] Christ." This has been possible thanks only to God, source of all light, who "has shone in our hearts" that are full of darkness. When writing this, Paul undoubtedly thinks of what happened to him on the road to Damascus: "a light from the sky suddenly flashed around him" and turned the persecutor into a believer (Acts 9:3). Immediately after his baptism, he "began at once to proclaim Jesus in the synagogues, that he is the Son of God" (Acts 9:20). The transformation was so radical and sudden that the hearers, "astounded," could not believe that they were dealing with the same man who only yesterday was devoured by zeal against the Church (Acts 9:21). Truly, such a light in such a darkened heart showed the intervention of God, who said, "Let light shine out of darkness." What happened in spectacular fashion to Paul happens again, secretly, to each believer. Indeed, how could we see God's glory in the face of a crucified man who is said to have risen from the dead if God did not reveal this to us? And how could we find credible those who announce such news if not because the inner light of their faith illuminates their words and especially their acts, whereas by themselves apostles are of little significance. Paul's case shows this, but it is not an exceptional case: he speaks in the name of all those who devote their lives to announcing the gospel.

"We are afflicted in every way, but not constrained; perplexed, but not driven to despair; persecuted, but not abandoned; struck down, but not destroyed." Is this a life that permanently verges on the miraculous? Not in Paul's view. What he sees in it is identification with the mystery of Christ, "always carrying about in the body the dying of Jesus, so that the life of Jesus may also be manifested in the body."

> Those that sow in tears
>   shall reap rejoicing.
> (Ps 126:5)

> Suffering in us is like a seeding: through it, something enters into us, without us, despite us; let us receive this something, even before knowing what it is. The farmer throws his most precious grain; he hides it in the earth; he scatters it so much that nothing seems to remain. But precisely because the seed is scattered, it remains without anybody being able to remove it; it rots to become fecund. Pain is similar to this dissolution necessary to the birth of a fuller action. Whoever has not suffered from something neither knows it nor loves it. This teaching is summed up in one word, which can be heard only with the heart: the meaning of pain is to reveal to us what escapes knowledge and self-centered will; to be the way to effective love, because it detaches ourselves from ourselves to give us to others and to invite us to give ourselves to others.[17]

The fecundity of suffering borne "for the sake of Jesus" and the gospel comes from the fact that it is full, conscious, and active participation in Christ's mystery announced and celebrated in the liturgy and through the whole of life.

"The Sabbath Was Made for Man, Not Man for the Sabbath"
The importance of the sabbath has too central a religious significance for Jesus not to give an authoritative teaching about it, in one way or another. He did it by his actions, explained in words when the opportunity arose. One thing must be noted first of all: Jesus assiduously participated in the synagogue services on the sabbath; he regularly celebrated Passover and the other religious feasts; he was faithful to the pilgrimages to Jerusalem that pious Jews made—and still make—every year. In a word, he was what we call an exemplary practicing Jew, in whom the strictest

observers of the Law could recognize a kindred soul, and who remains a model for us. However, what he sometimes happened to do on this holy day shocked certain persons, as this Sunday's Gospel relates (Mark 2:23–3:6).

"As he was passing through a field of grain on the sabbath, his disciples began to make a path while picking the heads of grain." This is an ordinary scene; who has not, during a walk, picked flowers on the roadside or a few samples from a fruit-laden tree? Nobody takes offense at this, provided, of course, that there be no pilfering or damaging whatsoever to the fields or trees during the innocent picking. But here are some indignant Pharisees who call out to Jesus, "Look, why are they doing what is unlawful on the sabbath?" The seventh day was indeed a day of rest on which no work was allowed (Deut 5:12-15).

Any law of this kind, formulated in a general way, calls for particulars that lawmakers and competent commentators are to enunciate in order that, being instructed, all may live in peace while observing the obligations laid upon them. The whole art consists in being precise enough without niggling, leaving to each one the proper margin of responsibility.[18] Besides, and especially, we must never forget that the letter of the law and the explanation given of it are at the service of its spirit, of the good it aims at promoting. The weekly rest—whether sabbath or Sunday—is intended to liberate us from the constraint of daily work, without, for all that, devaluing it, in order to allow everyone to be busy with the things of God—a holy day in honor of the Lord (Deut 5:12-13)—and to take the time to enjoy living. "By forbidding every kind of work, the sabbath does not tend to depreciate work but, much to the contrary, to affirm, to exalt its divine dignity. It is one and the same commandment that orders both work and respect for the sabbath. . . . The duty of working for six days belongs to the covenant with God as much as the duty of not working on the seventh day."[19] Some people, supported by a whole legalistic current, had made of the law of weekly rest an insufferable constraint. As later on for Sunday, there were lists of prohibited works.[20] The gesture of the disciples plucking a few heads of grain while crossing a field is deemed forbidden because it is probably likened to the harvester's work. We have here the ever-recurring conflict of letter and spirit. Mark does not record this episode to make these lawyers targets for Christians to jeer at, those who could put on airs and say, "O God, I thank you that I am not like the rest of humanity," particularly not like these Pharisees with their narrow and harmful legalisms (Luke 18:11). This would boil down to saying that the passage does not really belong to the Gospel and that Jesus' teaching on this occasion does not concern us. On the contrary, Mark has recorded this episode, and the Church makes us hear this story read in the assembly, because it remains always pertinent.[21]

Jesus first answers these reproaches in the rabbinical manner. In order to evaluate a case, the rabbis looked to the Bible for examples that could orient them toward a solution of the problem at hand. "Have you never read what David did when he was in need and he and his companions were hungry? How he went into the house of God when Abiathar was high priest and ate the bread of offering that only the priests could lawfully eat, and shared it with his companions?"[22] This is a type of exegesis difficult to practice, for one must carefully and honestly avoid comparisons that are only artificial similarities, clever and often facile, but objectively unjustified and proving nothing.[23] Nevertheless, the principle of "Scripture explained by Scripture" is not only legitimate and traditional, but fruitful.[24] This is the case for Jesus' reasoning. He is reproached for condoning the violation of the sabbath. He appeals to a biblical example in which necessity justified a notable exception to a sacred law relative to worship. The comparison is the more apt as, in both cases, it is a question of satisfying hunger. But in this particular case, Jesus goes further by enunciating a general principle.

"The sabbath was made for man, not man for the sabbath." To tell the truth, this pithy formula is not revolutionary. On the contrary, it conveys the manner in which the best tradition understood the sabbath.[25] But it is recalled with that authority that struck Jesus' hearers from the beginning (Mark 1:22, 27), an authority he owes, as we know, to his being God's Son. Besides, this formula can be applied to an almost unlimited number of instances, thus going far beyond what the casuists can explore with their lists of permissible and forbidden actions. This principle allows us, for example, to say by analogy that the sacraments are made for human beings, not human beings for the sacraments. But it cannot be invoked to justify everything and anything. For Jesus adds, "That is why the Son of Man is lord even of the sabbath." "That is why" the Father sent, gave, and delivered him up for humankind. From now on, everything is focused on the salvation, the liberation of human beings— everything, even the most sacred religious institutions. We are therefore equally far from a rigid and oppressive legalism—the law is an absolute to which all must submit at whatever price—as from relativism and subjectivism that reject all law—only my intention and my personal evaluation of the moment count. In fact, this principle proves to be more exacting than all catalogues of commands and prohibitions that one could hope to agree with or at least to find a compromise over. It opens infinite perspectives to human freedom and responsibility; it invites all to a perfection always sought but never obtained, in imitation of the Lord, who personally is *the* Law, its fulfillment. This way is directly opposite to those of legalism and formalism, which impair both God's and humans' liberty.

> The moment rules of salvation, cult and communal pattern are fixed, one is tempted to believe that their strict observance is already holiness in the sight of God. The moment there is a hierarchy of offices and powers, of tradition and law, there is also the danger of confusing authority and obedience with the kingdom of God. The moment human norms are applied to holiness, inflexible barriers drawn between right and wrong, the danger of laying hand on divine freedom, of entangling in rules and regulations, that which falls from God's grace alone becomes considerable. No matter how noble a thought may be, once it enters the human heart it stimulates contradiction, untruth and evil. The same fate awaits that which comes from God. Order in faith and prayer, in office and discipline, tradition and practice is of genuine value; but it opens up negative possibilities. Wherever a decisive either-or is demanded in the realm of sacred truth; where the objective forms of cult, order and authority are all that count, there you may be sure, is also danger of "the Pharisee" and his "Law." Danger of accepting outer values for intrinsic; danger of contradicting attitude and word; danger of judging God's freedom by legal standards—in short, danger of all the sins of which Christ accuses the Pharisees.[26]

To this episode Mark adds another one that is also concerned with the observance of the sabbath. This time, it is no longer the disciples' behavior that is questioned but that of Jesus himself. The scene is no longer in the country but inside a synagogue in which Jesus has come to celebrate the holy day of the sabbath. There is a man there whose hand is paralyzed or (as they said then) "withered." Is Jesus going to cure him and thereby break the Law? If he dares to, he risks being accused of publicly violating the sabbath and, to make things worse, in a synagogue. Jesus feels the eyes of all fixed on him, and he guesses the hostile intentions of some of the people.[27] Therefore, he makes the first move and calls the man to "Come up here before us," so that everyone may plainly see what is going to happen. Then he addresses the others: "Is it lawful to do good on the sabbath rather than do evil, to save life rather than to destroy it?" This is not a genuine question, because no one ever said that there was a day on which to commit evil and kill. But to do such things on the sabbath would be an abomination.[28] Jesus knows full well that all his hearers think the same. But to abstain from doing good, is it not evil?; and not to save a life when one could do so, is not that to kill?[29] Truly, if there is a day on which to do good and to save is more binding than ever, it is the sabbath and, for Christians, Sunday.[30]

As they remain silent, Jesus "[looked] around at them with anger and grieved at their hardness of heart." He has come to do good, to heal, and to save those who are lost. How is it possible for people not to recognize him. "If you do not believe my words, at least believe because of the works themselves" (see John 14:11). This angry look manifests Jesus' profound indignation at such lack of comprehension on the part of those he could legitimately expect to be better disposed.[31] Then Jesus "said to the man, 'Stretch out your hand.' He stretched it out and his hand was restored."[32]

The conclusion of the narrative is unexpected. "The Pharisees went out and immediately took counsel with the Herodians against him to put him to death." The juxtaposition of the two groups is surprising.[33] Herod certainly humored the Pharisees for political reasons. But he was never able to consider them convinced and reliable partisans. Besides, although they changed from having a reserved but somewhat favorable attitude to open hostility toward Jesus, the Pharisees did not take any part in his judgment and condemnation.[34] Nevertheless, it remains that Jesus, condemned for the stands he had taken against certain ways of understanding and practicing the Law, would be put to death because the Pharisees had recourse to those who held political power. All this urges us to become conscious of the high stakes involved in the practice of the Day of the Lord and to test our ideas and conduct against Jesus' teaching.

When we attentively listen to a whole Gospel passage proclaimed in the liturgy, we are in for many surprises. We were ready to hear the already known account of an old discussion concerning an observance we are no longer subject to. And there we are, faced with the realization that on the contrary, we are directly and seriously challenged. Week after week, we continue to celebrate Sunday, the Day of the Lord, the day of rest in God's honor, and the memorial of Christ's pasch. The observance of this sacred day involves our faith in the One who came to heal and save humankind and to establish the new, and eternal, covenant in his blood. To celebrate the Day of the Lord is to welcome with thanksgiving and publicly confess God, who "shone in our hearts to bring to light the knowledge of the glory of God on the face of [Jesus] Christ." The manner in which we celebrate the holy day of Sunday and its im-

pact on our daily lives depends largely on the Christian's degree of belief in Christ and the Church. The keeping of Sunday is therefore neither
an obligation to be fulfilled willy-nilly in a legalistic frame of mind nor
a religious custom that is to be taken lightly.

> If the Christian Sunday wants to fully receive the heritage of Israel's sab-
> bath, it must be a holy day on which humankind more particularly fulfills
> its vocation of image and child of God. Sunday will be the heir of the sab-
> bath in the freedom of God's children toward the necessary, objective regu-
> lations; with a joyful openness to all the values of the visible world, in which
> nothing is impure by itself; in a fraternal charity giving of itself to all with-
> out discrimination; with a joyous thankfulness to a God who invites his
> children to imitate him.[35]

But Sunday also invites the disciples of Jesus, the Son of Man, who
will appear in the last times, to look farther than this day that the Lord
has made. Their eyes already behold God's rest, into which Jesus has
led them through his pasch (Heb 3:7-11). It is a day of freedom on which
we must do good, a festive day, the Day of the Lord, which announces
and sacramentally anticipates the endless feast in the fully realized kingdom.

> Go today toward the joy that comes near:
>   Christ is risen!
>
> And, if they are reborn in him, humans discover
>   Eternal childhood.
>
> The work of the seven days
> Is completed
> In the awakening of Sunday!
> Time can resume its course,
> But all is transformed.
> Here are new signs:
> Bread, seed
> Of God's harvests,
> And wine, sap of the vine.
>
> Live today in the memory of Easter:
>   Christ is risen!
>
> And, if they travel with him, humans discover
>   Their native land.
>
> The work of the Living One,
> Announced by the promise,
> Is accomplished.
> It is for us now to draw
> Our lives from his life.

Love has a ready table,
Its voice invites us
To God's banquet:
Day of joy, day of Paschal offering!

Sing today the ineffable marvel:
  Christ is risen!

And, if they lose themselves in him, humans discover
  A new life.[36]

Tenth Sunday

Recognizing Jesus, Who Crushed the Evil One

The Certain Victory of Good at the End of a Merciless Struggle
The problem of the confrontation between good and evil, of its outcome, and of a possible redemption wished and waited for, is at the heart of the most ancient literary traditions that constitute the Book of Genesis and to which belongs the excerpt read this Sunday.[1] Reflection on the problem of evil stems from the experience of suffering, the painful character of work, death, the evil desires that haunt the human heart, revolts against God, and of a universal perversion that takes many forms. As to belief in the mystery of redemption, it results from the deep conviction that "God writes straight with crooked lines,"[2] is able to transform the series of repeated human failures into a history of salvation (Gen 3:9-15).

In the beginning, we find disobedience to God's order—sin—instigated by a mysterious, cunning, intelligent, and malevolent being—the serpent[3]—who causes the fall of man and woman. The event is recorded in the manner of a popular tale whose apparent simplicity reveals, to anyone with eyes to see, the depth of the author's reflection and his talent as a narrator. God must come on the scene for Adam to become aware of his fault and perceive that it is the origin of the malaise he feels. "The Lord God then called to the man and asked him, 'Where are you?' He answered, 'I heard you in the garden, but I was afraid because I was naked.' " The sudden fear of God, who only yesterday was familiar, and the shame of himself, hitherto unknown, are the first manifestations Adam feels of the disorder introduced by sin; for it is true, he has eaten of the forbidden fruit. But immediately, reflex of self-defense comes into play, to transfer to God the responsibility of the happening: "The woman you put here with me—she gave me fruit from the tree, so I ate it." As a father faces his children who, having committed some foolishness, seek to exculpate themselves by accusing one another, God turns to the woman, "Why did you do such a thing?" And she, too, finds an excuse,

"The serpent tricked me into it, so I ate it." Obviously, the author wants to get to the origin of sin. By interrupting the reading after God sentences the serpent, this Sunday's liturgy stresses the promise of the complete defeat of the one through whom sin entered the world. This way of proceeding is entirely consonant with the tradition that has seen in this narrative the first announcement of the gospel, the *proto-evangelium.*

> Christians can never speak of sin and guilt without speaking of the for-giveness promised and granted in Christ to human beings. It is precisely in the misery of sin—this too is the revelation of the first pages of the Bible—that the promise of God's salvation is given to humankind. God has pity on humankind; and this is why justification, redemption, and salvation can-not come from humans' own strength or from the merit of their own ac-tions. Thus on the one hand, sin reveals human weakness and, on the other hand, in sin, God reveals the greatness of his grace. Human guilt becomes in Christ a happy guilt (*felix culpa*). Augustine even speaks of the "neces-sary sin of Adam that gained for us so great a Redeemer " This text has been incorporated into the Easter Liturgy.[4]

Finally, God and the serpent join in battle. Man and woman will be punished for their fault, but the instigator of their disobedience will be cursed. The fact that it moves by crawling is considered to be the sign—and the punishment—of its heinous crime. It is destined to an attitude of permanent humiliation. All the days of its life, it will be reduced to eating dirt and condemned to fight a losing battle against those it had hoped to subject to itself by taking them away from God. An enmity will be established between their two progenies. The woman's offspring will strike at the serpent's head, but the serpent will be able to strike only at the offspring's heel.[5] To the end, the author remains faithful to the picturesque and symbolic literary genre he has chosen, the only one pos-sible, no doubt, that is appropriate to conveying his reflection on the sub-ject and to sharing it with large numbers of readers. Everyone indeed can understand that, though strenuous, the struggle will end with the defeat of the serpent whose head will be crushed, as God foretold.

But what must we—or what can we—understand by "offspring"? Does the term designate an individual or more than one person? That it refers to an individual is supported by the fact that one of the protagonists of the battle—the serpent—is an individual character. We are therefore justi-fied in understanding that the serpent will one day be confronted by a being who will prevail over it. Moreover, at the time the literary tradi-tion of which this story is a part was set down in writing—at the time of Solomon, David's son—old hopes had become more focused and intense:[6] a conqueror would rise from the people born of Abraham, and through him, the progeny of the ancient serpent would be overcome.

And who is the woman who will give birth to this progeny? Eve, projected beyond herself into a faraway future, disappears in favor of a Woman—we must capitalize the word—who will appear in messianic times. Like the victor who will overpower the serpent, she will be an unusual character, the mother of the great conqueror. Such a place given to a woman must not surprise us. Let us remember, among others, Sarah, Abraham's[7] wife; Rebekah;[8] Rachel;[9] "the virgin [who] shall be with child, and bear a son, and shall name him Immanuel,[10] that is, God with us; and finally, Micah's prophecy concerning Bethlehem of Judah, which will witness the birth of the son of her "who is to give birth."[11] Each of these played an important role in the fulfillment of the plan of salvation. The Bible stresses this, and we cannot forget it. A woman has been the first to be tainted by sin: through a woman, the first in the order of grace,[12] will come the salvation promised from the beginning and toward which our hope is directed.

> *With the Lord there is mercy*
> *and fullness of redemption.*
>
> Out of the depths I cry to you, O LORD;
>   LORD, hear my voice!
> Let your ears be attentive
>   to my voice in supplication:
> If you, O LORD, mark iniquities,
>   LORD, who can stand?
> But with you is forgiveness,
>   that you may be revered.
> I trust in the LORD;
>   my soul trusts in his word.
>
> ———
>
> More than sentinels wait for the dawn,
>   let Israel wait for the LORD,
> For with the Lord is kindness
>   and with him is plenteous redemption;
> And he will redeem Israel
>   from all their iniquities.
> (Ps 130:1-5, 6c-8)

God Builds for Us an Eternal Dwelling in Heaven

The Genesis account of sin's entrance into the world opens up on perspectives of salvation. The problem of evil, suffering, and death receives an initial and precious light from the onset of the biblical narrative. The paschal mystery of Christ not only decisively resolves the problem but also shows how these distressing trials open on a future of happiness and glory (2 Cor 4:13–5:1).

"For we who live are constantly being given up to death for the sake of Jesus, so that the life of Jesus may be manifested in our mortal flesh. So death is at work in us, but life in you" (2 Cor 4:11-12).[13] Believers' sanctification is achieved through Paul's human sufferings and miseries. How can he speak in this way? He borrows his answer from the psalmist, "I believed, therefore I spoke" (Ps 116:10), not without immediately adding that all apostles are inspired by the same faith that urges them also to speak. For they know—it is the good news which they announce and which the disciples have welcomed—that they will share in Jesus' pasch after having gone through a death similar to his (Rom 6:5). All believers have the same certitude: through suffering and all manner of trials, they are going toward life in the footsteps of Christ. Hence the extraordinary fecundity of their lives. "Everything indeed is for you, so that the grace bestowed in abundance on more and more people may cause the thanksgiving to overflow for the glory of God." This thought does not make them impervious to suffering; but it prevents them from becoming disheartened, for "although our outer self is wasting away, our inner self is being renewed day by day." Despite the pain, sometimes barely tolerable, that our trials entail and always will entail, "this momentary light affliction is producing for us an eternal weight of glory beyond all comparison."

Let us sincerely admit it: such words remain difficult for us to hear and, even more, to make our own. We cannot shake an indefinable impression of discomfort. Can persons who speak thus be really and totally sincere? Do they not—at least in part and to a certain point—say these things to encourage themselves and their hearers? We are reminded of very sick persons whose state is critical and who say or hear others say, "This is nothing, only a difficult moment to go through; then all will be perfectly well." Others react violently, "Lie! Despicable attempt to make bearable the unbearable!" We must be honest and humble enough to recognize that we must call on all the resources of our faith not to be misled by so many voices around us and to overcome the temptation to despair when suffering and adversities crush us. On certain days, we can only repeat in a cry or a whisper, "What is seen is transitory but what is unseen is eternal." We know it—we believe it, we cling to this hope—"for we know that if our earthly dwelling, a tent, should be destroyed, we have a building from God, a dwelling not made with hands, eternal in heaven." Happy are we if we are granted the grace to receive one day this message of hope, more convincing than any word. Neither should we be astonished if our words do not succeed in shaking, even in the slightest, the position of those who do not have faith but, on the contrary, arouse in them an irritation, often mixed with pity. Authentic witnessing to our faith is the only worthwhile preaching, here even more than in other areas.

> And I heard a voice coming out of night
>   loud as the breath of the world,
>
> that was crying, "Who wants to carry the Savior's crown?"
>
> And my love said, "Lord, I want to carry it."
>
> And I carried the crown in my hands
> and the dark thorns bloodied my fingers.
>
> But the voice cried again,
> "You must wear the crown on your head."
>
> And my love answered, "Yes, I want to wear it."
>
> And I lifted the crown and placed it on my brow:
> then a dazzling light appeared, white as the mountain stream.
>
> The voice cried, "See, the dark thorn has bloomed."
>
> And the light ran from my brow,
>   became wide as a river
>   and reached my feet.
>
> Then I cried in great dread, "Lord,
>   where do you want me to carry the crown?"
>
> The voice answered, "You must carry it into eternal life."
>
> Then I cried, "Lord, this is a crown of suffering,
>   let me die close against it."
>
> But the voice told me, "Don't you know that suffering
>   is immortal? I have transfigured the infinite:
>   Christ is risen!"
>
> Then the light carried me away.[14]

Jesus Victorious Over Satan—Sign of Contradiction

It is understandable that certain actions, certain attitudes of Jesus shocked people, especially when they challenged a practice as steeped in tradition as the sabbath. (By the way, we must recognize that Jesus' conduct and words contain a precious teaching for our own observance of Sunday.) But it is hard to believe that his own family declared him out of his mind; that he was accused of expelling demons by their chief, Beelzebul, and of being himself possessed by an unclean spirit. Would it not be better to forget these sorry facts that the Gospel writer has recorded (we wonder why)? And why mention them to Christians assembled for the liturgy? They know that Jesus was endowed with the divine authority and power of the Holy Spirit. They are now gathering to welcome with thanksgiving the salvation first announced by God from the beginning, then accomplished by Jesus. But for that very reason, must we not apply ourselves to hear this Gospel anew with our attention free from all prejudice, trusting the judgment of the Church, which offers it to us in this Sunday liturgy (Mark 3:20-35)?

"A prophet is not without honor except in his native place and among his own kin and in his own house." As the four Gospels[15] attest, Jesus verifies the pertinence of this proverb, which has remained famous. This is not surprising since—human among humans—he has known all the limitations of the human condition, such as the difficulty of making oneself always well understood; there is always the risk of being misjudged, even by one's kin, at least by some of them. We would be ill-advised to indignantly revile them as if similar misunderstandings never took root among us. Mark, who does not mince his words, goes so far as to say that Jesus' family, learning that he was in a house where he was surrounded by a crowd and could not even eat in peace, "set out to seize him, for they said, 'He is out of his mind.'" Do Jesus' relatives act only out of concern for him, whom they want to protect against himself and bring to a more reasonable attitude? "Let him at least take the time to feed himself instead of allowing all those people to devour him." Or do they really think that Jesus is demented? Do they speak thus in order to divorce themselves, in the eyes of suspicious religious authorities, from any responsibility for Jesus' words and actions?[16]

Mark says nothing that would allow us to answer such questions. He needs to introduce Jesus' family at this point and to mention their lack of comprehension,[17] in order to insure the sequence and coherence of his narrative. By arranging his material in this way, Mark has reached a twofold goal. On the one hand, he reminds his readers that to understand Jesus is not to be taken for granted, for his behavior defies human reason (1 Cor 1:5). By making us face Jesus' relatives and their reactions, Mark implicitly poses the question that cannot be answered lightly: "And you, sincerely, what do you think?" On the other hand, according to his custom, Mark obliges us, as it were, to be direct witnesses of what is going on inside the house, when he invites us to join the group of Jesus' relatives.

Mixed with the crowd, "scribes who had come from Jerusalem[18] said, 'He is possessed by Beelzebul' and 'By the prince of demons he drives out demons. . . . He has an unclean spirit.' "[19] One could not think of an accusation graver and more loaded with serious consequences concerning a man who presents himself as sent by God. He is labeled an impostor, to be condemned, or the devil's victim, to be exorcised. His followers are under the same malevolent influence unless—and this is serious—they are feeble-minded or deranged, easy prey for this sort of visionary.[20] They are known by their works.[21] Jesus answers his detractors, "Your calumny is not only hateful but also ridiculous." For how could Satan cast himself out, destroy his own power? "Wolves do not devour one another," popular wisdom rightly says, spontaneously applying this criterion of discernment to unmask secret and unacknowledged complicities. The conduct of God, Jesus, the Church, saints sometimes seems contrary to accepted norms. But does it not manifest a higher wisdom? To decide the case, we must not blindly and solely trust conventional ideas. Rather we must take into account the resulting good in the light of the revelation and the work of Christ. Where evil recedes and Christian values flourish, there Christ is together with the invisible but efficacious action of the Spirit that no one can fetter or confine. This is not to say that we should appropriate to ourselves the work of others in order to take credit for ourselves or for the Church: we must discern the presence of the Spirit, and to it alone we must attribute whatever develops. This is why to blaspheme against the Spirit by identifying it with Satan is to become "guilty of an everlasting sin."

Jesus' relatives, still standing outside, ask for him. Jesus does not directly answer their request. He does not send them a message like "Please be patient for a while and I shall be with you." He is at his Father's business (Luke 2:49); nothing, nobody can turn him away from it. He thinks only of those around him, seated in the attitude of disciples who listen to the word. These are now his family, for which he has left everything (Mark 10:29) and "emptied himself, taking the form of a slave" (Phil 2:7). "Whoever does the will of God is my brother and sister and mother." "Blessed are those who hear the word of God and observe it" (Luke 11:28). All are called to participate in this beatitude, applied to Mary, model of believers and figure of the Church, provided they follow the way of Jesus, whose whole life was a fulfillment of the Father's will.

The end time has come, that of the decisive confrontation between the vanquished Satan and the Woman and her offspring, whose coming has been announced from the beginning. All can and must join this battle, siding with Jesus. This battle is strenuous. It requires wrenching separations, painful choices, whose weight and value in the last analysis are light compared to the eternal glory assured us in "a building from God, a dwelling not made with hands, eternal in heaven," so that we may live forever with his Son.

> God's wisdom
> is foolishness to humans.
> It came to his own
> and his own did not accept it.
>
> *Lord Jesus,*
> *Lead me into the will of the Father.*
>
> Take me away from the road of lies,
> grant me the grace of your law.
>
> Teach me the path of your commands;
> my reward will be to keep them.
>
> Never shall I forget your precepts,
> through them you give me life.
>
> I am running in the way of your decrees
> because you have set my heart at large.[22]

On these four Sundays, from liturgy to liturgy, we have attempted to follow Jesus in order to better discover the secret of his mystery. His way of acting unceasingly raises the same question for us, with an ever-increasing insistence and renewed acuity: "For you who profess to be Christians, who participate in the Sunday assembly, who really is Jesus Christ?" Such a question is not answered with book knowledge. The answer must be given by everyday life, through total and unconditional adherence to the person of the Lord, in whom all of God's promises have found their "yes." Under these conditions, we take earthly realities and tasks with the utmost seriousness, but without becoming enslaved by them; our eyes are fixed upon the day when the eternal wedding of the Lord and his people will be celebrated; we are already invited to this wedding, whose sacrament is the Eucharistic meal, and whose desire it expresses. The risen Christ's life and glory, already manifested during our earthly existence burdened by suffering and trial, will be resplendent in our risen bodies.

The Eleventh and Twelfth Sunday in Ordinary Time

The preceding sequence was constituted by a series of scenes showing Jesus healing the sick and expelling demons. His way of acting with an unprecedented authority, his initiatives, his sovereign freedom of action, particularly on the holy day of the sabbath, at first intrigued the bystanders—"Who is this man acting in this manner?" But this question rapidly began to connote suspicion—"By what right does he take the liberty of ignoring the strict norms that the most pious take such pains to maintain and to impose on all?" Jesus' trial has already begun: the accusations of blasphemy and contempt for the Law have begun to be whispered. Mark has led his readers into the midst of the crowd, who witness in silence this beginning of conflict, which forebode grave risks for Jesus, especially after scribes came from Jerusalem to observe for themselves this strange man's conduct. The way the narrative is handled challenges us, as disciples, to choose our side, to verify or to ratify, with a better appreciation of what is at stake, the steadfastness of our original option. Now, in the short sequence of the Eleventh and Twelfth Sunday, we are invited to listen to an excerpt from the teaching given in parables (Mark 4:26-34), then to meditate on this new manifestation of the authority of Jesus, "whom even wind and sea obey" (Mark 4:35-41).

The first readings prepare us to welcome this preaching because each of them insists, in its own way, on the absolute confidence we must place in him who manifests his power in so many ways (Ezek 17:22-24; Job 38:1, 8-11).

For his part, Paul, in the Second Letter to the Corinthians, which we continue to read, recalls how faith in Christ, and the resulting hope, animates and guides Christians' lives, oriented toward a new world that is already here (2 Cor 5:6-10; 5:14-17).

The Present and the Future of the Word Sown by God

A Great Treeful of Birds, Planted by the Lord

On a high mountain stands a great, magnificent tree; in its large branches, laden with fruit, such a multitude of songbirds perch that one would think they assembled from the ends of the earth; in the shade of its leaves there are birds of every kind. This is a fascinating spectacle, one that causes us to daydream and resist waking up. We would love to photograph or paint it in order to share our wonderment with others. The prophet Ezekiel has certainly admired or imagined a solitary and majestic cedar that is the prize sight of this high place in Israel, especially in a spot where one does not expect to find such a tree. "Whim of nature or chance," some say. Religious people reply, "No. God planted this beautiful tree in this desert place." The prophet sees there an allegory of the future that God has revealed to him and which will surely come to pass, "As I, the LORD, have spoken, so will I do."

Every allegory is enigmatic in part, even when one knows for certain to whom and to what it alludes. It is not—far from it—the case of this particular allegory in the Book of Ezekiel.[1] But the obscurities that remain and the discussions on its interpretation do not affect its general sense, and the choice of this text for this Sunday's liturgy is therefore justified. God promised to intervene in person. His initiative will go much beyond yet another restoration of the royal power that, in any case, can never be considered completely trustworthy. The series of disappointing experiences with the monarchy widens the vision of messianic hope. People certainly continue to wait for someone sent by God who is different from others. But at the same time, they see that the people themselves will have a more important and active role to play, that the image of the great tree can also apply to themselves. A certain democratization of the messianic ideal takes place.[2]

> I will heal their defection,
>   I will love them freely;
>   for my wrath is turned away from them.
>
> I will be like the dew for Israel:
>   he shall blossom like the lily;
> He shall strike root like the Lebanon cedar,
>   and put forth his shoots.
> His splendor shall be like the olive tree
>   and his fragrance like the Lebanon cedar.
> Again they shall dwell in his shade and raise grain;
> They shall blossom like the vine,
>   and his fame shall be like the wine of Lebanon.
> (Hos 14:5-8)

Taken outside of its original historical and literary context, the allegory of the great tree full of birds is reread in the liturgy of this Sunday and applied to the present experience of salvation wrought by Christ and celebrated by the Christian assembly. This sort of reading does not do violence to the text: it prolongs its meaning in the light of the decisive event, the Son, who was from the beginning in the bosom of the Father and whom God sent to earth to save humankind. Moreover, the Bible itself has constantly observed past oracles by confronting them with the present, in the perspective of the future. Moreover, we cannot forget that Jesus himself used ancient traditional images in order to reveal their fulfillment, especially when he borrowed, on his own terms, the allegory of the vine, ''I am the true vine, and my Father is the vine grower. . . . I am the vine, you are the branches'' (John 15:1-8). In this way of speaking, we find again what has characterized the evolution of the extension given the image of the great tree in the Old Testament: it is God who has acted to plant the young shoot; this new plant is a descendent of David, Jesus of Nazareth, born in Bethlehem, ''the city of David'' (Luke 2:4, 11). Finally, the image applies at the same time to all who, attached to the trunk of the vine, receive from it salvation and life.

> *O Lord, it is good to give thanks to you.*
>
> It is good to give thanks to the LORD,
>   to sing praise to your name, Most High,
> To proclaim your kindness at dawn
>   and your faithfulness throughout the night.
>
> ———
>
> The just man shall flourish like the palm tree,
>   like a cedar of Lebanon shall he grow.

They that are planted in the house of the LORD
  shall flourish in the courts of our God.
They shall bear fruit even in old age;
  vigorous and sturdy shall they be,
Declaring how just is the LORD,
  my Rock, in whom there is no wrong.
(Ps 92:2-3, 13-16)

Exiled Far from the Lord, Yet Full of Trust

More than we today, the early Christians lived in the intense expectation
of the Lord's return and viewed their stay on earth as a painful exile.[3]
Moreover, everyone, and particularly the apostles, had to reckon with
difficulties and sufferings of all kinds. Paul often mentions these, declaring at the same time that these tribulations authenticate his apostolate
and insure its fecundity. He adds that his experience and this certitude
are to serve as example and encouragement to his correspondents.[4] He
insists on the subject, showing what must be the attitude of believers and
how they must take advantage of their present condition (2 Cor 5:6-10).
"We walk by faith, not by sight." We would prefer to be "at home,"
that is, "with Christ,"[5] near him.[6] This is perfectly normal. But we must
nonetheless have total confidence.

The foundation of such confidence is the certitude that God loves us
and has given us his Spirit (Rom 5:2-5). This faith and hope shapes our
behavior in the world and with regard to earthly realities; we must not
scorn them, but we must use them without getting attached to them since,
as we know, all this is transitory.[7] We are promised a heavenly city.

> We are citizens of this heavenly city, since we are Christians; we are exiled
> from it as long as we are mortal, but we tend toward it. For a long time,
> overgrown with brush and brambles, the road could not be found until the
> day on which the king of this city became himself our way so that we may
> reach the city. Therefore, let us walk in Christ, always exiled until we ar-
> rive, sighing, longing for the ineffable rest that resides in the city, rest in
> which we shall possess, according to divine promises,
>   "What eye has not seen, and ear has not heard,
>   and what has not entered the human heart . . . (1 Cor 2:9)"
> As long as we are on the way, let us sing to enflesh our desires. For he
> who desires, although silent, always sings in his heart. He who does not
> desire, whatever noise he may make, is mute before God.[8]

We find ourselves in an in-between state: between what we have already
received and what we are expecting, between baptism and life in our
homeland.[9] This time is given us to please the Lord, so as to be found

irreproachable[10] on judgment day when we will all appear "before the judgment seat of Christ, so that each one may receive recompense, according to what he did in the body, whether good or evil," during the time of exile. Our vocation is to make of our life "a living sacrifice, holy and pleasing to God" (Rom 12:1); this is the only good way of leading our earthly existence, in whatever condition we find ourselves.

> The true, the only perfection is not to embrace such and such way of life; it is to do God's will. It is to lead the kind of life that God wants, where he wants, and in the manner in which he himself would have led it. . . . Whenever he leaves us free to choose, then, yes, let us seek to follow him step by step, as exactly as possible, to share in his very way of life as the apostles did during his life and after his death. Love impels us to this imitation. If God leaves this choice, this freedom, to us, it is because he wants us to unfurl our sails to the wind of pure love. Moved by him, he wants us to run after him, in the fragrance of his perfumes, in an exact imitation, like Peter and Paul. . . . When he wants us elsewhere, let us go where he wants; let us lead the sort of life he will indicate; but let us draw near to him with all our strength; and let us be in every state of life, in every condition as he himself would have been, as he himself would have behaved, if the will of his Father had placed him there as it places us.[11]

Tending toward the encounter with the Lord, Christian life is marked by hope. The prospect of judgment is not anxiety-ridden for those who seek to please God. Merit is not a haggling with the one who will give everyone their deserts, for we are waiting for "what God has prepared for those who love him" (1 Cor 2:9).

The Seed Placed in the Earth Grows in Silence

After they have followed Jesus from synagogue to synagogue on the byways of Galilee, this Sunday's Gospel suggests that Christians sit down for a while in the attitude of disciples who attentively listen to the Lord's word so that it may enter their hearts.[12] The two short parables read today deal precisely with the burial of the word and the conditions of its growth (Mark 4:26-34).[13]

The kingdom of God began on the day the "sower went out to sow" (Mark 4:3).[14] In the Gospels, this refers to Jesus and his ministry. This does not mean that, before him, the word had not yet been sown, provided the soil had been prepared—plowed and harrowed; the whole of the Old Testament is opposed to such an interpretation. But, with Jesus' coming, the last sowing of the last season is taking place. Now is the time of sprouting and growth, after which will come the harvest and the storing of the fruits in God's granary on the day of judgment. Therefore, as we are admonished in the beginning of this discourse in parables (Mark 4:3), we must attentively listen to Jesus' teaching.

The parable of the seed growing by itself places God at center stage.[15] He is there in the beginning to sow the field, there at the time of harvest, when he wields the sickle in the field, that is, at the time of judgment evoked by these two images.[16] Meanwhile, the soil and the seed do their mysterious work; the seed germinates and grows, one "knows not how" "night and day," whether the sower sleeps or wakes. As often happens in parables, we may notice here some details that do not fit the situation described. Any farmer knows that after having sown the good grain, one cannot remain idle and be content with waiting for the earth to produce of itself "first the blade, then the ear, then the full grain in the ear." Jesus also knows this, as we see in the parable of the sower. We must further work the earth or at least prevent weeds from overrunning it. But the focus here is not on this point. We do not hasten the growth of a developing plant by looking at it; rather we are faced with the mystery of the transformation in process: a seed is buried in the ground and soon sprouts, becoming in a few weeks a long stem with a heavy ear, if the sower has selected quality seed. "This is how it is with the kingdom of God"—the seed carries within an extraordinary force of fecundity beyond any comparison.

God, therefore, trusts the seed. He knows that it can produce up to a hundredfold (Mark 4:8). His inaction does not imply any lack of interest for the outcome of the sowing, as if it were going to happen automatically; still less does it imply any sort of fatalism. "Happen what may!" If the harvest is bad or poor, he will attribute it to the soil's lack of fertility. There are "the ones on the path . . . Satan comes at once and takes away the word sown in them"; the ones who have no root; the ones who let "worldly anxiety, the lure of riches and the craving for other things" choke the word, and it therefore bears no fruit (Mark 4:15-19). Accounts will be settled in due course, at the "harvest." The present resting of God is like an implicit exhortation to watchfulness and an appeal to everyone's responsibility. Any questions regarding this divine discretion will, perhaps, be answered by a second parable.

God is not absent and distant. Invisibly, he insures the growth of the work in all those who receive it "with a generous and good heart" (Luke 8:15).

In truth I tell you, that one offends
My dear Hope,
Who refuses to trust me with the management of his night.
As if I had not proved myself.
Who refuses to trust me with the management of one single night.
As if more than one person
Who had left his affairs in a very bad state upon going to bed,
Had not found them in a very good state upon rising.
Because perchance I had wandered by.[17]

The kingdom of God is "like a mustard seed that, when it is sown in the ground, is the smallest of all the seeds on the earth. But once it is sown, it springs up and becomes the largest of plants and puts forth large branches, so that the birds of the sky can dwell in its shade." When one thinks of it, the kingdom of God began in a puny manner. In a relatively obscure province of the Roman Empire, for some three years, a man, surrounded by a handful of Galileans, walks through the region preaching and working miracles. The popular enthusiasm that he arouses for a time does not prevent him from being betrayed by one of his own and condemned to die on a criminal's cross. Bewildered by this tragic end, not knowing what to think, those whom Jesus had chosen and called apostles try to drop out of sight. The announcement of their Lord's resurrection, far from reassuring them, adds to their confusion, as unexpected good news they cannot believe. The risen Christ's apparitions give them the assurance that the crucified one is really alive. But he leaves them again. Then comes the event of Pentecost and the beginning of a wonderful adventure. Christian communities sprout throughout the entire Mediterranean world—even to Rome—as a result of preaching by the Eleven and those who join them. Among them is a recent persecutor, Saul of Tarsus, who will become the Apostle Paul. The minuscule seed in a corner of the earth has become in a few years the Church that gathers believers of all races, peoples, and tongues.

The development of the Church and the spreading of the gospel will not always continue at such a pace. There will be all sorts of crises, often so grave that they will seem deadly. Paganism will be reborn out of its own ashes, even sometimes in a land sown for a long time with the word of God, covered with trees that once bore marvelous fruit; beautiful gardens will become deserts again. Gloominess, fearful withdrawing into themselves, if not despair, will sometimes threaten the oldest Churches, which in time will see their adherents' numbers shrink.

We have not completely awakened from the dream of a flawless Christian West. As a consequence, we often fly into ill-timed rages when something comes to cloud our dream. We seek to materialize, through inadequate means and in inadequate places, the model of our desires; and we apply our striving to the wrong spot. . . .

For example, such and such an effort aimed at bringing one stone to the building of an homogeneous Christian West can be ill conceived, but it is possible that sometimes other reasons make it perfectly legitimate and necessary. . . .

But it remains understood that we must not consider the condition of Diaspora in which Christianity finds itself merely a regrettable fact inevitably calling forth an attitude of fierce hostility. We must consider it a necessity (I do not say an "obligation") inherent to history and foretold.

"With many such[18] parables he spoke the word to them as they were able to understand it. Without parables he did not speak to them, but to his own disciples he explained everything in private." This conclusion repeats what had already been said after the parable of the sower: "And when he was alone, those present along with the Twelve questioned him about the parables." Jesus explains why he uses this teaching device (Mark 4:10-13). "To those outside" who have ears but do not hear, parables remain enigmas; this is what explains the meager success of Jesus' teaching and the incomprehension he suffers. This fulfills Isaiah's prophecy:

> They may look and see but not perceive,
>   and hear and listen but not understand,
>   in order that they may not be converted and be forgiven.
> (Mark 4:12; see Isa 6:9-10)

Jesus, therefore, did not teach in parables because everybody immediately understands that form of language, i.e., as we might speak at a child's in telling them stories. Everyone has learned that parables are not the simple little stories they appear to be. We need perspicacious minds to comprehend their deep meaning, not the perspicacity of intellectuals— "the wise and the learned"—but that of the simple ones, in the evangelical sense of the term, the little ones who are open to God's things, to the mysteries God reveals to them (Luke 10:21). To penetrate their meaning, we must listen to them or read them with the desire to be taught like a disciple, by the light of the Spirit, in a climate of prayer.

In Mark's Gospel, the teaching in parables pertains to what has been called "the messianic secret."[19] Jesus addresses himself to everybody, to the crowds. There is no problem as long as his teaching is perceived as rather general and standard, as a confirmation of what is already known. It is quite another thing when we suspect that it implies a novelty that runs counter to accepted ideas, well-established ways of judging and acting. This strange newness upsets us, especially when it concerns the religious domain. We become defensive and either cease to pay attention to the teacher or argue against him: ''By what right does he speak in this manner?'' But the simple ones, those free of prejudices, are struck by Jesus' authority in words and acts, and they react differently. They perceive that Jesus knows the secrets of the kingdom, the secrets of God. They put questions to him and Jesus explains everything to them in private. The parables then cease to be enigmas for the disciples; they reveal to them ''the mystery of the kingdom of God'' (Mark 4:10-11). As to the ''secret'' that is thus unveiled for them, they must not jealously keep it for themselves or for a few privileged initiates. ''What I say to you in the darkness, speak in the light; what you hear whispered, proclaim on the housetops'' (Matt 10:27). ''For there is nothing hidden except to be made visible'' (Mark 4:22). ''Whoever is ashamed of me and of my words in this faithless and sinful generation, the Son of Man will be ashamed of when he comes in his Father's glory with the holy angels'' (Mark 8:38).

The rapid expansion and the vast diffusion of the gospel must not fool us; there remains a great deal to do before the sown word may germinate everywhere. The slowness of the germination and the rejection of the word must not dishearten us—do we not see branches culled by God from aging great cedars being planted in faraway lands, putting forth branches, bearing fruit, and becoming magnificent trees in which all sorts of birds build their nests? Our time is that of patience, not that of harvest and accounts. We must believe in the hidden fecundity of the word: a minute seed, it will grow beyond all hope. However, this certitude is not meant to generate or justify a lazy fatalism. We are journeying in faith, without seeing, but we must be confident that we can apply ourselves to please the Lord. Then the power of the gospel will unfold in us and around us, even if we cannot accurately appreciate its extent. Here we have an absolute certainty because it is founded upon God, who scatters the grain in his field.

> This grain is the kingdom of heaven,
> it is the grace of the divine Spirit.
> The garden is the heart,
> that of each man or woman,

the place where those who receive it
sow the Spirit and hide it in their innermost depths,
in the recesses of their guts,
so that no one can see it;
and they keep it with utmost care
so that it may germinate,
so that it may become a great tree
and reach up to the sky.
Therefore, should you say, "It is not here below,
but after death,
that all those who will have fervently desired it
will receive the kingdom,"
you turn upside down the words
of the Savior our God,
for if you do not take the seed,
this mustard seed he has spoken of,
if you do not sow it in your garden,
you remain completely sterile.
When, if not now,
will you receive the seed?[20]

Fear Not! A New World Has Already Been Born

The Sea and Its Storms—God Masters Everything

On the Fifth Sunday, we read an excerpt from the Book of Job concerning the scandal of suffering.[1] The passage we read today evokes in a few words, but in a striking way, the sovereign mastery that God exercises over the elements, particularly over the sea, which appears to be the most difficult to control (Job 38:1, 8-11).[2]

Often in the Bible, God manifests himself to frightened human beings from the midst of a storm.[3] By raising his voice in the din of unleashed waves, he shows that he dominates them, that he remains alive—standing when nothing resists the flooding of the waters that submerge and engulf everything, whose violence is so extraordinary that nothing or no one can tame it except God, who fearlessly speaks over the destructive roar.

Nothing so struck ancient peoples' imagination as the sea, immense without known limits, on which one ventured only in case of absolute necessity, for crossings as short as possible, and in the favorable season only, because its sudden fury turned any voyage into an uncertain undertaking.[4] To top it all, there were stories of sea monsters that certain persons swore to have encountered. As a consequence, the sea was regarded as the abode of the most redoubtable forces of evil, manifesting themselves by capricious and tumultuous waves in order to harm humans who dared to violate their domain. Such terror on the ancients' part is no laughing matter, for today the sea remains most impressive and is one of the natural forces that continues to inspire new and dreadful mythologies. It is not always considered—far from it—the "quiet roof where doves saunter."[5]

Many times, particularly in the psalms,[6] the Bible says and shows that God rules the sea and all the forces that break loose in the oceans: wind, rain, thunder, lightning, and darkness that, especially during a tempest, heightens a sailor's fears. This mastery allows God to submit the great waters to his own plans: he started and ended the Flood; he parted the waters of the Red Sea so that the people could cross it dry-shod, ordering the waters to come back together to prevent the Egyptians from following the people to the opposite shore; he saved Jonah from the turbulent waters by sending a huge fish to take him back to land. Without losing its frightening character, the sea is a docile instrument in God's hands,[7] not because he subdued it one day after a battle but because he created it.

The Book of Job poetically describes this creation as a birth. The sea "burst forth from the womb," and God "made the clouds its garment / and thick darkness its swaddling bands." At the same time, he imposed on it boundaries not to be transgressed.

> . . . Thus far shall you come but no farther,
>   and here shall your proud waves be stilled!

For God has "fastened the bar of its door."

> Give thanks to the Lord,
> his love is everlasting.
>
> They who sailed the sea in ships,
>   trading on the deep waters,
> These saw the works of the LORD
>   and his wonders in the abyss.
> His command raised up a storm wind
>   which tossed its waves on high.
> They mounted up to heaven; they sank to the depths;
>   their hearts melted away in their plight.
>
> ———
>
> They cried to the LORD in their distress;
>   from their straits he rescued them.
> He hushed the storm to a gentle breeze,
>   and the billows of the sea were stilled;
> They rejoiced that they were calmed,
>   and he brought them to their desired haven.
> Let them give thanks to the LORD for his kindness
>   and his wondrous deeds to the children of men.
> (Ps 107:23-26, 28-31)

Life Centered on the Dead and Risen Christ

Throughout the Second Letter to the Corinthians, Paul insists on his apostolic labor, sustained amid all sorts of trials. Where does he find so much energy and the inspiration for his zeal? In the brief passage read on this Sunday, in which we hear his heartbeat, he reveals the secret of his life, which should also be that of any Christian life (2 Cor 5:14-17).

"For the love of Christ impels us." This concise formula exactly expresses the deep and ultimate reason for our being Christians, even though those of us who were baptized at birth or in early infancy and have, so to speak, always known Christ, have the impression of not having chosen him any more than they chose their parents. Of necessity, there comes a day on which one has to make a personal choice;[8] lacking which, one bears the name of Christian simply as one bears one's last name. Some might honor and assume without difficulty, faithfully and generously, all the implications of their loyal and consciously accepted belonging to the Christian family—this is not negligible. But is it possible to remain for all one's life, or even for a long time, attached to one's Christian condition by these bonds alone? The question arises but remains rather theoretical because no one can fathom the deep motives of others' faithfulness to their condition as baptized persons, and no one has the right to judge others. Besides, do we always succeed in seeing clearly the sincerity of our own motivations? When we read what Paul writes, we can recognize that he expresses what is, in truth, inside us all: the awareness and the certitude of the love that Christ has manifested to us. When we think of it, how should we not make of our life an answer of love—albeit an awkward and imperfect one—to his infinite love of which he gave us the proof (John 15:13) and which we have done nothing to deserve?

Vocations are different, but all of us, wherever we are, must center our lives not on ourselves but on Christ, that is, "the love of Christ must come before all else."[9] Concretely, this means that we must have the Lord as our central point of reference, and not only our personal desires, our instincts, our interests. Such a Christ-centered life necessarily leads us to go beyond ourselves, to deny ourselves, to confront difficulties of all kinds. Is this in order to be consistent with ourselves, with our convictions? Hardly. Rather, it is to let Christ live in us. We are therefore far from the outlook of a cold and rigid moralism or of a tense voluntarism, that in the last analysis remain subtly self-centered. Consciously or unconsciously, those norms of conduct we practice aim at building ourselves according to our own moral scheme, according to our own human, or even religious, ideal. That such a way of life may be meritorious does not change the fact that it is utterly different from what Paul teaches, "I live, no longer I, but Christ lives in me" (Gal 2:20).

"Consequently, from now on we regard no one according to the flesh; even if we once knew Christ according to the flesh, yet now we know him so no longer." In the glory to which he has been raised to God's right hand, the risen Christ has kept his human nature; Christians cannot forget this or have a diminished esteem for the humanity of the risen Christ. Some who deny all value to the flesh have done this, going as far as thinking that Jesus had taken only the appearance of humanity, as a kind of disguise that he would eventually cast off. Paul does not fall into this error contrary to faith in the incarnation of God's Son, "true God and true man." On the way to Damascus, Paul heard not a spirit but "Jesus the Nazorean" speak to him (Acts 22:8). On the other hand, we cannot stop at the Lord's humanity. Paul was still at that stage when he was "zealous for God" (Acts 22:3) and pursued the disciples to imprison them. To see Christ the Lord in the man Jesus, to which history bears witness, requires that we go beyond human experience, beyond the merely human way of knowing him. It is thus that today we know Christ through faith.[10]

Faith also gives us a knowledge—a knowledge beyond the merely human—of ourselves, of others, of everything. It reveals the radical transformation wrought by the incarnation, the death, and the resurrection of the Lord. "So whoever is in Christ is a new creation: the old things have passed away; behold new things have come."

Why Are You Asleep, Lord? Speak to the Wind and the Sea!

If we read this episode rapidly, we learn that the Lord's calming of a storm at sea is a miracle that shows his extraordinary power: he has dominion over even the unleashed forces of nature. But a more attentive reading reveals that this miracle has a much wider meaning. To detect it, we must take into account the way in which Mark structures his narrative and inserts into it many details and numerous biblical allusions (Mark 4:35-41).

We are speaking of the sea, this frightful force of nature that only God can master because he created it and fixed impassable limits regarding it; its unfathomable depths evoke the abyss where infernal powers reside.[11] Jesus is asleep, his head resting on the cushion at the stern of the boat. This description is surprising. We can understand that he might sleep undisturbed by the usual rolling and pitching of a boat. But who is the sleeper who, even if exhausted, does not awaken in a boat tossed in all directions by a furious sea and, moreover, filling with water? The commotion of his companions around him, their probable yells in order to communicate above the din of wind and waves with one another and with people in other boats should be enough to arouse him from his deep sleep. Obviously, Mark is not bothered by these unlikely circumstances. On the contrary, he seems to voluntarily exaggerate the picture in order to emphasize the contrast between the anguish of the disciples, who think they are lost, and the unimaginable serenity of Jesus, whom the storm disturbs not a bit. We are reminded of another night in which, after the Lord's arrest and death, the disciples were filled with a terrible anguish. Then again, and even more than on the Sea of Galilee, they thought that all was over for them. This sleep of Jesus in the stern of the boat evokes that sleep of death and of Jonah in the monster's belly to which Jesus himself had referred when he was speaking in veiled terms of his stay in the tomb (Matt 12:40). Attentive readers discover in these coincidences—whether or not Mark intended them—a first enlightenment on the meaning of this episode. As a conclusion of the discourse in parables, he shows Jesus victorious over everything evoked by a stormy sea: the demons' attacks and death.

Awakened, Jesus "rebuked the wind and said to the sea, 'Quiet! Be still!' " He speaks here in the same way he had addressed the demon who possessed the man in the synagogue at Capernaum. At that time, Jesus had "rebuked him and said, 'Quiet! Come out of him!' " The account of the calming of the sea thus makes us think of an exorcism by which, in a single word, Jesus sends back all the infernal powers to the depths of their dwelling into which the sea wanted to engulf the disciples. And, as after driving out the demon, "there was great calm." But Jesus addresses his disciples, "Why are you terrified? Do you not yet have faith?"

This twofold reproach surprises us. How can Jesus reproach his disciples with being afraid when they were in such danger? Moreover, when they wake him up, they speak to him in terms akin to those of the psalmist entreating God for help,

> Awake! Why are you asleep, O LORD?
>   Arise! Cast us not off forever! (Ps 44:24)

> Awake, and be vigilant in my defense;
>   in my cause, my God and my Lord (Ps 35:23).

> Rouse yourself to see it, and aid me . . . (Ps 59:5).

But in the disciples' case, reproach predominates, "We are lost; don't you care about it?" They feel that they are abandoned to their own devices, powerless against the hostile, furious sea. Again, we are thinking of the distress of the disciples, "slow of heart to believe" even after the first announcement of the resurrection. "But we were hoping that he would be the one to redeem Israel; and besides all this, it is now the third day since this took place" (Luke 24:21). Seeing the great calm that succeeds the storm, the disciples are "filled with great awe." But they further ask themselves, "Who then is this whom even wind and sea obey?" On Easter day also, the women's report that they had found the tomb empty "astounded" the downcast disciples who were walking on the road to Emmaus, "Then some of those with us went to the tomb and found things just as the women had described, but him they did not see" (Luke 24:22-24).

Mark did not write this story in order to transport us to the shores of the Sea of Galilee and have us recreate in our imaginations the storm quelled, one evening, by Jesus. The Church for which he wrote was experiencing other storms that were shaking its trust, its faith. It ran the risk of being overwhelmed by skepticism, fear, unable to understand why it had still so many trials to undergo: "Where is the promise of his coming? From the time when our ancestors fell asleep, everything has remained as it was from the beginning of creation" (2 Pet 3:4). Peter's two letters strive to protect Christians against those who make similar insinuations. At the same time, the letters stress the "normal" character of persecutions that must not be seen as a tempest about to submerge everything.[12] History witnesses to the fact that at all times, the Church has been shaken by storms, in the midst of which God seems to forget it. The crises and disturbances afflicting the physical world and society can also trouble minds and provoke reactions of fear and panic. When we feel like a boat caught in a squall that dangerously makes sport of it, everything reels, and we may come to the point of doubting God, of wondering whether God has lost control of the boat.[13]

> Why therefore be disturbed? Your heart is agitated by the tribulations of the world, as the boat in which Jesus Christ was asleep. Here is, foolish man, the true cause of your heart's dismay. This boat in which Jesus Christ is sleeping is your heart in which faith is slumbering. What news do you hear, O Christian, what news do you hear?
>
> Since the beginning of the influence of Christian religion on the world, the world has been prey to those devastations; it has been nearing its end. Did not your Lord predict this ruin of the world? You used to believe these predictions when they were made, and now that they are fulfilled, you are

disturbed? The storm is brewing in your heart, watch out for shipwreck, awaken Jesus Christ.

"That Christ may dwell in your hearts through faith . . ." (Eph 3:17). Jesus Christ dwells in you through faith. Faith present in your heart is Jesus Christ present. Watchful faith is Jesus Christ watching. Sleeping faith is Jesus Christ asleep. Therefore, wake him up, arouse yourself and make this prayer, "Teacher, . . . we are perishing."[14]

When the bishop of Hippo spoke thus, the Church and the West were in the throes of one of the gravest crises in their history: schisms and heresies undermined Christian unity; the flood of invasions was beginning to shake the world's foundations, the world that, having been patiently built throughout centuries, seemed to promise an endless duration, despite a few crevices here and there. Today, we know upheavals that do not unsettle minds any the less. The Church's influence on society, which for so long was apparently natural for it and defined its identity, diminishes more and more. The world is in the midst of evolution in all domains. In our Western nations, Christianity, which has ceased to be the religion of the majority, is no longer the fundamental cultural center of reference. On the contrary, it must seek, laboriously and humbly, but also courageously, ways of new dialogue with the diverse cultures of today's world. This task is certainly more arduous and more complex now than in past centuries, when the gospel and its preaching confronted similar challenges.[15]

The passage toward other shores cannot be done without the risk of disturbances and storms that violently shake the boat of the Church and seem about to engulf it. This is not the time to yield to panic by clinging to old routines unduly mistaken for the Church's living tradition, which for its part pushes forward. Today as yesterday, the living tradition can, on the contrary, inspire new attitudes in response to new situations, allow us to discern with the aid of the Spirit, what must be kept, what must be adapted, what must be rejected. This is the hour for more instant prayer, "O God, come to our assistance." It is also the hour for listening to the Lord, who says from the midst of the tempest, "Do not be afraid."[16]

We all come to the liturgy with our worries and preoccupations, our joys and sorrows, sometimes our fears and anxieties. The celebration—the proclamation of Scripture; general intercessions; and Eucharist, the memorial of Christ's pasch offered for the whole world—assumes them all, by integrating them into a vision that encompasses the history of salvation and its unfolding in space and time until its fulfillment at the Lord's second coming. This broadening of perspectives does not dissolve or minimize the importance of our personal difficulties. We can clearly see the trials the Church and Christian communities are undergoing today. But the liturgy of the Twelfth Sunday in Ordinary Time reminds us that we are still at sea, still in the process of navigating to the other shore. It is impossible to accomplish such a crossing without being buffeted by contrary winds and storms. The Lord is always with us—his Church—in the boat tossed by the waves. He is watching even when he is "in the stern, asleep on a cushion." We should never doubt it in spite of appearances to the contrary. Such a certitude causes us to cry to him with faith and trust—with one word he can dispel all storms, quell all tempests. This assurance must give us the boldness to go ahead without being disheartened by anything.

> To invent other spaces
> In which bodies will rise,
> He stretched out his arms:
> The wall crumbled down
> On which had been written
> God is dead!
> Why should you grieve any longer?
> From the day when blood was poured out,
> You know full well that all is grace.
>
> To keep you out of dead ends
> And guide you in deserted places,
> He stretched out his arms:
> The waters stood up,
> His people crossed the seabed
> On the marvelous path
> That he reopened.
> Why should you not cross the sea?
> From the day when blood was poured out,
> You know full well that all is grace.[17]

The liturgy of the Eleventh and the Twelfth Sunday cannot but revive in disciples faith and trust in the Lord, while helping them to exorcise the demons of discouragement. These whisper in the ears of those who stubbornly cling to hope, "Look objectively at the situation. Twenty centuries have elapsed since Christ sent his apostles to preach the gospel to the whole world. Not only is the world not yet evangelized, but entire blocks of Christianity have crumbled. Countries in which for a long time churches flourished have become deserts. One speaks today of a 'new evangelization.' Is not this an admission that the prior sowing has failed and that everything is to be done anew and with what chance of success? Battered by waves, the boat of the Church is adrift. Where is your God, as people already said to your forebears?'' (Ps 42:11).

When such thoughts find an echo in our hearts, we must reread and meditate on the parables of the seed that sprouts and grows in silence day and night, and of the mustard seed, ''the smallest of all the seeds on the earth.'' Weeds grow rank. The kingdom of God takes deep root in the soil sown with the word. At harvest time, but not before, we shall see the results of the work accomplished and the fruits of patience garnered.

The violence of tempests would dishearten us if we alone were at the rudder. The Lord's sleep in the stern would disquiet us if it were a sign of indifference or a confession of helplessness to guide the boat to the opposite shore. After our initial surprise, we are rather reassured by this sleep. We know that Jesus will wake up in case of peril; only a word will be sufficient to abate the squall. He was dead, he rose from the grave, and henceforth he unceasingly watches over his Church and acts in it through the Spirit he sent.

It is enough for us to raise our eyes, to look beyond our limited horizon to see the wheat growing and the young trees already large enough for many birds to begin nesting in them.

The Thirteenth and Fourteenth Sunday in Ordinary Time

From the beginning of this year's Ordinary Time, every liturgy asks the same question with an ever-growing insistence: "Who therefore is Jesus of Nazareth to speak and act as he does?" The narrative of the calming of the storm recapitulates, so to speak, and allows us to better understand the meaning of the events Mark has reported. Jesus manifests that his authority is not just that of an uncommon man. The elements obey him with a docility that only he who created the universe and its mysterious forces of nature can evoke. When he silences the turbulent sea, an image of the abyss into which infernal powers have been cast by God, we understand that with Jesus' coming, Satan is utterly vanquished; he is tied; his domain is plundered (Mark 3:27). Finally, the account of the calming of the storm evokes, in a hidden manner, the pasch of Christ, who will wake up, victorious after the sleep of death during which he seems to abandon his own to distress. Besides, this story introduces what follows in Mark's Gospel, particularly the two excerpts selected for the Thirteenth and Fourteenth Sunday. Only faith enables us to discern who Jesus is. It is indispensable if we want to benefit by Jesus' saving power (Mark 5:21-43—Thirteenth Sunday) to the point that he cannot exercise his power when faith is lacking (Mark 6:1-6—Fourteenth Sunday).

By healing the sick and recalling to life Jairus' daughter, Jesus reminds us that "God did not make death . . . [f]or he fashioned all things that they might have being." "God formed man to be imperishable"; the power of death cannot rule on earth because "justice is undying" (Wis 1:13-15; 2:23-24—Thirteenth Sunday). Like many others, Jesus has not been welcome by all those to whom God has sent him. "Whether they heed or resist—for they are a rebellious house—they shall know that a prophet has been among them" (Ezek 2:2-5).

Christ's liberality fills our poverty with the abundance of spiritual gifts. How then should we not, in our turn, be lavishly and joyously generous toward the poor (2 Cor 8:7, 9, 13-15—Thirteenth Sunday)? We are weak, it is true. But this weakness manifests God's strength at work in us (2 Cor 12:7-10—Fourteenth Sunday).

Arise! Your Faith Has Made You Whole

God Has Not Created Death: He Is Saddened to See People Die
If God is good, if he loves human beings, how can he tolerate the death of these creatures to whom he has given life? Whence does this seed of death come that everyone carries from the moment of conception? And why does he cause us to be born with this deep desire to see life continue on and on forever? This is what constitutes our torment: we want to live forever, but we know that we are going to die. The author of the Book of Wisdom ponders these grave questions, aided by traditions that have been recorded in the narratives of the creation in the Book of Genesis, and witness to a long reflection guided by experience (Wis 1:13-15; 2:23-24).[1]

Looking at ourselves and all around us, we are first struck by human frailty and the precarious human condition. Such observations lead to a certain pessimism that finds frequent expression in the Bible.[2] But at the same time, they attest to another experience people have had, especially during the Exile and the liberating Exodus: God watches over his people. He never ceases to warn the people against the deadly perils to which infidelity to the covenant exposes them. He lifts them up—raises them—at the slightest sign of conversion when, despite all admonitions, ruin has overtaken them. Really, death is an abnormal phenomenon. God did not make it.

> Because God did not make death,
> neither does he rejoice in the destruction of the living.
>
> For he fashioned all things that they might have being.
>
> For God formed man to be imperishable.
>
> For justice is undying.

This conviction, based on experience, is expressed in the opening narrative of Genesis (1:1-31). Everything that exists came out of the creator's hands good, very good and beautiful. God has made of man and woman together[3] an image of what he is in himself, "a living being" (Gen 2:7) who was not supposed to know death.[4] However, death has appeared in the world. Satan bears the responsibility for this upheaval, having seduced the human couple into spurning God's command, assurance of immortality.[5]

> By the envy of the devil, death entered the world,
> and they who are in his possession experience it.[6]

> All human beings do not experience death, but only those who side with the devil. What is meant here, therefore, is something other than bodily death, which is the common fate of the just and the impious and which is only an appearance of misfortune for the just (Wis 3:2). The incorruptibility discussed here is not a privilege of bodily immortality; and for those who still believe in it, it is a life whose essential activities must not know any decline, whatever may be the fate of the body. The sage leaves the destiny of this secondary part of the human compound outside his expressed preoccupations. His fundamental optimism is not lessened by the obvious fact that death or even physical suffering do exist. The true evil is injustice; the true death is that caused by sin, not the immediate moral and religious disorder of the sinful act but its disastrous consequences.[7]

The creator's plan has been thwarted by sin. A day will come when Christ, a human being who is the perfect image of God,[8] whom Satan's assaults will not be able to lead away from the Father's plan, will, through his obedience, redeem the sin of the world and will conquer death.[9]

> Let us, therefore, have our eyes fixed on this image of God so that we may be formed anew in his likeness. For if man, created in God's image, became like the devil through sin by looking at the devil's image—a thing contrary to human nature—there is a better reason to think that by looking at the image of God, in whose likeness he was created, he will receive back from the power of God's Word the form that he had by nature. Let no one, discovering that he resembles the devil more than God, despair of recovering God's image, since the Savior "did not come to call the righteous but the sinners" (Matt 9:13).[10]

God "brought you to life along with [Christ], having forgiven us all our transgressions" (Col 2:13). We are no longer speaking about reasoning but about looking at Christ on the cross and seeing that God wants life, at any cost, for humans created in his image.

> *I will praise you, Lord, for you have rescued me.*

> I will extol you, O LORD, for you drew me clear
> and did not let my enemies rejoice over me.

O LORD, you brought me up from the nether world;
  you preserved me from among those going down into the pit.
Sing praise to the LORD, you his faithful ones,
  and give thanks to his holy name.
For his anger lasts but a moment;
  a lifetime, his good will.
At nightfall, weeping enters in,
  but with the dawn, rejoicing.

―――――

"Hear, O LORD, and have pity on me;
  O LORD, be my helper."
You changed my mourning into dancing.

―――――

   O LORD, my God, forever will I give you thanks.
(Ps 30:2, 4-6, 11-12a, 13b)

He Became Poor to Make Us Rich

Paul has committed himself to helping the Church in Jerusalem, which is struggling with serious material difficulties. Therefore, he organizes a collection and asks the Corinthians to join in this gesture of mutual aid between brothers and sisters.[11] To encourage them, he invites them to examine how Christ behaved toward them (2 Cor 8:7, 9, 13-15).

Christians are enriched by the priceless gifts due to "the gracious act of our Lord Jesus Christ": "faith, discourse, knowledge." To gain for us these invaluable riches, the Lord became poor for our sake—for us[12]— "so that by his poverty . . . [we] might become rich." Indeed,

> [He], though he was in the form of God,
> did not regard equality with God
>   something to be grasped.
>   Rather, he emptied himself,
> taking the form of a slave . . .
> (Phil 2:6-7)

so that we might "come to share in the divine nature" (2 Pet 1:4). Meditation on this mystery of the self-abasement of God's Son very early on led the disciples to the way of voluntary abnegation and poverty.

> Look at Church history. All the Christian renunciations were born from the imitation of Christ, thus understood. Saints only wanted to be "his original but incomplete followers" (Bergson). We want to know Christ, said Paul (see, Phil 3:10). And all the saints have done nothing but repeat this cry: to know him in his mercy or his truth, in his meekness or his poverty. And

how can we know him if not by imitating him? His beloved person works this miracle. It is in this light that we finally must see the attraction of poverty for so many souls. "I love his poverty because he loved it," Pascal said. Outside this active love of Christ, there are only paper flowers, not authentic saints.[13]

All are not called to go that far; and those who by vocation live in poverty, on account of Christ and their brothers and sisters, are careful not to condemn others who have not made the same choice. But they do not fail to remind people that no one can be reconciled to the blatant inequalities between humans, many of whom are hungry while others are surfeited. Exhorting the Corinthians to generosity toward their needy brothers and sisters in Jerusalem, Paul writes, "not that others should have relief while you are burdened, but that as a matter of equality your surplus at the present time should supply their needs." The surplus of the ones must compensate the want of the others. Paul evokes the way the manna was equitably divided among all. "He who had gathered a large amount did not have too much, and he who had gathered a small amount did not have too little" (Exod 16:18). Together with solicitous attention to the teaching of the apostles and to the breaking of the bread, this ideal of equality among all and of sharing between brothers and sisters characterized the first Christian community.[14] This ideal was not limited to a just allotment of material resources. Having shared in the spiritual goods of their brothers and sisters in Jerusalem, Christians of pagan origin were now obligated to relieve their material needs (Rom 15:26-27). The exchange must be mutual and take place at all levels. The field of application of this principle is extensive. We cannot jealously keep the gifts of the gospel and of faith to ourselves alone; as a consequence, every Christian community is bound to be missionary. Similarly, those churches that are richer, for example, in the number of priests and religious, cannot evade the duty to supply the needs of the other churches. Experience shows that this generosity is a source of benefits for the communities that dare to risk sharing even at the price of being poorer in the immediate future.[15] Finally, this demand of Christian solidarity requires that we diligently pray for each other. This cannot be limited to the mere recitation of a formula of intercession or to the inclusion of an intention in the general petitions at Mass. Prayer, as an expression of faith that remains dead "if it does not have works" (Jas 2:14-18), impels us to commit ourselves and to act where we are, under God's initiative, so that what is asked from God's goodness and mercy may come to pass.[16]

Once more, Paul shows us how the most concrete questions must be placed in relation to the mystery of God and Christ. He does not resort to any of the usual and often successful arguments—for instance, those appealing to sensibility and compassion—in order to stimulate generosity in those whom he approaches. He says, "Look at Christ, and you yourselves will see what you must do." Such an appeal to faith and to each one's free decision is full of risks: it does not allow us to shirk our duties once and for all under facile excuses, for Christ's example urges us to always go farther, to go beyond ourselves. Such is Christian morality: it is a search for the perfection exemplified by Jesus and not the observance of a series of precepts—maybe numerous, even costly—with which, at least in theory, we might hope to definitively put ourselves right some day. It is impossible for us to place ourselves or to remain stuck in that perspective when we hear the Apostle's preaching proclaimed to us, especially during the celebration of the pasch of Christ, dead and risen so that human beings may have life in fullness and may lack none of the treasures of grace.

Believe and You Will See Christ Conquer Evil and Death

Several times, Mark constructs short sequences according to a literary process similar to that of the slow dissolve used in film montage or in a series of slide projections: an image is progressively substituted for another; then it fades in its turn as a third takes its place.[17] This way of proceeding not only enlivens the narrative but also leads the readers to a deeper understanding of the recorded facts and to a more and more personal commitment, thanks to this smooth linking of images. This applies to the narrative we read today (Mark 5:21-43).[18]

First, we are in the middle of the crowd gathered around Jesus, who has come back to the shore of the lake at the spot from which he had gone when the boat ran into a violent storm. "One of the synagogue officials, named Jairus, came forward. Seeing [Jesus], he fell at his feet and pleaded earnestly with him, saying, 'My daughter is at the point of death. Please, come lay your hands on her that she may get well and live.' " The bold action of this important person,[19] who comes to Jesus and falls at his feet in front of the crowd while entreating him, could be explained by the distress of a father whose child is in danger of death. But there is much more. The sick girl is "at the point of death"; there is no hope that she will pull through. However, this man asks Jesus to lay his hands on her "that she may get well and live." Such a request proves the faith of the synagogue official; Jesus has the power not only to cure the sick but to bring the dying back to life. Immediately Jesus goes off with him. The crowd, which "pressed upon him," follows the lead of those who have been able to witness the amazing conduct of Jairus and wants without doubt to observe what is going to happen at Jairus' house.

At that moment, "a woman afflicted with hemorrhages for twelve years" appears on the scene. She, too, is at an impasse. She has spent all her fortune in medical consultation. She has suffered a great deal, and instead of the hoped-for improvement, she has seen a worsening of her ailment. Having learned what is said about Jesus, she thinks that she will obtain the impossible cure if she can only touch his garment after discreetly working her way toward him in the crowd. She succeeds and feels "in her body that she was healed of her affliction." Nobody notices anything, except Jesus, who turns around and asks, "Who has touched my clothes?" The question seems silly in the midst of a crushing crowd. But Jesus is "aware at once that power [has] gone out from him": one cannot steal a benefit from him by taking advantage of his inattention. He turns around "to see who had done it." The woman comes forward "in fear and trembling. She [falls] down before Jesus and [tells] him the whole truth. Then Jesus says to her, 'Daughter, your faith has saved you. Go in peace and be cured of your affliction.' " Jesus does not rebuke her for having approached him on the sly;[20] it is faith that pushed her to do so. And this is why she gains the salvation signified by the cure of this illness that human beings were unable to remedy.[21]

> This woman touched the Lord's garment and she was cured, freed from a long-standing illness. But we, unhappy people that we are, we touch and take the Lord's body everyday, and in spite of that our wounds do not heal over. If we are weak, it is not Christ that is failing us, it is faith. For now that he dwells in us, is it not evident that he can cure our wounds, he who in the past made whole the woman who was hiding herself?[22]

In the meantime, people arrive from Jairus's house, announcing his daughter's death. "Why trouble the teacher any longer?" In other words, "Even supposing that Jesus might have been able to do something when the child was still alive, it is too late now. There is nothing more to expect from him." However, Jesus, ignoring this message, says to the synagogue official, "Do not be afraid, just have faith." He allows no one to accompany him except Peter, James, and his brother John.[23] The news of the girl's death must have spread among the multitude and cooled its curiosity. Perhaps it even spontaneously disperses. But, accepting without a word what Jesus tells him, Jairus shows an admirable faith. Mark records all these details for our benefit. It is a trial for our faith when a first approach, made with deep conviction, does not produce the result expected with trust. We need a really solid faith not to be stopped by this disappointment and to believe that everything is still possible. The evangelist asks us, ''Are you ready to go to the house with the synagogue official?'' What Mark is speaking of in this narrative, whose conclusion we know, is our faith.

In the house, the ritual of mourning is already in full swing with its wailing and lamenting. The mourners have not waited for the father's return. Jesus ''went in and said to them 'Why this commotion and weeping? The child is not dead but asleep.' '' Such a remark causes jeering, for indeed, the little girl is actually dead. In those days, resurrection from the dead belonged to the common faith of Israel, although it was still a subject for debate and was even denied by certain people (Mark 12:18). Besides, in certain circles at least—that of the Pharisees in particular—it was part and parcel of the messianic hopes.[24] But we must face the fact that with Jesus' coming, death has become a sleep from which we shall be awakened with him and like him.[25] This is not clearly spelled out here. But how do we, today's Christians, read this narrative? Does Jesus' word elicit from us a remnant of skepticism or a frank confession of faith? ''You are, Lord, the resurrection and the life; whoever believes in you will never die.''[26]

Jesus ''took the child by the hand and said to her, '*Talitha koum,*' which means, 'Little girl, I say to you, arise!' '' She immediately gets up, begins to walk about, and eats.[27] Here, too, Christian readers are reminded of an old baptismal hymn,

> Awake, O sleeper,
>   and arise from the dead,
> and Christ will give you light.
> (Eph 5:14)

When Jesus rises, the meaning of the resurrection of Jairus' daughter will be completely unveiled. At that time, it will be the moment to announce to the whole world what was first accomplished secretly in the presence of only a few witnesses who had still a long way to go before acquiring the paschal faith.

> Master, you come near me and say to me as you said to Jairus' little girl, ''Arise.'' And taking her by the hand, you called her back to life. The child

whom everyone believed dead, immediately arose and began to walk. Here I glimpse the mystery and the power of the Resurrection through the daily act of waking up.

You, too, have risen up, living and glorious. And the glory of your Resurrection rests upon every one of our mornings. . . . It was "very early when the sun had risen"; Lord, grant that no new morning dawn on me without my going, in spirit, toward the empty tomb in the garden with my little bit of spices!

For it is the risen Christ who comes to me, everyday, at dawn. Whatever perplexities, whatever dangers surround me, the beginning of all my days will be radiant if I remember—with all my soul and all my mind—that my Savior has conquered the powers of evil and death. My first act of faith, every morning, will be an act of faith in your final victory.[28]

The whole of life is an unceasing struggle against the assaults of death, now violent, now more insidious, but never relenting. The joy of victories does not fool us: our "resurrections" after grave illnesses always remain provisional and precarious. Death will end up having the last word.

> Seventy is the sum of our years,
>   or eighty, if we are strong,
> And most of them are fruitless toil,
>   for they pass quickly and we drift away.
> (Ps 90:10)

The edge of pessimism and disillusion these words show does not detract from their aptness. However increased it may be, "the sum of our years" will remain limited. Nonetheless, the Bible proclaims that God has not created death but that "he fashioned all things that they might have being" and that "the creatures of the world are wholesome / and there is not a destructive drug among them" (Wis 1:14). These assertions, which run counter to what everyone cannot help but observe, lead us to look at the problem of death under another light.

Jesus healed numerous sick persons, but it is not said that he immunized them against all recurrences of their illnesses. This Sunday's Gospel records that he brought the child of the synagogue official back to life. But whatever the number of years granted to this twelve-year-old girl, she was subject to our common fate—like all of us, like Lazarus, whom Jesus ordered to come out of the tomb. When he heals a sick person, Jesus says, "Your faith has made you whole"; and, "Arise," when he addresses a dead person. He came to bring salvation to the world, health and life, which neither disease nor physical death can hold in check. Only faith allows us to understand and to help others to understand the meaning of the cures and resurrections worked by Jesus—in the measure in which we recognize that he is the Resurrection and the Life, the Living One, whom death was unable to vanquish and who gives us to share in his victory. This is why we must believe in him in spite of everything.

We have been liberally gifted with "faith, discourse, knowledge." This divine liberality makes it a duty for us to generously share with others the goods granted us, to remember that Christ "became poor although he was rich, so that by his poverty [we] might become rich." This sharing concerns material goods, which can relieve the needs of those who have less than we. But even if we have nothing, we still can allow not only a few but all to have a part in the more precious goods that have been given us, together with faith. Through our life, we can announce to all that the good news of salvation is for them as well as for us.

> People can tell you, too, "Whoever you are, if you are in good health, you are at liberty to think of other things; but if the malaise you feel leaves you no doubt about the seriousness of your state, first of all you must care about your health." Your health is Christ. First of all, think of Christ. Take his saving cup: "He heals all your ills." If you want it, you may obtain this kind of health. You are seeking honors and riches: they will not come at your bidding. Here is something far more precious and it is yours for the wishing. "He heals all your ills." "He redeems your life from destruction." All your ills will be healed when this corruptible body is clothed with incorruptibility: your life has been redeemed from corruption; from now on be without fear. "He redeems your life from destruction." Showing by his example the reward promised to us, "handed over for our transgressions and . . . raised for our justification" (Rom 4:25). Let the members hope for what has been realized in the head. How could he not heal the members when he has lifted their head up to heaven?[29]

Fourteenth Sunday

This Man Is the Son of God

A Prophet Must Speak, Whether or Not People Listen

Unless one is a simpleton or a self-styled visionary, no one lays claim to the title and mission of a prophet. Indeed, who would dare speak in the Lord's name unless they were truly assured that God has commissioned them when they absolutely were not seeking such a call? For prophets are often sent where they do not want to go, charged with announcing a message which will cost them dear and which has all chances of exposing them to trouble and dangers, to persecution. Ezekiel has this painful experience. God duly warns him that he is giving him a mission particularly unpleasant to fulfill, and even impossible (Ezek 2:2-5).[1]

"As he spoke to me, spirit entered into me and set me on my feet." Ezekiel, a priest, is in the land of the Chaldeans, among the exiles. "There the hand of the LORD came upon [him]" (Ezek 1:3). He has a terrible vision and falls upon his face (Ezek 1:28). Then the spirit enters him and sets him on his feet; and the Lord tells him what his mission was to be:[2] "I am sending you to the Israelites, rebels who have rebelled against me; they and their fathers have revolted against me to this very day. Hard of face and obstinate of heart are they to whom I am sending you." They are the very opposite of a welcoming and well-disposed audience. Now this prophet sent by God is himself a frail, vulnerable, and mortal being: a "son of man."[3] But when he addresses them, he will be able to say, "Thus says the Lord GOD." To show that the prophet's words will not be his own, the oracle uses a bold image. God orders Ezekiel to eat a scroll on which is written what he will have to say and which he will have to regurgitate, as it were. If he had not been coerced to assimilate the scroll, how could he pronounce such words? For the scroll contains "lamentations and wailing and woe" (Ezek 2:10; 3:1-3). "Son of man, go now to the house of Israel, and speak my words to them" (Ezek 3:4). The prophet is neither a flatterer nor a demagogue; he proclaims what God has ordered him to say. Therefore, he must expect not to be well received by all. God does not entertain illusions. But neither does he get discouraged. He is like the sower who throws the seed by the handful, although he knows that a part of it will fall upon ground in which it will not germinate (Mark 4:1-9). Is this wastefulness, lack of realism, disregard of the elementary demands of sound management that requires one to balance efforts and expenses against reasonably calculated hopes of success? By no means. God wants to give everyone a chance. He cannot resign himself to seeing the least plot of land remain fallow. His love causes him to hope against all hope. He knows the fecundity of the Word that, in any event, will bear fruit.

> What you are asking, Lord,
> is not easy.
> It is not easy
> to liberate your people
> when your people prefer
> to live in slavery,
> as long as they have enough
> to eat and drink.
> And we are not well equipped
> —when we count the troops—
> we are like David
> confronting the giant.
>
> It is not easy,
> Lord.
>
> However we are certain
> of the triumph and the victory:
> You are with us,
> you fight at our side.
> If people make fun of us,
> if we are labeled "daydreamers,"
> it is because we take after you.
> We are utopians, no doubt,
> but much less than you.[4]

"And whether they heed or resist . . . they shall know that a prophet has been among them." When someone turns a deaf ear to our advice and warnings, we may happen to say, "In any case, you have been warned." Usually, it is a way of freeing ourselves from any responsibility and withdrawing, as it were, into our tent. If, in the course of time, events show us to have been right, we can hardly guard against a certain feeling of satisfaction mixed with aggressiveness, i.e., "Too bad for you! I told you so!" God does not think, speak, or act in this manner. The fact that he sends a "son of man" as a prophet in the midst of the people shows, on the contrary, an unflagging solicitude. The presence of his spokesperson shows to all that he remains ready to welcome those who will listen, even after having first rejected the prophet. God is not naive, but knows that through hearing his unceasing calls, every sinner can finally experience a movement of wisdom, abandon bad ways, and be converted. All sinners will always find near at hand a prophet ready to help them and welcome them in the Lord's name. God places harsh words in his prophets' mouths in order to lead the most obdurate sinners to an awareness of grave consequences should they remain blind. Acting in such a way, God manifests his mercy. He puts "the message of reconciliation" in the mouths of his emissaries. "So we are the ambassadors for Christ, as if God were appealing through us. We implore you on behalf of Christ, be reconciled to God" (2 Cor 5:20).

Our eyes are fixed on the Lord,
pleading for his mercy.

To you I lift up my eyes
    who are enthroned in heaven.
Behold, as the eyes of servants
    are on the hands of their masters,
As the eyes of a maid
    are on the hands of her mistress,
So are our eyes on the LORD, our God,
    till he have pity on us.
Have pity on us, O LORD, have pity on us,
    for we are more than sated with contempt;
Our souls are more than sated
    with the mockery of the arrogant,
    with the contempt of the proud.
(Ps 123)

When I Am Weak, Then I Am Strong

Paul was favored with signal graces and extraordinary revelations. Otherwise, we cannot see how the converted persecutor could have become in such a short time so great an apostle and gain so profound an understanding of the Christian mystery. He himself is the first to recognize that his journey was a singular one, because against all expectations, he was selected to announce the good news to the nations. "Now I want you to know . . . that the gospel preached by me is not of human origin. For I did not receive it from a human being, nor was I taught it, but it came through a revelation of Jesus Christ."[5] Paul willingly recalls the exceptional way in which God has dealt with him. It is not to boast about it, but to express his understanding of these graces as a manifestation of divine glory and power.[6] Besides, it is a guarantee for the communities Paul addresses: they can trust the one who evangelizes them. But Paul does not hide from his correspondents the fact that he remains a weak man whom God is guarding against pride (2 Cor 12:7-10).

The revelations he received are exceptional. "Therefore, that I might not become too elated, a thorn in the flesh was given to me, an angel of Satan, to beat me." Since these lines were written, people have not ceased to speculate on the nature of this cross carried by the Apostle.[7] Some suggest a disease or a handicap especially trying and humiliating. Others think that Paul is alluding to the constant persecutions that follow him wherever he goes, as if Satan were dogging his very steps in an effort to discourage him. Some have even supposed that assaulted by numerous and unceasing troubles, Paul was like a man flayed alive, owing to his extreme sensibility. In any case, what he wrote to the Galatians suggests that he suffered enormously and that to keep going, he needed the comfort and support of the community. "You know that it was because of a physical illness that I originally preached the gospel to you, and you did not show disdain or contempt because of the trial caused you by my physical condition, but rather you received me as an angel of God, as Christ Jesus" (Gal 4:13-14).

Be that as it may, Paul entreated the Lord three times to take away this "thorn" that tormented him to the limit of the tolerable. We are reminded of Jesus during his agony in Gethsemane. "Troubled and distressed . . . sorrowful even to death," he begged the Father three times also to take away, if possible, the hour of his ordeal (Mark 14:32-42). The Lord did not reject Paul's prayer. He did not lift the burden of the cross bearing down on Paul, but he assured him of his effective help, "My grace is sufficient for you, for power is made perfect in weakness." Paul's prayer, as well as the Lord's answer, are to be seen in the perspective of the mystery of the cross of Christ, who has revealed God's power. "For indeed he was crucified out of weakness, but he lives by the power of God. So also we are weak in him, but toward you we shall live with him by the power of God" (2 Cor 13:4). "For we who live are constantly being given up to death for the sake of Jesus, so that the life of Jesus may be manifested in our mortal flesh" (2 Cor 4:11).[8] To dare speak in this manner, we must have personally lived this mystery in our flesh and in our souls. But we must not forget that the strength given by this faith does not prevent us from feeling, to our innermost depths, the anguish of fear. All saints bear witness to this, even those who underwent martyrdom. "I am not in the slightest displeased, Margaret, that your frailty causes you to fear. God gave us both the grace to despair of ourselves and to entrust ourselves entirely, in utter dependence, to the strength of hope."[9] "I will rather boast most gladly of my weaknesses." Such speech is absurd in the judgment of human wisdom, which demands to the contrary that we hide our weakness, for we must be and must appear to be strong in order to gain admittance in a world dominated by the spirit of competition. But what Paul says implies no morbid complacency in misery, no lack of dignity. He speaks with his head held high.[10] He boasts of his weakness "in order that the power of Christ may dwell with [him]." Here is why he is "content with weaknesses, insults, hardships, persecutions, and constraints, for the sake of Christ." And he concludes, "For when I am weak, then I am strong." Paul often experienced the truth of this in the course of his life and ministry. He recalls this for the benefit of those who, faced with grave difficulties, could be threatened with discouragement because of their own weakness. His experience should be heartening to them and give them a new reason for hoping against all hope. At bottom, this is the faith that Christians profess. Their assurance in weakness rests on the certitude of sharing in the pasch of Christ, who through the humiliation and annihilation of the cross, has passed into the Father's glory. "Whoever boasts, should boast in the Lord" (1 Cor 1:31). "Let orators keep their eloquence, philosophers their wisdom, kings their kingdoms; for us, Christ is glory, riches and kingdom; for us, wisdom is the folly of the gospel; for us, strength is the weakness of the flesh and glory is the scandal of the cross."[11]

The Announcement of the Gospel at the Risk of Faith

In spite of the popular enthusiasm he aroused, Jesus knew bitter failures. The evangelists do not attempt to hide or minimize them, because they are also an essential aspect of the Lord's mission, of the Church, and finally of salvation. The good news is announced at the risk of faith, of the freedom of human beings who can receive or refuse it, open or close their hearts to it, and by the same token allow or prevent its bearing fruit (Mark 6:1-6).

Still in the company of his disciples, Jesus comes back to "his native place," Nazareth, where he grew up, where everyone knows him, where his mother and other members of his family live.[12] On the sabbath, he goes to the synagogue, like all villagers, and he begins to teach. In Capernaum, the hearers were struck by his authority.[13] In Nazareth, this teaching arouses astonishment, and the inhabitants of "his native place . . . [take] offense at him." At *him*, not at what he did. "Where did this man get all this? What kind of wisdom has been given him? What mighty deeds are wrought by his hands?" Their astonishment is understandable. Jesus grew up among them; the son of a family like theirs, he has received the same education and the same instruction as they, acquired mainly in the synagogue. If he had enrolled, in Jerusalem or elsewhere, in the school of a renowned master, the face would be known. In this case, even if they felt a tinge of jealousy, they would be rather proud to see one of their own give the lie to the proverbial question, "Can anything good come from Nazareth?" (John 1:46). But the hitch is that no one knows where he has gotten his wisdom and his power to work miracles. All this is most suspicious.

"Jesus said to them, 'A prophet is not without honor except in his native place and among his own kin and in his own house.' " If the lack of success he meets with at home verifies a proverb expressing common experience, he ought not to be surprised. But Jesus "was amazed at their lack of faith." Moreover, he feels, as it were, powerless. "So he was not able to perform any mighty deed there, apart from curing a few sick people by laying his hands on them." Obviously, Mark records this fact and composes his narrative in this way to transmit a definite teaching. For a simple mention would be sufficient to describe the occasion when Jesus' preaching meets with failure; in this case, the proverb would be just the thing to explain the failure and to show that such a lack of welcome is not extraordinary, let alone dramatic. Such disappointments are scattered all through the history of the prophets and of the Church. This is sad, of course, but it does not discourage the apostles and the preachers of the gospel. Rather, they are encouraged to persevere by knowing that even Jesus has known this sort of disappointment. And without any doubt, this is one of the lessons we should draw from this episode. For when instructing the disciples he is sending on a mission, Jesus will tell them, "Whatever place does not welcome you or listen to you, leave there and shake the dust off your feet in testimony against them" (Mark 6:11). But what happens on that day in Nazareth suggests other reflections.

> On only two occasions does the Gospel tell us that Jesus was astonished at anything. In both cases, it is about faith. The first episode is when Jesus comes back to Nazareth . . . "He was amazed at their lack of faith." . . .

The second episode is at Capernaum. The Roman centurion implores the cure of his paralyzed servant. "I will come and cure him," Jesus says. The centurion protests, "I am not worthy to have you enter under my roof; only say the word and my servant will be healed." Having heard the centurion, Jesus "was amazed." He cures the servant from afar and he declares that even in Israel he has not found such faith (Matt 8:5-13).

The orthodoxy of Nazareth is not the living faith, the faith that saves. If such a faith had animated them, the people in Nazareth would have opened their hearts to Jesus. But they are content with a correct and sterile belief. Their hearts remain closed.

We know nothing of what exactly the centurion believed. About Jesus he did not know what it has been given us to know. But he opens his heart to Jesus. He feels that in him there is a Savior and a Lord.

Jesus sees what is in us. Does he find in us the centurion's faith or the incredulity of the Nazareth townsfolk? By what is Jesus going to be amazed: by our faith or by our lack of it?[14]

The Gospel constantly confronts us with Jesus' mystery: "But who is he?" He had his family in Nazareth of Galilee, but he said, "Before Abraham came to be, I AM" (John 8:58). Our creed clearly proclaims that Mary's son—the brother of James and Joses and Judas and Simon—is also the Son of God. But such a faith is daily subjected to dispute, to the ironical or virulent manifestations of astonishment: "How can you be so sure? What allows you to be so assertive?" The debate that began in Nazareth will last as long as there are humans on earth. Jesus, who was amazed at the lack of faith of his townspeople, said, "But when the Son of Man comes, will he find faith on earth?" (Luke 18:8). And today, among us, does he find this faith without which the Lord cannot perform any miracle, beyond the cure of a few sick persons?

For twenty centuries, eternally, Yeshua, you
    make us your contemporaries.
Adam himself says through the Baptist's
    voice: He who is before me comes after me.
Certainly it is hard for Abraham's posterity
    to hear: Before Abraham was, I AM.
To us—eternal worshippers of Reason—to
    hear that you are from and by yourself
    sounds like blasphemy and wounds us.
But it is your way of being present among us
    that forces us to believe, in spite of
    ourselves, that you are coming

Both from Nazareth and from the glory of the
  Unique who generated you without
  separating you from himself.

Both from the Unique in glory and from
  Nazareth: the proof in our eyes that you are the Absolute
Is that people wonder where your wisdom comes
  from, you the brother of James, Jude, and Joses.
Yes, the same hands that worked these
  miracles are the carpenter's.
My Father and I are one, says the one whose
  father and mother are known to all.
The Light of the world testifies to itself
  through these eyes of a craftsman
  engrossed in his work
Who shows us that Today the Word is
  fulfilled, although nothing seems to
  have budged since yesterday.[15]

Assembled to celebrate the liturgy, Christians publicly proclaim their faith in Jesus Christ. "The only Son of God, eternally begotten of the Father . . . was born of the Virgin Mary and became man." Again and again in the celebration, we sing his power and his glory, for through his death and resurrection, God realizes the plan of his love: to destroy death and renew life. Those who are strangers to faith are surprised. They can admit that certain persons believe all these things. But that the believers affirm them with such assurance, as if their truth was obvious, is beyond their comprehension. As a consequence, they cannot suffer that believers look down on them and seem to say while addressing them, "How is it possible for you not to have faith?" They retort: "Where are these great miracles you speak of, and this wisdom that is supposed to fill us with admiration? More than ever, death and violence dominate the world. Where are the prophets in your midst? And if there are any, how much of an audience do they have in your communities? For if the world is mad, as you say, you seem to adjust without too much pain to that madness in the way you live."

These objections and these challenges, along with others as serious, resound in the Church's celebration even if the carefully closed doors ward off rumors from without. The assembly gathers around the Lord, who has convoked it. He teaches us and renews for us the work of his pasch. To listen to him, to receive him under the signs of bread and wine are acts of faith. But every liturgy is also a renewed challenge to the truth and authenticity of the faith of those participating in it. The goal is not to dishearten them and arouse guilt in them but, on the contrary, to incite them to renew and deepen their attachment to the person of the Lord so that they may be in the world his credible and indefatigable witnesses. Their weakness is great, no doubt, but they can do anything with the grace of God, who is their strength.

Fifteenth and Sixteenth Sunday in Ordinary Time

The Gospels of these two Sundays are dedicated to the mission that Jesus entrusts to the Twelve in the course of his preaching. At the moment of their departure, he gives them precise and strict instructions concerning the manner of living incumbent on missionaries of the gospel and the way they must behave toward their hearers (Mark 6:7-13—Fifteenth Sunday). Upon returning, the disciples report to Jesus what they have done and taught. The Lord wants to lead them to a place apart, to a desert spot, to take some rest. But the crowd catches up with them. They must renounce the idea of taking a break. Jesus does not avoid the situation: immediately, "he began to teach them many things" (Mark 6:30-34—Sixteenth Sunday). The Sundays during which the liturgy presents the two sides of this diptych constitute a unit, a well-defined sequence, that concludes the reading of the first part of Mark's Gospel. For from the Seventeenth Sunday through the Twenty-first, the liturgy presents chapter 6 from John's Gospel, the "Discourse on the Bread of Life."[1]

The first mission entrusted to the Twelve by Jesus, discharged under his direct supervision, and whose smooth operation he himself verified, announces and prefigures those which, afterwards, will be conducted by a multitude of others, to announce the gospel to the whole world. Two texts from the Old Testament show that Jesus' initiative continues God's plan and fulfills it. The first text recounts how the prophet Amos was chosen by God, even though his past did not prepare him in the least for this ministry, and sent where he was neither expected nor, to say the least, wanted (Amos 7:12-15—Fifteenth Sunday). The other is an oracle from the Book of Jeremiah. It announces that God himself will conduct his people, gather them under the care of one of David's descendants, and call upon other shepherds to guide them (Jer 23:1-6—Sixteenth Sunday).

Finally, on the Fifteenth Sunday, we begin the reading of excerpts from Paul's Letter to the Ephesians.[2]

Fifteenth Sunday

Missionaries of the Gospel— Sent by God

The Lord Seized Me to Speak His Word

If it is difficult to be accepted as a prophet in one's own country, it is no less difficult when one comes from elsewhere, especially from a sister nation with which there is conflict, or from another Church. Amos experienced this fate (Amos 7:12-15).

The time is that of "the schism of Israel."[1] A native of Judea, Amos comes to proclaim oracles of a rare virulence against the neighboring nations, and against the northern kingdom itself, its leaders, its priests, and its inhabitants (Amos 1:3–7:9).[2] His preaching and his predictions of punishment for a kingdom whose economy has become remarkably prosperous—but at the price of what injustices and what compromises with conscience!—constitute an intolerable provocation in the eyes of high-placed people. When Amos attacks the local sanctuary, the priest Amaziah enters the fray. He denounces Amos to King Jeroboam II.[3] "Amos has conspired against you here within Israel; the country cannot endure all his words. For this is what Amos says:

> Jeroboam shall die by the sword
>   and Israel shall surely be exiled from its land."
> (Amos 7:10-11)

And without waiting for the King's reaction, Amaziah makes it his business to intimidate Amos so that the latter will cross the border as fast as possible. He speaks to him in spiteful words in order to make him aware that his plan has been thwarted. If, as Amaziah hopes, Amos flees in panic, he will lose all esteem in the eyes of those who might have lent him a willing ear. "Off with you, visionary . . ." Which means, "You are only one of these overwrought visionary prattlers who say anything and mistake the constructs of their demented minds for visions."[4] "Flee to the land of Judah! There earn your bread by prophesying . . ." This is biting irony: "We are not duped by you, a man who has been paid to make trouble among us. Go back where you come from. People back there might pay you to play this game with them." This sort of reaction and discourse is usual with those who have placed themselves at the service of the established power,[5] a good excuse for nonintervention or, at least, for police actions, disguised under very honorable pretexts, designed to discredit those who upset the established order: these are low agitators bought by foreign powers, high-strung persons, false prophets.

"I was no prophet, nor have I belonged to a company of prophets; I was a shepherd and a dresser of sycamores. The LORD took me from following the flock and said to me, Go, prophesy to my people Israel." Amos' answer is humble but firm. He has nothing to do with the bands of visionaries that haunt the sanctuaries. He used to have a job to earn his living. He did not quit the work he was well qualified for because of need or because of the lure of profit. He was "taken" by God, in some way plucked from his flock and his groves of sycamores, without having resisted in the least. That is what prophets are: they speak about God "not with extrinsic proofs, but with an inner and immediate feeling."[6] He cannot prevent himself from being a prophet. Nothing and no one can cause him to elude his mission.

> The Lord calls forth my voice
> His word tears my heart apart.
>
> Shall I tell him that his step crushes me?
> No, the Lord is plowing his field.
> Life in me has responded,
> Groaning life has spoken.
>
> As a tree testifies before the sky
> To the light hidden in the earth,
>
> My human voice testifies before the Lord
> To his descent into the bosom of creation.
>
> And the word of God arouses my memory,
> His humbling himself arouses the ascent of my psalm.
>
> I add to the cry of my life,
> For I am a field of the Lord.
>
> And he gathers all my ages,
> He tears apart a grown-up heart to find the child again.
>
> He crosses my property to reach my cry of misery,
> That of my birth and that of my end drawing near.
>
> The secret of the Lord has dug my secret:
> May his word take root![7]

Prophets are troublesome people. One is often tempted to reject them, to tell them to shut up. But they will not be intimidated. "Whether it is right in the sight of God for us to obey you rather than God, you be the judges. It is impossible for us not to speak about what we have seen and heard" (Acts 4:19-20). This is fortunate for us, because the coming of a prophet is always a grace: it attests to the faithfulness and love of God, who never abandons his own. He calls "my people" those he has charged Amos with reproving by foretelling the calamities that will strike them if they remain obstinate in their sins.

> *Lord, let us see your kindness,*
> *and grant us your salvation.*

> I will hear what God proclaims;
>   the LORD—for he proclaims peace.
> To his people . . .
> Near indeed is his salvation to those who fear him,
>   glory dwelling in our land.
> Kindness and truth shall meet;
>   justice and peace shall kiss.
> Truth shall spring out of the earth,
>   and justice shall look down from heaven.
> The LORD himself will give his benefits;
>   our land shall yield its increase.
> Justice shall walk before him,
>   and salvation, along the way of his steps.
> (Ps 85:9a-b, 10-14)

The Inexhaustible Grace of God for the Praise of His Glory

The Letter to the Ephesians is a general exposition of the Christian vision of salvation history: the plan of God, set from all eternity, realized by Christ, unfolds in the Church. This letter is a precious witness to Paul's reflection, which here reaches its apex;[8] it remains relevant because it presents an overview of the whole mystery.[9] Finally, although quite didactic, this letter is not as austere as this kind of exposition often is, requiring on the part of the readers or hearers a serious effort in order to remain attentive. Because of its lyricism, the doctrinal explication of Ephesians engages the readers from the very first, and its interest does not flag for a single instant. The tone is set from the beginning by a long thanksgiving that is the model of all Christian Eucharists (Eph 1:3-14).

"Blessed be the God and Father of our Lord Jesus Christ, who has blessed us in Christ with every spiritual blessing in the heavens . . ."[10] This Christological and Trinitarian perspective, corresponding to the dynamism of salvation history, characterizes the Eucharistic Prayer and the

whole liturgy. The Father is at the origin and at the end of this vast movement in which we are caught. "He chose us in him, before the foundation of the world, to be holy and without blemish. In love he destined
us for adoption to himself . . ." Such is the project formed from all eternity. He revealed it to Abraham, father of believers, when he said to him,

> "All communities of the earth
>   shall find blessing in you" (Gen 12:3).[11]

In his inexhaustible grace, he revealed his plan by making us the recipients
of this blessing in the fullness of time.

Christ is actively present in this immense work of salvation, from the
moment the Father decided upon it until the day of its full realization.
It is "in him," that, "in the heavens," he conceived his plan and foresaw everything for its unfolding. "In him," "he chose us before the creation of the world" and "has destined us for adoption to himself." "In
him," he redeemed us and filled us with grace. "Through him," he unveiled "the mystery of his will." "In him," we have listened to "the word
of truth, the gospel of [our] salvation," we have become believers, we
were "sealed with the promised holy Spirit." "In him," he has summed
up "all things in Christ, in heaven and on earth."

> The Word, who was in the beginning with God, through whom all things
> came into being, and who always was present to humankind, this same
> Word, in the last times, at the hour decreed by the Father, united himself
> to his own handicraft and became a human being liable to suffering. We
> have therefore rejected the objection of those who say, "If Christ was born
> at that moment, he did not exist beforehand." We have, indeed, shown
> that God's Son did not begin at that moment, since he was from all eter-
> nity with the Father; but when he became incarnate and human, he recapit-
> ulated in himself the long history of humankind and opened a shortcut to
> salvation so that we might regain in Jesus Christ what we had lost in
> Adam—that is, the image and likeness of God. As it was impossible for
> humans, once conquered and broken by disobedience, to be fashioned anew
> and gain the prize of victory, and as it was equally impossible for humans,
> fallen under the weight of sin, to have part in salvation, God's Son did
> both things. He who was God's Word came down from the Father's side,
> he became incarnate, he went down even into death, and thus he consum-
> mated the "economy" of our salvation.[12]

Through Christ and in him, God, who created us, gives us life, sanctifies
us; in the Son, he makes children of us and co-heirs of the promised kingdom. The Spirit is "the first installment of our inheritance toward redemption as God's possession . . ." In all that happens in the order of

salvation, the Holy Spirit is present, as the proximate agent of God's work and its progress. This is why it is always invoked in sacraments and the Eucharist. "Send your Spirit to bring to birth the new peoples who are about to be born for you out of the baptismal fountain."[13] "Be marked by the Spirit, God's gift."[14] "Send upon him, Lord, the Holy Spirit. May he thus be fortified with the seven gifts of your grace in order to faithfully discharge his ministry."[15]

> And so, Father, we bring you these gifts.
> We ask you to make them holy by the power of
> your spirit
> that they may become the body and blood
> of your Son . . .[16]

In a less explicit way, the Holy Spirit is equally present and active in the Church of Christ and the world to bring about the kingdom of God.

Finally, everything, through Christ and in the Spirit, goes back to the Father, from whom come "all good giving and every perfect gift . . ." (Jas 1:17). What God has willed, what he has done, what he will complete when we enter into possession of our heritage on the day of full deliverance is "to the praise of his glory."

> Father, we acknowledge your greatness:
> all your actions show your wisdom and love. . . .
> Father, you so loved the world
> that in the fullness of time you sent your
>   only Son to be our Savior. . . .
> In fulfillment of your will
> he gave himself up to death;
> but by rising from the dead,
> he destroyed death and restored life.
> And that we might live no longer for
>   ourselves but for him,
> he sent the Holy Spirit from you, Father,
> as his first gift to those who believe,
> to complete his work on earth
> and bring us the fullness of grace. . . .[17]
> Through him,
> with him,
> in him,
> in the unity of the Holy Spirit,
> all glory and honor is yours,
> almighty Father,
> for ever and ever.

Jesus Entrusts the Announcement of the Gospel to the Disciples
Mark proceeds in a pedagogical manner to help his readers progress in
their personal discovery of the mystery of Jesus and his work. First he
leads them, in the company of a small group of disciples, to follow the
Lord, who in the region around the Sea of Galilee at Capernaum and
Nazareth, then in the surrounding villages, taught the crowds, healed
the sick, freed those possessed by demons. We thus witness the enthusiastic reactions of the people, the first suspicions cast on Jesus' authority,
the misunderstanding on the part of the inhabitants of Nazareth and even
of his own relatives. But along the way, we also witness the faith of a
woman hoping to steal a miracle from Jesus without being noticed and
of a synagogue official begging the cure of his daughter, who was at the
point of death. The news of the child's death does not take away his hope.
With Peter, James, and John, we enter the room where the young girl
is lying and we see her rise—alive—at Jesus' command. With a few privileged persons, we profit by the teaching given in parables. The sending
of the disciples on their mission constitutes a new phase in the revelation of the mystery (Mark 6:7-13).

Up to now, only Jesus has acted and taught. It is true that he has chosen
twelve disciples "that they might be with him and he might send them
forth to preach and to have authority to drive out demons" (Mark 3:14-
15). But now he "began to send them out two by two" to exercise the
ministry he has told them about.[18] Was it not necessary for them to begin
to "learn on the job," as it were, by watching Jesus? Was it not necessary for them, also, to see him confronted with contestation, calumny,
and even failure? His warnings and his instructions have a concrete basis
in these experiences.

He "gave them authority over unclean spirits." This is probably not
the priority we would have expected. Certainly, Satan is the major obstacle on the way of salvation; Jesus came to conquer him and give us
the means to share in this victory in us and around us. But although the
unavoidable battle is fierce, we do not envision it today under the form
of exorcisms. Evil seems to us more interior, less easy to oust and even
to diagnose. Evil has, in us and in the world, such profound and entangled
roots that it seems illusory to us to want to pull them up all at once. How
could we, by one exorcism, free someone from his or her inner demons?
It is, however, let us admit it, what many would wish when they say,
"I don't know what I have inside me, what obscure force impels me to
do evil against my will." Faced with such anxieties, we remain not only

powerless but speechless. However, should not our first action be to denounce evil wherever its presence is obvious, to dare to openly confront it by appealing to the force of Christ? This requires courage, boldness, self-denial, faith, and also much humility, because one should not undertake this battle for self-promotion or any similar intention, but only to contribute to the salvation of others.[19]

This courageous denunciation of the evil that one confronts is always the prophets' mission and task.

> Today we speak a lot about the "power" of the ministers. It is curious: the only power given to ministers in Mark is one we do not exercise, that of driving out demons. This conception of the missionary's task, according to Mark, is in conformity with that of the Acts of the Apostles or Paul's letters. Paul had the certitude that he worked miracles on his way by preaching the gospel. We, for our part, have difficulty seeing things this way. Miracles make us uncomfortable . . . Our attitude is in contrast with the attitude of the sects that make abundant use of miracles. When we read the gospel, we feel estranged and we ask: By any chance are the sects closer to the gospel than we are? Do they not represent a reaction aimed at reestablishing a balance which we ourselves have lost?
>
> We get the impression that what, in Mark, formed a beautiful unit is now scattered: there are specialists in preaching and specialists in miracles—a loss for all concerned. A yen for miracles can be unwholesome (John will be very reticent on this point). But on the other hand, perhaps we are not attentive enough to the fact that the preaching of the gospel must have repercussions on human equilibrium. I know that we have replaced the healing of the sick with the will to create a world more just and kinder to one's brothers and sisters. It is, no doubt, legitimate to seek for signs of the coming of the kingdom into our world in the improvement of human life. But under the condition that we not forget the potency of the gospel: it is a power of action against the reign of evil.[20]

"He instructed them to take nothing for the journey but a walking stick—no food, no sack, no money in their belts. They were, however, to wear sandals, but not a second tunic."[21] Such reduced equipment allows for a brisk pace and gives the missionaries the possibility of freely going from one place to another. "Wherever you enter a house, stay there until you leave from there. Whatever place does not welcome you or listen to you, leave there and shake the dust off your feet in testimony against them." The zeal of the missionaries and their message are not guaranteed success everywhere and always, " 'No slave is greater than his master.' If they persecuted me, they will also persecute you" (John 15:20). Far from being disturbed to the point of doubting their vocation, missionaries will be strengthened by this participation in the Lord's destiny.[22] Furthermore, disciples sent on a mission must not give the appearance of important personages who seek to impress others by their magnificence or of propagandists who command considerable material means. Missionaries appeal to the free commitment of faith and not to the persuasive force of their discourses. They propose a message of salvation with conviction, but they do not impose it. Then they move on to where other people are waiting. Those who will not have listened to them will at least know that messengers had stopped by one day. Perhaps later on, when remembering, they will welcome others better. A sowing does not always succeed at the first try. The missionaries of the gospel accept in advance not to see the fruits of their labors: "For here the saying is verified that 'One sows and another reaps' " (John 4:37). "I planted, Apollos watered, but God caused the growth. Therefore neither the one who plants nor the one who waters is anything, but only God, who causes the growth. The one who plants and the one who waters are equal, and each will receive wages in proportion to his labor" (1 Cor 3:6-8).

"So they went off and preached repentance." The Twelve sent on their mission repeat the message given by Jesus himself when he began to preach in Galilee after John the Baptist had been arrested. "This is the time of fulfillment. The kingdom of God is at hand. Repent, and believe in the gospel" (Mark 1:15). As they had been instructed, they "drove out many demons, and they anointed with oil many who were sick and cured them." By speaking of anointing with oil, Mark refers to the practice of the Church as attested by James' letter (5:14). This is also a way of reminding us that apostles and missionaries do not accomplish miracles by virtue of their own power: they must not let any doubt remain on this point; on the contrary, should there be the slightest risk of erroneous interpretation concerning their actions, a clear and explicit reaction is necessary. "When Peter saw this, he addressed the people, 'You Israelites, why are you amazed at this, and why do you look so intently at us as if we had made him walk by our own power or piety? . . . by faith in [Jesus'] name, this man, whom you see and know, his name has made strong, and the faith that comes through it has given him this perfect health, in the presence of all of you' " (Acts 3:12, 16).

The Eucharistic Prayer addresses God, the Father of our Lord Jesus Christ, saying: "All things are of your making, all times and seasons obey your laws."[23] "In him you have renewed all things and you have given us all a share in his riches."[24] Through him, "you have founded your

Church on the apostles . . . as the living gospel for all men to hear."[25] The mission of the Twelve directly continues Jesus mission.[26] Therefore, they, too, are in "the beginning of the gospel of Jesus [the Son of God]," whom we have received in faith because the Father has granted us the "spiritual blessing." The Eucharistic Prayer embraces the totality of God's plan conceived "before the foundation of the world," realized in his Son when the time was fulfilled and in which we participate today and which unfolds until its full realization, when "all things [are summed up] in Christ, in heaven and on earth."

Christians who, in their hymns and thanksgivings, celebrate this magnificent plan that love inspired in God and from which no one is excluded, cannot constitute a closed society. Our faith demands a universal evangelization. Already during his lifetime, Jesus widened his field of action by sending the disciples to carry the good news of salvation to places he himself could not reach. Later on, at the moment of going back to his Father, he will tell them, "Go into the whole world and proclaim the gospel to every creature" (Mark 16:15). He will then renew their power over evil spirits and their power to cure the sick (Mark 16:17). "They went forth and preached everywhere, while the Lord worked with them and confirmed the word through accompanying signs" (Mark 16:20). The sending of the Twelve on their mission has a general scope, without restriction of time or place. We belong to a Church sent to others; we are all constituted witnesses of Christ in the day-to-day work of mission.[27]

The effective response to this Christian and ecclesial vocation often places us in difficult situations: "Go and prophesy elsewhere! We have no use for your discourses!" The refusal to receive the messengers of the gospel and to listen to them will not always be expressed in words only and with irony: "We should like to hear you on this some other time" (Acts 17:32). "You are mad, Paul; much learning is driving you mad" (Acts 26:24). All kinds of trials—ill treatment, imprisonment, even death—can become the form taken by rejection of the gospel and of the missionaries. It is because a number of them accepted everything through faithfulness to their mission that "the word of truth, the gospel of . . . salvation" has reached us.

> Your call has thrust them
> on the ways and byways;
> bearers of your word,
> without any other support than your love,
> they speak your joy
> to those who receive them.

Marvels of your grace!
You entrust God's secrets to humans.

Messengers of the good news,
they announce peace to the ends of the world.

The forgiveness they proclaim on earth,
God accomplishes in heaven.

Happy the people who welcome your emissaries,
happy the people whose God you are.[28]

Sixteenth Sunday

No Rest for Christ and His Apostles

God Will Not Leave His People Without a Shepherd

In all peoples whose origins are pastoral and nomadic, shepherds are important personages. Usually they are the heads of families who work at their tasks with the help of their sons and daughters. If they must have recourse to strangers, these must be trustworthy persons because they are charged with an important responsibility.[1] As a consequence, among those people, in the Ancient East in general and among the Hebrews in particular, the image of the shepherd is naturally used to designate the chiefs, the kings, and even God.[2] The people whose vocation and story the Bible reports was the property of God, who had chosen it, who had acquired it. It follows that its leaders could only be the Lord's intendants. They were held to observe his instructions and give him an account of their management. If the flock was ill-cared for, exhausted by too long a drive; if sheep got lost, the shepherds in charge, accounted responsible, deserved to be dismissed, even punished when the losses were too severe, or worse, when the shepherds were convicted of neglect or dishonest dealings. The prophet Jeremiah speaks in this cultural and religious context (Jer 23:1-6).[3]

"Woe to the shepherds who mislead and scatter the flock of my pasture, says the Lord." This is a most grave accusation. Those to whom God entrusted his people[4] are declared guilty of criminal negligence: ewes are dying for lack of care and those left to wander off are sure to die of hunger and thirst or to be devoured by wild beasts.[5] "I will take care to punish your evil deeds," says the Lord. The oracle does not dwell on the fate reserved for them; delay will not lessen the punishment. The Lord first takes care of the flock that needs emergency intervention: "I myself will gather the remnant of my flock from all the lands to which I have driven them and bring them back to their meadow; there they shall increase and multiply." Therefore, God personally takes in hand the disastrous situation into which the bad shepherds have placed the flock.

147

First of all, what is left must be gathered. This is a task that only the Lord can successfully undertake, for the ewes are scattered throughout all lands. This way of speaking shows that the oracle goes much further than the historical situation and future of a small people: its population was exiled in Babylon and not scattered throughout all lands. This widening of perspective should not surprise us, for, in the Bible, the Exile has taken on a religious meaning. The true cause of the Exile lies not in the strength of the conqueror's arms but in the sin of the people and their unfaithfulness to the covenant. They have turned away from God and placed their trust in others. Hence, the catastrophe—the ruination of the land and the deportation of its inhabitants. This was to be expected, the more so as the prophets had never ceased to warn the people and their leaders against the disastrous consequences of their aberrations. The Exile was the opportunity for the people to become aware of these deviations and to understand that there is salvation only in God, that only conversion and renewal of fidelity to the covenant are the conditions of a new gathering of the exiles in the Promised Land. This is why the Exile remains for today's believers, as well as for yesterday's, a subject for salutary meditation. Yes, only God can gather those whom sin disperses in all lands; only he can make of them a saved people.[6]

In order to accomplish this work, God chooses and sends shepherds charged in his name with leading the sheep on the roads of life where they have nothing to fear from anything or anyone, if they do not succumb to the temptation to leave these ways laid down and marked by the Lord, their only Master. Then it happens that, among these leaders of the flock, the still indistinct form of the Elect of God is silhouetted on the horizon; born of the stock of David, he will distinguish himself, however, from all others. He will act "wisely," concerned only with establishing "what is just and what is right in the land." In other words, he will behave exactly like God. No longer will schism set north and south in fratricidal antagonism.

> In his days, Judah will be saved,
> Israel shall dwell in security.[7]

This marvelous future is in direct relation to the promises formerly made to Jesse, David's father,[8] promises never to be forgotten. As time passes, the people realize that no king can correspond truly and for a long time to the hopes placed in him.[9] They will understand that the promise, and the oracles that regularly confirm it, will have their fulfillment only with the coming of a Messiah, born of David's race, but so much according to God's heart that he will be above human standards. He will be the "good shepherd" (John 10:11).[10] It is, therefore, toward God and his Christ that Jeremiah's oracle turns our eyes, reread within the tradition and with the additional light of ulterior revelations, the hope and the prayer of believers.

> *The Lord is my shepherd;*
> *there is nothing I shall want.*

> The LORD is my shepherd; I shall not want.
>   In verdant pastures he gives me repose;
> Beside restful waters he leads me;
>   he refreshes my soul.
>   He guides me in right paths for his name's sake.
> Even though I walk in the dark valley
>   I fear no evil; for you are at my side
> With your rod and your staff
>   that give me courage.
> You spread the table before me
>   in the sight of my foes;
> You anoint my head with oil;
>   my cup overflows.
> Only goodness and kindness follow me
>   all the days of my life;
> And I shall dwell in the house of the LORD
>   for years to come.
> (Ps 23)

The Universal Reconciliation Through Christ in the Spirit

The experience of divisions, factions, etc., belongs to all ages and to all environments—in the world, between believers, and in the Church. Separated from each other by walls with often deep foundations, humans spend their lives closed in upon themselves and their respective positions. Mutual distrust prevents any form of dialogue. Intolerance sets in, leading to fanaticism, to aggressive feelings and words, to hidden or violently exploding hatred. Must we become resigned to this state of affairs and say, unfortunately, that it will always be so as long as there are human beings? No, answers Paul, because it is completely alien to God's will and because Christ came so that his will might be accomplished (Eph 2:13-18).

The world was divided into two sides: on the one side, those who believed in the true God and submitted to the prescriptions of the Mosaic Law; on the other—the rest of humanity—those we call pagans. From these two, Jesus, who "is our peace . . . made both one and broke down the dividing wall of enmity, through his flesh, abolishing the law with its commandments and legal claims," which in fact closed the access of salvation to pagans. He did not abolish the Law; on the contrary, he brought it to its fulfillment (Matt 5:17-19). "You shall love the Lord your God, with all your heart, with all your soul, and with all your mind. This is the greatest and the first commandment. The second is like it: You shall love your neighbor as yourself. The whole law and the prophets depend on these two commandments" (Matt 22:37-40).

God, therefore, did not send his Son to promulgate new juridical prescriptions. But in him, he created "one new person," the first-born of a new humanity. Henceforth, it is not by reading a code, however venerable, that we discover God's will, but by looking at Christ. By his cross, he has reconciled human beings with God; better still, he has—personally—become their reconciliation.[11] In him, all human beings form "one body" and "have access in one Spirit to the Father." To build walls of division and hatred between human beings is to rise up against God, blaspheme against Christ, and seek to oppose the Spirit. Christians cannot in any way—be it by their silence and passivity—cooperate in such undertakings. They do not have the right to resign themselves to them, as if they were unavoidable strokes of fate. Rather, they have the strict duty to work at abolishing, in and around themselves, everything conducive to divisions, antagonisms, wars small or great: inequality, injustice, egoism. Our faith demands this of us.[12]

Jesus, the Apostles, and the Crowds

Mark gathers into two simple tableaux the traditional data on the mission that Jesus entrusted to the Twelve. Here again they are "gathered together with Jesus."[13] Everything is said in a few lines. But this brief account is not as inconsequential as a rapid reading might lead us to believe (Mark 6:30-34).[14]

Mark, who up to now has spoken of the Twelve, here calls them apostles,[15] which means emissaries, envoys.[16] Indeed, they have just exercised this function at Jesus' command. They "reported all they had done and taught." It would be of no interest to us to amplify or sum up this report. The apostles have proclaimed that one must be converted; they have driven out many demons and healed the sick (Mark 6:12-13). Simply, they have transmitted the teaching given by Jesus himself as later on the evangelists and other preachers of the good news will do.[17] Mark's comment reminds us that all envoys must act and teach only as faithful spokespersons who must give the Lord an account of what they say and do. "Thus should one regard us: as servants of Christ and stewards of the mysteries of God. Now it is of course required of stewards that they be found trustworthy" (1 Cor 4:1-2).[18]

Jesus tells them, " 'Come away by yourselves to a deserted place to rest a while.' People were coming and going in great numbers, and they had no opportunity even to eat." This thoughtfulness of Jesus toward the Twelve is the more remarkable, as he did not care in the same way about himself, which prompted his family to say, "He is out of his mind" (Mark 3:21). We also can think that this attentiveness and Jesus' words, reported by Mark with quiet satisfaction, carry a general teaching that is always timely.[19] We have already seen that after teaching the multitudes, Jesus takes the disciples apart to explain everything to them "in private" (Mark 4:34).[20] He himself regularly goes to a deserted spot to pray in a silent face-to-face encounter with the Father after days in which he has not had a free moment (Mark 1:35).[21] Jesus teaches the apostles that they must adopt a rhythm of life similar to his, with a balanced alternation of time generously given to others and solitude, of intense activity and rest. But what kind of rest are we speaking about?

> In all things, Lord, you imitate the Father. If we seek what could be your rest, we must ask: Is there rest in God? What is it like?
>
> Now Scripture describes for us this rest of God. "God looked at everything he had made, and he found it very good . . . Since on the seventh day God was finished with the work he had been doing, he rested on the seventh day and made it holy, because on it he rested from all the work he had done in creation" (Gen 1:31–2:3).
>
> This text clearly indicates what is the rest of God, what is the rest of the Son of God and the Son of Man, and under what conditions God blesses the rest of human beings. "And whoever enters into God's rest, rests from his own works as God did from his. Therefore, let us strive to enter into that rest" (Heb 4:10-11).
>
> The Creator's rest is tied to the perception of the completion of the work he had willed. God rests because all has been done and well done. Likewise, Lord, you had a right to rest because you saw your work being successfully accomplished. Through you salvation was entering souls and the world.
>
> Your disciples, too, had the right to rest. For they had just completed their first mission. They had preached repentance, they had driven out demons, they had cured the sick, they had come back with joy. You appreciated their

work by saying, "I have observed Satan fall like lightning from the sky" (Luke 10:18). As well as the Creator, as well as yourself, they could rest, seeing that their work was good.[22]

In fact, Jesus and the apostles are unable to go away without being noticed. "People saw them leaving and many came to know about it. They hastened there on foot from all the towns and arrived at the place before them." By reporting this with a dash of humor, might Mark not want to suggest that the time of mission is not that of contemplative rest? Such an intention is improbable when we speak about such a serious subject and about Jesus, who by his example is training his apostles.[23] It is enough to continue reading the text to be completely convinced of this. Seeing the crowd, "his heart was moved with pity for them, for they were like sheep without a shepherd." This pity does not resemble a feeling mixed with condescension, somewhat humiliating for those who arouse it. Rather than the pity felt at the sight of misery and misfortune, the pity mentioned in the Scriptures is an extremely deep feeling and an attitude of active benevolence that impels us to do everything possible to relieve the sufferers by a total commitment of ourselves. Pity characterizes God: we appeal to it when we are in distress and when we seek pardon for our sins.[24] It impels Jesus to heal the sick,[25] to multiply loaves for the crowd that has nothing to eat (Mark 8:2). Here Jesus, "moved with pity for them, for they were like sheep without a shepherd, . . . began to teach them many things."

"Every word that comes forth / from the mouth of God" is food (Matt 4:4), "bread of life."[26] By his word—the Law; the teaching of the prophets, his spokespersons—God as a good shepherd, prudent and self-assured, guides his people through all the dangers of their exodus, leads them "beside restful waters" that refresh their souls so that they may "dwell in the house of the Lord for years to come" (Ps 23). The liturgical practice of the Christian assemblies surely attests to this faith and this tradition. The Eucharist always includes the two tables of the shared word and bread.[27] Jesus' disciples are sent on their mission for the same ministry: to teach the crowds and supply them with life-giving food.[28]

> His teaching is certainly not an intellectual teaching that would conceal propositions on divine nature or the secrets of the world. According to the gospel, it is made up of diverse, impressionistic touches, as if words only brushed against a much deeper reality but did not succeed in breaking through it. As human being, Christ was unable to go beyond the fundamental inadequacy of any language: his words are human words that find mean-

ing and weight only because they express the truth of a person, in this case the truth of the Son of God; perhaps it is there that the mystery of Christ as shepherd resides. In him, every word reflects, with absolute authenticity, the existential truth of a love relationship with the Father and all human beings.

To live in faith, one's bond to Jesus Christ is to recognize the one who has so totally lived his relation of Son and brother that his word is truth: not an abstract, narrow truth, a quasi-magical formulation of the divine mystery, but a concretely lived Truth, the ultimate point where experience joins the Absolute.[29]

To express God's solicitude toward the human beings he loves, the Bible uses, among others, the image of the landowner, whose flock of sheep is his dearest possession. He entrusts it to shepherds charged with carefully watching over it in his name and according to his directions: to keep it together in a fruitful peace by leading it in the ways of justice. Woe to those shepherds who would show themselves unfaithful to their mission! The warnings and denunciations of the prophets of old still resound today in the Church, relayed by the admonitions of Peter's first letter (5:2-4), admonitions that echo those of Jesus himself (Matt 7:15; John 10:12).

The Son of God was sent to earth to announce the good news of peace to those who were much "like sheep without a shepherd" and to give them "access in one Spirit to the Father." He formed the apostles for this ministry by awakening them to pity for the crowds that were hungry for word and bread, and by teaching them, through his example, what they were to do and teach. This urgent mission has priority over all the rest. When the multitudes are here, waiting for the food the shepherds are supposed to give them, it is not the time for rest and self-absorption.[30]

This is not to say that the missionaries of the gospel do not have the right to seek solitude. On the contrary, it is indispensable for them to enjoy a well-deserved rest—this will come in due course, when the work is finished—but to get closer to God and to Christ and, in a more intimate communion, to learn what it means and what is demanded of them when moved with pity for the crowds.

Thus in and through solitude we do not move away from people. On the contrary, we move closer to them through compassionate ministry.

In a world that victimizes us by its compulsions, we are called to solitude where we can struggle against our anger and greed and let our new self be born in the loving encounter with Jesus Christ. It is in this solitude that we become compassionate people, deeply aware of our solidarity in brokenness with all humanity and ready to reach out to anyone in need.

The end of Anthony's story shows him, after years of compassionate ministry, returning to his solitude to be totally absorbed in direct communion with God. . . . It is therefore to solitude that we must return, not alone, but with all those whom we embrace through our ministry. This return continues until the time when the same Lord who sent us into the world calls us back to be with him in a never-ending communion.[31]

God convokes the Christian assembly to celebrate the Eucharist, when Christ, Word and Bread, having fed his faithful by giving himself to them, sends them into the world to announce to the crowds, wandering without shepherds, the good news of salvation, so that all of us may one day share the same joy and unite ourselves to the thanksgiving of God's children finally gathered.

You were far from the source of life,
wandering and dispersed.
Now, rejoice:
by his cross the Lamb
gathers the flock,
and all those who follow him proclaim:

Jesus, our shepherd,
you lead us to the father!

All of you who are hungry and thirsty,
come quickly:
God's justice is revealed to you.

The walls are destroyed,
the barriers are down:
God reconciles you
through the blood of the Lamb.

Joyous news for those who were far
and for those who were near:
one body unites them.[32]

From the Seventeenth to the Twenty-first Sunday in Ordinary Time

On the Seventeenth Sunday in Ordinary Time, Year B, we temporarily set aside Mark's Gospel in order to read in John's the account of the multiplication of the loaves and, afterwards, for four Sundays, the discourse on the Bread of Life (John 6:1-69).[1] "This insertion is a natural one, because the narrative of the multiplication in John's Gospel takes the place of [the first multiplication] in Mark's."[2]

On the other side of the lake, where he went with the Twelve, people who have seen Jesus leave catch up with him (Mark 6:33). A great crowd finds itself gathered around him. Where, in this sequestered place, can anyone get the wherewithal to feed such a mob? There is a young boy who has five barley loaves and two fish: it is pitifully meager. But it is enough. With so little, Jesus feeds the crowd; there are even leftovers. Seeing this miracle, the crowd swells with immense enthusiasm. Jesus understands that they want to carry him off forcefully to make him king. "He withdrew again to the mountain alone" (John 6:1-15—Seventeenth Sunday).

There the crowd finds him, on the opposite shore, in Capernaum. "You are looking for me . . . because you ate the loaves and were filled," says Jesus, "whereas you should ask yourselves what the sign I accomplished means. You are worried only about material food instead of working for that which endures for eternal life and that I can give you, for 'I am the bread of life' " (John 6:24-35—Eighteenth Sunday).

This statement arouses murmurs. How can this man, whose parents we know, say such a thing? Jesus does not answer their astonishment by saying that they must understand his words in a symbolic sense. On the contrary, he insists, "I am the living bread that came down from heaven; whoever eats this bread will live forever" (John 6:41-51—Nineteenth Sunday).

His hearers understand that Jesus' language is not symbolic: "How can this man give us [his] flesh to eat?" This is true, "for my flesh is true food, and my blood is true drink." "Whoever eats my flesh and drinks

155

my blood has eternal life, and I will raise him on the last day'' (John 6:51-58—Twentieth Sunday).

There is a crisis among Jesus' disciples. Many go away and no longer accompany him. He turns to the Twelve. '' 'Do you also want to leave?' Simon Peter answers him, 'Master, to whom shall we go? You have the words of eternal life. We have come to believe and are convinced that you are the Holy One of God' '' (John 6:60-69—Twenty-first Sunday).

Old Testament texts, especially well chosen, shed light on each successive part of the sixth chapter of John's Gospel.[3] Whereas there is a famine in the land, Elisha feeds one hundred persons with twenty barley loaves he has been offered (2 Kgs 4:42-44—Seventeenth Sunday).

The recalling of the gift of the manna is unavoidable: thanks to this mysterious food from heaven, God feeds his people during the forty years of their march through the desert (Exod 16:2-4, 12-15—Eighteenth Sunday). Similarly, the prophet Elijah, exhausted and disheartened, finds ''at his head'' a hearth loaf and a jug of water, which give him the strength to walk ''forty days and forty nights to the mountain of God, Horeb'' (1 Kgs 4:8—Nineteenth Sunday).

Jesus' invitation to his hearers to ''eat the flesh of the Son of Man and drink his blood'' reminds us of the pressing call of Wisdom,

> Come, eat of my food;
>   and drink of the wine I have mixed!
> (Prov 9:1-6—Twentieth Sunday)

When, at the end of the discourse on the Bread of Life, Simon Peter proclaims, in the name of the Twelve, his unshakable attachment to Jesus, we think of the solemn renewal of faithfulness to the covenant that took place at the time of Joshua, at the great gathering of the twelve tribes of Israel in Shechem: ''We also will serve the LORD, for he is our God'' (Josh 24:1-2a, 15-17, 18b—Twenty-first Sunday).

From the Seventeenth to the Twenty-first Sunday, we read five excerpts from Paul's Letter to the Ephesians. They are exhortations addressed to all faithful by the Apostle who is ''a prisoner for the Lord.'' Strive ''to preserve the unity of the spirit through the bond of peace'' (Eph 4:1-6—Seventeenth Sunday). ''Put on the new self, created in God's way in righteousness and holiness of truth (Eph 4:17, 20-24—Eighteenth Sunday). ''Do not grieve the holy Spirit of God, with which you were sealed for the day of redemption'' (Eph 4:30-5:2—Nineteenth Sunday). Give ''thanks always and for everything in the name of our Lord Jesus Christ to God the Father'' (Eph 5:15-20—Twentieth Sunday). Finally, Paul addresses married Christians. Let them follow the example of the relation between Christ, who is the head, and his body. Grounded in mutual respect and love, their lives as couples will acquire their full significance. For "this is a great mystery, but I speak in reference to Christ and the church" (Eph 5:21-32—Twenty-first Sunday).

In the course of this long sequence, placed in the middle of Ordinary Time, Year B,[4] we progress at a rhythm quite different from that of the preceding and following passages. With Mark, we are constantly moving; it is quite another thing with these five Sundays. Having left the shore of the Sea of Galilee, where Jesus has multiplied the loaves and fish, we remain in Capernaum. But the difference does not stop here. The discourse on the Bread of Life develops as if in a spiral.[5] We often have the impression of not progressing, even of going backwards, of hearing again and again what has already been said. It is worthwhile to disregard this impression and to strive to enter into the particular movement of John's style.

The liturgy does not leave to everyone the time necessary for the study and meditation of the scriptural texts that are proclaimed. This is normal. These texts are elements of the liturgical action, which has its own dynamism and must go on, although it does provide for moments of silence and meditation. Moreover, the homily, short in principle, cannot exhaust all their doctrinal and spiritual riches. All it can do is open ways for the hearers to understand them and make them their own, suggest developments and applications to daily life. Its aim is to say, "Today this scripture passage is fulfilled in your hearing."[6] To help us see the mystery we celebrate and for which we give thanks[7] together. Happy are we if our attentive listening to the proclaimed word and the homily incite us to go back to the texts, clarified by the homily, and to the liturgy itself in order to meditate upon them, to make them ours by personal meditation or by sharing with brothers and sisters.[8] The necessity for this will probably be more keenly felt on these five Sundays in Ordinary Time, Year B.

Seventeenth Sunday

Plenty of Bread for All

The Bread of First Fruits Will Never Fail

In the biblical tradition, Elisha, who played an important role in the northern kingdom, is presented as a person whose life was marked by many miraculous episodes.[1] The liturgy has chosen the miracle of the multiplied loaves as a counterpart to Jesus' miracle (2 Kgs 4:42-44).[2]

The episode itself is most simple. "There was a famine in the land" (2 Kgs 4:38). A man offers Elisha "twenty barley loaves made from the first-fruits, and fresh grain in the ear." Elisha has this providential food distributed among his prophet-brethren[3] who are with him, numbering one hundred. Not only is the small quantity of food sufficient for all, but remnants are collected. If we stop at the fact itself, the interest of this narrative does not exceed that of other similar stories that we read in the *Golden Legend* about saints of all times. But a certain number of details catch our attention and give to the episode a precious significance in the framework of today's liturgy.

We are dealing with bread multiplied in order that it might be shared, which is already a highly symbolic fact for any human. "Bread plays so many roles! We have learned to recognize, in it, an instrument of the human community, because of the bread we break together. We have learned to recognize, in it, the image of the nobility of work, because of the bread we earn by the sweat of our brow. We have learned to recognize, in it, the essential vehicle of pity, because of the bread we distribute in times of want. The taste of shared bread is without compare."[4] In the Bible, bread, gift of God to humans to strengthen them (Ps 104:14-15), symbolizes intelligence and wisdom (Prov 9:5). It is a sign of a concluded peace, of life (John 6:35).[5] The barley loaves are those of the bread offering.[6] The gesture of the man who brings to Elisha the first-fruits "which earth has given and human hands have made" has a definite liturgical connection.[7] Finally, the abundance of the bread that will feed the poor has come to suggest, in a later tradition, the banquet of the end times, when at last God himself will liberally satisfy all human needs.

The hand of the Lord feeds us;
he answers all our needs.

Let all your works give you thanks, O LORD,
    and let your faithful ones bless you.
Let them discourse of the glory of your kingdom
    and speak of your might . . .
The eyes of all look hopefully to you,
    and you give them their food in due season;
You open your hand
    and satisfy the desire of every living thing.
The LORD is just in all his ways
    and holy in all his works.
The LORD is near to all who call upon him,
    to all who call upon him in truth.
(Ps 145:10-11, 15-18)

Following God's Call

Sin has introduced division everywhere: in the universe, in the human heart, between human beings. The history of salvation is that of the return to unity. Salvation has been gained once for all by Christ, dead on the cross for the multitude.[8] But now, salvation must develop in his body, whose members are to ward off any assault of the evils that could compromise unity.[9] The second part of the Letter to the Ephesians begins with a vibrant exhortation by Paul, "a prisoner for the Lord," addressed to all Christians, "Strive to preserve the unity of the spirit through the bond of peace" (Eph 4:3).

First, Paul enumerates some concrete attitudes that express and insure faithfulness to God's call: humility, gentleness, patience, and mutual forbearance "through love." We have here genuinely evangelical values in accord with the Beatitudes, and not modes of behavior recommended by sages—philosophers, ethicists—in order to live in harmony with ourselves and, inasmuch as possible, with others around us. Such human wisdom is very valuable: Christians rejoice to see it taught and, especially, put into practice by people who do not share their faith. They must even recognize that some have reached admirable degrees of inner peace, meekness, patience, and benevolence toward all, virtues marvelously radiant. But the exhortation does not rest on a comparison, however stimulating, between the perfection of the ones and the mediocrity of the others. These virtues, fruits of the Spirit, opposed to those of the flesh, are inseparable from life in Christ, into which Christians have been born.[10] By gathering them in the unique body of Christ, the Spirit establishes them in peace with God and among themselves, the ultimate goal of their calling.[11]

All this is condensed in an extremely pithy formula, easy to memorize, its origin probably liturgical and, in all likelihood, baptismal: "one body and one Spirit, as you were also called to the one hope of your call; one Lord, one faith, one baptism; one God and Father of all, who is over all and through all and in all." When seeds of division arise in the Church, we must cling to this fundamental profession of faith. All problems and difficulties will not be automatically resolved. But as long as all members repeat together and with deep conviction what Paul recalls here, their foremost care will be to reject any action that would break the unity of children born into the same family. And if, unfortunately, walls have been raised, they will take no rest until they have leveled these walls. United to other believers, Christians must unceasingly proclaim by words and especially by their way of life, "One God and Father of all." This is without doubt the only argument—and the most convincing—able to expose the monstrosity of aggressive behavior toward any person, because we are all, without any distinction, children of the same Father.

The Bread Multiplied for the Crowd and the Pasch in Galilee

The multiplication of the loaves occupies an exceptional place in the Gospels.[12] To his own narrative, John adds a long discourse pronounced by Jesus in Capernaum. The full significance of the event is thus progressively revealed. Indeed, the multiplication of the loaves is not only a miracle—with the meaning of a manifestation of power above the ordinary, supernatural—but a "sign." By sign, we understand that because of its content and the circumstances surrounding it, and of the context into which it is inserted, of the persons involved, and in particular of it's principal actor, the sign expresses superior realities—realities of another order. These are not clearly enunciated, but suggested through the mediation of symbols and allusions. It is not that the author wants to hide something or prevent all but initiates from grasping the intended meaning. It is that the realities in question are too lofty to be enclosed in common propositions and definitions. Moreover, we must be open to the realities that are alluded to in order to comprehend the sign; otherwise, we do not even see that we are in the presence of a fact that could have meaning. Finally, the sign appeals not only to reason, but to the whole being, the whole person. This is why the sign can be understood by all, even—especially—the simplest.[13] We must keep all these things in mind when we read the account of the multiplication of the loaves in John's Gospel (John 6:1-15).

In a sign, the details often have great importance: they, too, are bearers of meaning. "Jesus went across the Sea of Galilee [of Tiberias]." We remember that "Jesus did . . . the beginning of his signs in Cana in Galilee and so revealed his glory, and his disciples began to believe in him."[14] This sign took place at a wedding feast. Now his disciples are with him also, but "on the mountain" and not in a closed banquet hall. There is no longer only a restricted number of guests selected in advance, joined by a group invited at the last minute. Here we have a whole crowd who spontaneously followed Jesus and his disciples "because they saw the signs he was performing on the sick." Did these people really see these cures as signs, to use John's term for them? It does not matter: Christians must understand Jesus' miracles as signs, and this one in particular. They must remember what Isaiah had announced.

> Then will the eyes of the blind be opened,
>   the ears of the deaf be cleared;
> Then will the lame leap like a stag,
>   the tongue of the dumb will sing.
> (Isa 35:5-6a)[15]

The messianic expectations must be strong in this multitude, fired by Jesus' miracles. By following him to the mountain, the people perhaps expect to see some extraordinary manifestation of Jesus' authority and power: a great discourse as that of the Beatitudes?[16] a startling revelation as when the covenant was established?[17] John takes special pain to tell Christians within what context we must read the sign. "The Jewish feast of Passover was near." This feast celebrates the coming out of Egypt and recalls the signs that accompanied it, in particular, that of the manna. But let us remember also that "before the feast of Passover, Jesus knew that his hour had come to pass from this world to the Father. He loved his own in the world and loved them to the end," giving them a sign during a meal (John 13:1-2). "Jesus raised his eyes" toward the multitude. "Where can we buy enough food for them to eat?" In the desert, Moses had already met with a similar problem; he had turned to God, interceding for the people (Num 11:13).[18] Jesus addresses one of the Twelve, Philip. "He said this to test him, because he himself knew what he was going to do." We must pause here—as John probably did, when he was speaking of this sign to the gathered brothers and sisters—in order to allow everyone to understand that this request for a vote of confidence is addressed to us today.[19]

Humanly, the situation is without solution. "Two hundred days' wages worth of food would not be enough for each of them to have a little [bit]." Coming after this statement, the intervention of Andrew, "the brother of Simon Peter," would be ridiculous if it did not suggest that we must always keep a glimmer of hope in our hearts, even though we do not see how it can ever come true. "There is a boy here who has five barley loaves and two fish; but what good are these for so many?" Nothing, apparently.[20] But these are barley loaves like those used for the offering.[21] One would think that Jesus was only waiting for this generous and symbolic offering of a few modest fruits of human work: everything is in readiness for his intervention. He commands the apostles to have the people sit down, for "there was a great deal of grass in that place."[22] Then Jesus took the loaves, gave thanks, and distributed them to those who were reclining, and also as much of the fish as they wanted. These gestures vividly remind us of those Jesus makes when he institutes the Eucharist, "on the night he was handed over" (1 Cor 11:23).[23] Similarly, the conclusion of this narrative is especially significant. The disciples "filled twelve wicker baskets with fragments from the five barley loaves that had been more than they could eat." The guests are "about five thousand in number." This detail highlights the abundance of the bread multiplied by Jesus. As to the remaining pieces—the "fragments"—that Jesus orders to be collected "so that nothing will be lost," they make us think of the ancient appellation of Eucharist: "the fraction of the bread."[24] Finally, Christian tradition has seen the relation between those pieces carefully gathered and the Eucharistic meal that Christian communities, scattered through time and space, continue to celebrate until the day when Christ will assemble the elect at the heavenly table.[25] The Eucharistic bread, "the food that endures for eternal life" (John 6:27), will never fail in the Church; everyone is abundantly fed with it today, and there will still be plenty of it tomorrow and the day after tomorrow. "When we take this true bread, each one does not have less than all together; a single person has it in its entirety; two, several receive it, whole, without diminishment; for the blessing of this sacrament can be distributed, but cannot be exhausted in this distribution."[26]

Not surprisingly, the miracle of the loaves multiplied superabundantly excites the enthusiasm of the crowd: "This is truly the Prophet, the one who is to come into the world." Immediately Jesus escapes; "he withdrew again to the mountain alone." For he "knew that they were going to carry him off to make him king." This is not what the sign he has performed is about. He is not going to leave any possible doubt on this point. In this atmosphere of exacerbated messianism, any explanation or attempt at clarification is doomed to failure. Once calm returns, he will explain; this is what the long discourse we shall read on the following Sundays will try to do.

As Elisha before him, Jesus multiplied the loaves in order to satisfy the hunger of those around him on the mountain; they were not just one hundred, but a crowd of about five thousand who had followed him to a desert place, where he was teaching them. But the liturgy does not invite us to a comparison of the two miracles. For his part, John alludes to past events, in particular to the gift of the manna in the desert after the Exodus. However, Jesus' miracle is not a repetition of the prodigy of former years. There is more than Moses here, more than a prophet. He is the one the Father sent to gather all human beings into the unity of one body, in one Spirit, but not by wielding over them the temporal power of a king. Jesus flees when they want to forcefully carry him off to make him king. Nobody has any power over him, unless this power is received from above (John 19:11). People will capture him, but at the hour decreed by the Father; and then the cross will be his throne of glory.[27] It is toward this major sign that all other signs lead us; we must learn to understand them by renouncing human ways of seeing and judging.

> Having followed him without food
> The multitude was hungry
> He took pity on them
> > I was there and you too
> > When he shared with us
> > The two fish and the five loaves
> > He gave thanks
>
> No one was forgotten
> Everyone received from his hand
> What they wanted
> > When all were satisfied
> > Twelve baskets were filled
> > With the remaining bread
> > So that nothing be wasted
>
> This remnant that is the whole Thing
> Is broken for us everyday

Unceasingly undivided
  Formerly as today
  We forget as soon as we have eaten our fill
  And ceasing to believe in him
  We demand signs.[28]

Eighteenth Sunday

"I Am the Bread of Life"

The Daily Bread Come Down from Heaven

Exodus, the liberation from slavery in Egypt, is the event upon which Israel and its faith are founded. Each one of the other liberations wrought by God in the course of time has been considered a new exodus, more marvelous than the first and, in its turn, foreshadowing and announcing another one, the ultimate. This last one will assemble God's people in a Promised Land where the Lord will make them dwell for ever, in peace and happiness. The Old and New Testament tradition has reread the Exodus and scrutinized the meaning of the various events that punctuated the long march of forty years in the desert.[1] The gift of the manna is one of these events. Ancient traditions thus gave rise to narratives amplified and progressively enriched with new details as they were recounted. The sacred writers have recorded a certain number of reflections and exhortations that these accounts have suggested to the sages. So we find in the Bible little homilies on such and such event of the Exodus and the subsequent march in the desert, for example, the one we read today concerning the gift of the manna (Exod 16:2-4, 12-15).[2]

This intervention of God in favor of his people, who did not find food in the desert, is presented as the divine answer to grumblings "against Moses and Aaron." This corresponds to a tradition that depicts the Exodus and the ensuing march in the wilderness as a succession of extraordinary manifestations of the power of God, leading his people "with a mighty hand and an outstretched arm" (Ps 136:2), but also as a period during which the people never stopped murmuring and even rebelling against their God. One can accent now one, now the other of these two phases of history, but one cannot separate them. For the Exodus and the following period were the times when God revealed himself through his works and in the great manifestations of his majesty that culminate with the promulgation of the Law on Sinai. But these are also times when the people had to learn to live in a freely accepted faithfulness to the covenant, and to place their trust only in God. The manna is especially significant from this last point of view.

To set a whole people on the go through a desert in order to reach an unknown place is an insane undertaking. The crossing of the Red Sea had, of course, shown that nothing is impossible for God. But other difficulties, day in day out, had not been long in coming: water and food for the immense caravan had to be found. On certain days they were lacking. Then the people began to grumble against Moses and Aaron, accused of having led them into a deadly adventure: "Would that we had died at the LORD's hand in the land of Egypt, as we sat by our fleshpots and ate our fill of bread! But you had to lead us into this desert to make the whole community die of famine!"³ Let us not voice too loudly our indignation at this reaction and this nostalgia for a slavery that at least had the advantage of insuring an indispensable food allowance to all and perhaps a relative abundance to some who were more skilled at managing or at pleasing their overseers. It is too easy and cruel to criticize the lack of trust and the mutterings of others in a redoubtable trial that one does not have to endure and of which one knows the happy end. On the other hand, we must have the honesty to recognize that we have shown, more or less often, a behavior similar to that of the Hebrews during their march in the desert: bondage is better than hunger! To trust God completely is never an easy matter.

God hears the recriminations of his people. "In the evening quail came up and covered the camp. In the morning a dew lay all about the camp, and when the dew evaporated, there on the surface of the desert were fine flakes like hoarfrost on the ground. On seeing it, the Israelites asked one another, 'What is this?' [that is, 'man hu?'] for they did not know what it was."⁴ This popular etymology underlines the mysterious character of the food God gave to his people.⁵ A manifestation of the Lord's solicitude, this gift is also a test of the faithfulness of the people. All are assured of their daily ration of food,⁶ but they cannot keep it. Those who break this prescription are doomed to disappointment on the morrow, when they find that the food they unduly saved has become "wormy and rotten" (Exod 16:16-20).⁷

Manna is a powerful symbol; it evokes the trial to which believers' faith is forever subject: that of getting tired, in the long run, of "the bread which the LORD has given [them] to eat" and finding it tasteless. Then the temptation creeps in to look elsewhere for other foods more flattering to the taste. Their disappointment will be great and dramatic on the day when they will see—too late—that the earthly manna was preparing them for the fare of the Lord's table, in eternity. "The manna was piling up on the ground, higher than the water of the Flood; and the peoples of the East, as of the West, saw God feeding his people with his heavenly food. Thus, on Judgment Day, the evil ones will see the just seated at the Lord's table; for the manna is ground in the third heaven in the Angels' mills, and the Saints will feed upon it during eternity."[8] The Book of Revelation also speaks of "the hidden manna" that the Lord will give to "the victor" (Rev 2:17). Christians ask God for it with their "daily bread." The Eucharist is both the sign and the pledge of this heavenly manna.

The Lord gave them bread from heaven.

What we have heard and know,
    and what our fathers have declared to us, . . .
    we will declare to the generation to come
The glorious deeds of the LORD and his strength
    and the wonders that he wrought.

He commanded the skies above
    and the doors of heaven he opened;
He rained manna upon them for food
    and gave them heavenly bread.
The bread of the mighty was eaten by men;
    even a surfeit of provisions he sent them.

And he brought them to his holy land,
    to the mountains his right hand had won.
(Ps 78:3, 4b-d, 23-25, 54)

Adopting the Behavior of the New Self

Humans must unceasingly struggle to become or even to become anew what they are, what they resolutely have chosen to be. This characteristic fickleness comes from the fact that the freedom that is their dignity and places them above all other creatures has been wounded by sin. This is why, in contrast with God, who created them in his image, they do not always follow the good and the just, infallibly perceived and willed with full lucidity.[9] But they have the ability to take hold of themselves, to correct their errors, and, with God's grace, to take again and again this salutary step called conversion. For it is not enough to be converted once.[10] We must continually test and rectify the orientation of our lives toward God, Christ, and the gospel. This is what Paul says (Eph 4:17, 20-24).

Paul speaks to recently converted Christians who risk lapsing back into the pagan customs they have rejected. Our condition is not exactly the same. But the danger of our becoming pagans in our way of thinking, judging, and acting is not any the less. For we are not living in a society clearly divided into pagans and Christians standing on either side of a neatly defined line. We live in a world saturated with neo-paganism, to such—and often so subtle—a degree that we must practice unflinching watchfulness and keep a strong, enlightened will to avoid being contaminated and to remain Christian through and through. At the same time, in all domains of personal and social life, we are confronted with ever new questions and situations. In such an impenetrable maze, concealing traps, there are few well-marked trails and roads that would allow us to walk without looking where we set our feet. Furthermore, everything changes so fast that up-to-date maps showing the latest details are not readily available. And we do not have the leisure to wait for the new edition because we must make a decision and choose our road here and now. Among others, this is the case with grave and complex problems arising from the progress of science and its application—for instance, in biology and genetics. To have a position in principle is one thing. But what are we to do when we find ourselves—and this is frequent—in a real emergency where we must make a decision? These topics, which are much spoken about today and much discussed in passionate public debates, cannot make us forget that many other questions, absolutely central to Christian authenticity, arise every day. As an example, we think of the use of money and material goods in a society of unbridled consumption and competition, extolling luxury, ease of life, comfort, instant gratification as so many uncontested values.

"You must no longer live as the Gentiles do, in the futility of their minds." The business at hand is to "put away the old self of your former way of life, corrupted through deceitful desires, and be renewed in the spirit of your minds, and put on the new self, created in God's way in righteousness and holiness of truth." "That is not how you learned Christ." We cannot be and remain Christian if we do not take and keep Christ and the gospel as our proximate and ultimate references. Christian identity and singularity are bought at that price.[11] It is not possible "to serve the living and true God" without turning away from idols (1 Thess 1:9). Under other names than those of former times, these idols claim to bring, together with happiness, all the goods that we desire for ourselves and others; these claims are supported by publicity that is often aggressive and always clever. These idols arouse and heighten "deceitful desires." To denounce them, not only with words but with acts, not to be seduced by them, is an obligation for Christians. Being thus faithful to their vocation, they efficaciously contribute to pave the way for a more human art of living that the world longs for.

> Yes, the time has come for conversion, for personal transformation, for inner renewal. We must get used to thinking in a new way, of humanity, of common life among humans, of the roads of history and the destiny of the world, according to Paul's word, "Put on the new self, created in God's way in righteousness and holiness of truth."
>
> The hour has come for us to stop, to collect ourselves, to reflect, almost to pray: to think anew of our common origin, of our history, of our common destiny. Never as urgently as today has it been necessary to appeal to human moral conscience, in these times marked by such great progress. The peril does not come from progress or science; on the contrary, well utilized, they can solve a great number of problems facing humanity. The true peril is inside the human heart which is in possession of tools ever more powerful, capable of bringing about either ruin or the highest conquests.[12]

The Christian message is not theoretical or abstract; it does not advocate conformity to external norms of life. What it is about is for us to "learn Christ," to let ourselves "be renewed in the spirit of [our] minds" according to the truth of Jesus himself. He is the new Adam of a world where "new things have come" (2 Cor 5:17); whose citizens we are and which we must build; whose customs, spirit, and laws we must adopt.[13] Paul often comes back to this mystery of newness[14] that, far from immobilizing us in a given situation, drives us always forward and incites us to continuously invent, because God always remakes anew in his image the human beings he has created. Paul's call is therefore more timely than ever in a world in constant change, in which, individually and together, humans confront unheard-of situations, new challenges. To let ourselves "be renewed in the spirit of [our] minds" means, "Show courage, imagination, boldness, true freedom, drawing your inspiration from the tradition received from the apostles, and from the certitude that God, who, through Christ, makes 'all things new' (Rev 21:5) is always creating new things."

To Believe in Jesus, the Bread of Life

After the multiplication of the loaves, Jesus, in the company of his disciples, gets away from the enthusiastic crowd that wants to carry him off to make him king. When they notice his absence, those who have been so wonderfully fed on the mountain become agitated. After a new crossing of the sea, new searches in the area of Capernaum, they find him in the town. Then begins an exchange of questions and answers, in the course of which Jesus' words and clear statements will be less and less understood and will end up eliciting an unequivocal reaction of refusal. But he is not shaken or misled by the words addressed to him. On the contrary, the discourse on the sign of the multiplied loaves is a patient effort on his part to make the people understand its meaning (John 6:24-35).

"Rabbi, when did you get here?" Jesus does not reply to this question. The important thing is for all to become sincerely conscious of the deep reasons why they are there: "You are looking for me not because you saw signs but because you ate the loaves and were filled." Today, those who claim to be Christians and participate in the Sunday Eucharist cannot be reproached with the same thing. However, Jesus' remark provokes reflection. It is not rare to hear people say: "What is the use of being Christian and of remaining assiduous to the teaching of the apostles and to the breaking of bread?[15] It is a waste of time." This sort of consideration does not always remain without an echo in ourselves; we must admit it. There are so many things to do—immediately and tangibly useful and necessary—that we do not find time for what indeed serves no purpose, from a material point of view. Thus we easily dispense with prayer and Sunday Mass.[16] What follows invites us to pursue our reflection.

"Do not work for food that perishes but for the food that endures for eternal life, which the Son of Man will give you. For on him the Father, God, has set his seal." What exactly does Jesus mean when he speaks in this manner? He knows that humans must work to earn their bread. But earthly foods, necessary though they are, can sustain for only a lifetime, a life that eventually flows away and ends with death. There is another food that "endures for eternal life." We must receive and welcome this food as a gift of the Son of Man, whom the Father has marked with his seal,[17] to whom we must listen.[18] It is work; we cannot be content with passively waiting for such food. Jesus' hearers understand this very well. "So they said to him, 'What can we do to accomplish the works of God?'" This question unavoidably crops up under one form or another when we talk of religion, "Good teacher, what must I do to inherit eternal life?" (Mark 10:17). It can be the expression of a perfect and unconditional openness to God's will, but often it simply shows the desire to know what precepts to observe, the demands placed on us. When there is a spiritual guide, a prophet, or a charismatic person near at hand, we address ourselves to that one, who perhaps knows the secret of a short cut—easy access—that will save us the trouble of going through the maze of multiple commandments and thou-shalt-nots through which we unceasingly risk getting lost.[19]

"This is the work of God, that you believe in the one he sent." Therefore, Jesus comes neither to propose, in God's name, new works to accomplish, nor to abrogate any precept whatsoever (Matt 5:17); God demands faith in Jesus, whom he has sent. It is an unprecedented demand; what is asked is total commitment to him in whom we believe, and no longer just the observance of a certain number of particular precepts, the list of which can be drawn up, even if it is a long one. This faith must be manifested by concrete acts—otherwise it is dead (Jas 2:14-26)—but what must be done or rejected is not written in a book, in a code. To be able to decide what to do and what not to do, we must look at the Lord and imitate him all the time, in all circumstances, always. "So be perfect, just as your heavenly Father is perfect" (Matt 5:48).

"So they said to him, 'What sign can you do, that we may see and believe in you? What can you do? Our ancestors ate manna in the desert, as it is written: "He gave them bread from heaven to eat."'" This question surprises us because the evangelist has just stressed the enthusiasm of the crowd that wanted to make Jesus their king. In fact, things always take such a turn. In the course of the march through the desert, the signs accomplished by Moses' hand were forgotten one after the other. Present-day miracles regularly appear less awesome and less convincing than those of the past, amplified, as they are, by imagination. Anyway, God has never done anything to coerce anybody. "I have set before you life and death, the blessing and the curse" (Deut 30:19). "For freedom Christ set us free" (Gal 5:1).

Jesus does not allow himself to be led into establishing a meaningless comparison between the signs worked by Moses and the one he has just accomplished before their eyes. He is content with reminding his hearers that the gift of the manna should not be attributed to Moses but to God: "My Father gives you the true bread from heaven," prefigured by the manna. "For the bread of God is that which comes down from heaven and gives life to the world." The manna and the multiplied barley loaves can satisfy only the hunger of the moment. There is another manna, an-

other bread, that gives life: the Word of God, food that gives true life.[20]
Who would not want "this bread always"?

"I am the bread of life; whoever comes to me will never hunger, and
whoever believes in me will never thirst." This solemn declaration constitutes a first summit in Jesus' discourse, which through circuitous discussion, develops in a coherent and progressive manner. The manna God
gave through the intermediary Moses orients us toward another food that
comes directly from God: his life-giving Word unto eternal life. Jesus,
God's Word made flesh, is this promised bread. The only indispensable
condition to feed on it is to believe in him. Like God at the revelation
to Moses at Mount Horeb, he says, "I am" (Exod 3:14). And he says this
to invite the crowd surrounding him to come to him because he is able
to fulfill all the needs of those who will believe in him.[21]

The words and the signs that Jesus accomplished, particularly the multiplication of the barley loaves, are, as God's miracles that accompanied
the people in the Exodus and the march through the desert, appeals to
faith, to the free commitment to follow him. In order to perceive their
meaning, we must "be renewed in the spirit of [our] minds" and not
be guided by "deceitful desires" that do not rise above earthly realities,
immediate experience. The Lord does not propose to us a body of dogmas
or a code of laws: he offers himself as food to those who receive him with
faith. He invites them to the table at which he is, personally, the Word
and the Bread.

> Stretch out your hands, brother and sister,
> and keep them open:
> receive the manna of new times,
> the bread served at the Father's table,
> welcome the Word of God
> who gives us his flesh
> and becomes our life.
>
> *To welcome you with praise, Lord,*
> *here are our outstretched hands.*
>
> The bread of life comes down from heaven,
> it gives life to the world.
>
> Come near to the bread of life,
> those who receive it will never hunger again.
>
> To whom shall we turn if not to Jesus?
> He is the true bread.[22]

"Whoever Eats This Bread Will Live Forever"

"Get Up and Eat"

In the Bible, Elijah is a historical personage, legendary in stature. The diverse accounts of his prophetic activity—his deeds—form an ensemble called a "cycle."[1] Elijah is a figurehead in the biblical tradition, and the New Testament sees in him a precursor of the Lord.[2] The first reading of this Sunday reminds us that he was fed with a mysterious bread that restored his strength and allowed him to go "to the mountain of God, Horeb" (1 Kgs 19:4-8).

In the ninth century B.C., "like a fire there appeared the prophet / whose words were as a flaming furnace" (Sir 48:1). It was a tragic time for the religious future of Israel and the survival of the covenant. Under the influence of a dynasty of impious kings and queens, God, who had made Israel his people, whose sole Lord he was to remain,[3] saw the competition of the worship of Phoenician and Canaanite gods—the Baals—that personified natural forces.[4] At the risk of his life, Elijah rose with vehemence against this intolerable apostasy: "I have been most zealous for the LORD, the God of hosts, but the Israelites have forsaken your covenant, torn down your altars, and put your prophets to the sword. I alone am left, and they seek to take my life" (1 Kgs 19:10).[5] He had believed that the manifestation of the Lord's power and the public demonstration of the nothingness of the Baals at the sacrifice on Mount Carmel (1 Kgs 18:20-40), then the end of the drought obtained through his intercession (1 Kgs 18:41-46), would bring King Ahab back to the worship of God. But he had not reckoned with Queen Jezebel. Learning that Baal's priests have been put to the sword, she sends a message to Elijah, "May the gods do thus and so to me if by this time tomorrow I have not done with your life what was done to each of them" (1 Kgs 19:2). He saves his life by precipitously fleeing to the Negeb desert.

Exhausted after a day's march, at a fast pace no doubt, he sits down in the shade of a bush. Discouragement overwhelms him, along with the feeling of lamentable failure: " 'This is enough, O LORD! Take my life for I am no better than my fathers.' He lay down and fell asleep under the broom tree, but then an angel touched him and ordered him to get up and eat. He looked and there at his head saw a hearth cake and a jug of water." Probably quite unaware of what he is doing, he eats and drinks, then falls back to sleep. The angel comes back with the same injunction, "Get up and eat." This time, there is no doubt: God is answering his cry, but also is making him understand that his resignation is not accepted, "Get up and eat, else the journey will be too long for you." Elijah "ate and drank; then strengthened by that food, he walked forty days and forty nights to the mountain of God, Horeb."[6]

"This is enough." This cry had been that of Moses, bent under the weight of the load that God had placed on his shoulders,[7] as it later will be that of Jeremiah, whose faithfulness to his mission exposes him to sarcasm and persecution.[8] It is ours, too, even if we are not battling against difficulties as momentous. The bread of the strong is given to us.

> The Eucharist gives us the One who, taken over by the absolute darkness of death, said, "Father, into you hands I commend my spirit" (Luke 23:46); and he is here with his death. We are sad because we are unable to love. But the Eucharist gives us the One who on the night on which he was handed over (for us all), loved his own to the end. We would like to be faithful to the earth, not to see the work of our hands crumble? But the Eucharist shows us in the glorified flesh of the Risen Christ the world already transfigured, and it inaugurates the definitive harmony of earthly things, the harmony of glory. Rise, my soul, take and eat the pledge of salvation and glory for all flesh.[9]

It is in the desert that the bread from above is given to Elijah, who, strengthened by this food, is able to walk for forty days toward the encounter with God. This place and this number remind us of the years following the Exodus, during which the Israelites ate the manna;[10] of the forty days that Moses spent on Sinai, eating only bread and water;[11] of the fast of Jesus, comforted after forty days by angels.[12] The life of the Church and of the believers in an exodus, a time of trial, often a crossing of the wilderness. But God remains near those who do not despair of him, even when the burden that crushes them leads them to say, "It is enough, Lord."

> *Taste and see the goodness of the Lord.*
>
> I will bless the LORD at all times;
>   his praise shall be ever in my mouth.

Let my soul glory in the LORD;
 the lowly will hear me and be glad.
Glorify the LORD with me,
 let us together extol his name.
I sought the LORD, and he answered me
 and delivered me from all my fears.
Look to him that you may be radiant with joy,
 and your faces may not blush with shame.
When the afflicted man called out, the LORD heard,
 and from all his distress he saved him.
The angel of the LORD encamps
 around those who fear him, and delivers them.
Taste and see how good the LORD is;
 happy the man who takes refuge in him.
(Ps 34:1-9)

Not to Grieve the Spirit, but to Seek to Imitate God

In the "ordinary time" of their daily lives, most Christians do not behave much differently from other humans whose conduct is honorable.
Like most Christians, they strive, for example, to base their relationships
to others on justice and mutual respect, without duplicity or guile. Some
come to the point of considering the gospel morality a form of humanism that can be perfectly adhered to without espousing a faith. One has
only to strip the Christian code of morality of its religious language. On
the other hand, even among Christians, certain positions are regarded
as questionable and indeed unacceptable because they do not correspond
to the prevalent ideas and contradict the norms commonly observed by
a fair number—or a majority—of honorable persons. And opposite viewpoints seem endless. The morality preached by Paul is set on an altogether
different plane (Eph 4:30–5:2).

You have received "the holy Spirit of God, with which you were sealed
. . ." This fact must motivate and determine Christians' behavior. They
must remove from their lives anything that grieves the Holy Spirit. The
seal they are marked with authenticates their quality as baptized persons.
Modes of behavior in contradiction with this seal of the Holy Spirit constitute, in the same way, a grave breach of trust. "All bitterness, fury,
anger, shouting, and reviling must be removed from you, along with all
malice." All this opposes and injures the Spirit. For "the fruit of the Spirit
is love, joy, peace, patience, kindness, generosity, faithfulness, gentleness, self-control" (Gal 5:22). The generosity and the tenderness with
which Christians must be filled may take the same forms of expression

as anybody else's. But Christ's disciples know from whom they received these gifts: they are conscious of their strict obligation to make these gifts produce good works. The motivation of their conduct is really theological. "Be kind to one another, compassionate, forgiving one another as God has forgiven you in Christ." And Paul insists, "Be imitators of God, as beloved children." Christian moral teaching is the opposite of a tense and joyless voluntarism, as well as the opposite of a conformity to values that fluctuate with the times and the evolution of the surrounding culture.

"Live in love, as Christ loved us": this is the fundamental principle that is valid in all times and places, in all circumstances. Therefore, there is no need for codes, lists of duties to fulfill and faults to avoid. "Love as Christ loves" is a sufficient center of reference for each one to be able to determine, in a fully responsible way, the conduct to adopt here and now, in the very real and unpredictable circumstances of life. This is not to say that each one behaves as dictated by a personal conscience, that Christian moral conduct is a matter of free enquiry.

First of all, conscience needs to be unceasingly formed and refined; second, it is not sincerity but truth that makes us free (John 8:32), the truth that comes down from God—the God of truth—and not that of sinful humans, for sin distorts our faculties of judgment and discernment. The search for this saving truth, for "what is pleasing to the Lord" (Eph 5:10), is done within the Church. "Some people God has designated in the church to be, first, apostles; second, prophets; third, teachers" (1 Cor 12:28). He has distributed the ministries and diverse charisms for the good of all (1 Cor 12:4-11) so that we may learn from each other to "live in love, as Christ loved," offering ourselves "as a living sacrifice, holy and pleasing to God" (Rom 12:1).

> The return of the soul to God is her conversion to the Word in order to be recreated by, and made similar to, the Word.
>
> By what means? By love. For it is written, "So be imitators of God, as beloved children, and live in love, as Christ loved us" (Eph 5:1-2). This conformity weds the soul to the Word; already similar to it by nature, it becomes so also by her will when she loves it as she has been loved. There is no greater joy than this similarity, no more desirable good than this love through which the soul, no longer content with listening to human teachings, dares to trustfully address the Word itself, to closely cling to it, to ask it questions with familiarity, to make queries on everything, and be the bolder as she feels her intelligence able to understand. It is a true "spiritual marriage": more than a contract, it is a total union in which the same will, the same refusals melt two spirits into one . . .

Love is fully sufficient to itself; when it enters the heart, it absorbs all other feelings. The soul who loves, loves and knows nothing more.

To God alone, honor and glory. But God accepts these only when seasoned with the honey of love. Love, for its part, suffices to itself; it pleases by itself; it is its own merit; it is its own reward. Love does not look outside itself for its raison d'être and its end. The fruit of love is love: I love because I love, I love in order to love.[13]

The Bread Is My Flesh for the Life of the World

The discourse on the Bread of Life progresses, thanks to a subtle interplay of questions and answers reminiscent of that in parables. "Christ pronounces a formula that is profound, enigmatic, picturesque or metaphorical, or one referring to an Old Testament symbol; then the hearers misunderstand the true meaning of the words; then, Christ explains."[14] But his explanations raise new questions, even vehement protests. No matter. Jesus continues, not because he is indifferent to such incomprehension but because he owes it to himself to speak the truth, even if it is shocking, and also to have regard for those who, in spite of the difficulties, remain open to his revelation. We are thus progressively led toward the summit of this long discourse and the moment of decision: to continue to follow Christ, or to leave him (John 6:41-51).

"I am the bread that came down from heaven." This statement causes a strong reaction on his hearers' part. Up to now, Jesus certainly has made some strange, enigmatic pronouncements. But it was still possible to question him and ask for clarification. Now, this is too much. How can a man—Jesus, the son of Joseph, whose father and mother are known—say that he has come from heaven? All take their neighbors as witnesses to the inadmissible character of such a pretense. Indeed, this is difficult to accept. We can see in Jesus an outstanding man by reason of his message, adopted by so many men and women in all walks of life for centuries, a message that, year in year out, bears plentiful and remarkable fruits. But to accept or recognize that this man comes from heaven—that he is God, Son of God—is a matter of faith. Now, the power of faith is derived neither from evidence nor from the logical and necessary conclusion of reasoning nor from irrefutable proofs nor from the persuasive and irresistible force of works and miracles.[15]

Jesus knows it and says, "No one can come to me unless the Father who sent me draw him." Faith is a gift from the Father. But we must well understand what this means. We are not speaking here of a present received by certain persons and not by others, as we speak of a "gift" to do such and such a thing. Rather, faith is akin to love: to believe and to love go hand in hand. One is imperceptibly caught or suddenly seized; one fights what is happening or one is, as it were, incapable of resisting this attraction. However, this marvelous gift is received from one's own free will and with thanksgiving. Afterwards, one can become aware of reasons for believing and loving, explain what one finds lovable in the loved one, what justifies this attachment to God, Christ, the gospel. Nevertheless, the deep cause of faith and love lies elsewhere. This is why these reasons may disappear one after the other without causing the death of love and faith, though these may be shaken for a time by the trial. The analogies between human love and faith are great. But the difference is greater. To believe is to allow oneself to be drawn—captured—by him who alone is infinitely worthy of love.

> How can I freely believe, if I am drawn?
> Freely is to say too little: you are attracted even by pleasure.
> What is it to be attracted by pleasure?
> Take delight in the LORD and he will grant you your heart's requests.
> (Ps 37:4)

> There is a certain pleasure for the heart which has tasted the sweetness of this heavenly bread. Now, if the poet was able to say, "Everyone is drawn by pleasure," not by necessity but by pleasure, not by coercion but by charm, how much more must we say that those are attracted by Christ who delight in truth, in beatitude, in justice, in eternal life, all things that Christ is. Or else would the bodily senses have their pleasures while the senses of the soul would lack theirs? . . .

> Give me persons who love and they will understand what I am saying. Give me persons who desire; who are hungry; who, after a pilgrimage in the wilderness, are thirsty and pine for the source of the eternal homeland; give me such persons and they will understand what I am saying. But if I speak to cold hearts, they do not know what I am talking about. Such were those who murmured among themselves. "No one can come to me unless the Father who sent me draw him."[16]

"Stop murmuring among yourselves," Jesus simply says. God himself neither can nor wants to coerce anyone to get attached to him. "Do not murmur, saying, 'This man cannot be who he pretends to be and what we affirm he is, we who believe in him.'" Such is the only possible and licit reaction when faced with doubters and unbelievers. When we find a person lovable, when we love that person, we think it impossible that all do not show the same appreciation. And yet, it is so. Nothing we can do or say will change this attitude in any way. "You tell me that this person is trustworthy; you list all of his or her qualities, you refute all my prejudices one after the other. You may be right. But I am not capitulating; I remain on my guard. One day perhaps, although this seems improbable, I shall share your feelings." And this happens. In this case, the cause of the reversal is not that the reasons offered by others suddenly appear convincing, but that we have been seized. This is why believers do not have the right either to judge or to despise, in any way, those who do not have faith.[17] Christians must only instantly and humbly pray that all humans may be drawn to Christ by the Father.

It is written in the prophets:
"They shall all be taught by God."[18]

The time is now because Jesus is the Word of God, whom nobody has ever seen except him who came from his side.[19] From now on, whoever listens to God receives his Son's teaching. In other words, the ultimate fulfillment of faith in God is faith in Christ, in the same way as Christ leads to faith in his Father.[20] Whoever comes to Jesus and recognizes in him the one sent by the Father, who receives the Word, already has eternal life. For faith is intimate adherence of the whole being to a person, and not merely assent given to that person's teaching: it is a vital communion to be understood in the most concrete way. It is participation in eternal life—God's life—assured by a certain food. In the desert, God gave manna to our fathers. This wonderful bread sustained their life during their years of wandering. But this was a perishable food, and those who ate it died. Jesus declares that he himself is the food offered to those who believe in him, a food that does not decay and that really confers eternal life to those who eat it: "I am the bread of life . . . so that one may eat it and not die. . . . I am the living bread that came down from heaven; whoever eats this bread will live forever."

Our life is a long march, often monotonous, sometimes painful. In any case, it is filled with trials. On certain days, weariness, discouragement gnaw at us; despair is just around the corner. When we have the feeling that we have made a mess of our lives, that we have been forsaken by all and by God himself, like Elijah and so many after him and around us, we could willingly lie down under the first bush we come to in order to sleep as long as possible, forever. At such times, we must cling with all our strength to the certitudes faith gives us. We have been marked with the seal of the Holy Spirit. We are God's beloved children. Christ delivered himself up for us. He knew the throes of the most painful of agonies, and he died on a cross, surrounded by God' silence. Risen, he is the bread that every day restores our strength to get up again and go on, until the day of the encounter on the mountain, where he is waiting for us.

> Back from my innermost depths,
> I lift up to the day my night canticle

> "Before your baptism in death,
> You made a Eucharist of your whole being.

> "You submitted to the great abyss
> When you breathed the breath of life on the waters.

> "You subjected death to wear its sign
> And you rose to transmit it to your friends.

> "Since that time, you create life in them,
> Their mortal hollowness is made fecund.

> "The cells that we are in the body of creation
> Are sacrificed in you.

> "A disturbing sense is at work in us,
> Pushing aside our senses in order to grow.

> "But it also takes nurture from them,
> It makes of them its sap and its blood.

> "We enter into his food:
> If he exhausts us, he renews us.

> "When people think we are done with,
> You will give birth to that sense.

> "And all those who will have carried it
> Will know your feast of love."

> Lord, when we are on the brink of the abyss,
> Hold us in your Eucharist.[21]

The Body and Blood of Christ for Eternal Life

All Come to Be Nourished at the Banquet of Wisdom

This Sunday's liturgy takes a text from the Book of Proverbs, only the title of which is familiar to most Christians.[1] It suggests a collection of sayings we dig into now and then but do not read as an ordinary book.[2] We are even surprised to find such a book in the Bible: Is it not just a compilation of sundry adages that are devoid of originality, seemingly nonreligious and uninspirational? This impression is first of all due to the fact that in our Western culture, lessons from secular and religious experience are not transmitted in this way, however popular; our methods of education are completely different, more systematic, more discursive. The sayings in the Book of Proverbs do not constitute treatises; it is even difficult, not to say impossible, to group them in order to obtain well-structured ensembles.[3] We must judiciously choose from this reserve of wisdom garnered through the centuries, take the time to extract the juice of the plants we pick, and assimilate it. Then we shall discover that these biblical proverbs repeat and transmit, under a popular form, teachings that we also find in Deuteronomy and in the Prophets, particularly Isaiah and Jeremiah. Finally, the book is not entirely made up of a series of brief sayings. The first part is chiefly formed by several poems.[4] The text we read this Sunday is excerpted from one of these (Prov 9:1-6).

Biblical authors have naturally taken advantage of the experience transmitted by the sages of the various civilizations and cultures with which history has put them in contact. They have compared it to their traditions and their experiences; to the teachings of the Law, its commentators, its preachers. The art of living that their sayings seek to inculcate is, at the root, founded on the fear of God, a general attitude of reverence toward the Lord that inspires the daily conduct of those who acknowledge him as the only true God. This fear of God blossoms into wisdom, the source of understanding and happiness.[5] It is the opposite of those foolish attractions that can be the ruin of those who allow themselves to be seduced.[6] This wisdom is personified to make it clear that it is at once transcendent and close at hand, very lofty and at the level of daily realities. It is Wisdom. By God's side from the beginning, Wisdom has been his artisan (Prov 8:22-31); he is present on earth where she has a house, a true royal palace with "seven columns."[7] Wisdom has even prepared a great feast and sends her maids to proclaim her invitation "from the heights out over the city."[8]

"Come." This message is addressed to every human being devoid of wisdom and "understanding," to all who lack judgment, discernment, clearsightedness in the management of their lives, an easy prey for folly and its allurements. They do not need beautiful speeches or grand theories,[9] but a very accurate art of living. Therefore, the message of Wisdom is the simplest:

> Come, eat of my food,
>   and drink of the wine I have mixed!
> Forsake foolishness that you may live;
>   advance in the way of understanding.

In a word, she offers them to freely partake of what she is.

> Brethren, let us desire, let us seek, let us unceasingly love "the source of wisdom, the word of God who is in heaven" (see, Sir 1): in it are hidden, as Paul says, "all the treasures of wisdom and knowledge" (Col 2:3). It invites all those who are thirsty to come and draw from it. If you are thirsty, drink from the fountain of life; if you are hungry, eat the Bread of life. Happy are those who are hungry for this bread and thirsty for this fountain! They do not stop eating and drinking and yet they still desire to drink and eat. How good is that which one can unceasingly eat or drink without losing either thirst or appetite, that which one can continually taste without ceasing to desire it! The prophet king says:

> Taste and see how good the LORD is;
>   happy the man who takes refuge in him.
> (Ps 34:9)[10]

Jesus—whose relationship to wisdom Luke highlights several times[11]—will use a similar invitation, "Come to me" (Matt 11:28). Finally, the liturgy of the feast of the Body and Blood of Christ evokes or quotes this text from the Book of Proverbs when speaking of the Eucharist,[12] the table to which the Lord himself invites us, welcomes us, and gives his very self to us as food.

> *Taste and see the goodness of the Lord.*
>
> I will bless the LORD at all times;
>   his praise shall be ever in my mouth.

Let my soul glory in the LORD;
  the lowly will hear me and be glad.

———

Fear the LORD, you his holy ones,
  for nought is lacking to those who fear him.
The great grow poor and hungry;
  but those who seek the LORD want for no good thing.
Come, children, hear me;
  I will teach you the fear of the LORD.
Which of you desires life,
  and takes delight in prosperous days?
Keep your tongue from evil
  and your lips from speaking guile;
Turn from evil, and do good;
  seek peace, and follow after it.
(Ps 34:2-3, 10-15)

Living Wisely in the Present Time

Faith opens our eyes to the divine light and uncovers God's plan realized in his Son, Jesus Christ our Lord, "to sum up all things in Christ, in heaven and on earth."[13] Baptism turns believers into new creatures.[14] Nonetheless, we are still living in this world in which light and darkness mercilessly struggle, in which the powers of evil multiply their desperate assaults.[15] As a result, Christians find themselves in an uncomfortable, difficult situation. They must conduct themselves wisely in a world that remains stamped with madness (Eph 5:15-20).

Paul advises us not to leave the world but, on the contrary, to "[make] the most of the opportunity." To know the will of God is a matter of reflection and, to observe it, a matter of wisdom. Whenever we encounter evil days, we must eschew all impulsive behavior and cling to what does not risk being carried off by the violence of the storm. It would be particularly serious to let ourselves go, to yield to the temptation of numbing ourselves so as not to think, in order to forget. "Do not get drunk on wine, in which lies debauchery." We must not be surprised or shocked by such a warning. We know very well that in times of crisis—and we live in a world that has lost its bearings—many seek to evade reality by having recourse to all sorts of drugs, among which we must include that frenzy of work or activity, so that they may avoid confronting the true problems and decisions that would necessarily ensue. Although it seems paradoxical, we need courage and clear thinking to stop, to free ourselves from the infernal rhythms—of which we complain in any case—in order to take the time to "be filled with the Spirit," to listen to it in silence and prayer.

Address "one another [in] psalms and hymns and spiritual songs, singing and playing to the Lord in your hearts." It would seem that Paul is referring only to the liturgical form of prayer. But after what he has just written on the dangers of drunkenness, we understand that he insists on sober prayer, contrasting with the excesses of certain pagan feasts and celebrations. In any case, in his First Letter to the Corinthians, Paul preaches moderation—we could say temperance—in the expression of prayer.

> [For] if I pray in a tongue, my spirit is at prayer but my mind is unproductive. So what is to be done? I will pray with the spirit, but I will also pray with the mind. I will sing praise with the spirit, but I will also sing praise with the mind. Otherwise, if you pronounce a blessing [with] the spirit, how shall one who holds the place of the uninstructed say the "Amen" to your thanksgiving, since he does not know what you are saying? For you may be giving thanks very well, but the other is not built up (1 Cor 14:14-17).

In any case, liturgical prayer is objectively under the sway of the Holy Spirit, inasmuch as it is constituted, for a large part, by inspired songs: the psalms and other scriptural canticles. Finally, this prayer of the Church is the teacher of personal and spontaneous prayer; it teaches us to regulate our spontaneity, which does not mean batter it, still less, sterilize and repress it. Liturgical prayer opens the way to the Spirit's freedom. "Having left aside the lyre and the cithara, soulless instruments, God's Logos regulated, through the Holy Spirit, our world and, in particular, this microcosm: human beings, soul and body. He uses this many-voiced instrument to celebrate God, and himself sings in harmony with this human instrument."[16] "Give thanks always and for everything in the name of the Lord Jesus Christ to God the Father." Thanksgiving is at the heart of every Christian prayer and of the liturgy; it is especially developed in the Eucharist. It is continual and universal, cosmic; it orients the entire universe to the praise of God.

> Bless the Lord, all you works of the Lord,
>   praise and exalt him above all forever.
> (Dan 3:57)
>
> Father, all-powerful and ever-living God,
> we do well always and everywhere to give you thanks.
>
> We see your infinite power
> in your loving plan of salvation.

You came to our rescue by your power as God,
but you wanted us to be saved by one like us.
Man refused your friendship,
but man himself was to restore it
through Jesus Christ our Lord.

Through him the angels of heaven offer their prayer of adoration
as they rejoice in your presence for ever.
May our voices be one with theirs
in their triumphant hymn of praise.[17]

Flesh and Blood of Christ—True Food of Life

To Christians reading it today, the discourse on the Bread of Life is, from its beginning, focused on the Eucharist. Little by little they see its outlines become clearer. But now, Jesus speaks explicitly of this mystery of faith (John 6:51-58).

"I am the living bread; . . . the bread that I will give is my flesh for the life of the world." Again, this is an enigmatic saying that arouses amazement, "How can this man give us [his] flesh to eat?" If we take into account all that went before, we see that this question has a very different ring from that of Mary humbly asking the angel, "How can this be?" (Luke 1:34). It is a renewed refusal to believe in Jesus' word (John 6:40-45), which is, moreover, understood in a grossly material sense. It is normal: when we deny credibility to a person, we immediately take any saying that is at odds with all we hold dear as absurd or at least give it short shrift. Then, all attempt at explaining proves useless: the only result will be more ambiguities and more quibbling, in which the gainsayers often take pleasure by insidiously continuing arguments. Accordingly, Jesus stops all discussing. Far from softening his preceding affirmation, he solemnly reiterates it with fresh insistence. "Amen, amen, I say to you, unless you eat the flesh of the Son of Man and drink his blood, you do not have life within you. Whoever eats my flesh and drinks my blood has eternal life, and I will raise him on the last day. For my flesh is true food, and my blood is true drink." The extraordinary force of each of these statements is further increased by repetition. Jesus is the Son of Man. In the fourth Gospel, this way of designating Jesus evokes his heavenly origin,[18] his being "lifted up" on the cross,[19] his resurrection,[20] his glorification by the Father.[21] Christians, especially those somewhat familiar with John's Gospel, understand that Jesus' words here must be understood in reference to the mysteries of the incarnation and Easter celebrated in the Eucharist.[22] They also notice their accord with the vocabulary of the accounts of the Last Supper.[23]

We are speaking of really eating the flesh of the Son of Man, now risen in the Father's glory, and of really drinking his blood. The realism of the words used leaves no doubt on the subject.[24] The fact is that Jesus—John strongly stresses this point—the Son of Man, has really assumed human flesh and not only human appearance.[25] It is impossible to separate in Jesus human nature—flesh and blood—from divine nature: "Whoever eats my flesh and drinks my blood has eternal life." In the cultural depths common to all peoples, blood is the most immediate symbol of that life which we have within ourselves, which we share with others whom we call "consanguineous," which we ourselves lose, which we voluntarily give, or which we violently take away when blood is poured out. A pact sealed in blood is for life. To mix even a drop of our blood with that of another is a gesture, a rite, the seriousness of which even children understand. To drink the blood of the Son of God become human is to share in his life to the utmost, in the life that he possesses in its fullness. "Whoever eats my flesh and drinks my blood remains in me and I in him. Just as the living Father sent me and I have life because of the Father, so also the one who feeds on me will have life because of me." "I shall raise him [on] the last day." "Your ancestors ate the manna in the desert, but they died; this is the bread that comes down from heaven so that one may eat it and not die." This is why tradition calls the Eucharist "remedy of immortality," the living bread that gives life forever: "May this mingling of the body and blood of our Lord Jesus Christ bring eternal life to us who receive it."[26]

Jesus does not say here how—through what sign, what sacrament—this true food and this true drink will be given. The revelation will come at Jesus' "hour," during this last meal when he will show his own to what point he has loved them (John 13:1-2). But we know it, we who share the bread and the wine, "which earth has given and human hands have made," changed for us by the invocation, the epiclesis, of the Holy Spirit, into the Body "delivered up," the Blood "given" for the life of the world.[27]

> We speak of the real presence of Christ in us: if he himself has not taught this to us, we utter only foolishness and impiety. But he himself said: "For my flesh is true food, and my blood is true drink. Whoever eats my flesh and drinks my blood remains in me and I in him" (John 6:55-56).
>
> The reality of his flesh and his blood leaves no room for doubt, both according to the Lord's teaching and our faith. We are speaking of true flesh and true blood. When we receive and absorb these substances, they put

us in Christ and put Christ in us. Is this not the truth? Perhaps it is not true for those who do not recognize the true God in Christ. But he is in us, through his flesh, and we are in him; and with him, what we are is in God.[28]

"Come, eat of my food, / and drink of the wine I have mixed!" Thus the announcement proclaimed by the maidservants of Wisdom when they are sent on the mountains to carry her invitation to human beings lacking understanding. "Come to me," Jesus says in his turn. But now it is to call us to eat his body and drink his blood that give eternal life.

Today's Christians—like the original hearers of John's Gospel—know that in the discourse following the sign of the multiplication of the loaves, Jesus intends to speak of the Eucharist. The slow pace of John's spiral-like development and of his progression may disconcert us; we would like the evangelist to come to the point more rapidly. But no: we must adopt this rhythm without trying to outrun it by ignoring the red traffic lights. Otherwise, we will lose a great deal of the teaching he has transmitted to us. His rhythm allows us to calmly reflect, taking our time, on the mystery of faith, which the Church has celebrated since its beginning and in which we participate. It is rooted in the long history of the marvelous deeds worked by God since the Exodus and in the unfolding of the revelation of God, who leads his people. In order to plunge deeper into the understanding of the Eucharist, we must regularly revive our comprehension of all the preceding signs that, from near or far, prepared this day on which the Son of Man says, "I am the living bread," as he said, "I am the way, the truth and the life" (John 14:6). Strengthened by this food from heaven, we shall be able to make the most of the opportunity and, whatever the difficulties of the journey, to walk at a brisk pace, reciting "psalms and hymns and spiritual songs." Traveling from Eucharist to Eucharist, we shall arrive at the promised day of eternal life.

> Happy those who come to light
> Through the night of Jesus,
> Happy those who receive their selves
> From the hand of their God,
> Happy those who find their lives
> In the death of Jesus:
>
>> Roads open up in their hearts,
>> They fear nothing of the second death.
>> In God's Paradise,
>> Victorious, they will eat from the Tree of Life.

Happy those who are born from above
And from the blood of Jesus,
Happy those who are grafted
On the Body of their God,
Happy those who are the prey
Of the Spirit of Jesus:

  Roads open up in their hearts,
  They will taste the hidden manna.
  In God's Paradise,
  Victorious, they will receive the Stone with the blessed Name.

Happy those who owe their names
Only to the Name of Jesus,
Happy those who are happy
With their God's happiness,
Happy those who set their steps
In the steps of Jesus:

  Roads open up in their hearts,
  They will hold power over nations.
  In God's Paradise,
  Victorious, they will receive the morning Star.[29]

Twenty-first Sunday

To Whom Should We Go, Lord? You Have the Words of Eternal Life

The Choice of Keeping Faith with God

Sacred history is the story of a covenant proposed by God to a people whom he freely chose and who, for their part, freely committed themselves to remain faithful to it, after due consideration of its conditions. This faithfulness is expressed in daily life by the observance of the Law of the Lord. Each of the important steps in the history of salvation is marked by a solemn renewal of the initial commitment, according to a rite that recalls and actualizes what happened for the first time on Sinai. This is the case, in particular, at the time of the people's entering the Promised Land. The hour is a historic one. A long period of uncertain wanderings through the desert is ending; a new era is beginning. Now, scattered through their God-given land, the liberated people must preserve their unity. No longer insulated from foreign influences as before, but living in the midst of pagans, they have to keep their identity, avoiding contamination from the worship of local gods. Joshua, Moses' successor, entrusted by God with the inauguration of this long-awaited phase of the realization of the promises made on Sinai, convokes all the tribes at Shechem for a solemn renewal of their commitment of faithfulness to God. Being reminded of this assembly, Christians do not turn their eyes toward a past event—even a signal one—but toward Christ and their own circumstances (Josh 24:1-2a, 15-17, 18b).[1]

Whatever its other motives and immediate and concrete objectives,[2] a reunion of "all the tribes . . . before God," as that which takes place at Shechem, retains a permanent significance: salvation is given and unfolds in a people whom God gathers while revealing himself. This conviction, shared by all believers, must be expressed and, at the same time, needs to be renewed. Therefore, the assembly is fundamentally what we could call a "sacrament," a visible manifestation of a pre-existing reality—

189

the gathering of a people—which makes this reality happen in and by this very gathering, and always has the character of a ritual celebration. It proclaims that although dispersed, the faithful are members of God's people. Therefore, the assembly is of necessity a reality of the religious order, and not only or foremost of the social order.[3] Belonging to a church—the word means a calling together—is loosened and finally dissolved by a habitual and prolonged abstention from attendance at the assembly. To find again the way to the Church, in current parlance, means to come back to the assembly and once more assume one's identity as a member of God's people.[4]

When they assemble at Shechem, the tribes of Israel acknowledge their belonging to a people who owe their existence to God's initiative. They are, in some way, the children who recognize their father and who state their resolve to remain attached to the one who gave them life. This is why the plan of this renewal of the covenant is in the form of a memorial, a thanksgiving—we could say an "anamnesis," a Eucharist. Joshua enunciates these themes: "For it was the LORD our God, who brought us and our fathers up out of the land of Egypt, out of a state of slavery. He performed those great miracles before our very eyes and protected us along our entire journey and among all the peoples through whom we passed." Following his example, all proclaim, "We also will serve the LORD, for he is our God."

But it is a personal commitment taken on in complete freedom: "If it does not please you to serve the LORD, decide today whom you will serve, the gods your fathers served beyond the River or the gods of the Amorites in whose country you are dwelling." The question is to know whether they ratify their conversion from ancestral paganism or do not, and to decide whether they want to remain faithful to their conversion or do not. Every participation in the assembly implies the renewal of this commitment, for it is a public profession of one's well thought out decision to belong to God's people.[5] This is done in a solemn and explicit manner at certain gatherings, especially at the Easter gathering.

Finally, the assembly at Shechem captures Christians' attention because tradition has seen in Joshua, Moses' successor, a figure of Christ, the new Moses (Heb 3:7–4:11). The comparison is the more natural since Joshua and Jesus are two forms of the same name.

> God has given our Lord Jesus Christ a name that is above all names. Jesus is this name which is above all names. And this for this reason:
>   "that at the name of Jesus

every knee should bend,
of those in heaven and on earth and
   under the earth.''
(Phil 2:10)

We encounter this name of Jesus for the first time when we see him as an army leader. Therefore, where I encounter the name of Jesus for the first time, I learn at the same moment the mystery of its symbolism. Indeed, Jesus commands the army. To what is all this leading? To the fact that this book does not so much recount the deeds of Jesus, son of Nun, as it describes the mysteries of Jesus, my Lord. It is he who leads the army and triumphs over Amalek and who, foreshadowed by the hands extended on the mountain, vanquishes principalities and powers by nailing them to the cross in his person.[6]

Recalling the wonders wrought in the past for his people and for us is still at the heart of the Christian assembly today. It can only reinforce our enthusiastic determination.

Taste and see the goodness of the Lord.

I will bless the Lord at all times;
   his praise shall be ever in my mouth.
Let my soul glory in the Lord;
   the lowly will hear me and be glad.

———

The Lord has eyes for the just, and ears for their cry.
The Lord confronts the evildoers,
   to destroy remembrance of them from the earth.
When the just cry out, the Lord hears them,
   and from all their distress he rescues them.
The Lord is close to the brokenhearted;
   and those who are crushed in spirit he saves.
Many are the troubles of the just man,
   but out of them all the Lord delivers him;
He watches over all his bones;
   not one of them shall be broken.
Vice slays the wicked,
   and the enemies of the just pay for their guilt.
But the Lord redeems the lives of his servants;
   no one incurs guilt who takes refuge in him.
(Ps 34:2-3, 16-23)

Subject to One Another Out of Respect for Christ

Faith in Christ, baptism, and the gift of the Spirit establish new relationships between Christians. To know it and to proclaim it are not enough. We must put into practice what we have learned from hearing the gospel, in our daily lives and, first of all, in the family, the basic social cell, the first place where everyone's Christian conduct is tested. This is why, at the end of his long development on Christian behavior in the present world, Paul comes to these considerations in his Letter to the Ephesians (Eph 5:21-32).

"Be subordinate to one another out of reverence for Christ." This is the great principle that everywhere and always must inform everyone's conduct. This is not to say that to live thus we must leave the present world or create new social structures alongside the existing ones; rather, we must "[make] the best of the opportunity" by understanding correctly "what is the will of the Lord" (Eph 5:16-17).[7] Now, the Lord has radically changed the nature of relationships between believers: "For all of you who were baptized into Christ have clothed yourselves with Christ. There is neither Jew nor Greek, there is neither slave nor free person, there is not male and female; for you are all one in Christ Jesus" (Gal 3:27-28). This change would be in vain if all went on behaving toward others as they did before, continuing to act according to the ways of the world, which ignores Christ and his gospel. However, Paul does not preach social revolution.

> Only, everyone should live as the Lord has assigned, just as God called each one. I give this order in all the churches. . . . Were you a slave when you were called? Do not be concerned, but, rather, even if you can gain your freedom, make the most of it. For the slave called in the Lord is a freed person in the Lord, just as the free person who has been called is a slave of Christ. You have been purchased at a price. Do not become slaves to human beings. Brothers, everyone should continue before God in the state in which he was called.
> (1 Cor 7:17, 21-24)

Paul does not envision—how could he?—a change in society. But he knows that in all conditions, slave or free, we can live in bondage to our passions, to our egotism, to the insane ways of this world. From all these, Christians have been delivered through baptism and their incorporation into Christ, who redeemed them at the price of his blood, so that they may no longer be Satan's slaves. However, this liberation is not only an interior one, because everyone must consider and treat others as free persons. Mutual submission, then, replaces the relations of strength between dominating and dominated, between slaves and free persons, "out of reverence for Christ." This can mean two things: to respect the law of Christ and to honor in everyone the image of Christ according to which

they have been shaped by baptism. As a consequence, relationships between Christians are not ordained by social status but by the regard for
their common dignity as children of God and servants—slaves—of the
same Lord. Mutual submission, as Paul speaks of it, is an expression of
charity that "builds up" (1 Cor 8:1), that "is not inflated . . . believes
all things, hopes all things, endures all things" (1 Cor 13:4-7).

It is by the light of these data of faith that we must look at realities,
such as conjugal relationships, in order to discover their meaning.[8] Paul
speaks to Christian women and men living in a cultural milieu that no
one, at that time, is contesting. The family structure is pyramidal: the
man is the head to which the woman is subject; children owe him obedience. Such is the established order that everyone accepts without asking any questions. The apostle first addresses wives: "Wives should be
subordinate to their husbands as to the Lord. For the husband is head
of his wife just as Christ is head of the church, he himself the saviur ot
the body. As the church is subordinate to Christ, so wives should be
subordinate to their husbands in everything." Today, this discourse
shocks because the modern tendency is rather in the direction of egalitari-
anism, according to which "the one is the other."[9] But what Paul says
does not amount to an ideological canonization of the submission of
woman to man, as if this were a "natural law," so that the eventual eman-
cipation would be "against nature." He wants to show Christian women
in what perspective they must understand and live their condition as
wives. Moreover, we must not separate what is said to wives from what
is said to their husbands.[10] "Husbands, love your wives, even as Christ
loved the church and handed himself over for her . . . So [also] husbands should love their wives as their own bodies. . . . even as Christ
does the church . . .

> 'For this reason a man shall leave [his]
>   father and his mother and be joined to his wife,
> and the two shall become one flesh.'

This is a great mystery, but I speak in reference to Christ and the church."
Paul speaks with the language and in the context of his time. But the submission he preaches to wives has nothing in common with the subjec-
tion imposed by an authoritarian power. Husbands are not the lords of
their wives; this title belongs to Christ alone. Husbands must behave toward their wives as Christ behaves toward the Church. "Christ loved
the church and handed himself over for her." The relations between

women and men have not stopped evolving since the beginning of humanity. Today in the West, they are undergoing mutations whose causes we scrutinize in order to foresee the possible or probable consequences.[11] Whatever happens, the principles Paul deduces from the mystery of Christ in his relation to the Church will remain a safe point of reference; for, on closer inspection, their value is not linked to any given cultural situation.

> At their wedding table,
> Your friends keep in their hearts
> Your place, Lord!
> Come and sit down, it is the nearest one,
> Come down to their house since they want you
> To be a permanent guest.
>
> One single heart, since they lift to you
> One cup to be shared:
> You, be the first!
> They carry it to your lips,
> Enter deeper into their feast:
> Drink to their joy of loving one another.
>
> Show them also your own cup
> You have given them faith in you,
> They thirst after you!
> May they discover, since they love you,
> That from your place in themselves
> It is really you who welcome them.
>
> One takes breath from the other,
> And their breaths are one:
> It seeks yours!
> May they hear from your own mouth:
> Drink together from my cup
> The best wine of the end times.
>
> Do you know at whose house you are
> And why I speak thus
> With my friends?
> At the table of my feast,
> Already their places are reserved:
> I too am waiting for my wedding.[12]

The "Sign" of the Living Bread and the Decision of Faith

Throughout the whole of the discourse on the Bread of Life, questions have been put, difficulties and misunderstandings voiced—to some of which we are not strangers. At certain moments, we even have the impression that the narrative has been written so as to give time for these various questions to resound long enough to eventually arouse an echo in us. And at this point the disciples, up to now strangely absent from the discussions caused by Jesus' statements, break upon the scene (John 6:60-69).

Many among the disciples who had heard Jesus say "Whoever eats my flesh and drinks my blood" cry out, "This saying is hard; who can accept it?" They are disciples, John notes; they have been accompanying Jesus for quite some time already. But their sympathy has been mixed with a certain reserve; they have been waiting before making up their minds in earnest. Now their conviction is brought to a stop: "There is nothing to hope from this man. What's the use of continuing to follow him?" Disappointed, they perhaps go back home. They have lost, not their faith, but their illusions; for "faith is not a conviction; it is its own proof, light and life; it gives the joy that lifts up life only if it is risked in a living history."[13] It is with faith as it is with love. To believe is to commit one's whole life, not because one is sure of oneself but because one is sure of the other. This gives us food for thought: even when Jesus was living on earth, certain disciples were not ready to take this decisive step, to trust themselves unreservedly to his person and his word.

"Since Jesus knew that his disciples were murmuring about this, he said to them, 'Does this shock you? What if you were to see the Son of Man ascending to where he was before?'" The sentence remains unfinished, but for us, today, its meaning is perfectly clear. The cross on which Jesus will be lifted up in order to return to his Father is the permanent scandal, the obstacle to be surmounted to reach the faith that believers often find again and again on the road of life. To believe in Christ is indeed to exclaim while looking at the Crucified, "Truly, this man was the Son of God!" (Mark 15:39). Today, the place for this profession of paschal faith is no longer Calvary, but the liturgical assembly at the moment when commemorating the death and resurrection of the Lord, Christians share the bread of eternal life and the cup of salvation, "the body and blood of Christ. Amen."

"It is the spirit that gives life, while the flesh is of no avail. The words I have spoken to you are spirit and life." Jesus gives himself as food under the sign—the sacrament—of the bread and wine made holy by the Holy Spirit, thus becoming for us "the body and blood of our Lord Jesus Christ,"[14] the Son of Man, who ascended to the Father through his pasch and resurrection.

It is, therefore, with absolute assurance that we participate in a certain way in the body and blood of Christ. For under the form of bread, the body is given to you, and under the form of wine, the blood is given to you so that you may become one single body and one single blood with Christ by having shared in the body and blood of Christ. So we become Christ-bearers when his body and blood spread into our body. In this manner, according to Blessed Peter, we ''come to share in the divine nature'' (2 Pet 1:4).

Therefore, do not regard the bread and wine as natural elements because they are, as the Master declared, body and blood. Our senses suggest the former; may your faith reassure you. In this domain, do not judge by taste but by faith; be fully assured, you who have been judged worthy of the body and blood of Christ.

You have received the teaching and you are absolutely certain: what appears to be bread is not bread, although it tastes like bread, but the body of Christ; what appears to be wine is not wine, although it tastes like wine, but the blood of Christ . . . Therefore, strengthen your hearts, taking this bread as a spiritual bread, and gladden the face of your soul. And you, your face uncovered in a pure conscience, reflect as in a mirror the glory of the Lord, and advance from glory to glory in Christ Jesus our Lord, to whom may glory be for ever and ever. Amen.[15]

''There are some of you who do not believe.'' This is still another word addressed by Jesus himself to some disciples. ''Jesus knew from the beginning the ones who would not believe and the one who would betray him.'' With Jesus, it is impossible to cheat, to feign; he sees what is in everyone's heart. When doubt and temptation sneak into our souls, the good reflex is to turn to Christ in a humble and trusting prayer. It is not necessary for us to know how to express ourselves well or even to clearly see what is happening inside. This twofold incapacity hampers recourse to others' help, but not recourse to God's. The Father does not need our explanations in order to take away from our hearts what impedes our going to his Son, but he cannot give this grace to whoever does not desire it.

''Do you also want to leave?'' At the end of the discourse on the Bread of Life, we are asked in a straightforward way for our vote of confidence. Simon Peter intervenes as the spokesperson for the disciples who remain firmly attached to Jesus: ''Master, to whom shall we go? You have the words of eternal life.'' This answer is admirable; it expresses what real faith is. Knowledge of dogma is not a precondition of faith. What Simon Peter adds is certainly exact, ''You are the Holy One of God.'' However, this is not a formula that will be kept by the first Christian generation.

On the other hand, for believers, faith in Christ always consists in recognizing Jesus as the only Savior, the only one to possess "the words of eternal life." All converts give witness to this: first they were seized by Christ and gave him their complete trust; only afterwards did they become more familiar with him and his teaching.

The liturgical assembly is a "sacrament" of the Church, the people of God convoked to welcome his Word; give thanks by recalling the death and resurrection of Christ; receive, under the signs of bread and wine, his body and blood unto eternal life. By participating in the assembly, we renew and revive our belonging to the Body of Christ, whose members are baptized persons, placing at the service of all the gifts of the Spirit given to them. Really, the mystery of faith is great (see Eph 5:32).

> Above all, let us pray Him to draw us to Him, and to give us faith. When we feel that His mysteries are too severe for us, and occasion us to doubt, let us earnestly wait on Him for the gift of humility and love. Those who love and who are humble will apprehend them;—carnal minds do not seek them, and proud minds are offended at them;—but while love desires them, humility sustains them. Let us pray Him then to give us such a real and living insight into the blessed doctrine of the Incarnation of the Son of God, of His birth of a Virgin, His atoning death, and resurrection, that we may desire that the Holy Communion may be the effectual type of that gracious Economy. No one realizes the Mystery of the Incarnation but must feel disposed towards that of Holy Communion. Let us pray Him to give us an earnest longing after Him—a thirst for His presence—an anxiety to find Him—a joy on hearing that He is to be found, even now, under the veil of sensible things,—and a good hope that we shall find Him there. Blessed indeed are they who have not seen, and yet have believed.[16]

The liturgy is not primarily catechesis, but it has a great catechetical value. Better than all explanation, the celebration of the Seventeenth to the Twenty-first Sunday in Ordinary Time of this year makes us understand this. As usual, we have celebrated the Eucharist. But the Gospel has not ceased speaking of the Bread of life. Not in any systematic way, as one expands upon a topic point by point before a listening audience without interrupting the speaker. At the end, a few questions are eventually put and explanations are requested. The discourse on the Bread of Life, on the contrary, takes as its point of departure a misapprehension of the meaning of the multiplication of the loaves and, by the same token, of the mission and person of Jesus: he has not been sent to become king and to procure daily bread for his followers through his miraculous powers. The discourse further develops, following the rhythm of the hearers' successive misunderstandings and increasingly aggressive questioning of the Lord. The multiplied bread is a "sign" of contradiction.

From the beginning of the Church, the account of the multiplication of the loaves and the long discourse that follows it have been read with a Eucharistic perspective that obviously corresponds to John's intention in writing this passage of his Gospel. Moreover, as the discourse progresses, it speaks more and more explicitly of the Eucharist. But in the framework of the Sunday celebration, Jesus' words, together with his hearers' objections, take on a particularly striking character. All participants in the Eucharistic celebration feel personally and directly challenged. It is impossible to listen to this discourse coldly. All are led to become lucidly aware of the thoughts of their hearts, to ask themselves, not so much what they know about the Eucharist, but what sense it has truly and practically in their daily lives; finally they are led to question themselves on their faith in Jesus Christ risen, "living bread," who has given his flesh for the salvation of the world and poured out his blood for the salvation of all human beings. Really, the Eucharist is the "sacrament of faith," "the source and summit of the Christian life,"[17] nourishment for the Christian community who "go to the Father with Christ,"[18] "foretaste of the heavenly banquet."[19]

> Let us take the words
> That love says;
> *Here is the time*
> *When God shows favor*
> *To our earth.*
> Jesus died,
> The Book has been read;
> *Here is the time*
> *To give thanks*
> *To our Father.*
> One same Spirit
> Speaks to our hearts;
> *Let us take the time*
> *To live in grace*
> *With our brothers and sisters.*
> Let us take the bread
> That gives everything;
> *Here is the time*
> *When God shows favor*
> *to our earth.*
> Jesus died,

Jesus comes to us;
Here is the time
To give thanks
To our Father.
Let us dwell in the body
Where all are bonded together;
Let us take the time
To live in grace
With our brothers and sisters.[20]

The Twenty-second
and Twenty-third Sunday
in Ordinary Time

After an interruption of five Sundays, we come back to Mark's Gospel today and continue reading it through the Thirty-third Sunday.[1] But the reading of John's sixth chapter does not constitute a hiatus, because the thread of the narration has not been severed. The account of the multiplication of the loaves (Mark 6:35-44), which Mark places after the return of the Twelve to Jesus, who had sent them on a mission (Mark 6:30-34—Sixteenth Sunday), has been read in John's version. After this miracle, Mark reports the walk on the water (6:45-52), and he rapidly mentions that Jesus works cures in Gennesaret (6:53-56). It is at this point that we return to Mark's Gospel. It records first the discussions on clean and unclean that Jesus has with some Pharisees and a few scribes who have come from Jerusalem (Mark 7:1-8, 14-15, 21-23—Twenty-second Sunday) and the cure of a deaf and mute man (Mark 7:31-37—Twenty-third Sunday).

The two episodes are related. In the first one, the topic is the correct practice of the prescriptions of the Law, which must be a witness to God in the eyes of all peoples (Deut 4:1-2, 6-8—Twenty-second Sunday). The second shows that Jesus accomplishes the works foretold of the day when God will come to save his people (Isa 35:4-7a—Twenty-third Sunday).

We begin reading James' letter, which will continue through the Twenty-sixth Sunday. It has sometimes been viewed as a sort of first Christian examination of conscience because of the concrete character of the situations and actions that are the subject of the author's reflections and often sharp criticisms.[2] "Be doers of the word and not hearers only" (Jas 1:17-18, 21b-22, 27—Twenty-second Sunday). Hold the poor in honor instead of judging according to false values (Jas 2:1-5—Twenty-third Sunday).

In this brief sequence, we dwell on putting into practice God's word, which we regularly hear proclaimed in the liturgy. At baptism, our deafness was healed: may our hearts not be deaf to the teaching and exhortations of the Lord and may our tongues be prompt to praise God.

Twenty-second Sunday

Putting into Practice the Word Sown in the Heart

The Lord's Law, Wisdom and Life

The Law of God, or Code of the Covenant, designates the whole of the legal dispositions—prescriptions and interdicts—recorded, in particular, in the first five books of the Bible—the Pentateuch—precisely called the Law, the Torah. But although belonging to the same literary genre as other ancient Middle Eastern legal codes, this law of God differs fundamentally from all others. These latter only require an external obedience: they rule acts, not intentions.[1] Besides, and most importantly, these other codes do not establish any personal bond between those who observe or ignore them and the lawgiver. Deuteronomy strives to make its readers aware of this difference; today, we read a passage significant in this regard (Deut 4:1-2, 6-8).[2]

"Now, Israel, hear the statutes and decrees which I am teaching you to observe." We have here an urgent appeal to conversion, enhanced by the recalling of the ancestors' unfaithfulness and the misfortunes it has caused.

> Oh, that today you would hear his voice:
> "Harden not your hearts as at Meribah,
> as in the day of Massah in the desert,
> Where your father tempted me;
> they tested me though they had seen my works.
> (Ps 95:7d-9)[3]

Taught by their experience, we shall avoid committing the same errors and the same sins. For our life is an exodus that must bring us to the promised land into which the Lord will lead those who, eschewing the mirages of the past, walk in the way of his commandments. "Every person must come out of Egypt everyday."[4] To guide us, the Lord is here "close to us every time we invoke him." His word too, ever new,[5] is close to us, calling to each one's responsibility for the advent of salvation.

> Grounded in the word of the Talmud that it is enough that all humans re-
> pent to bring about the coming of the Messiah, I decided to act with them.
> I was sure to succeed in this. But where should I begin? The world is so
> vast I shall therefore begin with the land I know best: my own. But it is
> enormous. Well, I shall begin with the city that is closest to me: my own.
> But it is large and I hardly know it. Well then, I shall begin with my street.
> No: my house. No: my family. There it is, I shall begin with myself.[6]

People will carefully guard against adding anything to this law or taking
anything from it, because it comes from God himself, and also because,
when properly understood, it orients us toward a never attained perfection. It keeps the people from the temptation of settling into any sort of
self-satisfaction, into an introverted complacency. Unceasingly, it projects
into the future the fulfillment that God will realize when he wills, as he
wills. Through the Law, God teaches his children to walk so that taking
at every hour of every day, at every phase of life, the step they can and
must take, they may reach the end of the journey. Scrupulous faithfulness to observances can certainly turn into formalism, invite criticism,
and fall prey to narrow-mindedness and ridicule. It would be wrong to
base one's judgments on these caricatures that the genuine followers of
the Law are the first to denounce. The humble and persevering observance
of God's law and its prescriptions gives its adepts the strength to stand,
to walk for a long distance, because they keep a regular pace. Their example carries others along, or at least shows the way.[7]

Faithful observance of the Law is, moreover, a witness to God shown
before all peoples ''who will hear of these statutes and say, 'This great
nation is truly a wise and intelligent people.' . . . For what great nation
has statutes and decrees that are as just as this whole law which I am
setting before you today?'' The Law is the pride of God's people and
is the ground for its responsibility in the world.

> It is our duty
> to glorify the Master of the universe,
> to praise the grandeur
> of the Creator of the beginnings.
> He has not made us like
> to the other nations of the earth.
> He has not limited our portion
> to the same measure as theirs.
> He has not made our fate like
> to their whole tumult.
> As for us,
> we bow,

we prostrate ourselves,
we give thanks
before the face
of the King of kings, of all kings,
of the Holy One, Blessed be He.
He is above in the heavens;
the abode of his victory
is our lofty grandeur.
He is our God
and no other.
He is truly King
and nothing exists without Him,
as His Torah says:
"This is why you must know
and fix in your heart
that the Lord is God
in the heavens above
and on earth below,
and that there is no other (Deut 4:39).[8]

Word of God, source of wisdom, school of savoir-vivre, of savoir-faire, by keeping their cultural and religious identity, the Law has empowered the Jewish people to confront the innumerable and tragic events of their history without losing their soul. Its teaching bears upon all aspects of life. It speaks of a God who is close to humans, not only without losing anything of his transcendence but, on the contrary, because of it. Rabbi Yehuda Ben Tema said, "At five years of age, one learns the Scriptures; at ten years of age, one learns the Mishna; at thirteen years of age, one keeps the commandments."[9]

Psalms vie with one another to sing the Law of God.

The law of the LORD is perfect,
refreshing the soul . . . (Ps 19:8).

I see that all fulfillment has its limits;
broad indeed is your command (Ps 119:96).

Truly, faithful observance of the commandments enlarges the heart and fills it with joy.

He who does justice will live in the presence
of the Lord.

He who walks blamelessly and does justice;
who thinks the truth in his heart
and slanders not with his tongue;
Who harms not his fellow man

nor takes up a reproach against his neighbor;
By whom the reprobate is despised,
   while he honors those who fear the LORD;
Who, though it be to his loss, changes not his pledged word;
who lends not his money at usury
   and accepts no bribe against the innocent.
He who does these things
   shall never be disturbed.
(Ps 15:2-5)

Putting God's Word into Practice

In the Bible, as in all the ancient East, wisdom is the exact knowledge that allows us to appreciate everything at its just value and, as a consequence, to lead upright and peaceful lives. Being the fruit of personal reflection and experience nourished by tradition, it is akin to the divine knowledge that does not stop at appearances and the outer layer of realities, but penetrates their very depths. The intent of wisdom is of the practical order: it determines a savoir-vivre.[10] James' letter decidedly belongs to this tradition (Jas 1:17-18, 21b-22, 27).

Human wisdom is acquired, only in part, for it is also—even mostly—a gift that some people have known how to patiently cultivate and make fruitful. This is why one expects to find it among aged persons rather than young ones. Their long years of life have given them experience. They have seen so many things and met so many persons, that they have learned to show discernment, to distinguish good from evil, what is opportune, and what should be set aside or avoided. They have acquired the art of living that only life can teach. They listen more than they talk, and their words often take the shape of aphorisms, sayings that give food for thought. The first words of this Sunday's reading could be one of these maxims, "All good giving and every perfect gift is from above." But the author of the letter immediately adds that they "com[e] down from the Father of lights, with whom there is no alteration or shadow caused by change." The gifts that interest him and that must be sought after by Christians are of divine origin: those that we designate "graces."[11] They come from the creator, the transcendent and inexhaustible source of all light, of all good, of all perfection. Supernatural by their origin, they are also supernatural in their effects.

The Father "willed to give us birth by the word of truth that we may be a kind of firstfruits of his creatures." In the Old Testament, the Law is called "the word of truth." In the New Testament, this expression is a synonym for the gospel[12] and even, in John's Gospel, for the person of Christ.[13] It is through him that believers become new creatures, "children of light and children of the day" (1 Thess 5:5), the firstfruits of a new creation (see Rev 14:4). The word of God is a seed we must welcome in ourselves as does a well-prepared soil, freed beforehand from "all filth and evil excess" (Jas 1:21a).[14] Then the word will be able to germinate and produce abundant fruit[15] because it has, by its very nature, an extraordinary efficacy.[16] But in order that it may unfold its full potential, it must be put into practice. That this is so, the Gospels often remind us, particularly Matthew's, which, like James' letter, insists on the illusory character of faith separated from practice, and especially from active charity.[17] "Be doers of the word and not hearers only, deluding yourselves."

As any good catechesis, James' letter does not stop at the mere enunciation of a general principle. "Religion that is pure and undefiled before God the Father is this: to care for orphans and widows in their affliction and to keep oneself unstained by the world." The practice of religion goes much farther than what we habitually understand: faithfulness to liturgical worship, to Sunday Mass. What is meant here are the acts that correspond to the worship "in Spirit and truth" (John 4:23-24), the complete list of which cannot be laid down. James several times denounces the illusion of those who multiply acts of devotion but neglect certain points of the Law they regard as secondary. This is a vain, ineffective, untrue[18] religion and, we must add, one that scandalizes unbelievers. All will be judged by their acts, by what they will have done or omitted to do for the most destitute (Matt 25:31-46).

Good and Evil Come from the Heart

The question whether certain traditional religious practices were of permanent value arose with urgency in the beginning of the Church, when pagans received the gospel. It was resolved at the assembly called the "Council of Jerusalem," after an arduous debate.[19] "It is the decision of the holy Spirit and of us not to place on you any burden beyond these necessities, namely, to abstain from meat sacrificed to idols, from blood, from meats of strangled animals, and from unlawful marriage" (Acts 15:28-29). The obligation of circumcision was the central object of the debate; the council decided that it was not to be enjoined on converts from paganism. The interdict concerning the meats from sacrifices, sold at the market, did not last long.[20] As to the obligation to eat kosher, it is mentioned neither in Acts nor in the other New Testament writings. This sort of debate might appear to have been totally obsolete for a long time. In fact, history shows that it has often reappeared under one form or another: Must churches impose all their traditions on the peoples they evangelize? How can we distinguish between the necessary ones and the others? These questions are again in the forefront today. We have become sensitive to the duty of respecting diverse cultures and of avoiding anything that could resemble religious colonialism or imperialism.[21] Jesus' words recorded in this Sunday's Gospel are most timely in denouncing the formalism threatening certain practices and the danger of confusion between human traditions and divine commands (Mark 7:1-8, 14-15, 21-23).

Some Pharisees and scribes, coming from Jerusalem, therefore belonging to the circles most strictly attached to traditions,[22] reproach Jesus with the conduct of his disciples, who do "not follow the tradition of the elders,[23] but instead eat a meal with unclean hands." The evangelist takes the trouble to explain that what is discussed are ritual practices. This washing of the hands when returning from the town or marketplace, as well as the washing of cups, jugs, and kettles, was intended to purify persons and everyday objects from all risk of legal impurity contracted by chance. The intent is an excellent one.[24] But the gesture has meaning only inasmuch as it expresses the purification of the heart. Of itself, it is unable to confer purity of soul, still less replace it. Now this is what is discussed here: we must honor God in our heart, and not only with our lips. No rite, regardless of how sacred, has value or efficacy if the inner disposition does not correspond to what it signifies.[25]

Addressing the crowd, Jesus enunciates the general principle to which we must adhere: "Hear me, all of you, and understand. Nothing that enters one from outside can defile that person, but the things that come out from within are what defile." This is clear; what is bad in things can stain us only from the moment we allow their impurity to enter into us. Or in other words, morality resides in the use we make of things and in our intention. Thus for instance, a substance can be taken either as a remedy or as a drug. However, this principle does not allow us to justify everything. People say, "Only the intention counts." It is true in this sense: we must act according to our conscience, but this must be well formed.[26] Moreover, nothing can justify certain actions; what harms our neighbor remains, always and objectively, an evil.

> From a controversy on the clean and unclean, on good and evil, on tradition and newness, Jesus leads us into an altogether different perspective:

that of an examination of one's life and of a conversion of the heart. From concrete attitudes that each one is tempted to assume, from simplistic slogans to which each one is tempted to reduce truth understood in an individual way, Jesus leads us back to a critical scrutiny of our interior and spiritual motivations.

Reality is the meaning that things, events, persons, and we ourselves have before God and for God. In the name of this reality, we must attempt to track down our hidden hypocrisies, this ever renewed need to cheaply justify ourselves.

Hypocrisy of liturgical worship and private prayer, if they are only a way of washing our hands, if they are only an opportunity to hear the Word of God without allowing it to germinate in us and really produce a merciful attitude and merciful actions.

Less well-noticed hypocrisy—and the more dangerous for it—of our presence to the world and of human solidarity if those cover a mere conformism to all the prevailing ideas and to all the current slogans, or self-complacency, or the obsession to ingratiate ourselves with non-Christians. . . .

Hypocrisy of those who multiply the rules in order to pacify themselves and to feel superior to those who do not observe those rules.

Hypocrisy of those who reject rules and laws, if it is simply to live according to their impulses and desires, while taking pride in their freedom. What freedom?

It is what comes out of a human being, out of a human heart, that is pure or impure, free or servile, healthy or unhealthy.[27]

Taking his disciples aside—"away from the crowd"—Jesus tells them, "From within people, from their hearts, come evil thoughts, unchastity, theft, murder, adultery, greed, malice, deceit, licentiousness, envy, blasphemy, arrogance, folly." Here, Jesus does not merely explain what he just stated in a general way. He shows how far the concern for inner purity must go. The heart is the place where evil is consummated, and not only the place where it originates. The evil desire, the base intention, hatred, greed make persons unclean even though they do not act upon them. "Everyone who looks at a woman with lust has already committed adultery with her in his heart" (Matt 5:28). This does not mean that intention is purely and simply identical with action.[28] For on the one hand, as long as neighbors are unaware of our evil desires, they are not affected by them.[29] On the other hand and more importantly, a wicked thought may be just a temptation that, being fought back, represents a victory over evil. Watchfulness over our hearts—our desires, our thoughts—is an obligation, because we are called to become perfect as our heavenly Father is perfect (Matt 5:48).

> The source and point of departure of all faults are evil thoughts; for if they do not overcome us, there will be neither murder nor adultery nor any other sin. This is why we must stand guard with the utmost watchfulness over our own hearts. For on the day of judgment, "the Lord . . . will bring to light what is hidden in darkness and will manifest the motives of our hearts": (1 Cor 4:5), and also "God will judge people's hidden works . . ." (Rom 2:16).
>
> "To eat with unwashed hands does not defile [a person]" (Matt 15:20), but if we must boldly speak, what does defile a person is to eat, without washing one's heart, anything that our reason is naturally apt to eat.[30]

The liturgy for this Sunday urges Christians to a rigorous examination of their lives and behavior. God's commandments are a grace that assigns to us a considerable responsibility toward the whole world. If they are humbly received and faithfully kept, they render witness to the wisdom of God who gave them, at the same time as they insure salvation in truth. For Jesus is a free man who frees others and calls them to act responsibly by conforming their lives to the desires of their hearts in which the Word has been sown.

> The Son of man
> knows the thoughts of humans.
> When our hearts are naked before him,
> let us implore his pity.
> Without ceasing, let us cry:
>
> *Purify us, Lord,*
> *Draw us near to you.*
>
> Listen to my word,
> practice it and you will live.
>
> If any love me,
> my Father will love them and we shall dwell in them.
>
> Love one another,
> and so you will remain in my love.[31]

Twenty-third Sunday

Signs of New Times in Pagan Lands

Here Is Your God—Take Courage

In the Bible, history and prophecy are engaged in an unceasing dialogue.[1] We must refer to the past in order to interpret and comprehend the present, itself pregnant with promises of the future. History is propelled by a single dynamism and goes toward its fulfillment because God leads us to realize his plan of salvation for humankind and the whole universe. Creator of all things, he has absolute mastery over them. For him, there are no historical vicissitudes. Nothing, not even the malice and sin of humankind can and will ever be able to thwart his work, still less to wreck it. For believers, history is not the simple succession of facts eventually linked together to render intelligible their sequence, their reciprocal influences and their direction. Only a reading done with faith and under the guidance of the Spirit, a reading to which the inspired sages devoted themselves, allows us to unveil its deep meaning. The particular mission of prophets consists in uncovering this meaning in order to lead their hearers to live the present, to be converted, to be with God and in conformity with God's views, the actors and beneficiaries of a future of resurrection, of salvation. They announce what must happen and denounce what delays or hinders its occurrence.[2] Therefore, the ancient prophetic oracles retain all their relevance. They shed an indispensable light on the mystery of Christ and the Church and, at the same time, show today's believers how to receive it and become part of it.[3] The text from the Book of Isaiah chosen for this Sunday must be read in this perspective (Isa 35:4-7a).

> Say to those whose hearts are frightened:
>   Be strong, fear not!
> Here is your God,
>   he comes with vindication;
> With divine recompense
>   he comes to save you.

Clearly, such a message was addressed in its time to people in a dire situation, the meaning of which they did not see.[4] The prophet's gaze discerns signs promising a liberation close at hand; therefore, instead of being dejected by the length of the trial, people must take courage.[5] This manner of speech is evidence of a constant religious reflection on the causes and the meaning of the Exile, whereas the reach of the promise expressed by this oracle goes much farther than the horizon of immediate history. God himself is coming to bring salvation, and not only deliverance after this prolonged exile. The powerful of this world, whatever may be the reasons for their politics, are instruments in the Lord's hands to accomplish his plans. This is a recognition of the fact that the true cause—the happy events as well as the misfortunes of the history of God's people—is to be sought in their attitude toward the covenant. When a king carries off the inhabitants of the land, it is, in fact, God who is punishing them for their unfaithfulness.[6] When another king arises to liberate them, it is, in fact, God again who is at work: he "comes" to "save" them.[7]

The description of what the Lord is about to do clearly evokes a work of salvation.

> Then will the eyes of the blind be opened,
>   the ears of the deaf be cleared;
> Then will the lame leap like a stag,
>   then the tongue of the dumb will sing.
> Streams will burst forth in the desert,
>   and rivers in the steppe.
> The burning sands will become pools,
>   and the thirsty ground, springs of water. . . .

These are not words and images normally used to speak of the end of a time of exile. But the cure of the blind, deaf, and lame is one of the signs that the Messiah must perform.[8] Jesus mentioned this sign when he preached for the first time in Nazareth (Luke 4:18); he also mentioned it to those sent by John the Baptist to ask him whether he was the expected one.[9] God sent his Son into the world in order to cure human beings of these grave infirmities caused by sin: blindness that prevents our seeing the Light; deafness that closes our hearts to the Word; lameness that hinders us from walking unerringly and joyfully in the steps of him who said, "I am the way" (John 14:6).[10]

> *Praise the Lord, my soul!*
>
> [The God of Jacob] keeps faith forever,
>   secures justice for the oppressed,

gives food to the hungry.
The LORD sets captives free:
  the LORD gives sight to the blind.
The LORD raises up those that were bowed down;
  the LORD loves the just.
The LORD protects strangers;
  the fatherless and the widow he sustains,
  but the way of the wicked he thwarts.
The LORD shall reign forever;
  your God, O Zion, through all generations. Alleluia.
(Ps 146:6c-10)

Imitating God by Honoring the Poor

"Religion that is pure and undefiled before God" comes to the aid of whoever is in need, beginning with those who because of their circumstances are abandoned to their fate, defenseless.[11] But assuming the charge of the most destitute cannot stop at insuring the material help they surely need, to which they have a right, which in any case those richer than they have the strict duty to bring them. For there are ways of acting that, while rendering an indispensable service, leave, or even maintain, those who benefit by them in a state of inferiority. Many among them would become reconciled to paternalism and would even play its game, as long as the benefactors do not exercise an obvious power of domination over them under the pretense of assisting them.[12]

James' letter requires much more: we must, in all circumstances, render the same honor to the poor as we do to others. Faith in Christ demands this. The way we receive and treat the poor in liturgical celebrations proves to be, on this point, particularly revealing (Jas 2:1-5).

"My brothers, show no partiality as you adhere to the faith in our glorious Lord Jesus Christ." The Law enjoins especially on those who render justice that they not show favor to some at the expense of others: rich or poor, each one must be judged with equity.[13] For God does not treat human beings differently, not when he judges them[14] and not when he calls them to salvation. Peter was given proof of this when he received the order to go to Cornelius, a centurion, a pagan (Acts 10:32). Moreover, Jesus has shown that he acts with impartiality (Matt 22:16). Henceforth, undue biases are incompatible with the "faith in our glorious Lord Jesus Christ." Again, we are not speaking of vague generalities or fine sentiments but of concrete modes of behavior. The letter's author gives an example. Let us suppose that "a man with gold rings on his fingers and in fine clothes comes into your assembly, and a poor person in shabby clothes also comes in.'' To rush toward the former to seat him in a place of honor, while one tells the latter to remain standing where he is, near the door, unless he can find a corner to sit on the floor, is acting as ''judges with evil designs.'' The scene is so vividly sketched that it seems to have been drawn from life. Who, at some time or other, has not witnessed similar obsequious attentions lavished on a personage entering church and the off-handedness with which a lowly person, entering at the same time, was relegated to the last pew? The worst part of this is probably that we act in this way without any awareness of our behaving badly, so molded are we by the standards of the world. In any case, two centuries after James' letter, the ecclesiastical constitution called ''The Teaching of the Twelve Apostles'' will state, making reference to James' letter: ''If poor people come in, whether they belong to your parish or another one, especially if they are getting on in years and if there is no place for them, make room for them wholeheartedly, O bishop, even if it means that you have to sit on the ground. You must not be a respecter of persons if you want your ministry to be agreeable before God.''[15]

The example of conduct fitting to the liturgical assembly is completely pertinent because ''it is through the liturgy especially that the faithful are enabled to express in their lives and manifest to others . . . the real nature of the true Church.''[16] The way we behave toward others during the liturgy, especially toward the poor, is, therefore, an excellent mirror of our heart and mindset. If, at church, we judge according to false values, what of our daily lives? A liturgical assembly offering the same spectacle as a worldly gathering in which the poor, the lowly, do not have a place, while the rich and powerful are honored, causes harm to the true nature of the Church, a community of brothers and sisters in which there is no longer any difference between slave and freeborn, employer and employee, rich and poor, man and woman (see Gal 3:28). It is not enough to know and say it: we must show it. The behavior of the assembled community must confirm the variety of witness given, in daily life, by scattered Christians.

''Did not God choose those who are poor in the world to be rich and heirs of the kingdom that he promised to those who love him?'' Jesus not only taught the eminent dignity of the poor.[17] ''He became poor . . . so that by his poverty [we] might become rich'' (2 Cor 8:9).

> Jesus is poor. He is infinitely and rigorously poor. Poor with an absolute poverty. The Prince of poverty, the Lord of perfect poverty. Poor with the

poor, having come for the poor, speaking to the poor, giving to the poor, working for the poor. Poor among the poor, destitute among the destitute, beggar among beggars. The poor one of eternal poverty. The poor one, happy and rich, who accepts poverty, wants it, espouses it, sings it. The beggar who gives alms. The naked one who covers the naked, the hungry one who nourishes others. The miraculous and supernatural poor one who transforms the rich into as many poor and the poor into as many truly rich.[18]

The Deaf Hear, the Mute Speak

Jesus, as portrayed in Mark's Gospel, is always on the move. Hardly has he arrived somewhere than he leaves to go elsewhere, farther. The evangelist does not give us the leisure to consult a map on which to mark the itinerary of these unceasing comings and goings; he does not even take the trouble to give us particulars that would allow us to locate exactly the places where Jesus stops. Obviously, Mark wants our attention to remain, at every moment, wholly concentrated on what Jesus says and does. The meaning and reach of his teaching are better understood if we know who the persons around him are, so the evangelist does not fail to tell us. The same holds true in the accounts of miracles in which the actions and words of Jesus usually hold a larger place than those of the cured persons. On the other hand, Mark mentions in what region such and such an incident takes place when the location proves significant. This is the case in the account of the healing of a deaf and mute man (Mark 7:31-37).

At the end of a rather complicated itinerary, Jesus arrives in "the district of the Decapolis." He has left the region of Tyre and Sidon on the boundaries of Galilee, whose population was a mixed one. Now Mark leads us, following Jesus' steps, into undeniably pagan territory. We must remember this fact, for it is important in helping us understand what is about to happen. "People brought to him a deaf man who had a speech impediment and begged him to lay his hand on him." This opening sentence surprises us. Who is this man, where is he coming from, who brought him? Our surprise becomes greater as we read on. Not only the sick man and the persons with him remain completely anonymous, but no word of theirs is recorded. It is clear that Mark wants to focus our attention uniquely on what Jesus does and says, on the manner in which he cures the sick man.[19] Perhaps Mark wants to suggest to each one of his readers, "You might very well be this deaf and mute man or one of those who bring him to Jesus." Jesus "took him off by himself away from the crowd."

The way Jesus proceeds is somewhat disconcerting. We would be content with the laying on of hands, and we know that one single word of Jesus is sufficient to cure the man. Why does he take this infirm person away from peoples' eyes, put his fingers in his ears, and touch his tongue with saliva? To say that these gestures were commonly used by healers at this time is not a satisfying answer because, precisely, Jesus is not a healer among others.[20] But is not reasoning in this way tantamount to considering this healing exclusively as something Jesus did in the past, singled out for the telling for no reason we can discover? For it is neither especially spectacular nor, it seems, very significant.

But Mark says Jesus "looked up to heaven and groaned, and said to him, 'Ephphatha!' (that is, 'Be opened!')." "Ephphatha" is an Aramaic word that the evangelist has preserved as we would do with a ritual or sacred formula that has meaning for its readers.[21] In fact, for a long time, it was used, just as it is, in the baptismal liturgy. Besides, this word proves to be immediately effective: "And [immediately] the man's ears were opened, his speech impediment was removed, and he spoke clearly." This healing of a nameless deaf-mute seems to be a parable for the cure of another deafness and of another speech impediment that only grace can heal. Jesus often reproaches his disciples with their lack of understanding of the word.[22] And if they confess, along with Peter, that Jesus is the Christ, the Son of the living God, they do so because God has placed this profession of faith in their mouths.[23]

> I now come to the explanation of the sacraments that you have received. . . . What did we do last Saturday? The opening. These mysteries of the opening were celebrated when the bishop touched your ears and nostrils. What does this mean? When a deaf-mute was brought to him, Our Lord Jesus Christ in the Gospel touched his ears and mouth: the ears because he was deaf, the mouth because he was mute. And he said, "Ephphatha." This is a Hebrew word that means "Be opened." Therefore, the bishop touched your ears so that they might open to the bishop's words and speech. But you ask, "Why the nostrils?" . . . In order that you might receive the good odors of divine goodness, so that you might say, "For we are the aroma of Christ for God," as the holy apostle says (2 Cor 2:15), and so that there might be in you all the perfumes of faith and devotion.[24]

The narrative ends with the mention of the praise that this cure arouses, a praise at first sight rather disconcerting. Henceforth, this praise freely rises in the Christian assembly that has just commemorated, once more, the marvels accomplished by the Lord since the day he cured a nameless deaf-mute: "He has done all things well. He makes the deaf hear and

[the] mute speak." This cry of admiration has the stamp of a liturgical hymn of the Christian community that spontaneously occurs to Mark. The deeds formerly accomplished by God at the Exodus and announced by the prophet as belonging to messianic times[25] are unceasingly renewed by the holy humanity of the Lord and the sacraments, which are the saving gestures of Christ.

> The deaf-mute healed by Christ felt his fingers of flesh touch his ears and tongue; but when his ears were unstopped, he reached the inaccessible divinity through the intermediary of this finger that his senses perceived. The very artisan of his body, the maker of his limbs had come to him; he had found him deaf, and with a soft voice, without the slightest pain had opened his hard ears. Immediately, his blocked throat, up to now unable to let any sound through, burst out in praise of him who, with one word, had cured him of his helplessness.[26]

The Bible is the history of the difficult dialogue between God and his people. God, who by his word has created everything, never ceases to address human beings. He adapts his language to the measure of their understanding. He multiplies signs and prodigies that manifest his tenderness and his power, his determination to accomplish his plan of salvation. When he falls silent for a while, he hopes that humans will renew their cries to him and thus allow him to resume the dialogue for which he is always ready. But the sad thing is that human beings have a short memory; that the din from below, to which they lend a complacent ear, ends by making them deaf to their God's voice; that, finally, they do not even know how to say his name. The time will come, say the prophets— God's spokespersons—when the ears of the deaf will be opened and the mute will cry for joy. "And the Word became flesh" (John 1:14). Jesus' cure of a nameless deaf-mute in "the district of the Decapolis" becomes a sign of new times. All those who up to the present have been deaf, can now hear his word, confess that he is the Messiah, the Son of God, and go into the whole world to proclaim the good news, in their turn, and sing his praises. "He has done all things well." He chooses "those who are poor in the world to be rich in faith and heirs of the kingdom that he promised to those who love him." All barriers down, he assembles them around the table of the Word and the Bread shared in thanksgiving.

> In your footsteps
> justice for the poor has bloomed;
> you say, "Ephphatha,"
> and ears are opened;
> you listen: tongues are loosened

for your praise;
you stretch your hand,
and we are healed.

Marvelous are your works,
Lord, Master of life!

You are the joy of your faithful,
you hear their cry, you save them.

You cure the broken-hearted
and tend their wounds.

You unbind those who are chained,
you open to captives the door of happiness.

Let us bless the Lord at all times,
May his praise be always on our lips.[27]

From the Twenty-fourth to the Twenty-sixth Sunday in Ordinary Time

This new sequence of Ordinary Time, Year B, begins by reminding us of Peter's declaration to Jesus in the region of Caesarea Philippi: "You are the Messiah." This profession of faith is in contrast to the hesitations of the crowd that continues to ask "Who then is this man?" But Peter and the disciples still have a long way to go before they can accept a humiliated Messiah who will save the world by dying on a cross (Mark 8:27-35—Twenty-fourth Sunday). The idea of an earthly kingdom is so deeply rooted in their minds that they continue to speculate on each one's chances of securing the first place for himself once their Master is victorious. "If anyone wishes to be first, he shall be the last of all and the servant of all," Jesus says (Mark 9:30-37—Twenty-fifth Sunday). On the one hand, there are no reserved places—whoever accomplishes in Jesus' name the same works as the Lord is ranked among the disciples. On the other hand, whoever is an occasion of falling for others will be severely condemned (Mark 9:38-43, 45, 47-48—Twenty-sixth Sunday).

These Gospel passages are chosen in connection with first readings from the Old Testament. The Book of Isaiah has painted the portrait of the Lord's Servant who cannot be turned away from his mission because of his unshakable trust in God, his defender (Isa 50:5-9a—Twenty-fourth Sunday). In fact, just persons have often been persecuted, sometimes condemned to an infamous death; but in spite of appearances, they were never abandoned by God (Wis 2:12, 17-20—Twenty-fifth Sunday). He pours out his Spirit with incomparable liberality and sovereign liberty. We are sometimes surprised by his choices, but we cannot impugn them by claiming the right of deciding who should receive what gifts (Num 11:25-29—Twenty-sixth Sunday).

Over these three Sundays we continue—and complete—the reading of James' letter. Without actions faith is dead: it cannot save (Jas 2:14-18—Twenty-fourth Sunday). The authenticity of faith is proved by its fruits—in the first place, charity, justice, and peace (Jas 3:16–4:3—Twenty-fifth Sunday). So that these may thrive, we must break away from the false values of the world that place material riches above everything else. The desire we have for them engenders the worst disorders and leads to ruin those who are enslaved to them (Jas 5:1-6—Twenty-sixth Sunday).

Twenty-fourth Sunday

For You, Who Is Christ?

The Obedient Servant, Meek and Humble of Heart
Among Old Testament texts, few have been commented on more often
than the four poems of the Book of Isaiah called "Songs of the Suffering
Servant."[1] The mysterious character of the person presented in these four
songs, the torments he undergoes, his unwavering attachment to God's
will in the midst of his suffering, the certitude with which he expects to
see his righteousness recognized and rewarded make of him an unusual
person.[2] Therefore, Christian tradition has seen in the just one, persecuted and then exalted by God, one of the most striking figures of Christ.
In particular, it has pondered these poems in conjunction with the Gospel
readings of the passion, and as a parallel to the announcements of his
pasch. The latter is the case for this Sunday, on which we read the third
poem of the Servant (Isa 50:5-9a).

In this poem, the Servant himself speaks. He evokes the ill treatment
that his torturers have inflicted on him, resorting to blows in order to
crush him by physical pain, and to insulting actions in order to overwhelm
him under their contempt. This evocation is more dramatic in its restraint
than would be a detailed description of the tortures undergone: so much
fury and cruelty make us shudder. But the way in which these torments
are spoken of shows us a man of extraordinary grandeur and dignity:
physically reduced to nothing in his body, he has not been injured in
his soul. What is more, he remains serene beyond what we can imagine.
No violence has succeeded in altering in the slightest his nonviolence.
Obviously, his endurance is not that of an impassive and haughty Stoic
confronting his merciless fate. What is his secret? The Suffering Servant
indicates from what sources he draws the strength of his non-violence
and his serenity in the worst tribulations.

> The Lord GOD . . . opens my ear that I may hear;
> And I have not rebelled,
>   have not turned back.

Therefore, this man has heard God revealing both his plan and the mission to which he calls his servant in view of accomplishing his work. At

the same time, this man learned of the difficulties he would have to face. God never deals with anybody in a disloyal manner. But he expects a complete trust and a total commitment of being, soul and body,[3] from those he calls: "Behold I come." Then, in spite of their weakness, humans become able to do anything. The servant experiences this certitude again and again.

> The Lord GOD is my help,
>   therefore I am not disgraced;
> I have set my face like flint,
>   knowing that I shall not be put to shame.

Faith in the future, the conviction of not suffering and dying in vain have always been the source of a superhuman strength for all those who have devoted their lives to a just cause. They feel certain that others will arise to continue their work and bring it to completion. They seem not to be touched by the abuse and humiliation they are made to undergo, even when pain engulfs them. Their torturers are taken aback by this. They cannot understand—nor tolerate—the faces "like flint" of these non-violent persons who silently reveal the failure of the violence that was supposed to crush them. God's Servant is unshakable because he knows he can count on the Almighty, who never abandons the just. When reproaches rain upon him, along with blows, God's Servant even defies his persecutors: "Who disputes my right? / Let him confront me." Assured of being in the right, apparently abandoned to himself, but certain of God's presence and assistance, the one whom human beings condemn dares to cry out without fear of being contradicted, "Who will prove me wrong?"

Psalms abundantly prove that the exemplary experience of God's Servant presented in the Book of Isaiah is not exceptional. All believers who seek to remain faithful to God will know trials and will be called, although usually in less tragic circumstances, to trust themselves to God alone with a confidence equal to that of the Servant, proclaiming, "[I know] that I shall not be put to shame."

> *I will walk in the presence of the Lord,*
> *in the land of the living.*
>
> I love the LORD because he has heard
>   my voice in supplication,
> Because he has inclined his ear to me
>   the day I called.

The cords of death encompassed me;
  the snares of the nether world seized upon me;
  I fell into distress and sorrow,
And I called upon the name of the LORD,
  "O LORD, save my life!"
Gracious is the LORD and just;
  yes, our God is merciful.
The LORD keeps the little ones;
  I was brought low, and he saved me.

  ———

For he has freed my soul from death,
  my eyes from tears, my feet from stumbling.
I shall walk before the LORD
  in the land of the living.
(Ps 116:1-6, 8-9)

Faith and Works

Today's passage from the Letter of James deals with the relationship between faith and works. Here we have a question that very early in the Christian community was the subject of intense debates. For it arose not in a theoretical and serene manner but in a polemical context. Some, owing to their previous formation, tended to give to works—in particular, to the observance of the Law—such an importance that the role of faith unto salvation was devaluated. Others, on the contrary, judged actions to be quite secondary, if not negligible, for those who had faith. Paul brings things into focus while addressing the former.[4] James, especially in the passage we read today, also seeks clarification, while addressing the latter (Jas 2:14-18).

At the very first, the question is vigorously put: "What good is it, my brothers, if someone says he has faith but does not have works? Can that faith save him?" In the catechetical and eminently practical perspective that characterizes his letter, James does not bother with long explanations. To this question, he responds with a concrete example. "If a brother or sister has nothing to wear and has no food for the day, and one of you says to them, 'Go in peace, keep warm, and eat well,' but you do not give them the necessities of the body, what good is it?" It serves no purpose obviously, except that it exacerbates the suffering of those to whom one speaks in this way and arouses fully understandable feelings of resentment. "So also faith of itself, if it does not have works, is dead." Persons who behave thus believe in God who is love and proclaim themselves disciples of him who said that the great commandment is to love

God and one's neighbor. But their faith does not bear the fruits of love. They are like dead trees. James' letter is a direct continuation of the prophets' preaching: the fast that pleases the Lord is

> releasing those bound unjustly,
>   untying the thongs of the yoke;
> Setting free the oppressed,
>   breaking every yoke;
> Sharing your bread with the hungry,
>   sheltering the oppressed and the homeless;
> Clothing the naked when you see them,
>   and not turning your back on your own.
> (Isa 58:6b-7)[5]

On judgment day, the sentence will be pronounced according to what each one will have done or not done for those who were hungry, thirsty, naked, sick, or imprisoned (Matt 25:31-46).[6]

In no way can we call on Paul, when he writes of salvation through faith and not works, to contradict or water down James' teaching. Paul's words are addressed to those who think they will be saved by their own strength, by the accumulation of merits gained through their faithful observance of the Law. No, says Paul. Salvation is a grace, a gift, acquired for us by Christ, shared by us in the measure in which we are united to the Savior through faith. Paul himself protests against distorted interpretations of his teaching. "Serve one another through love. . . . live by the spirit and you will certainly not gratify the desire of the flesh (Gal 5:13, 16). He frequently exhorts Christians to the "work of faith."[7] The connection between faith and works can be looked at from different points of view, with the result that one stresses one or the other of the two terms, especially when addressing persons who tend to minimize the importance of one of them. But Scripture and tradition unanimously affirm that faith and works, to believe and to do, are inseparable.

The way in which James' letter insists on the necessity of works is intentionally caricatural. It is hard to imagine that one could treat a poor person with such unfeeling curtness. But a similar indifference may well lie hidden under our ways of speaking and acting. Thus, when we rest content with praying for those in need or when we think that a particular vocation exempts us or prevents us from acting. True contemplatives warn us against such illusions.

> When I see souls very earnest in trying to understand the prayer they have and very sullen when they are in it—for it seems they don't dare let their

minds move or stir lest a bit of their spiritual delight and devotion be lost—it makes me realize how little they understand of the way by which union is attained; they think the whole matter lies in these things. No, Sisters, absolutely not; works are what the Lord wants! He desires that if you see a Sister who is sick to whom you can bring some relief, you have compassion on her and not worry about losing this devotion; and that if she is suffering pain, you also feel it; and that, if necessary, you fast so that she might eat—not so much for her sake as because you know it is your Lord's desire. This is true union with His will. . . .[8]

To completely convince his readers, James challenges them, "Demonstrate your faith to me without works, and I will demonstrate my faith to you from my works." Faith without works is spineless. To "be hearers of the word only and not doers" is to delude ourselves and, at the same time, contribute to the undermining of our credibility (cf. Jas 1:22-24).

Faith and charity are the beginning and the end of life: the beginning is faith and the end is charity. The two together are God, and everything else that leads to human perfection is only a consequence of faith and charity. None sin if they profess faith; none hate if they possess charity. "A tree is known by its fruits" (Matt 12:33): likewise, those who profess to belong to Christ will be known by their works. Now the work that is required of us is not that we merely profess our faith, but that we may be found engaged in the practice of the faith to the end.[9]

The Scandal of the Cross

The Gospel passage read this Sunday occupies a central place in Mark's work, and for several reasons. First, it is about in the center of his writing.[10] Second, from this point on, Jesus will leave Galilee, which he goes through for the last time,[11] in order to go to Jerusalem, where his ministry will end.[12] Third—and most importantly—we arrive here at a decisive point on the way that progressively leads us to the discovery of Jesus' true identity (Mark 8:27-35).

"Who, then, is Jesus?" All through the first part of Mark's Gospel this question recurs again and again. Most of Jesus' hearers ask themselves this question. Some people already have their answer: Jesus is a man under suspicion, a blasphemer (Mark 2:7), whose disciples observe neither the Sabbath (2:24) nor the traditions of the elders (7:1-23), a man possessed by the devil (3:22). Jesus knows all these answers, whether they were pronounced aloud or only whispered in the heart (2:8). He therefore does not need to be informed of what "people" say of him. The disciples are well aware of these divisions concerning their master because they must decide where they themselves stand with regard to

these contradictory verdicts. Jesus asks, "Who do people say that I am?"
They omit the mention of judgments obviously prompted by ill will because, they know that by saying "people," Jesus has in mind this multitude of women and men of good will who follow him. These people show
their enthusiasm at his miracles; they are struck by the authority of his
teaching; but they are probably troubled when they hear the peremp-
tory judgments of scribes and Pharisees who attack the young master.
For their own part, they are uncertain: John the Baptist? Elijah?[13] one of
the prophets?[14]

Jesus makes no pronouncement, either on this diversity of opinion or
on the indecision of the "people." The disciples must declare their opinion, come to a decision: "And you, what do you say? For you, who am
I?" It is no longer a question of reporting what others think; we must
make a personal choice, a personal commitment, move from opinion to
a faith decision, say what we really think and no longer repeat what we
have heard or read in a book.

> I was learning, learning.
> Our masters thought, with bad logic,
> That to acquire knowledge of you would cause
>   you to be born in us.
> But all was conceived to make us unlearn what
>   is life-giving, the knowledge of you.
> All was conceived to render boring the
>   immutable mystery of unflagging joy.
> We did not even read your book on the sly,
> But a textbook of religious instruction with
>   the imprimatur of the bishop of Bayeux.
> It was too meager a fare for us to really
>   know you although you were called Son of
>   God on every page.
> From dogmatics and apologetics I remember not
>   a single word today.
> And even when I knew you word for word, you
>   were less real for me than St. Louis.[15]

"Peter said to him in reply, 'You are the Messiah.' " This statement is
clearly different from the peoples' opinions. Jesus is not a prophet of old
come back to earth but he whom the prophets announced. From now
on, the true disciples, in whose name Peter speaks, are decidedly distinct from the crowd: they have taken a great step toward true knowledge of Jesus' identity. But they still have a long way to go, and the
hardest part for sure.[16] Jesus knows this. He "warned them not to tell

anyone about him." The same command recurs several times in Mark's Gospel after the accounts of healings and exorcisms.[17] The evangelist does not trust premature professions of faith that run the risk of being full of ambiguities, even equivocations. We must take into account the fullness of revelation before professing our faith. Here, for the first time, Jesus himself gives the reason for this delay. To his disciples who recognize the Messiah in him Jesus "openly" says "that the Son of Man must suffer greatly and be rejected by the elders, the chief priests, and the scribes, and be killed, and rise after three days." "Must": it is thus that he will be the Messiah—Savior—as God had him announced by the prophets, Isaiah in particular.[18] Only by the light of his pasch of death and resurrection can we correctly interpret and understand everything else. Lacking this, the commitment to the Lord, though sincere, remains, as it were, that of catechumens: we are still in the time of initiation, of novitiate, during which we are introduced to Christian life and at the end of which we shall be called to make a fully informed profession of faith.

In fact, Peter strongly reacts to this first announcement of the passion; he "rebukes" Jesus in the way one would rebuke someone who spoke in a thoughtless, wholly unacceptable manner. This rebuke of Peter strikes Jesus right in the heart. Peter's thoughts contradict God's. In the disciple's reprimand, Jesus perceives the echo of the perfidious words of the devil, who in the desert during the forty days had attempted to dissuade him from setting out on the way marked by the Father. "Get behind me, Satan." We are taken aback by the vehemence of this retort. We must place it side by side with what Jesus will tell Peter during the last paschal meal: "Simon, Simon, behold Satan has demanded to sift all of you like wheat, but I have prayed that your own faith may not fail; and once you have turned back, you must strengthen your brothers" (Luke 22:31-32).[19] The cross of Christ remains the great obstacle—the great scandal—on the road of faith. To surmount this obstacle without stumbling, we must, through God's grace and the Lord's entreaty, let our hearts be freed from human thoughts—exorcised—and penetrated by divine thoughts.

> You I have so often named
> Without knowing how to give you your Name
> Without knowing how to give you your Name
> When did I for the first time call you Christ and crucified?
> When did I for the first time see you, from below, hanging on the Cross?
> When did I for the first time see you tormented by me?

What made of this occasion "the first time"?
Beforehand, there had been so many others
Opaque face-to-faces, everywhere, nowhere
Never did the symbol leave my eyes but, ensconced there, it blocked the
    entrance to my being
He was before me against me
In museums cemeteries books refectories boarding-school chapels
On the classroom walls on the schoolmasters' pates
Even as a small child in the church of my native place I remember I think
    I remember
An enormous body with plaster muscles and a towel poorly attached around
    the loins
Which seemed ready to slide naked from the scaffold threatening us with
    its avalanche
Immeasurably greater than our puny sins
Unknowingly I caught his glance and he drew mine through the thorns
I almost felt he was contemplating me
I know it now you have contemplated me from my mother's womb
In the beginning your glance showed me, your glance seeking insignifi-
    cant me
Christ with hollow eyes horribly dilated with orbits hewn out of the world's
    misery
I know now that you have carved my orbits to place your eyes in them.[20]

Having begun to "openly" tell his disciples for the first time that he must
suffer his passion "and rise after three days," Jesus "summon[s] the
crowd" so that all may hear what he is going to add: "Whoever wishes
to come after me must deny himself, take up his cross, and follow me.
For whoever loses his life for my sake and that of the gospel will save
it." Therefore, these words of Jesus are addressed to all those who want
to become Christ's disciples. Early Christian tradition understood this
well; the evangelists have taken care to faithfully record these words.[21]
Not all will be called upon to shed their blood for Christ and the Gospel;[22]
but to prefer nothing to Christ, including one's life, is an obligation for
all Christians. Under one form or another, each one, in the ordinary circumstances of daily life, is confronted with crucifying choices.

> This word is not destined for virgins, to the exclusion of married women;
> for widows, to the exclusion of wives; to monks, to the exclusion of hus-
> bands; to clerics, to the exclusion of lay people. The whole Church, the
> entire body, all members, differentiated and situated according to their own
> tasks, must follow Christ. Let the whole Church follow Christ, she who
> is the only one, she who is the dove, she who is the bride; let her follow
> Christ, she who is redeemed and endowed by the Bridegroom's blood. The

virgin's purity has its place here; so has the widow's continence; so has the spouses' chastity.

May these members that have their places here follow Christ, according to their categories, their ranks, their own ways. . . . Let them love him, the only one who neither deceives nor is deceived, the only one who does not lie: let them love him because what he promises is true.[23]

Who is Jesus Christ for people today? In order to answer this question, it is not necessary to organize a poll; it is sufficient for all of us to think of what we hear in our own circles. For many, Christ is certainly one of the foremost religious figures of humankind, on a par with other founders of great religions. What the Church proclaims on his account—from his conception and birth to his death and resurrection, including the extraordinary actions that he performed, if we believe the Gospels—usually plays a minimal role in these judgments concerning the person of Jesus of Nazareth. Anyway, the same is true about other founders of religions. That there may be more or less mythical and legendary elements in the narratives about them does not bother people much. On the other hand, the way in which believers live in conformity with, or in contradiction to, their faith has a considerable importance. This is the perspective adopted to judge the value, or lack of it, of religious affiliations. Faith without works is dead, useless, says the Letter of James (2:26).

And for us Christians—each one of us—who is Christ? If we must give a really personal answer—and not one found in books—the question is often perplexing. Ancient scriptures have announced a Servant of God, doomed to a tragic destiny; the sufferings of this mysterious personage have so many common points with those of Christ that we cannot escape the comparison. But why was it necessary for Jesus of Nazareth to know such a fate? "On the third day he rose again," the Creed says. Many Christians admit that this resurrection is an added difficulty and that they really do not believe in its reality. And what about us? Finally, there is this obligation, stated by Jesus, to carry our cross and follow him. We cannot hear this without having a deep sense of fear, if not repugnance. We must not be ashamed of these struggles and fears. Jesus himself knew these, as shown by the agony at Gethsemane. He went through this pasch in order to open to us the way of life.

Jesus died to the world
that no one may live for the world,
and he lived in his flesh as if crucified
that no one may live in the flesh in lust.

He died to our world in our very body
that we may live to *his* world
in our own body.
He mortified the life of the flesh,
that we may not live in the flesh
in a carnal manner.
He became the master,
not through others' sufferings
but through his own sufferings.
And he himself has first tasted bitterness,
for he has explained to us
that we do not become disciples through titles,
but through suffering.[24]

The Son of Man Delivered into Human Hands

Trial of the Just, Trial of God

Those who do evil are intolerant of contradiction, whatever its form. They strive to silence it. But nothing is more unbearable to them than the living reproach and permanent challenge of the life of just persons in their midst. Unable to pressure the just to act as they themselves do, evildoers attempt to ruin the reputation of the just by showing them to be impostors whom God himself disowns (Wis 2:12, 17-20).

The Sage uncovers the intentions and the duplicity of evildoers who assail the just. In fact, they attempt to justify their attacks; they appeal to quite honorable reasons. Those whom they denounce they characterize as troublemakers who disturb the public order, dangerous malcontents who mislead the people. By not living like everyone else, they become marginal. They must be expelled, since they refuse to be assimilated into normality. "Lies, hypocrisy," says the Sage, letting the impious themselves reveal the true reasons for their behavior. Through their very lives, led in conformity with God's law, the just denounce the misconduct of the impious and their culpable contempt of traditions.

> To us [the just ones] is the censure of our thoughts;
>
> ———
>
> He judges us debased;
>   he holds aloof from our paths as from things impure
> He calls blest the destiny of the just. . . .
> (Wis 2:14a, 16)

This last claim is particularly intolerable. In fact, it is obvious that from their faith in a reward after death, the just draw patience and strength in persecution.[1] Besides, in thinking that there is no appeal against this supreme tribunal of evildoers, the accused, themselves, are transformed into self-assured accusers when faced with their persecutors, over whom looms the threat of an inescapable punishment. These "just" claim to be children of God, protected by the Lord, who will "deliver [them] from the hands of [their] foes." Their mere presence is insufferable (Wis 2:14).

As always in such cases, evildoers begin by trying to break down the disturbers by reviling and torturing them. These tortures, whether moral or physical, are the usual means used in the hope of overcoming the meekness and patience of the just, of getting the better of their determination. Those who have recourse to such measures believe them to be infallibly efficacious because, in their opinion, force can obtain anything and because they themselves are unable to resist similar pressures. The failure of these methods exacerbates their fury and unleashes their worst instincts.

> Let us condemn him to a shameful death;
> for, according to his own words, God will take care of him.

In the last analysis, they impugn God himself; they blasphemously challenge him by putting the just to an ignominious death.

This passage from the Book of Wisdom applies to a multitude of men and women of all times, persecuted, tortured, put to death because they stood, by their mere presence, unshakable witnesses to right and justice. It applies literally to the Just One par excellence.

Jesus declared that he was God's Son. He never stopped denouncing impiety and injustice by his teaching and his conduct; he was the defender of the little ones and the poor; he never ceased to trust and proclaim God. He suffered the sarcasms and insults of those who, putting him to death, thought they were through with him. "He trusted in God; let him deliver him now if he wants him. For he said, 'I am the Son of God'" (Matt 27:43). The cross of the Righteous One (see Luke 23:47), which from now on stands on the earth as God's answer to all the challenges of the powerful of the whole world, is God's testimony to the invincible strength of those whom brutal force will never cause to falter.

> Through what decaying process have we been able to speak of a meek Jesus? Is this not shutting our eyes to the interior violence that impels you to defy your adversaries, to risk to be scandalous, to attract thunderbolts? Hence, without doubt, these paradoxical, imprudent formulas, miles away from the sages' usual tone. "What is of human esteem is an abomination in the sight of God" (Luke 16:15). "Tax collectors and prostitutes are entering the kingdom of God before you" (Matt 21:31). "Whoever exalts himself will be humbled; but whoever humbles himself will be exalted" (Matt 23:12). And this prediction, which is so dear to you, "The first will be last and the last will be first." All this is meant to be shocking. Your words, the gospel admits, have often seemed incomprehensible, often discouraging.

Could you be an agent provocateur? an anarchist? Who knows, even a sort of "leftist"?[2]

"When I am weak, then I am strong" (2 Cor 12:10). All of us, in our own way, can verify the relevance of these words by Paul. This is why Christians tirelessly pray with childlike trust and humble boldness.

The Lord upholds my life.

O God, by your name save me,
 and by your might defend my cause.
O God, hear my prayer;
 hearken to the words of my mouth.
For haughty men have risen up against me,
 and fierce men seek my life;
 they set not God before their eyes.
Behold, God is my helper;
 the Lord sustains my life.

———

Freely will I offer you sacrifice;
 I will praise your name, O LORD, for its goodness. . . .
(Ps 54:3-6, 8)

Wisdom from God, Source of Justice and Peace

As faith proves itself by acts, so does "the wisdom from above." It is one of those good things that we must intently ask of the Lord by unwaveringly fighting against the "passions that make war within [our] members" (Jas 3:16–4:3).

Wisdom is that virtue which makes us appreciate everything at its just value and, as a consequence, is a norm for daily conduct. But what James speaks of is Christian wisdom. It is opposed to "jealousy and selfish ambition" leading to "disorder and every foul practice." One does not need to be a Christian or a believer to say this. The sages of all times also say that righteousness is the foundation of peace, tolerance, understanding of others; that such a way of living is "full of . . . good fruits, without inconstancy or insincerity"; and finally, that "the fruit of righteousness is sown in peace for those who cultivate peace." In fact, Christians have never claimed to possess a monopoly on wisdom. On the contrary, they know that they have a great deal to learn from others, particularly from the teachings and lives of believers of other faiths. All are equally searching for wisdom and confess that it comes from God. Perhaps it is here that all great religions meet at the deepest level in a sincere and fruitful dialogue, in prayer.[3] The question is not to look for what constitutes Christians' originality, what sets them apart. What God and the world expect of them is that the message of the Beatitudes animate their lives and that they may share it with the greatest possible number:

> Blessed are the meek . . .
> Blessed are the merciful . . .
> Blessed are the peacemakers . . .
> (Matt 5:4-9)

> Happy the soul who attains this peace that I do not think anyone can reach except by loving God, himself and in himself. All lovable Lord Jesus, I entreat you to give me peace, but may it be always peace with you. Having it, I shall at the same time, inasmuch as it depends on me, as Paul says, "live at peace with all" (Rom 12:18). If I have peace with you, my Lord, I can sincerely say what the prophet said, "I lived in peace even with those who hated peace" (see, Ps 120:6-7).

> The whole world cannot rob of its peace the soul who really rests in God's love; no attack of evil ones, no insult of demons will disturb it, even so slightly, because genuine love of God in God is for the soul a rampart that no violence can break down. Christ's peace is a rock, an impregnable fortress.

> I may be assaulted from all sides, but if Christ is my refuge, I am certain not to succumb; if I hope in God, I shall be saved.[4]

The root of peace, as that of conflict and war, lies in the human heart, the arena where the fight takes place against greed, jealousy, and evil instincts that unceasingly threaten peace. Peaceful persons radiate peace. Communities in which tolerance and mercy, mutual understanding and unselfishness reign contribute, even though modestly, to showing that peace is possible and to fostering the desire for it.

> Never again war. Never again war! Peace, and only peace, must direct the destiny of all nations and all [humankind]. . . .

> As you know, peace is not built up simply by political means and the balance of power and interests. It is built in the realm of the spirit, in the world of ideas, in the arena of peaceful activity. You are the promoters of this great work. You are still only at the beginning of your endeavors, however. Will the world ever succeed in changing its individualistic and warlike mentality which up to now has woven itself into so great a part of its history? It is difficult to be a prophet, but it is easy to state that it must set out with determination toward the path of that new history, that peaceful history, that history truly and fully human, which God has promised to [people] of good will.[5]

Prayer is the means for adjusting one's will to God's; and God's will is for peace among humans. Prayer is true and deserves to be heard in the measure in which it expresses the effective desire for conversion, a conversion for which one humbly but intently asks for God's grace and the Holy Spirit. God always hears such a prayer (see Luke 11:13).

To Be Servants of All, Like the Son of Man

Mark's Gospel has kept the memory of Jesus' crossing Galilee, incognito as it were, accompanied by disciples, among whom the Twelve are the most prominent. During this journey, he devotes himself to teaching the little group of those who travel with him and, for the second time, he clearly announces his forthcoming passion (Mark 9:30-37).

" 'The Son of Man is to be handed over to men and they will kill him, and three days after his death he will rise.' But they did not understand the saying. . . ." The disciples cannot imagine that Jesus will really be put to death;[6] consequently, the prediction of his resurrection shortly afterwards[7] is quite mysterious. Under these circumstances, the disciples probably think that these words have a hidden meaning that escapes them. But "they were afraid to question him." After all, for the gospel tradition, the important fact is not so much that Jesus knew beforehand what was to happen, but that he gave to his freely accepted death a meaning we must uncover.

> Jesus is an authentic man, and the unalterable nobility of human beings is to be able, even to feel a duty, to freely project the design of their existence into a future they do not know. If they are believers, the future into which they propel and project themselves is God in his freedom and immensity. To deprive Jesus of this opportunity and to see him advancing toward a goal known beforehand, comes down to despoiling him of his human dignity.[8]

Jesus must realize that the disciples do not understand what he is talking about, but he does not broach the subject immediately. He waits until they are "inside the house" at Capernaum before asking them, "What were you arguing about on the way?"[9] They remain silent, ashamed that Jesus overheard their conversation when they were discussing "who was the greatest." It is necessary to straighten things out on the spot.[10] Jesus sits down, as a master engaged in teaching, and calls the Twelve to himself in order to give them an answer to the question they were debating. "If anyone wishes to be first, he shall be the last of all and the servant of all." This teaching reaches beyond the Twelve to the whole Church.[11] In the ecclesial community there is not—there must not be—any other distinction than that of "ministries," a word that means "services"

(1 Cor 12:1-30). Those who are entrusted with a function must consider themselves and be considered by others "servants of Christ," "stewards of the mysteries of God," of whom it is required "that they be found trustworthy" (1 Cor 4:1-2). This responsibility, to which it is praiseworthy to aspire (1 Tim 3:1), entails duties, but does not give any right to material advantages or honors.

> If I am afraid of what I am for you, I am consoled by what you are for me. For you, I am a bishop; with you I am a Christian. The former title is that of the dignity I am invested with; the latter reminds me of the grace I received; the former is rife with dangers for me; the latter spells salvation and safety for me. . . . Seeing that I am entrusted with such important, numerous, and varied duties, help me with your prayers and your obedience; ask that I be affected less by the honor of giving you orders than by the happiness of serving you.[12]

Then Jesus calls a child to him, embraces him, and says to his disciples, "Whoever receives one child such as this in my name, receives me; and whoever receives me, receives not me but the One who sent me." By identifying himself with a child, Jesus shows what he himself is, without pretense: the Lord and the Master certainly, but as one who serves (see John 13:12-16). The disciples must conduct themselves in the same manner and rejoice at being welcomed as lowly persons, not seeking to cut an impressive figure or to assert themselves. "To follow Christ by bending down to our brothers and sisters, to be extended by action, to cut oneself into a thousand pieces, to be everything to everyone, to undervalue nothing that pertains to Christ; to be thirsty for only one thing, to be concerned with only one thing when dealing with the One Christ; to want to be at the service of Christ when dealing with the multiple Christ."[13]

The revelation of Jesus' person and work progresses at the rhythm of his comings and goings from village to village. After Peter's confession of faith at Caesarea Philippi, Jesus now is walking toward Jerusalem and his passion, leading the small group of disciples who have remained faithful to him. He supplements and explains "in the house" what he has told them on the way. In order to be the first in the kingdom opened by the crucified Messiah, we must, like him, become the last and the servants of all.

Such a message runs counter to the statements, the laws, and the mores of the world. To proclaim such a message is to invite sarcasm and contempt. Moreover, to practice such a doctrine is to become a nuisance.

There is nothing surprising in the fact that people seek to suppress, or more generally to neutralize, those who want to promote a way of living so contrary to the principles guiding world and society. Soon they will be labeled ridiculous or obnoxious persons whose example, should many follow it, would lead to a disastrous destabilization of the established order and to a dangerous slowing of progress.

However, experience shows that a system of relationships based on rivalries, competition to the finish, an unbridled race for the top positions inexorably leads to a world without peace, in which life becomes impossible.

Gathered around Jesus "in the house," let us take the time to listen to and become imbued with his teaching.

> To your disciples,
> you deliver the secret:
> the Son of the living God
> walks toward death,
> the Master of the universe
> is the servant of all.
>
> *Lead us, Lord,*
> *on the way to eternity!*
>
> Human beings will kill the son of Man,
> but he will rise from the dead.
>
> Those who want to be first,
> let them be the last of all.
>
> Those who welcome a child in my name
> welcome me.[14]

Twenty-sixth Sunday

The Lord Knows His Own

Do Not Hinder the Spirit: It Blows Where It Wills
Among the stories that enliven the Exodus history, the one we read today is among the most colorful. Replete with meaning, it shows that religious structures in no way limit the initiatives of God's freedom. Far from being offended by divine liberality, as if it detracted from the right of certain privileged persons, we must, on the contrary, rejoice and wish that all may be granted the same graces (Num 11:25-29).

Already, during the wanderings of the people through the desert, relationships with God were structured by an organization adapted to the nomadic status of the people. There were no sanctuaries; but at each stop, Moses pitched, at some distance from the camp, a tent called the "meeting tent." It was in the meeting tent that God gave Moses his instructions. There, also, God granted audiences to Moses in order to hear his requests and answer his questions.[1] God's presence was manifested under the form of a cloud that came to rest before the door of the meeting tent. On one of these occasions, God told Moses to choose seventy elders as helpers in the task of leading the people. Moses was to gather them at the meeting tent for their investiture. So it was done, and God took "some of the spirit that was on Moses" to distribute it to his helpers.[2] And immediately they entered into a frenzy.[3]

Now two men—Eldad and Medad—who had not gone to the meeting tent, although they were part of the gathering of elders, began to prophesy in the camp where they had remained. When Joshua, "who from his youth had been Moses' aid," heard this, he said, "Moses, my lord, stop them," probably because he feared his master's authority would be jeopardized. Such words betray a practical misunderstanding of God's freedom, of the nature and finality of his gifts. These gifts are ways and means for being of service to the community, and not personal prerogatives jealously guarded. God does not impoverish anyone by spreading his gifts among many. "Would that all the people of the LORD were prophets! Would that the LORD might bestow his spirit on them all!" No sacred precincts can imprison God's spirit. Everyone must humbly ask to receive his or her share of it.

> In me, I who am afflicted, full of sadness,
> Because your grace has left me
> Because of sins unceasingly committed
> In my soul that willfully loves the Evil One,
>
> Deign to send the Spirit in abundance,
> Which, for giving, is not the poorer,
> In order to console my dejected soul
> In order to purify it from evil thoughts.
>
> Renew with me the Spirit of righteousness
> That never grows old
> In me, old temple of sin
> And dwelling of the Wayward One.
>
> Through the Spirit strengthen my freedom,
> And do not withdraw the Spirit from me,
> But may your Holy Spirit, full of kindness,
> Be my guide to heaven.[4]

This gift of the Spirit is lavishly poured out over the earth. No religious barrier can hold in check its diffusion. Only sin is an obstacle in its way. Whoever faithfully keeps God's law receives it in abundance.

> *The precepts of the Lord give joy to the heart.*
>
> The law of the LORD is perfect,
>   refreshing the soul;
> The decree of the LORD is trustworthy,
>   giving wisdom to the simple.
>
> ———
>
> The fear of the LORD is pure,
>   enduring forever.
> The ordinances of the LORD are true,
>   all of them just.
>
> ———
>
> Though your servant is careful of them,
>   very diligent in keeping them,
> Yet who can detect failings?
>   Cleanse me from my unknown faults!
> From wanton sin especially, restrain your servant;
>   let it not rule over me.
> Then shall I be blameless and innocent of serious sin.
> (Ps 19:8, 10, 12-14)

Woe to the Rich

The last excerpt from the Letter of James read this year is a particularly harsh diatribe addressed to the rich; it is far from being the only one of its kind in the Old and New Testaments.[5] Still, one is surprised to hear such language in a liturgical assembly. However, what we have here is authentic gospel preaching (Jas 5:1-6).

The attitude we adopt with regard to riches shows our world view in full light. If we are attached to earthly goods, we manifest our lack of belief in another world toward which this present life is tending—''You have stored up treasure for the last days.'' This is what Jesus taught: ''Though one may be rich, one's life does not consist of possessions. . . . Where your treasure is, there also will your heart be'' (Luke 12:15, 34).[6] It is folly to rely on riches that will be without value in the kingdom to come. ''Come now, you rich, weep and wail over your impending miseries. Your wealth has rotted away, your clothes have become moth-eaten, your gold and silver have corroded, and that corrosion will be a testimony against you; it will devour your flesh like a fire. You have stored up treasure for the last days.'' Preachers of the gospel speak to the rich in that manner because they are concerned about their salvation. They talk loud in an effort to wake them up, to make them aware of the deadly danger in which they find themselves and which they seem to overlook. The author of the letter does not curse them: he adjures them to be converted.

But must we not define what we mean by rich? Can we accept the notion that there are ''innocent'' riches? Let us recognize that such questions are a way of defusing the message and redirecting toward other people the warnings aimed at us. ''Thanks be to God, I am not really rich. In any case, I am not one of those wealthy persons about whom it can be said, 'Harvesters have harvested your fields and you did not pay them.' If I have some money, I did not steal it from anyone.'' Neither the Letter of James nor Christian tradition says that owning property is a crime. Nevertheless, the Fathers of the Church do not excuse those who rightfully own legitimate property from the admonitions of Scripture.

> If everyone kept only what is necessary for ordinary needs and left the surplus to the poor, wealth and poverty would be abolished. . . . Are you not a thief? The bread you store belongs to the hungry. The cloak kept in your closet belongs to those who lack clothing. The money you keep hidden away belongs to the needy. Thus you oppress as many people as you are in a position to help.[7]

But if we go from the individual to the collective plane, we cannot refute any of the statements of the Letter of James, not even when it is said, "In the time of slaughter you went on eating to your heart's content."[8] We know it today more than ever: while multitudes of men, women, and children are dying of hunger, certain people grow richer and richer, are sated with goods and waste them.

> The cry of the oppressed is Gods's voice. . . . The cry of the voiceless and the hopeless is God's voice. . . . The protest of the poor is God's voice. . . . And the voice of the countries who are victims of these injustices is God's voice.[9]

The text from the Letter of James, which at first sight could seem out of place in a liturgical celebration, finally proves to be extraordinarily relevant. It reminds Christians that riches are always stained by sin and that they must, by reason of their faith, be in the front line of the battle against hunger and poverty born of the search for pleasure and luxury denounced in the Letter of James.

> "The poor you will always have with you" (Mark 14:7). Since this abysmal statement, no human being has been able to say what Poverty is. Saints who have wed her out of love and have had many children by her, affirm that it is infinitely lovable. Those who do not want her as a partner sometimes die of dread and despair under her kiss and the multitude goes "from womb to tomb" without knowing what to think of this monster. When the chaos of this fallen world will have been disentangled, when stars will seek for bread, and when only the most discredited mud will be allowed to reflect splendor; when it will be known that nothing was in its proper place and that the reasonable species lived only on riddles and appearances, then perhaps the torments of the poor will reveal the poverty of soul of millionaires, which in the mysterious roster of the apportionment of universal solidarity is the spiritual equivalent of their tattered clothes.[10]

Everything Will Be Justly Rewarded, but Beware of Scandal

The teachings of Jesus that Mark has gathered together after the second prediction of the passion, during the march toward Jerusalem, deal with the disciples' behavior in the Christian community. They constitute a catechetical ensemble whose diverse elements are connected together more by association of ideas, words even, than by logic, at least as we understand it today. This Sunday's excerpt is made up of two strongly contrasting parts. In the first one, Jesus shows great tolerance toward all those who, even though not belonging to the group of his disciples, bring some relief to others' lot. In the second part, he shows cutting severity toward those who cause scandal, and he enjoins upon his disciples to pitilessly eradicate in themselves everything that can lead them to sin (Mark 9:38-43, 45, 47-48).

"Teacher, we saw someone driving out demons in your name, and we tried to prevent him because he does not follow us." It is John who speaks in this way, protective as he is of Jesus' authority and of the authority of those Jesus has chosen by giving them the power of healing the sick and delivering those possessed by evil spirits (see Mark 6:7-13).[11] The intention is certainly good, but it betrays a narrow-mindedness that Jesus rejects.[12] "Do not prevent him. There is no one who performs a mighty deed in my name who can at the same time speak ill of me."[13] Who was this man? To what group did he belong? Whose disciple was he? No matter—the lesson is obvious: we must neither monopolize the right to do good nor belittle the good others do, although they may not belong to the fold.

> No condemnation must be brought to bear a priori upon any human being. It happens that we hear words from the Gospel quoted by people who are not assiduous churchgoers or even are church-bashers. This sometimes irritates us. As a result, they accuse us of monopolizing the Christian message. And they are right.
>
> A work of discernment is in order. Many of those who are inspired by the Gospel, in one domain or another, without adhering to the Catholic creed, act with good will and sincerity. We know people who have found in Jesus' conduct new incentives to increase their hunger and thirst after justice. We may suffer, of course, because they do not share our certitudes; however, let us not require of them their entrance ticket or an up-to-date passport. "There are," wrote St. Augustine, "those who seem outside the sheepfold yet are inside it, and those others who seem inside and are outside."[14]

All who do good must be recognized as brothers and sisters, but we must be careful to respect their freedom and their consciences. We do not have to put them on a Christian honor roll they do not ask for or lionize them so that they can make us look better. "Anyone who gives you a cup of water to drink because you belong to Christ, amen, I say to you, will surely not lose his reward." But it is for the Lord to reveal to them the value of the least gesture of a brother or sister. On that day, they will be able to hear Christ say to them, without any mental reservation, "For I was hungry and you gave me food, I was thirsty and you gave me drink, a stranger and you welcomed me, naked and you clothed me, ill and you cared for me, in prison and you visited me" (Matt 25:35-40). Rather than evincing touchiness, disciples must, for their part, generously serve whoever needs their help. For they know that any omission will be counted against them by the just Judge (see Matt 25:41-46).

> It is crucial
> To be alive.
>
> It is crucial
> That my face be the threshold and dial
> That every look, every ray show the time on it
> That the day have open house in my dwelling
> That my house be an oasis for the passerby
>
> It is crucial
> That I offer fresh bread with the salt of old age
> That I may never tire of sharing
> That the first passerby sit down at table to eat
> Then without paying continue on the way
>
> It is crucial
> To give everything without expecting anything even from God
> To be here for the homeless and the godless
>
> It is crucial
> To be alive.[15]

The infinite thankfulness that the Lord will show to anyone who will have given even a glass of water to one of those who belong to him allows us to understand his extreme severity toward those who would cause even one of his own to fall: they will have no excuse. There is no light matter, no venial sin in this domain: an apparently trivial obstacle can cause a weak person to fall gravely, mortally. This way of acting is the more unforgivable because it runs counter to the duty of charity, whose delicacy must be tailored to the weakness of the "little ones." We must renounce even our rights,[16] rather than risk causing even one person to fall.

> He had just spoken of the little ones who believe in him; and it is as if he suddenly saw in his mind's eyes the horrendous movie of the trampling of the little ones throughout the centuries by those who deem themselves wise, strong, clever, or who simply crush without noticing anything. For Jesus, *this* is sin. . . .
>
> How many little ones are mocked, scorned nearby, without our paying any attention to it?[17]

Then Jesus turns to each of his disciples: "If your hand, your foot, your eye cause you to sin, cut them off, gouge it out. It is better to enter life eternal maimed, lame, half-blind than to be thrown with your two hands, your two feet, your two eyes into Gehenna, where 'their worm does not die, and the fire is not quenched.' ''[18] Physical mutilations do not free us from malice and evil desires that come from the heart and lead to all sins (see Mark 7:21-23).[19] These are the things to be pitilessly eradicated, deep amputations more painful than the loss of a limb or an eye.

The meekness of Jesus and his sternness, his open-mindedness and the rigor of his demands are not opposed to one another. It is always one and the same Lord who speaks. The coherence of his teaching appears when we look at him, him whose zeal for the good and whose love for his own cannot admit any sort of compromise.

> "If you remain in my word . . . you will know the truth, and the truth will set you free" (John 8:31), he said. I believe this in the innermost part of myself. He who said, "Let your 'Yes' mean 'Yes,' and your 'No' mean 'No' " (Matt 5:37), has certainly not used ambiguous and equivocal language; he himself did not have multiple and contradictory personalities; there was not in him at the same time Jesus according to Bunuel and another Jesus according to Pasolini, a hippie Jesus and an inquisitor Jesus. Light gets fractured in our prisms and glass trinkets, not in its source. There were not two gospels taught by Christ: on the one hand, an easygoing, very human, somewhat gypsy-like gospel welling up in moments of smile and mildness; and on the other hand, a rigorist, fanatical teaching coming forth in times of anger and exasperation.[20]

It is a people of prophets God wished to gather through Christ, a people of men and women who by word and action announce the world to come, the laws of which are not those of the present world, slave to all sorts of lusts. These men and women have the Beatitudes and the Sermon on the Mount for their charter. They know that in these resides the true freedom of God's children. But their ideal is not a certain idea of human nature: it is a human being—Jesus, the Good News.[21] Others, who do not share their faith, also work at building a new world, purified from evil and injustice. The Spirit blows where it wills. May it make prophets out of more and more men and women!

> Free like the wind,
> the Spirit blows, unpredictable.
> From your cenacles,
> it carries the name of Jesus Christ.
> Do not quench the fire just ignited:
> it must set the world aflame!
>
> *Lord, call forth prophets!*

I shall make your sons and daughters speak,
The old will have dreams
and the young visions.

On the poor and humiliated
I am going to pour out my Spirit.

If you are insulted for the name of Christ, rejoice:
on you rests the Spirit of glory.[22]

Who is Jesus Christ? To this question, put to us from the beginning of Mark's Gospel, we are invited to give a personal answer, not only in words but also in our way of living. To recognize who Jesus Christ is, is to follow him, to walk with him, carrying his cross, on the path that his pasch opened; it is being open to losing our life in order to save it; it is to be the servant of all; it is to prefer nothing to the love of Christ. This is the narrow way, the royal way of an exodus where the luminous cloud guides the redeemed people, commissioned to announce to the world the good news from which no one is excluded.

Christ became our paschal sacrifice.
In him a new age has dawned,
the long reign of sin is ended,
a broken world has been renewed,
and man is once again made whole.[23]

Christ our Pasch has been sacrificed:
by destroying a fallen world,
he made a new creation;
from him we now have
the life he possesses in fullness.

The Twenty-seventh and Twenty-eighth Sunday in Ordinary Time

The Gospel readings for the Twenty-seventh and Twenty-eighth Sunday in Ordinary Time, Year B, occur, in Mark's Gospel, between the second and third predictions of the passion (Mark 9:30-32; 10:33-34). Accompanied by his disciples, having started on the way to Jerusalem, the Lord resolutely moves on. They are following—"afraid" (Mark 10:32). Between these two predictions, according to Mark, some Pharisees approach Jesus: "Is it lawful for a husband to divorce his wife?" Indeed, the Law had foreseen such a possibility and had prescribed the procedure to follow (see Deut 24:1-4). Jesus does not deny this. He does not enter into the casuistry of the manner to use—or abuse—this concession.[1] He refers his questioners to the original intention of God when he created man and woman. Back at "the house," the disciples ask him about it again. Jesus takes this opportunity to say that one cannot contravene God's intention in this matter without committing a grave sin. Then people bring him children for him to touch. He embraces and blesses them, placing his hands on them; for he sees in them an image of the disciple who welcomes the kingdom without pride or ulterior motive (Mark 10:2-16—Twenty-seventh Sunday).

From the Twenty-seventh Sunday to the Thirty-third, we read excerpts from the Letter to the Hebrews, one of the longest in the New Testament.[2] This piece of writing has the earmarks of a treatise rather than a letter. It raises a certain number of problems debated by exegetes:[3] its author unknown,[4] its date uncertain,[5] its addressees unmentioned.[6] It disconcerts modern readers by its frequent allusions to the Temple sacrifices and by its use of a subtle symbolism to interpret ancient texts and events in order to suggest connections between earthly and heavenly realities, history and eternity. But if we overcome this feeling disorientation here, we find ourselves captivated by the doctrinal and spiritual wealth of this treatise that has not really become obsolete; the seven excerpts selected by the Sunday Lectionary give a good sampling of this letter.

The structure of this letter, in which doctrinal developments and exhortations unceasingly intermingle, is too complex to be given a definitive outline. But at least we can discern four main lines of reflection. The Son through whom "God spoke" is above all creatures: we must therefore firmly cling to his teaching, a source of salvation (chs. 1 and 2). He is the true, unique, faithful, and compassionate high priest.

> Oh, that today you would hear his voice:
> Harden not your hearts. . . (chs. 3–10).

Then, the author eulogizes faith (chs. 11 and 12). Finally, comes a series of exhortations concerning fraternal love, marriage, poverty, docility to leaders, rejection of greed and "strange teaching[s]" (ch. 13).

To start with, we read an excerpt from the first part (Heb 2:9-11—Twenty-seventh Sunday); then, from the Twenty-eighth Sunday on, six texts taken from the second part (Heb 4:12-13; 4:14-16; 5:1-6; 7:23-28; 9:24-28; 10:11-14, 18).[7]

These second readings have no connection with the other two readings for each Sunday. But they were chosen because of the light they shed on the mystery of Christ and salvation celebrated by the liturgy.

Twenty-seventh Sunday

Faithfulness of the Covenant of God and Spouses

In the Beginning, God Made Them Male and Female

The first pages of the Book of Genesis were written by sages at the end of long meditations on the origins of the universe and of humankind, on life, evil and death—all the great questions humans keep asking themselves. To set down the outcome of their reflections, they had recourse to a literary genre that was both popular and sophisticated. Indeed, while they are accessible to even the simplest people, these narratives are in no way naive. These inspired sages were believers, endowed with an already long experience of the initiatives and solicitude of God toward his own. Thus they learned that all that happens in the world and history is willed or permitted by this personal and transcendent God, who made himself known to humanity precisely by the interventions of his sovereign power. The ultimate explanation of the world and humankind is here. Everything happened because the creator "in the beginning" so willed it. Consequently, in spite of all appearances, nothing is the result of chance or accident.[1] The sages then pondered the mystery of man and woman and the deep-seated impulse that attracts them to each other. This, too, has been willed by God (Gen 2:18-24).

The Book of Genesis relates two accounts of creation. The text read today belongs to the older tradition (Gen 2:5-24).[2] Much shorter and less elaborate than the other, this account immediately addresses the question of the origin of humankind. "Then the LORD God formed man from the dust of the ground, and breathed into his nostrils the breath of life; and the man became a living being."[3] The emphasis is on the fact that the creation of humans was anterior to the appearance of any other form of life. Only afterwards, according to this tradition, did God plant the garden in which he placed him who was to till it and care for it. He was alone, and in spite of the splendor of the domain, irrigated by a great river dividing into four branches, and trees bearing excellent fruit (see 2:8-17), this solitude was not good for him. God therefore decided to create "a suitable partner for him." Then, "the LORD God formed out of the ground various wild animals and various birds of the air, and he brought them to the man to see what he would call them." The "wild animals and various birds of the air" are made of the same matter as humans, but God does not breathe into them the same "breath of life." He has them march past the man, who names each of them. Majestic in its simplicity, the scene expresses in a highly picturesque and vivid way that God himself, who created heaven and earth, has given to the human race mastery over all the living beings populating earth and sky. But among all these living beings that he observes, the man finds no "suitable partner." By discovering the world around him, its riches, its abundance of life, the man is faced with the realization that he is a creature apart, a living being of a kind other than the innumerable living beings that populate sky and earth. An arresting scene is sufficient for the author of the narrative to evoke in the man the emergence of the consciousness of his singularity, of the transcendent otherness of his being—in a word, of his humanity. He enjoys the power to define all other living beings, to call them by names of his own making. But among them, none is able in its turn to name him, to act as someone with whom he can have dialogue on an equal footing, saying "You and I." Lacking such a suitable interlocutor, he would not really be made in the image of God.

> Through its "vertical" dimension, personal existence plunges into God's fullness. But in himself our God is not solitude. The ocean of his essence vibrates with an infinite "movement of love." The abyss is not undifferentiated darkness; a reciprocity, an exchange is in him, the other is in him, and the overcoming of duality in the communion of the uni-Trinity. . . .
>
> This reciprocity of the singular and the plural is written in the Bible from the first chapter of Genesis. . . .
>
> The mystery of the singular and the plural in humans mirrors the mystery of the singular and plural in God.[4]

From the beginning, the creator had said, "I will make a suitable partner for him." Therefore, it is not man who caused God to create woman. Everything indicates rather that God had awakened man only to make him aware of his need for another being with whom he would form a "we," without absorbing this other being. The "deep sleep," a sort of profound lethargy, would in some way bring man to the previous stage in which, fashioned "out of the clay of the ground" and having become "a living being" (2:7), he had not yet opened his eyes on the world.[5] In any case, again acting without witness—the act of creation always escapes detection; it is accomplished outside of time—God, with man's rib rather than clay, "[builds] it up into a woman" and, like a father at a wedding, presents her to the man who, waking from his "deep sleep" and recalling the multitude of beings he had previously seen, cries out in wonder, "This one, at last, is bone of my bones / and flesh of my flesh"; and he gives her a name that expresses this admirable similarity.[6] Each account emphasizes in its own way the equal dignity of man and woman whom God made, from the beginning, as perfectly matched partners.[7]

The narrative of the creation of woman could have stopped here. But the writer added a conclusion—"That is why"—that reveals the nature of his reflection on the mystery of man and woman: Where does the powerful and primordial attraction between the sexes come from, this tendency that leads man to break all other bonds—leave his father and mother—to cling to the woman in whom he recognizes what corresponds to himself? This, too, comes from God; because they derive their origin from one single flesh, man and woman are impelled by their nature to recover their original unity. This narrative attests to a remarkably lofty vision of the human couple and sexuality. It is the search for communion that drives man and woman toward union, and not the impulse of a carnal, uncontrollable, and blind instinct.

> A man and a woman make a world
> As soon as they are one flesh together.
> From the time humanity exists, there is only one encounter,
> One horizon, one undivided gaze,
> One modesty, one underlying love,
> One holy ring of silence—life.
> When we see them kneaded in each other,
> Where is, pride says, the leaven of their dough?
> But love is often so humble and so discreet
> That it ignores itself and seems to get lost in the depths of being,
> The only birth whence death can make it rise
> Held in a furtive tear on the eyelashes.[8]

It is a masculine-feminine world, and not a uniquely masculine world that God has created. From the beginning, he has placed woman at the man's side, like to him, of the same nature, from the same flesh, as the Bible says in a more concrete and expressive manner. To break this unity, to harm this complementarity, to upset this dynamic and fecund balance introduces into God's work a grave disorder, because it generates endless conflicts, painful competition for supremacy, perturbations of all kinds.[9]

This text does not explicitly teach monogamy and the indissoluble character of the union between man and woman. The history of the patriarchs proves that the practice of having more than one wife was current.[10]

Polygamy will increase at the time of the kings, who will have numerous wives, as did other powerful and rich men of the Middle East.[11] It is the more remarkable, then, to see the origin of humankind depicted as a monogamous couple. We must add that the ideal of a monogamous society extolled by the wisdom books[12] is congruent with the prophetic representation of Israel as the one bride chosen by God.[13] The authors of the first chapters of the Book of Genesis were sages imbued with this tradition. They understood that the grandeur of the universe and humankind, the guarantee of their future and happiness were found in the blessing of God, who made all things beautiful and good.

May the Lord bless us all the days of our lives.

Happy are you who fear the LORD,
   who walk in his ways!
For you shall eat the fruit of your handiwork;
   happy shall you be, and favored.
Your wife shall be like a fruitful vine
   in the recesses of your home;
Your children like olive plants
   around your table.
Behold, thus is the man blessed
   who fears the LORD.
The LORD bless you from Zion:
   may you see the prosperity of Jerusalem
   all the days of your life;
May you see your children's children.
   Peace be upon Israel!
(Ps 128)

The Glory of the Redeemer

The Letter to the Hebrews is not easy reading for a modern mind[14] and requires preparation with the use of a good introduction.[15] But the effort is soon rewarded. For we have here a remarkable treatise on the work of redemption wrought by Christ and of the mediation that he does not cease to exercise for the benefit of those he redeemed. One also discovers that this long letter shows a rare understanding of the difficulties of Christian existence and of the temptations that beset it. To those threatened by discouragement and disconcerted by difficulties, the author does not direct vaguely moralizing speeches; he exhorts them to deepen their faith in the Lord who was and remains, before his Father, in solidarity with his brothers and sisters. The first of the seven excerpts selected for this and the following six Sundays sets the tone (Heb 2:9-11).

Hebrews begins with a vibrant hymn to Christ. "The very imprint of his being," the Son of God has been sent "in these last days."

> When he had accomplished purification from sins,
> he took his seat at the right hand of the Majesty on high,
> as far superior to the angels
> as the name he has inherited is more excellent than theirs.
> (Heb 1:3-4)[16]

Christ occupies an unequaled position in relation to God, not only because he is his Son, but also because he has accepted to see himself "for a little while lower than the angels." Moreover, he is "crowned with glory and honor because he suffered death." He has thus made possible the fulfillment of the plan of God, who wanted to "[bring] many children to glory." By his acceptance to personally experience death, in obedience to his Father, he has reversed the meaning of death. The terrible consequence of Adam's disobedience has become "by the grace of God" the cause of salvation for all. "He, for whom and through whom all things exist" has directly implicated himself in this work of redemption. He allowed his Son to become of the same race as human sinners in order to save them. The broken relationship between God and humankind is thus marvelously restored, thanks to the Son of God made human being, by the initiative of the offended one. From all eternity united with the Father in an indissoluble way, from now on one with humans through his incarnation and his experience of death, Christ has bridged the impassable abyss between heaven and earth.

> "God is love" (1 John 4:8). In order to introduce us into his divine life, he creates the world over which humans reign. Intelligent and created in God's image, they will be, in their own names and in those of all creatures, the adorers of the Infinite Being. But Adam does not want any other sovereign than himself: this is sin. The relationship is broken. The original order is destroyed. Who will reestablish the bonds with the Creator? Humans are incapable of doing so. But God, who has magnificently created everything, wants, in his mercy, to restore everything still more marvelously. He decides to send his Son to humans as pontiff, *pontifex*, which has often been rendered "bridge builder." He will be their ferryman, the passage between God and humankind. Christ himself explicitly acknowledges this, "*Ego sum via*—I am the way" (John 14:6). He is the only means, that is, the unique mediator between creation and its creator, and, therefore, the only incarnation. St. Augustine says it clearly, "Inasmuch as he is born

of the Father, [Christ] is God, not a priest. He is a priest because of the flesh he has assumed, the victim he has received from us."[17]

What God Has Joined Together, No One Must Separate

This Sunday's Gospel relates Jesus' position on divorce and his reaction one day when the disciples wanted to keep away children brought to him.[18] First, here is what he said on the indissoluble character of marriage (Mark 10:2-12).

The occasion was a question put by a group of Pharisees who approached him, asking, "Is it lawful for a husband to divorce his wife?" "They were testing him," the evangelist adds. We have here, indeed, one of these trap-questions we still ask today of someone we want to embarrass. We formulate it as if it were possible to answer yes or no; whereas, it is obviously complex. Moreover, two schools were at odds on this topic. One, the stricter, allowed recourse to divorce only for a grave reason; but according to the Book of Deuteronomy (24:1), divorce was apparently acceptable when, for instance, the wife no longer pleased her husband. Under these conditions, any answer Jesus could make would set him in opposition to one party or the other. Moreover, Jesus had recently arrived in Judea (see Mark 10:1), a region under Herod's jurisdiction. Remember that Herod had thrown John the Baptist into prison, ultimately beheading him, because he had reproached Herod for divorcing his wife and living with the wife of his brother Philip (see Mark 6:17-29). Here, too, Jesus could fall into a trap. Either he would disavow John the Baptist, whom the people venerated, or he would be a target for Herod's anger and the terrible Herodias' vindictiveness.

Jesus does not allow himself to be enmeshed in this net. He asks his questioners what they themselves think, why and at what level they are asking the question. This is not a clever ploy to evade a bad situation, but rather an honest reflex, so to speak. Without this preliminary clarification, the dialogue would be ambiguous, unclear. Knowing that he is dealing with lawyers and not with persons submitting an actual case to him, he asks, "What did Moses command you?" They answer unhesitatingly, "Moses permitted [the husband] to write a bill of divorce and dismiss her." This answer correctly expresses the content of the Law that, indeed, allowed a man to send his wife away if he found in her a hidden blemish.[19]

This legislation concerns a woman's status and rights in society. In Middle Eastern and Greek societies of that time, she was often treated as an inferior being; Aristotle (ca. 384-322 B.C.) even considers her a "failed man.''[20] The account of creation says that on a par with man, woman is an image of God. In practice, she had a subordinate position (see Gen 3:16) despite the esteem she enjoyed through becoming a mother.[21] We cannot forget, either, that certain women were honored as prophets.[22] But marriage was a business settled by men: the young girl's father and he to whom she was destined. Finally, adultery designated female misconduct or extraconjugal relations of a man with a married woman. In other words, the man was guilty only if he violated another man's rights; whereas, the wife was obliged to be faithful to her husband: what was punishable was an offense against a man's rights, not against a woman's.[23] However, the bill of divorce gave the dismissed wife the right to enter into another marriage. Such was the juridical and social context in which the question of the legitimacy of divorce was posed. To accept a discussion at this level would have dragged Jesus down into an interminable debate that was then going on between lawyers, which was not the object of his mission—he had come to reveal God's will.

"Because of the hardness of your hearts he wrote you this commandment. But from the beginning of creation, 'God made them male and female. For this reason a man shall leave his father and mother [and be joined to his wife].' '' Jesus suggests that divorce corresponds to a stage of human development marked by the weakness resulting from sin. In Jesus' time, divorce was routinely practiced. But, especially when followed by a second marriage, it was already forbidden, at least in certain milieux.[24] This development is evolving in the right direction, says Jesus. With the coming of messianic times, people must resolutely go back to the primordial purity of marriage and to the creator's intention: "Therefore what God has joined together, no human being must separate."

Such a clear-cut affirmation and such a radical condemnation of divorce struck the disciples. "In the house," they cannot help asking Jesus about what he has just said. And Jesus answers them, "Whoever divorces his wife and marries another commits adultery against her; and if she divorces her husband and marries another, she commits adultery.''[25] These words could not be clearer, and they say that we must strictly conform to the initial intention and will of God. At the same time, Jesus gives the exact interpretation of what the Book of Genesis says: man and woman were created equal by God with rigorously the same duties toward each other. No longer is it possible to consider only the unfaithful woman as guilty of adultery against her husband. The latter commits the same sin if he dismisses his wife in order to marry another. By the same token, marriage is given back all its dignity—its sacred character—as a divine institution.[26]

> Such is the response that Christ made in the past to the Pharisees. Today, listen to me, you merchants of marriage, who change wives as you change cloaks; you who build homes as flimsy as stands at a fair; you who marry wealth and traffick in wives; you who, at the least grievance, write a bill of divorce; you, in a word, who, still alive, leave widows. Be persuaded that only death and adultery can break marriage. A true and legitimate union is neither an encounter with a prostitute nor a fleeting pleasure. Marriage, my brothers, joins bodies and souls; it mingles two spirits and unites two bodies. How can you be separated without torment from the one you have knitted into your life not as a casual maid, but as a sister, as a wife? Sister, according to creation and origins. Both of you are made of the same earth, the same clay. Wife, through the conjugal bond and the marriage contract. What knot are you about to sever, you who are bound by nature and by law? How could you dare to betray the oath pronounced on your wedding day?[27]

The Kingdom of God and Children

The second part of this Sunday's Gospel relates an incident full of meaning. People bring children to Jesus so that he may touch them. The disciples brusquely push them aside. Jesus grows angry: "Let the children come to me; do not prevent them, for the kingdom of God belongs to such as these" (Mark 10:13-16).

This scene has often been depicted in ways that are sometimes insipid, other times silly. They do not convey the real teaching the situation embodies. Jesus becomes "indignant" because his disciples' attitude betrays a grave misunderstanding of the kingdom of God. Its door is open to all, especially to the little ones who seek it without guile, to the poor who have nothing to boast of, to those who resemble the children brought to Jesus. "Do not prevent them."[28] You are mistaken if you think your "adult" wisdom or your knowledge gives you rights! Rather, be thankful to the Father. "Although you have hidden these things from the wise and learned you have revealed them to the childlike."[29]

> If Christ sees as profound the kinship between the child, the kingdom, and baptismal faith, it is not only because he thinks that the child's qualities are the qualities of faith but because he himself has experienced this child-like spirit more deeply throughout his life. If I must now say what quality characterizes this childlike spirit, I would willingly plead for naïveté according to the Gospel.
>
> Make no mistake: the naïveté according to the Gospel has nothing in common with the foolishness of childish people lacking awareness. It is the extra-

lucidity of eyes that see farther then the immediate realism of so many persons, myopic in their view of life, who reduce the reality of humankind to its living conditions or who imagine they know life because they have a knack for business or politics.

Naïveté is the other name for hope when Christians, sharing all human hopes and fighting to realize a possible world, do not trust in the logic of the sages, but in that wisdom of which Paul says, "God chose the foolish of the world to shame the wise" (1 Cor 1:27). Naïveté, which is regarded as a defect by clever people, becomes a challenge for Christians. A challenge to the will-to-power before which Christ did not bow, because he sacrificed himself on the Cross.[30]

God created man and woman in his image in order to have a multitude of children to lead to glory. Sin did not cause the creator to renounce fulfillment of this plan. "In these last days, he spoke to us through a son, whom he made heir of all things" (Heb 1:2). Jesus, of the same race as his human brothers and sisters, is now " 'crowned with glory and honor' because he suffered death," a death freely accepted for the salvation of all (Second Reading). The Eucharist is the sacrament of this new and eternal covenant, sealed by the blood of Christ "the son of Adam, the son of God" (Luke 3:38). Firstborn of a humanity recreated by God in justice and truth.

Jesus came to announce to the world the good news and to show by his words and actions the way to follow in order to have a share, with him, in the heritage of children, by fulfilling, like him, God's will. New Moses, he has shed new light on the old Law that he freed from the excess weight of human traditions and from the heaviness of "the letter [that] brings death" in order to take it back to its original purity according to "the Spirit [that] gives life" (2 Cor 3:6). Thus, Jesus spoke of marriage as God instituted it "from the beginning." It cannot be reduced to a contract negotiated between a man and a woman that they can break whenever one or the other wants to. God is implicated in marriage, which refers to the mystery of the covenant concluded "from the beginning" between the creator and humanity and renewed by Christ.[31] The love that impels a man and woman to be united into one being is the reflection of the indefectible love of God for his creatures: spouses have received through grace the mission of witnessing to this love by living in faithfulness to their mutual commitment, as God remains faithful to those he has chosen through love. This is a vocation that the world finds hard to recognize and understand. To assume such a vocation for a lifetime entails all sorts of difficulties, which many married persons do not succeed in overcoming. Hence, these marriages are so often broken apart today, painful failures of a planned life together that was promised before God and blessed by him.

God proposes this ideal of marriage to weak human beings. But he places his trust in men and women created in his image and strengthened by the help of his grace, a trust inspired by his infinite love as a Father.

> Truly it is good
> that the trust and the joy of a wedding
> flow back from us toward you,
> Father of all covenants.
>
> For the life you give to everyone
> and the body whose keepers we are,
> for every communion possible in this world
> and every hope of happiness . . .
> we want to give you thanks
> and acknowledge that we come from you
> through Jesus, the Christ, our Lord.
>
> It is in him,
> the eternal Son of your tenderness,
> that you have concluded with humanity
> the Covenant of your first love.
> It is through him,
> Son of Man born in the flesh,
> that you save human loves
> by making them flow back into their source.
> It is in him,
> faithful spouse of your Church,
> that you change our hearts of stone
> and enable them to love as you love.[32]

Twenty-eighth Sunday

Because of Christ and the Gospel

Prefer the Gift of Wisdom Above All Else

The list of goods commonly considered useful or necessary to happiness is interminable: from health to a long and peaceful life, from means sufficient to easily satisfy daily needs to wealth guaranteeing the future, from freedom to a sharing in power itself. And how many more things besides? In consumer societies the list is constantly growing and there is no end in sight. The riches and lifestyles of the "haves" arouse envy and the conviction that one is in need when one does not have what others have in plenty.[1] And here, at the end of a long reflection,[2] the author of the Book of Wisdom asserts that nothing is comparable to Wisdom, the gift to be preferred above all other goods (7:7-11).

Here is a man who lives in a world flourishing economically and intellectually.[3] He belôngs to a Jewish community that plays an important role in the prosperity of a city founded on a system of artisans—weavers, papermakers, goldsmiths, potters—and trade. In this center of Hellenistic culture, Jewish thought thrived. Sages pondered the question of its originality and of its possible contribution to the ideological debates fostered by a concentration of schools, philosophers, and scientists.[4] Such a confrontation caused courageous but delicate questioning on the part of the Jews. The literate believers reread the Scriptures, reflecting on the pertinence of their teachings to their present circumstances and on the way of transmitting them to the people of their time.[5] In sum, they found themselves in a situation not unlike ours, confronted by challenges similar to those that modern cultures pose for today's Christians.[6]

The author of the Book of Wisdom is one of these believers who ask questions. The assiduous meditation on Scripture and a long reflection on experience have led him to this conviction: it is Wisdom that guides the world in the right direction, that direction corresponding to the creator's intention that is revealed by contemplating the universe, the way God acts since the beginning, and the Law. He then remembers what was related about the great Solomon. God appeared to him in a dream and said, "Ask something of me and I will give it to you." Without hesitation, the king answered, "Give me . . . wisdom."[7] Here is the supreme good. Compared to her, riches are worth nothing, precious stones do not deserve a glance,

> because all gold, in view of her, is a little sand,
>   and before her, silver is to be accounted mire.[8]

She is even preferable to health, beauty, light. For all these goods are transient and are not worth the effort made to secure them. Only Wisdom, which does not perish, deserves that one toil to obtain her.

> The pearl of great price lies deeply hidden.
> Like the pearl divers, O my soul, dive
> Dive deep!
> Dive deeper and search!
> Perhaps you will not find anything the first time?
>
> As a pearl diver, O my soul,
> Without tiring, persist and persist further,
> Dive deep, even deeper,
> And seek!
>
> Those who do not know the secret
> Will laugh at you,
> And you will be saddened;
> But do not lose heart
> Pearl diver, O my soul!
>
> The pearl of great price is hidden there,
> hidden at the very bottom.
> Faith will help you find the treasure,
> And it will allow what was hidden
> to be at last revealed.
>
> Dive deep, dive still deeper,
> Like a pearl diver, O my soul,
> And seek, seek without tiring![9]

If humans must ardently desire her and prefer her to other goods, Wisdom, as described by the biblical author, is not within human grasp; she is a gift from God for which we must pray: Solomon's example shows this.[10] Wisdom is an attribute of God. God himself. Nothing created could be the object of such a desire, such a love; nothing could allow us to share in all goods.[11]

> Oh, what is this reality hidden from all created essence?
> What is this intelligible light nobody sees

and what are these abundant riches that no one in the world
has ever been able to discover or totally possess?
It cannot be seized by anyone, the world cannot contain it.
It is supremely lovable, more than the whole world;
it is as desirable, as God is above
the visible things which he has established.

———

I have a share in the light, and also in the glory,
and my face is radiant like that of my beloved,
and all my limbs become bearers of light.
Then I finally become fairer than those who are fair,
richer than the rich and more powerful than all powerful ones;
I am powerful, and greater than kings,
and far more precious than all that is visible,
more precious not only than the earth or humanity, but than the heavens
and all the angels of heaven, for I possess the Creator of the whole universe
to whom are due glory and honor, now and forever. Amen.[12]

This wisdom is the spirit of discernment, understanding of the heart,
surety of judgment that shows with certainty what is good and what is
evil.[13] It particularly characterizes the leaders of his people to whom God
had given his Spirit and the prophets.[14] It would be given in overabundance to the Messiah in order that many might benefit by it. One day,
Jesus exulted with joy upon seeing the wisdom shown by the little ones
(see Matt 11:25-26), and he said that the Father would give the Holy Spirit
to those who asked for it (see Luke 11:13).

Fill us with your love, O Lord, and we will
sing for joy!

Teach us to number our days aright,
  that we may gain wisdom of heart.
Return, O Lord! How long?
  Have pity on your servants!
Fill us at daybreak with your kindness,
  that we may shout for joy and gladness all our days.
Make us glad, for the days when you afflicted us,
  for the years when we saw evil.
Let your work be seen by your servants
  and your glory by their children;
And may the gracious care of the Lord our God be ours;
  prosper the work of our hands for us!
  [Prosper the work of our hands!]
(Ps 90:12-17)

"The Word of God Is Living"

From the beginning, God has spoken to humankind "in times past in
. . . various ways . . . through the prophets; in these last days, he spoke
to us through a son whom he made heir of all things and through whom
he created the universe" (Heb 1:1-2).[15] The prophets' words, the meditations of the inspired sages who pondered them, the apostolic preaching and catecheses of those selected by the Lord, have been carefully set
down in writing under the movement of the Holy Spirit, who guarantees the truth and credibility of the holy Scriptures faithfully transmitted
from generation to generation by tradition.[16] The Bible contains the whole
of Scripture.[17] But we must not forget that Scripture is only what sup-
ports the living word (Heb 4:12-13).[18]

This word is living because it comes from the living God. That is why
it is "effective" and penetrates everywhere "between soul and spirit"
often painfully as a "two-edged sword"—a scalpel. It is impossible to
evade it, even if one refuses to listen. What God said once remains eternally. One cannot silence him nor nullify any of his words.

> Yes, this Word is living, living in the heart of the Father, in the mouths
> of those who proclaim it, in the hearts of those who believe and love. . . .
> When God's words are heard, they pierce the believers' hearts as the sharp
> arrows of the warrior (see Ps 120:4). They penetrate and remain in the hearts'
> innermost depths. This Word is sharper than a two-edged sword, more cut-
> ting than any force or power, more subtle than all the finesse of human
> genius, more pointed than every learned thrust of human discourse.[19]

The living word designates the living God for whom to say is the same
as to make. By his word he created the universe (see Gen 1:1-31), he
"gives to everyone life and breath and everything" (Acts 17:25).[20] This
is why the author of the Letter to the Hebrews writes that nothing escapes the notice of this living Word, that it is "able to discern reflections
and thoughts of the heart," that "we must render an account" to God.
It is impossible to flee to avoid hearing God's word, to cheat it. Often
scouring, it reveals to all their deep truth, what they are in the Lord's
judgment, what they are called to become everyday in order to correspond
to God's designs for them.

Eternal Life Is Priceless

On the road to Jerusalem, after the group of Pharisees came to question
him, here is a man who runs up to Jesus. He kneels down and asks,
"Good teacher, what must I do to inherit eternal life?" We readily identify with this man because all of us carry in our hearts the question he

takes the initiative to ask. But Jesus' response and the explanation given to the disciples later on hold many surprises and go far beyond what we expected (Mark 10:17-30).[21]

The manner in which this man addresses Jesus, before whom he kneels, appears exemplary. However, he is somewhat chided, "Why do you call me good? No one is good but God alone." This reaction on Jesus' part surprises us: Would it be inappropriate to give him the same title as the one we give God? No, when his true identity as Son of God has been recognized. Yes, when we see in him a man, even though an unusual one, or a rabbi endowed with unequalled authority.[22] Whatever the intention of his questioner, Jesus reminds him that in order to know how to act, one must consult the commandments of the Law: "You shall not kill; you shall not commit adultery; you shall not steal; you shall not bear false witness; you shall not defraud; honor your father and your mother." The enumeration is not complete, but it is sufficient to evoke the whole series of precepts.[23]

"Teacher, all of these I have observed from my youth." This statement is not inspired by pride. It reminds us of what the psalmist said:

> Yes, your decrees are my delight;
> they are my counselors.
>
> ———
>
> The way of truth I have chosen;
> I have set your ordinances before me.
>
> ———
>
> I keep your precepts and your decrees,
> for all my ways are before you.
> (Ps 119:24, 30, 168)

Perhaps this statement betrays a certain feeling of dissatisfaction and a hunch that there is another way to enter the kingdom. In any case, it appears that after having answered the man's question, seemingly absent-mindedly, Jesus suddenly sees in him one of those just of Israel, "molded by centuries of observance,"[24] who has the makings of a disciple—"Jesus, looking at him, loved him."

> This is not a banal formula; this look concentrates on the disciples the luminous arrow of divine holiness: in this look one can read the absolute demand that compromises neither with evil nor with mediocrity; in this look one also receives absolute love that forgives failings at every moment and comforts every conscience in its very depths by revealing to it that it is called to share in the life of the Father, the Son, and the Spirit.[25]

"You are lacking in one thing. Go, sell what you have, and give to [the] poor and you will have treasure in heaven; then come, follow me." Upon hearing this text, St. Antony (251-356), the "father of monks," left everything in order to lead a life of self-denial in the Egyptian desert.[26] Antony's action caused this word of Jesus to the rich man in the Gospel to be routinely perceived and quoted as a call to evangelical poverty in religious life. In fact, thus understood, it has led many to enter, like St. Antony, upon this way of life.[27] It remains that such an interpretation is anachronistic: neither Jesus nor the evangelists could then think of this particular option.[28] "To follow" Jesus, an expression that describes discipleship, demands that we prefer him over everything, that we accompany him without looking back, free from all attachment.[29] "At that statement [the man's] face fell, and he went away sad, for he had many possessions."

> The young[30] man had up to then shown an uncommon eagerness; he was like a lover. Whereas others approached Christ to test him or to tell him of their diseases, those of their parents or of still other people, he comes near Jesus to speak of eternal life. The soil was rich and fertile, but it was full of brambles ready to choke the seeds. . . . Our young man left, eyes downcast for sadness, a notable sign that he had not come with a bad disposition. But he was too weak; he desired Life, but a passion difficult to overcome was holding him back.[31]

Again, Jesus "looked around" and now addresses the disciples, " 'How hard it is for those who have wealth to enter the kingdom of God!' The disciples were amazed at his words." Is the faithful observance of the Law reduced to nothing by the possession of many goods? Far from withdrawing his astonishing statement, Jesus insists, " 'Children, how hard it is to enter the kingdom of God! It is easier for a camel to pass through [the] eye of [a] needle than for one who is rich to enter the kingdom of God.' They were exceedingly astonished and said among themselves, 'Then who can be saved?' " For the third time Jesus looks at them, "For human beings it is impossible, but not for God." In order to have access to the kingdom, we must free ourselves from earthly things, from material riches that tie us down. And we all know how difficult—no, impossible—it is to be really detached from what we possess, even if it is very little. But Jesus' word reaches farther: there exists no way of forcing open the door of the kingdom; salvation is a gift—a grace—that always comes from God.

We do not know what we should do to be saved. But there is nothing to do. . . . The only thing we can do is to welcome, there again, as a child, the Father's gift. Of course, it is asked of Christians that they let go of riches and many other things, but this is only a gesture of welcome, a preliminary condition to a rebirth that makes us over, renders us able to receive the salvation coming from God alone.[32]

If humans cannot by themselves, whatever they may do, acquire salvation, they know that God is powerful enough to save them. Many experiences have contributed to their acquiring this certainty. In particular, psalms delight in recalling these experiences with thanksgiving.[33] God is the Savior one entreats with humility and trust.[34] The temptation to rely—at least to a certain point—on one's own merits sometimes remains. One knows indeed how costly is a life led in faithfulness to God's law. And when one yields to the urge of comparing the rigor of one's own observance with the casualness of many others, one easily comes to conclude, if not to say, that so much generosity surely is worthy of some thankfulness on God's part. Such an attitude is a grave distortion of the relationship with God and of religion.[35] This is what Jesus forcefully proclaims.

But the reflection goes on. "Peter began to say to him, 'We have given up everything and followed you.'" Depending on the tone of voice with which this is said, this cry of the heart may signify two things. It can express a certain personal satisfaction, which is not reprehensible anyway; for it would be at the same time a profession of complete trust in Jesus. "As far as we are concerned, we are on the right track, are we not, since we have abandoned everything in order to follow you." But for Peter, this cry of the heart may also have expressed a secret worry, "What will happen to us who have renounced everything for your sake?" But in the end, it matters little to know what Peter's exact feelings were. For us, the important thing is Jesus' response. It is not in vain that one renounces what one holds dearest, "house or brothers or sisters or mother or father or children or lands." "Eternal life in the age to come" is assured to those who act in this manner. But Jesus specifies "for my sake and for the sake of the gospel." Many are the motives that can bring people to part with a portion or the totality of their possessions. Whatever the value of these various renunciations taken in themselves, the promise of eternal life supposes that the renunciations are accepted "for [the] sake [of Christ] and for the sake of the gospel."[36] Nothing outside this has currency in "the age to come." When the time for choices is at hand, we must weigh things on the scales of eternity revealed by Christ and the gospel.

What Jesus says afterwards should not come as too much of a surprise. Everything left for his sake will be restored a hundredfold "now in this present age: houses and brothers and sisters and mothers and children and lands." But according to Mark, he adds, "with persecutions." This unexpected addition—but one that corresponds to the experience of the first Christian communities—suggests that these new goods given "a hundred times more" are the same as those that delighted Jesus himself when people said of him, "He is out of his mind." "Looking around at those seated in the circle, he said, 'Here are my mother and my brothers'" (Mark 3:21, 34).

Wisdom is infinitely above all the goods humans may desire. It allows us to discern, often beyond deceptive appearances, what is true, just, and good. It is a participation in the intelligence of God, who searches the depths of all beings, it is "the splendor . . . [that] never yields to sleep" (First Reading).

But, even when one sincerely wants "to follow Christ," renouncing worldly riches remains difficult. We must accept this renunciation, however, when riches—even relative riches—are an obstacle on the way to salvation. Riches always remain a weight that prevents us from rising above earthly things. This is true to such an extent that we would be driven to despair of being saved without the certainty that nothing is impossible for God (Gospel Reading).

Our guarantee is God's word, which no thing or no one can escape; it is living and life-giving; it is powerful enough to work out the salvation of those who make room for it inside themselves (Second Reading).

It never ceases to resound in the liturgy, urging us to walk at a more and more lively pace toward the encounter with him who came and is coming, who gives us the viaticum of his Word and his Bread to restore our failing strength.

> The Lord is passing by . . .
> will you open
> when the stranger knocks?
> Can you ignore the voice
> that demands your faith?

> The Lord is passing by . . .
> will you hear the Spirit of Jesus Christ?
> He is hollowing poverty into you
> to teach you how to pray.

The Lord is passing by . . .
will you quench
the purifying love?
Will you flee and refuse
to be' gold in the crucible?

The Lord is passing by . . .
will you enter
into his Eucharist?
Remember that in his body
he receives your death.

The Lord is passing by . . .
will you dare
to cry out in joy?
Christ is alive, arisen,
who will give him a home?

The Lord is passing by . . .
will you wait
another meeting?
Why delay? Walk with him
on the road of life.

The Lord is passing by.[37]

The Gospels read on the Twenty-seventh and Twenty-eighth Sundays in Ordinary Time, Year B, relate the teachings that Jesus gave between the second and third predictions of his passion. This took place on the road to Jerusalem, toward which he was guiding his disciples. This framework sets in relief the true meaning and real object of the demands, often radical, of the gospel. They are absolutely not arbitrary. Jesus came to reorient lives toward God's will, the lives of human beings, whom he sanctified by becoming their brother. Those who follow him, free from earthly attachments, will receive "in the age to come," together with eternal life, a glory like that with which the Father crowned him "because he suffered death" (Heb 2:9) and "in this present age" the hundredfold of all the goods they have left behind.

Truly, it is within the Eucharistic celebration—a memorial of the death and resurrection of Christ, a meal in which the author of grace gives himself as a food, an announcement of his return and of a new creation—that the word of God fully reveals what it is and why it has made itself heard.

The Twenty-ninth and Thirtieth Sunday in Ordinary Time

In Mark's Gospel, three predictions of the passion punctuate the march of Jesus toward Jerusalem (8:31; 9:30-32; 10:32-34). Between the third prediction and Jesus' entrance into Jerusalem (Mark 11:1-11), Mark has inserted the two narratives we read on the Twenty-ninth and Thirtieth Sundays. Therefore, they form in the very texture of Mark's Gospel, a well-defined sequence. We are with Jesus and the disciples in the last phase of his journey to the city; what follows will take place in Jerusalem or its immediate surroundings. But the unity of this sequence has another basis. Jesus has just finished telling the Twelve what is in store for him at the end of the journey: arrest, insults, condemnation to death, and three days later—resurrection. The disciples are following, but they are terrified. James and John, who have their minds on other things, believe that Jesus is announcing the beginning of an earthly kingdom that has been the recurrent theme of certain messianic dreams. As a consequence, they approach Jesus to ask that they be closely associated with his glory, in the first two places nearest him. Obviously, they have not understood anything. Jesus then moves in to open the eyes of his blind disciples (Mark 10:35-45—Twenty-ninth Sunday).

Immediately afterward, Mark reports that at the moment Jesus "was leaving Jericho with his disciples and a sizable crowd, Bartimaeus, a blind man, the son of Timaeus, . . . began to cry out and say, 'Jesus, son of David, have pity on me.' " Moved by this man's faith, Jesus summons him and grants him what he asks: his sight. And the man begins to follow Jesus on the road to Jerusalem (Mark 10:46b-52—Thirtieth Sunday). In these two narratives what is meant is the light of faith that alone allows people to perceive the true meaning of the pasch of the Lord.

On each Sunday in Ordinary Time, the first readings have been chosen in connection with the Gospels. The beginning of the fourth Song of the Suffering Servant is a prophetic evocation of Christ's passover: he was lifted up into glory because he accepted to suffer in order to free the multitudes from their sins (Isa 53:10-11—Twenty-ninth Sunday).

Another prophetic oracle hails the new Exodus—the new Easter—of the people of God "father[ed] . . . from the ends of the world," which from then on, walks in the way of salvation without stumbling (Jer 31:7-9—Thirtieth Sunday).

The reading of the Letter to the Hebrews continues. ''We have a great high priest . . . Jesus, the Son of God'' (Heb 4:14-16—Twenty-ninth Sunday).

Invested with his priestly function by God himself, who has taken him into glory, Christ is the high priest who eternally intercedes for us with the Father (Heb 5:1-6—Thirtieth Sunday).

Twenty-ninth Sunday

The Son, Servant of God and of His Brothers and Sisters

From Suffering to Glory

Because the prophets have a keen insight into the significance of earlier Scriptures and of history, they are able to sense the deep meaning of what happens in the present. At the same time, they give us a premonition of the future whose promise this present contains. A particularly striking example of this threefold function of prophetic texts is found in the poems called the Songs of the Suffering Servant, from the Book of Isaiah,[1] from which this Sunday's liturgy selects a few lines (Isa 53:10-11).

"But the Lord was pleased / to crush him in infirmity." This poem begins as the praise of an exemplary and just person who remained faithful to God despite the persecutions he had to suffer.[2] We could indeed conceive that this was written of a martyr, saying "He or she has made of his or her life a sacrifice of atonement," even understanding this expression in its technical and cultic meaning.[3] Such words as "Because of his or her suffering, this person will see the light and will be richly blessed" would also be fitting in a panegyric. But this is not the case in what follows: "Through his suffering, my servant shall justify many / and their guilt he shall bear." Obviously, this is no longer a discourse of praise in honor of a just person. The prophet glimpses the coming of a mysterious servant who, although belonging to the lineage of past just persons, will nevertheless be unequalled. Indeed, he is not "smitten . . . and afflicted" (Isa 53:4) because of his own sins. Innocent, he offers himself voluntarily as a sacrifice to justify others. Through him, the will—the plan—of the Lord will be fulfilled; he is an artisan of the work of salvation in which God has been engaged from the beginning. For his part, owing to his expiatory immolation, "he shall see the light in fullness of days." What an extraordinary reversal! He will live because he delivers himself to death. Contrary to what normally happens, his death will allow him to "see his descendants."

Therefore, it comes as no surprise that the Songs of the Suffering Servant have played an important part in the understanding of Christ's passion and, early on,[4] in the preaching during apostolic times, and afterwards, in the elaboration of the theology of redemption. The insults and sufferings that Jesus, the Just One among the just, endured; his death on the shameful gallows of the cross of evildoers, forsaken by humans and, it seems, by God himself (see Mark 15:34) were a scandal for those who had placed their hope in him (see Luke 24:21). The Songs of the Suffering Servant offer the key to this terrible enigma defying reason. The prophet's oracle helps us to recognize that Jesus saved the world by dying on the cross; that far from abandoning him, God has exalted him above all things because of his obedience unto death (see Phil 2:6-11). Jesus on the cross appears at once as the supreme manifestation of God's love for the multitude and as the ultimate reason for our hope.

Lord, let your mercy be on us, as we place
our trust in you.

Upright is the word of the LORD,
  and all his works are trustworthy.
He loves justice and right;
  of the kindness of the LORD the earth is full.

———

But see, the eyes of the LORD are upon those who fear him,
  upon those who hope for his kindness,
To deliver them from death
  and preserve them in spite of famine.
Our soul waits for the LORD,
  who is our help and our shield. . . .
May your kindness, O LORD, be upon us
  who have put our hope in you.
(Ps 33:4-5, 18-20, 22)

Jesus, Son of God, the High Priest

"Through Jesus Christ, your Son, our Lord": this formula recurs so often and so regularly in the liturgy that it risks not holding our attention except as a cue for us to say "Amen." However, it is rich in meaning—Jesus, the Son of God, is the high priest thanks to whom we "confidently approach the throne of grace" (Heb 4:14-16).

The author of the Letter to the Hebrews expresses this dignity and this function of Christ by directly referring to the understanding of the priesthood as found in the Old Testament.[5] But even though it has received important nuances, the priestly mission is still, in the main, perceived as it was then: it renders those who are invested with it able to approach God,[6] to consult him and transmit his decisions,[7] to preside over worship.[8] The priest is thus the qualified intermediary between God and humankind; he serves as a bridge—pontiff—between heaven and earth. Accepted by God as a qualified interlocutor and spokesperson for his brothers and sisters, he still remains an earthly person; he has not crossed the threshold of God's dwelling. As for Christ, he "has passed through the heavens"; he is with the Father, whose glory he shares; he is his Son. In him, we have the high priest par excellence.

At the same time, only he is able "to sympathize with our weaknesses . . . [having] similarly been tested in every way, yet without sin." This is why his experience of our weaknesses and trials, including that of death, has with him a unique value. One could say that he knew weakness and trials in an unadulterated state without the aftertaste due to the consciousness of being sinners and thereby responsible, at least in part, for the evil one suffers. Although he freely delivered himself to his passion, he has also felt in his innermost depths the torment of injustice. Like millions before and after him, Jesus can say in truth that he knows what it means to suffer and die—his agony at Gethsemane is the proof of it (see Luke 22:39-44)—because he absolutely did not deserve to suffer. Thus, he is the true high priest through whom we may "confidently approach the throne of grace to receive mercy and to find grace for timely help."

> To mention Christ's priesthood, what is it if not to express the mystery of the incarnation in which the Son of God "[who], though he was in the form of God, . . . emptied himself, taking the form of a slave, . . . becoming obedient to death" (Phil 2:6-8). He lowered himself below the angels, he who was united to the Father as an equal. By wanting to become like humans, the Son abased himself while remaining equal to the Father. . . .
>
> Christ, inasmuch as he remains in his divine condition, is therefore the only Son of God, to whom we offer sacrifices as we do to the Father; but inasmuch as he takes the condition of a slave, he becomes the Priest through whom we may offer to God the living and holy host he approves. Now, we could not offer sacrifice if Christ had not become a victim for us, he in whom our human nature is the true salvific host.[9]

Servant of All, Like the Lord

The kingdom of God—announcement, expectation, proximity, arrival, definitive establishment, access open to believers—occupies a notable place in the Old Testament. The Synoptic Gospels place it at the center of Jesus' preaching. In English, "kingdom" is the name given to a land, a territory governed by a king; the regal dignity and power are called "kingship"; their exercise is designated by the word "reign."[10] It is important to keep these nuances of vocabulary in mind when we read the scriptural texts that speak of the "kingdom of God."[11] This is the case in particular for the Gospel passage of this Sunday (Mark 10:35-45).

After the rich man who did not have the heart to sell all his possessions departed, Jesus had said to his disciples, "How hard it is for those who have wealth to enter the kingdom of God!" Then he had said that no one would renounce one's dearest possessions without receiving eternal life "in the age to come" and "a hundred times more now in this present age" (10:29-30).[12] And he had added, "But many that are first will be last, and [the] last will be first" (10:31). After this, in Mark's Gospel, comes the third prediction of the passion to the Twelve, whom Jesus took aside (see 10:32-34). This revelation of what was to happen in Jerusalem was not calculated to restore equanimity in anyone following Jesus: The Twelve were amazed and those who followed "were afraid to question him" (10:32). The behavior of James and John—the two most intimate friends of Jesus, along with Peter[13]—appears even stranger within this context. Do they really understand nothing of Jesus' words; or else, because of what he had previously said, do they think that Jesus will extricate himself from this tight corner in order to enter his glory? Whatever, they leave the group behind, trying, it seems, not to be noticed by the others. They approach Jesus, who is walking ahead of them, "Teacher, we want you to do for us whatever we ask of you." Invited to state their request, they answer, "Grant that in your glory we may sit one at your right and the other at your left." "To register first on a waiting list is to be well advised. They are betting on Jesus, that is, on his success and glory. Even before having done battle, they want the guarantee of a reward. . . . They demand a good salary and substantial benefits in return for joining Jesus' company early on. . . . How well are we qualified to understand them!"[14] But Jesus answers, "You do not know what you are asking." Christ's glory has nothing in common with what we can gain here on earth by claiming our rights or resorting to undue favors, by competing with others to get the better of them or even push them away. "Can you drink the cup that I drink or be baptized with the baptism with which I am baptized?" Biblical symbolism of these two images suggests the forthcoming suffering and death of Jesus in obedience to his Father and in fulfillment of his redemptive mission.[15] "There is a baptism with which I must be baptized, and how great is my anguish until it is accomplished!" (Luke 12:50).[16] "Abba, Father, all things are possible to you. Take this cup away from me, but not what I will but what you will" (Mark 14:36). To follow Christ on this way is the disciple's concern. "We can," James and John unhesitatingly answer. Must we see in their assurance a sort of presumption or simply the spontaneous response of their generosity and attachment to the Lord, for whom they have left everything (see Mark 10:28)? The evangelist is not interested in subjective motivations. What he wants is for us to remember Jesus' words, "The cup that I drink, you will drink, and with the baptism with which I am baptized, you will be baptized." We cannot be Christ's disciples and have access to salvation without sharing in his death, that we might have a part in his resurrection: "If we have died with him / we shall also live with him" (2 Tim 2:11).[17]

> All sufferings have been undergone, but in him who is the head; there still remained the sufferings of Christ in his body. "Now you are Christ's body and individually parts of it," says Paul (1 Cor 12:27). We are therefore going where Christ preceded us, and Christ is still walking toward the goal where he preceded us. For Christ, being the head, preceded us, but his body follows suit. Christ is still suffering on earth; he was suffering on account of Saul when the latter heard, "Saul, Saul, why are you persecuting me?" (Acts 9:4).[18]

"But to sit at my right or at my left is not mine to give but it is for those for whom it has been prepared." No one has the right to encroach on the Father's prerogatives, not even the Son. It is into the Father's hands that we must, with a child's confidence, entrust the future.

In spite of the precautions taken by James and John, their request does not escape the notice of the other apostles. They are indignant and show it. Then Jesus calls them, because all must understand well what the nature of relationships must be in the Christian community that foretells and foreshadows the kingdom. The world is based on relations of power and domination: "You know that those who are recognized as rulers over the Gentiles lord it over them, and their great ones make their authority over them felt. But it shall not be so among you. Rather, whoever wishes to be great among you will be your servant; whoever wishes to be first among you will be the slave of all." Those responsible for Christian communities must conceive and exercise their responsibility not like a power—and still less a discretionary power—but like a service, like a diakonia. One becomes great by being others' servant; one obtains the first place by taking the last, that of a child (see Matt 9:33-36) and, better still, that of the "slave of all" who asks nothing in return for what he or she does.[19] "For the Son of Man did not come to be served but to serve, and to give his life as a ransom for many." There is no other motivation, and this one is decisive.

> Whether in our individual lives or in the communities that invoke his name or in international life, Jesus' word is endlessly subversive. What must be done is to plow humanity like hard and barren soil that must be opened to be able to receive and nurture God's seed. This God is not the faraway master, constructed by human fear, this God who so often seemed to back up the power of the powerful. Even before God Jesus is subversive, because he invites us to continually overturn the image we have formed of him. Through his whole life, as much as through his words, he directs us toward a God who became the servant of those to whom he gave birth through love.[20]

The three biblical texts proclaimed today give a remarkable unity to this Sunday's liturgy. The parallelism is striking—down to the vocabulary[21]—between the mysterious Servant of God described in the book of the prophet Isaiah (First Reading) and Jesus, who gave "his life as a ransom for many" (Gospel). Moreover, the excerpt from the Letter to the Hebrews—used by the liturgy since the Twenty-seventh Sunday—reminds us that Jesus, the Son of God, is the high priest who entered the sanctuary of heaven and whose sacrifice insures for us God's mercy (Second Reading). We have here three texts to read in parallel fashion. But their proclamation in the liturgy aims at illuminating the meaning and scope of the mystery of the salvation worked by Christ, celebrated here and now by the Church, in which we share and which must shape our way of living everyday in the Christian community and the world.

Jesus "has similarly been tested in every way," and he died although having never sinned. He freely accepted the cup that the Father, for whom everything is possible, could have taken away from him (see Luke 22:42) in order to justify the multitude of human beings imprisoned by sin, assuming the tragic destiny of all those who want to liberate their brothers and sisters from the powers that enslave them. The logic of these destructive forces and the infernal circle of violence generated by violence have been broken by the resurrection of the Crucified One who "has passed through the heavens" by going through the veil of death in order to enter the sanctuary of God's presence. He called his disciples to follow him by directing them to vie zealously with one another so that they might become like him, servants and slaves of all.

One day they would learn
the price of the last place.
They had not seen at their feet
the master turned slave.
They had not tasted
the cup of bitterness.
Today, the Spirit gathers you:
enter with Jesus
into his baptism of fire.

Everything is possible for those who believe!

The cup the Father gives me,
You too will drink.

With the baptism I shall receive,
You too will be baptized

Him who emptied himself
God has exalted.[22]

Do Not Stay There, Sitting by the Roadside

Save Your People, O Lord

To call on God for help, to cry out to him, beseeching him to intervene, is an act of faith in his mercy on which we know we can rely. We dare to pray assuredly in this way because he himself urges us to do so. He behaves as a father, so eager to lavish his tenderness on his children that he closely watches for the slightest opportunity. He sends them a messenger who had once manifested his anger toward them and who is now commissioned to bring the good news of forgiveness, "Proclaim your praise and say: / The LORD has delivered his people" (Jer 31:7-9).[1]

God is so happy to be able to pardon at last that he asks all nations to rejoice over what he does for his people. He speaks of his people as if they were the first, the most important of all peoples. And it is so for him because he loves them with a love of predilection.[2] He reluctantly decided to chastise them, but only that they might repent their aberrations.[3] Now, he is going to renew with them a fruitful dialogue and inaugurate a new phase of salvation. As so often, this reversal in the situation is presented as a new Exodus that must not be a journey rife with ambushes and rebellions against God,[4] but "a level road, so that no one shall stumble," directly leading to "brooks of water." This exodus will see those who were scattered all over the world return to their land. It will also put an end to the schism of the northern tribes[5] and reunite the people. Lastly, all will benefit by this salvation, all will be able to walk along this straight road, even the weak and the handicapped, those whom a legal impurity kept apart: "the blind and the lame . . . the mothers and those with child."

> The Being of Blessing passed in front of my house,
> My own house, belonging to me, the barber!
> I ran, he turned around and waited for me,
> I, the barber!
> I said, "May I speak to you, O Lord?"

And he said, "Yes."
Yes, to me, the barber!
And I said, "Does peace exist for a being such as I?"
And he said, "Yes."
Even for me, the barber!
And I said, "May I follow you?"
And he said, "Yes."
Even to me, the barber!
And I said, "May I stay near you, O Lord?"
And he said, "You may."
Even I, the poor barber?[6]

The great universal gathering announced by this oracle is in process throughout the ages. Coming "from the ends of the world," the multitude of believers continues its exodus toward God, who, through the voice of his envoy Jesus—whose name means "God saves" (see Matt 1:21), "God is with us" (Matt 1:23)—calls it to come back by following "the level road" from now on.[7]

The Lord has done great things for us;
we are filled with joy.

When the LORD brought back the captives of Zion,
  we were like men dreaming.
Then our mouth was filled with laughter,
  and our tongue with rejoicing.
Then they said among the nations,
  "The LORD has done great things for them."
The LORD has done great things for us;
  we are glad indeed
Restore our fortunes, O LORD,
  like the torrents in the southern desert.
Those that sow in tears
  shall reap rejoicing.
Although they go forth weeping,
  carrying the seed to be sown,
They shall come back rejoicing,
  carrying their sheaves.
(Ps 126)

Priest Forever and for All

Son of God made man, Jesus the Christ is the unique mediator between God and humanity. In order to render intelligible this ministry exercised by the Lord in the service of humans, the author of the Letter to the Hebrews compares it to the priestly ministry. "Therefore . . . we have a great high priest who has passed through the heavens. . . . So let us confidently approach the throne of grace to receive mercy and to find grace for timely help.''[8] To be correctly understood, this way of considering Christ's role requires some explanations (Heb 5:1-6).

''Every high priest is taken from among men and made their representative before God.'' This is the usual definition of the priestly ministry. Today, it is true, the necessity of this function is questioned often enough, certain persons deeming that they have no need of an intermediary in their relation with God. The author of the Letter to the Hebrews totally ignores such an objection. For him, as for the whole biblical tradition, it is through signs that a person reaches the transcendent domain of the sacred, in the same way that it is through signs that God, the All-Other, manifests his presence here below and sanctifies humans. Every radical challenge to this ''sacramental economy'' is equivalent—whatever may be said about it—to a negation or a misunderstanding of God's transcendence. By the same token, one fabricates a human-sized god or else one sets oneself up as god,[9] even though this consequence is probably less conscious.

''No one takes this honor upon himself but only when called by God.'' The author adds, ''just as Aaron was'' because he addresses Christians coming from Judaism.[10] This divine election is done through mediations: in the Old Testament, the fact of belonging to a priestly lineage; today, the call of the Church represented by the bishop, who is responsible for the local Christian community. ''In the same way, it was not Christ who glorified himself in becoming high priest, but rather the one who said to him: 'You are my son; this day I have begotten you.' ''[11]

Another psalm verse, says the author of the letter, shows the eminent superiority of the priesthood of Christ. Indeed, the statement of God, ''You are a priest forever, according to the order of Melchizedek'' (Ps 110:4), concerns him.[12] Melchizedek is a mysterious character who briefly appears in the story of Abraham: ''King of Salem,'' ''a priest of God Most High,'' he brought to the patriarch ''bread and wine'' and ''blessed'' him (Gen 14:18-20). Afterwards, he is never mentioned again in the Old Testament, save for this reference in Psalm 110.[13] In the New Testament, only the Letter to the Hebrews evokes his memory, but with a view to finding in it a teaching with regard to Christ.[14] Melchizedek was ''king of Salem,'' that is, ''king of peace'' (Heb 7:2). His origins remain as mysterious as his person; nothing is said either about his father or his mother or his genealogy (see Heb 7:3). All this, including the silence of the Scriptures, makes of him a figure of Christ. His priesthood, like that of Melchizedek, antedates every historical institution and, as a consequence, is not submitted to the ups and downs of history. Christ therefore is "priest forever."[15] Whatever the value of this argument, rather disconcerting for our modern minds,[16] the teaching of Hebrews remains. Besides, the reference to the mysterious personage of Melchizedek, named in the Roman Canon, opens interesting vistas to Christian reflection.

> In Melchizedek, it is the primeval cosmic religion that, under the Spirit's guidance, comes to hail biblical religion and render homage to it. It was indeed necessary that there be a transmission of tradition from one covenant to the other, and Melchizedek, arising from the mysterious depths of the covenant with Noah, "without father, mother, or ancestry," as noted in the Letter to the Hebrews, because all of humankind, not a particular race, is concerned, is the delegate of this primeval covenant.[17]

Going Toward Jesus Passing by and Following Him on the Road

The prophet Isaiah had foretold that the advent of the kingdom would be heralded by signs such as the cure of the blind.[18] Jesus recalled this fact in his inaugural preaching in Nazareth and in his response to the inquirers sent by John the Baptist.[19] The four evangelists have recorded at least one of those cures worked by Jesus.[20] That of Bartimaeus, the account of which we read today, is particularly important in Mark's Gospel because of the contrast it stresses with the attitude of the "sons of Zebedee" and with their blindness and lack of faith (Mark 10:46b-52), about which we read last Sunday.

The healing takes place when Jesus "was leaving Jericho with his disciples and a sizeable crowd" in order to begin the last stage of a meandering journey, undertaken after the arrest of John the Baptist (see Mark 1:14) and coming to an end in Jerusalem (see Mark 10:1).[21] Mark has already related the cure of a blind man in Bethsaida, on the shore of the Sea of Galilee (see 8:22-26). At that time, people had brought the man, asking Jesus to touch him. The healing was performed almost in secrecy—Jesus had led him "outside the village"—and progressively—he had first put spittle on the eyes of the man, who began to see; then he again laid his hands on him with the result that the patient saw clearly. Jesus ordered him not to go into the village. When Jesus leaves Jericho, everything happens very differently. The blind beggar sitting "by the roadside" hears the noise of a crowd. He learns that Jesus is passing by and begins "to cry out and say, 'Jesus, son of David, have pity on me.' And many rebuked him, telling him to be silent. But he kept calling out all the more, 'Son of David, have pity on me.' Jesus stopped and said, 'Call him.' So they called the blind man, saying to him, 'Take courage, get up, he is calling you.' '' Then the man "threw aside his cloak,'' which he probably used to collect the alms of the passers-by. He "sprang up, and came to Jesus.'' A brief dialogue takes place: "Jesus said to him in reply, 'What do you want me to do for you?' The blind man replied to him, 'Master, I want to see.' Jesus told him, 'Go your way; your faith has saved you.' Immediately he received his sight and followed him on the way.''

This narrative is extremely lively because of the succession of concrete details and the dynamic style of the text. The scene unfolds before the readers or hearers, who are led to take part in it in retrospect. It is similar to the way that eyewitnesses, still moved by emotion, relate in an animated way the extraordinary happening they have just observed. But Mark certainly used his narrative talents for a didactic purpose, which we can easily discover. Now that we are close to Jerusalem, we must go very fast. Everyone must become aware of being blind, of failing to understand the mystery of Jesus; everyone must stop sitting "by the roadside'' and run toward the son of David, crying, "Have pity on me.'' Overcoming all interior hesitation, ignoring the voices that would deter us from this decisive move, we must closely follow in the footsteps of the Lord, that is, act as resolute disciples and go with him on the road to Jerusalem.

> Rightly does this Scripture picture this blind man sitting by the wayside and begging; for Truth himself said, "I am the way'' (John 14:6). Thus, all who ignore the radiance of the eternal light are blind. If people already have faith in the redeemer, they are sitting by the way. But if these believers neglect to ask to be given back eternal light and do not pray, they may be sitting by the road, but they are not begging. But if they believe, if they know their blindness of heart and pray to receive the light of truth, then they are the blind man sitting by the road and begging. Therefore, let those who acknowledge the darkness of their blindness and feel the deprivation of eternal light, let them cry in the bottom of their heart, let them cry with their whole soul and say, "Jesus, son of David, have pity on me.''[22]

The time is no longer a time for silence (see Mark 8:30). We must now shout the gospel in public squares and in all the streets, we must encourage the blind, eager to see, so that they may confidently approach Jesus.

Surrounded by his disciples and a large crowd of witnesses, Jesus, invisible to the eyes of unbelievers, walks in our ways. God is calling a great exodus, an immense gathering of those coming from the ends of the earth. In spite of their infirmities, all walk at a brisk pace while singing the Lord's praises and crying out, "Save the remnant of your people" (First Reading). Let no one feel excluded and left by the wayside: the Lord stops and calls whoever want to recover their sight. Even if, on certain days, the road seems long and arduous, this is not the time to stop, disheartened, since we are in view of Jerusalem (Gospel).

The Lord, our high priest who offers himself in sacrifice to his Father, is well able to understand our wanderings and weaknesses. His body and blood are given to us to restore our strength.

> I never saw your face,
> but those who know it
> spoke of it to me.
>
> Since that day
> I expect your passage
> and I hear
> that today is the day.
>
> *Jesus, our light,*
> *Christ, our salvation!*
>
> Blinded by our darkness,
> far from God,
> we cry to him:
>
> Lost in the world,
> without horizons,
> we cry to him:
>
> Harboring hope,
> looking forward to the encounter,
> we cry to him:
>
> *Jesus, our light,*
> *Christ, our salvation!*[23]

The sequence constituted by the Twenty-Ninth and Thirtieth Sundays could be titled, "The End of the Preliminary Examination of the Case of Jesus after the Arrest of John the Baptist," (see Mark 1:14). The passion is in sight, at the end of the road; Jesus has just announced it to his disciples for the third time (see Mark 10:32-34). The time of waiting is over. Now we must take the risk of the faith adventure, be ready to drink the cup that the Lord himself is going to drink, receive the baptism in which he is going to be immersed, renounce the exercise of any kind of power in order to become the servants and slaves of all, as did the Servant of God, who made of his life a sacrifice of atonement.

Jesus is walking on the road to Jerusalem; this is no time for us to remain sitting by the roadside, held captive by our blindness. We must cry out to him, asking for a cure so that we can follow him to the source of life-giving waters. Of course, we are weak. But "since we have a great high priest who has passed through the heavens, Jesus, the Son of God, let us hold fast to our confession." He is able to understand those who sin through ignorance or error. Let us "proclaim [God's] praise and say: The Lord has delivered his people."

The Thirty-first and Thirty-second Sunday in Ordinary Time

Jesus makes his solemn entry into Jerusalem (Mark 11:1-11),[1] and comes to grips with those who will play an active part in the course of his trial: after his vehement treatment of the Temple merchants (Mark 11:15-19; 27-33), members of the priestly hierarchy, lawyers, and elders call his authority into question. There is no doubt that the drama is reaching a climax; the denouement is at hand and Jesus knows it, as shown by the parable of the murderous tenants (Mark 12:1-12). His adversaries seek to ensnare him by persuading a few Pharisees and Herod's supporters to ask him an insidious question concerning the legitimacy of Caesar's tax (Mark 12:13-17). Then some Sadducees question him about the resurrection from the dead (Mark 12:18-27).[2]

For the Thirty-first Sunday, the reading is that of Jesus' response to a scribe who asks him what is the first of the commandments (Mark 12:28b-34). His answer reminds his questioner of the *Shema*, the prayer that every Jew is to recite daily, morning and evening (Deut 6:2-6, First Reading).

On the Thirty-second Sunday we hear Jesus' admonition against lawyers' behavior and greed. In contrast, he eulogizes the poor widow who put two small coins into the Temple treasury, her entire livelihood (Mark 12:38-44). The first reading reports what happened to another widow in Elijah's time. She gave the prophet the little cake she was about to prepare for herself and her son along with whatever provisions remained to her, "a handful of flour . . . and a little oil" (1 Kgs 17:10-16).

Two more excerpts from the Letter to the Hebrews are read. Christ, the high priest, "holy, innocent, undefiled," possesses "a priesthood that does not pass away" (Heb 7:23-28, Thirty-first Sunday). "Now once for all he has appeared at the end of the ages to take away . . . the sins of many" (Heb 9:24-28, Thirty-second Sunday).

Thirty-first Sunday

To Love the One God
with All Your Heart

You Will Love the Lord with All Your Heart

The Book of Deuteronomy—"the Second Law"—is a code of civil and religious laws inserted into a great discourse attributed to Moses.[1] The passage read today immediately follows the recalling of the Ten Commandments God gave on the mountain.[2] We have here an urgent exhortation that is still pertinent because of what is said about the meaning of God's commandments and about the spirit in which we must receive and observe them (Deut 6:2-8).

Faithfulness to commandments is the daily expression of what the Bible calls "the fear of God." This phrase designates a feeling and an attitude with many components. We can attribute this fear to the sacred fright aroused in us by various manifestations of God's infinite grandeur and power and by our feelings of smallness and nothingness. But this instinctive fear is blended with trust and translated into adoration. It is akin to reverence, not that of a slave but of a child showing a deep and affectionate respect toward venerated parents. Finally, the fear of God embraces the whole of religion in spirit and truth. It is a gift of the Spirit, bestowed in its fullness on the Messiah (see Isa 11:2). As a consequence, those in whom this "fear of God" dwells consider none of his commandments negligible, since they express God's will here and now, what pleases him, and what is good for us to do.

God did not give commandments to humanity to impress it with his power and keep it in bondage. On the contrary, he promulgated them in the framework of a covenant, a pact of friendship proposed on his initiative, and based on mutual trust between partners. To those who accept this privileged relationship and express their daily assent to this covenant, God committed himself to give his best gifts, expressed here by the promise of a "long life." The people steady in their faithfulness to the commandments will "grow and prosper . . . [in] a land flowing with milk and honey.'' This way of speaking[3] evokes the agricultural prosperity of a land[4] in which the living is good. This does not mean that faithfulness to God's commands preserves us from everything that may bring pain and bereavement. But whatever they may be, unhappy events do not lessen the deep peace—the happiness—of those who live in faithfulness to God's covenant. Is not this the case when, under duress, we can rely on the closeness of faithful, thoughtful, and understanding friends?

In fact, it is love that is involved in our relation to God. ''Hear, O Israel! The LORD is our God, the LORD alone! Therefore, you shall love the LORD, your God, with all your heart, and with all your soul, and with all your strength.''[5] This text is the origin of the beautiful prayer of *Shema Israel*—''Hear, O Israel!''—that every pious Jew recites morning and evening; it is at once a profession of faith in the One God, a renewal of the commitment to the covenant, and a thanksgiving. Those who ''fear'' God ''listen'' to what he says and learn to love him. Christian spiritual tradition has preserved this teaching: through obedience to the commandments, one passes from fear to love.

> Hear, O Israel! The LORD is our God, the LORD alone! Therefore, you shall love the LORD, your God, with all your heart, and with all your soul, and with all your strength. Take to heart these words which I enjoin on you today. Drill them into your children. Speak of them at home and abroad, whether you are busy or at rest. Bind them at your wrist as a sign and let them be as a pendant on your forehead. Write them on the doorposts of your houses and on your gates (Deut 6:4-9).
>
> If, then, you truly heed my commandments which I enjoin on you today, loving and serving the LORD, your God, with all your heart and all your soul, I will give the seasonal rain to your land, the early rain and the late rain, that you may have your grain, wine and oil to gather in; and I will bring forth grass in your fields for your animals. Thus you may eat your fill. But be careful lest your heart be so lured away that you serve other gods and worship them. For then the wrath of the LORD will flare up against you and he will close up the heavens, so that no rain will fall, and the soil will not yield its crops, and you will soon perish from the good land he is giving you. Therefore, take these words of mine into your heart and soul. Bind them at your wrist as a sign, and let them be a pendant on your forehead. Teach them to your children, speaking of them at home and abroad, whether you are busy or at rest. And write them on the doorposts of your houses and on your gates, so that, as long as the heavens are above the earth, you and your children may live on in the land which the LORD swore to your fathers he would give them (Deut 11:13-21).[6]

"Take to heart these words which I enjoin on you today." Do not "let them slip from your memory as long as you live, but teach them to your children and to your children's children" (Deut 4:9). In order to remain engraved in the memory of the heart, these commandments will be learned by heart. The injunction to memorize is frequent in Deuteronomy.[7] This is not a method of teaching befitting only an oral civilization. Today as yesterday, we interiorize what we frequently ponder, and what has thus entered the heart springs up spontaneously to be translated into action. This word "is very near to you, already in your mouths and in your hearts; you have only to carry it out" (Deut 30:14).

I love you, Lord, my strength.

I love you, O Lord, my strength,
O Lord, my rock, my fortress, my deliverer.
My God, my rock of refuge,
   my shield, the horn of my salvation, my stronghold!
Praised be the Lord, I exclaim,
   and I am safe from my enemies

    ———

The Lord live! And blessed be my Rock!
   Extolled be God my savior.

    ———

You who gave great victories to your king
   and showed kindness to your anointed. . . .
(Ps 18:2-4, 47, 51)

Christ, the Unique Priest Who Lives Forever

In order to explain in what sense Christ is priest, the Letter to the Hebrews compares his priesthood with that of the priests of the Old Testament and, thereby, with that of priests of subsequent times. There are resemblances—otherwise, the term "priest" would be mistakenly used with a totally ambiguous meaning—but also considerable differences, which place Christ's priesthood on such an eminent level that he is the only one who truly deserves to be called Priest (the word must then be capitalized). This is what this Sunday's passage from Hebrews demonstrates (Heb 7:23-28).[8]

Because death puts a term to every human life, priests can exercise their ministry only for a rather brief time. Therefore, in order to insure the continuity of the priesthood, others must replace those who disappear, one after the other, and by different modes of succession.[9] The priestly lineage therefore is made up of many priests who receive holy orders one after the other.[10] Besides, being limited in time, the ministry of each priest can reach only a restricted number of persons who die in their turn.[11] The case is completely different with Christ. Through his incarnation, the Son of God became the mediator between humankind and his Father. At his resurrection, he was instituted Priest in the heavenly sanctuary.[12] Consequently, in contrast with all other priests, "he, because he remains forever, has a priesthood that does not pass away." Nothing, no limit of time or space, hinders the exercise of his priestly function. He is, without restriction, Priest once and for all, forever, for everyone. "It was fitting that we should have such a high priest: holy, innocent, undefiled." Before all else, holiness has always been what is demanded of priests. Prophets insistently recall this and severely reprove those who scandalize when they should be edifying.

> And now, O priests, this commandment is for you:
>   If you do not listen,
> And if you do not lay it to heart,
>   to give glory to my name, says the LORD of hosts,
> I will send a curse upon you
>   and of your blessing I will make a curse.
>
> ———
>
> But you have turned aside from the way,
>   and have caused many to falter by your instruction;
> You have made void the covenant of Levi,
>   says the LORD of hosts.
> I, therefore, have made you contemptible
>   and base before all the people,
> Since you do not keep my ways
>   but show partiality in your decisions.
> (Mal 2:1-2b, 8-9)[13]

The bishop publicly reminds the person about to be ordained of his duty of holiness.

> While you meditate on the law of the Lord, see that you believe what you read, that you teach what you believe and that you translate your teaching into action. Let your instruction serve as a nourishing diet for the people of God. Let the impact of your lives please the followers of Christ, so that by word and action you may strengthen the house which is the Church of God. In the same way you must carry out your mission of sanctifying the world in Christ. It is your ministry which will make the spiritual sacrifices of the faithful perfect by uniting them to the eucharistic sacrifice of Christ. That sacrifice of Christ will be offered sacramentally in an unbloody way through your hands. Understand the meaning of what you do; put into

practice what you celebrate. When you recall the mystery of the death and resurrection of the Lord try to die to sin and to walk in the new life of Christ.[14]

Yes, Jesus is really the high priest who was fit for us to have, possessing total holiness—that of the Son of God—beyond all we could imagine and wish for in a human being. He offered a unique sacrifice that does not need to be repeated, because it is perfect. The Eucharists that we celebrate do not reiterate his sacrifice and cannot be added to his. As the sacramental memorial of Christ's death and resurrection, a communion with his body and blood given as food under the form of bread and wine, the Eucharist unceasingly re-presents, in human time and until the last day, the one and perfect offering of Christ, our High Priest "who has passed through the heavens."

The First Commandment: To Love God and Neighbor

Whereas others came to put tricky questions to Jesus,[15] a scribe who has heard those discussions approaches him and asks without guile, "Which is the first of all the commandments?" The serene climate of this encounter, as related in Mark's Gospel, invites us to candidly enter the dialogue between Jesus and the scribe—as a child who hears again and again with renewed wonder an often-told story (Mark 12:28b-34).[16]

To ask the question of "the first of all the commandments"—and who does not ask this question?—does not necessarily denote a mind bent on casuistry. Such a one seeks to set up a hierarchy among duties, to determine principles of jurisprudence in order to appraise the relative importance of each duty and to discharge it at minimum cost: one will have to attend to what is more serious, and the rest will be treated with less attention, less scrupulously. The "first" commandment is that which is absolutely capital, which is binding on all, always; that to which all others are subjected without being canceled or considered more or less optional. In this sense, the first commandment is not determined by a list. On the contrary, it is the source of all other commandments, even those not listed. It is this first commandment that, in a novel situation—not foreseen by a code of law—will dictate or inspire the suitable concrete behavior. Therefore, it is very important—even vital—to know what commandment comes first. The scribe of the Gospel narrative is right to put this question to Jesus. No one can answer like him or with equal authority.

Jesus does not answer in the way a lawyer might make reference to a code of laws, but he recites the opening words of the best-known prayer—the *Shema*—which pious Jews know by heart.[17] "Hear, O Israel! The LORD our God is LORD alone! You shall love the LORD your God with all your heart, with all your soul, with all your mind, and with all your strength." It is a verbatim quote from the text of Deuteronomy (6:4-5)[18] that represents a progress and a deepening of faith in God. The Ten Commandments said: "I, the LORD, am your God, who brought you out of the land of Egypt, that place of slavery. You shall not have other gods besides me. You shall not carve idols for yourselves in the shape of anything in the sky above or on the earth below or in the waters beneath the earth; you shall not bow down before them or worship them. For I, the LORD, your God, am a jealous God . . ." (Exod 20:2-5a).[19] Experience and reflection progressively led to an understanding of God's unparalleled grandeur in a much stricter and more absolute sense. Not only is he above all others who claim to be or are considered gods. He is the only God. His name is "The One."[20] This name became progressively dominant. The experience of the Exile played an important role in this by leading the exiles to the realization that other gods were nothing. The Lord had bonded with his people, had concluded a covenant with them through a free choice "because [he] loved" the people (Deut 7:7-8).[21] This choice and this covenant created a bond comparable to the conjugal bond;[22] reciprocal, unfailing, exclusive, and total love, "with all your heart, with all your soul, with all your mind, with all your strength."

Jesus adds, "The second is this: 'You shall love your neighbor as yourself.'" Again, we are referred to the Law.[23] The notion of neighbor, it is true, has undergone an evolution. First "neighbor" meant those who belonged to the people of God (Lev 19:15-18) and the aliens residing in the land, who were placed on the same footing (Lev 19:33-34), which demonstrated an already noticeably high conception of relationship to others and what its practice entailed. Bringing the Law to fulfillment, Jesus further enlarged this notion of neighbor: every human being without any distinction.[24] From the beginning, the duty to love one's neighbors derives from the bond that God established with them. Therefore, it is understandable that the extension of the notion of neighbor was parallel to the revelation and realization of the universality of salvation. This extended notion presupposes that all human beings have an equal dignity,[25] whatever their race, religion, or culture. "And 'to love him with all your heart, with all your understanding, with all your strength, and to love your neighbor as yourself' is worth more than all burnt offerings and sacrifices." When one professes this faith and practices it, one is "not far from the kingdom of God." This assurance given here by Jesus has its concrete confirmation in Matthew's judgment scene. On that day the Lord will recognize those "blessed by [his] Father" and take with him all who will have truly treated others as neighbors (see Matt 25:31-46). For the love of neighbor cannot be satisfied with good feelings and beautiful but ineffectual intentions.

> I am sending you the resolutions of Madame N., which are good, but they would seem even better to me if they were more particularized. It will be good to train the retreatants at your house to enter into detail; all else is only a product of the mind which, having found some sweetness in the meditation on a virtue, flatteringly thinks itself to be quite virtuous. However, to become solidly virtuous, one must make good practical resolutions concerning particular acts of virtue and be faithful in accomplishing them. Lacking this, one only imagines oneself to be virtuous.[26]

> Where pondered and not practiced, virtues are more harmful than useful.[27]

To love all human beings, even enemies, is to behave as "children of [our] heavenly Father, for he makes his sun rise on the bad and the good, and causes rain to fall on the just and the unjust." To act in this way is to "be perfect, just as [our] heavenly Father is perfect" (Matt 5:43, 48). Is this ideal above our strength? Certainly, in the same way it is impossible for humans to save themselves. But "all things are possible for God" (Mark 10:27)[28] if we ask him through Jesus Christ, his Son, our high priest who intercedes for us.

> What is the heart that can possess the fullness of love for the children of its flesh? What is the soul that can bring to fruition in itself, toward all other souls, the love sown in it by this precept that engenders charity: "You shall love your neighbor as yourself" (Matt 22:39)? Of themselves, our faculties are incapable of being the instruments of the quick and rich volitions of the Deity; the fruit of charity, sown by God is the only thing equal to the task. God can, by nature, accomplish what he wishes; now he wants to give life to his human children.[29]

He Gave Everything, Even His Own Life

The Pagan Woman Who Gave the Little She Had

The story read at the beginning of the Liturgy of the Word on this Sunday is one of the best-known passages of the "Cycle of Elijah," which tells of the prophet's adventures and miracles.[1] He vigorously condemned the impiety of King Ahab and his wife, Jezebel, who favored the worship of local gods, called baals, and who sought to destroy all of Yahweh's prophets.[2] Elijah has announced to the king that there will be a drought of several years, a punishment decreed by God for Ahab's evil conduct. At the Lord's command, he immediately flees and takes refuge near a stream where God-sent ravens bring "him bread and meat in the morning, and bread and meat in the evening." But owing to the drought, the stream runs dry. Then God tells Elijah to go to Zarephath, a Phoenician port some ten miles from Sidon; there he will find a widow who will see to his survival.[3] Today, the liturgy has us read the story of this meeting (1 Kgs 17:10-16).

From the start, the narrative is on the level of faith. Elijah has to have total trust in God to seek shelter in this region governed by Jezebel's father, Ethbaal, who has an implacable hatred for the prophet. At the same time, he must be convinced of the power of the Lord in order to hope that a pagan woman of this region will come to the aid of this baal-basher, she who worships the baals. But Elijah sets out on his journey to Zarephath. At the entrance of the city, he sees a widow—easy to spot because of her mourning clothes[4]—who is gathering wood. She must be the one the Lord has designated. He calls to her, "Please bring me a small cupful of water to drink." This is a service no one refuses to render in hot climates. To ask for water is a simple way to start a conversation with the people one meets. Depending on the way they respond, one can judge their disposition and, eventually, one may ask for more than water.[5] But Elijah does not wait. As the woman goes to fetch water, he says, " 'Please bring along a bit of bread.' 'As the LORD, your God, lives,' she answered,

'I have nothing baked; there is only a handful of flour in my jar and a little oil in my jug. Just now I was collecting a couple of sticks, to go in and prepare something for myself and my son; when we have eaten it, we shall die.' "

This tragic situation does not shake Elijah's faith. God told him that a widow would help him. He knows this woman's extreme destitution. Without any doubt, the Lord will give her the means necessary to fulfill her charitable mission. Therefore, Elijah repeats his request, adding to it an extraordinary promise: "For the LORD, the God of Israel says, 'The jar of flour shall not go empty, nor the jug of oil run dry, until the day when the LORD sends rain upon the earth.' "

Nothing more is needed for the poor widow to believe what this stranger tells her in the name of the God of Israel, more powerful than the local baal. She immediately carries out what the man, whose word transmits the Lord's oracle, has requested. "She was able to eat for a year, and he and her son as well; the jar of flour did not go empty, nor the jug of oil run dry, as the LORD had foretold through Elijah."

What a marvelous story! The most admirable part is not the miracle itself, but the faith of the protagonists, especially the poor widow's. Elijah, of course, believed in the Lord; but the Lord had spoken to him and, by the bank of a stream, had just given him a signal proof of his power and solicitude. But this woman was a pagan. She believed God's word— an unlikely promise—transmitted by an unknown person, a stranger who spoke to her in the name of a God locked in combat with the baal she served. On this word, she risked her life and her son's life. This is an admirable faith on the part of a simple and poor woman, and it reminds us of all those who, forgetting themselves, accomplish the acts of mercy that God expects.

> However, they stand under the Cross
> And are the first at the empty tomb.
> They are those who wash the dead
> Delighting in those ultimate caresses.
> Visceral is their glance
> And visceral are their anger
> And their gentleness, both born of earth.
> The man born of them knows he must be reborn.
> Whether he sees them as womb or tomb matters little.
> The whole obsession is that he must know why
> It is from them that he expects the rites of passage
> Toward the Other absent from this side of the landscape.[6]

Lastly, this narrative is remarkable because of the religious universalism it manifests. God's work exercises its power in pagan lands. It is welcomed in the hearts of the poor everywhere; it arouses the faith that brings salvation.

> *Praise·the Lord, my soul!*
>
> [The LORD] keeps faith forever,
> secures justice for the oppressed,
> gives food to the hungry.
> The LORD sets captives free;
>   the LORD gives sight to the blind.
> The LORD raises up those that were bowed down;
>   the LORD loves the just.
> The LORD protects strangers;
>   the fatherless and the widow he sustains,
>   but the way of the wicked he thwarts.
> The LORD shall reign forever;
>   your God, O Zion, through all generations. Alleluia.
> (Ps 146:6c-10)

The Unique Sacrifice of the Perfect Priest

Jesus' death on the cross is the decisive event of salvation history, the perfect sacrifice offered once for all, thanks to which sin was definitively destroyed. In order to express what constitutes a true fulfillment, the author of the Letter to the Hebrews compares with the sacrifices of the previous worship what Christ was able to do. But this comparison also sheds great light on the liturgy the Church celebrates today (Heb 9:24-28).

The great sacrifice of the Temple was that of the Day of Atonement, Yom Kippur, celebrated in the fall.[7] The high priest entered the inner sanctuary—the holy of holies beyond the veil—for an offering of incense and the sprinkling with the blood of a young bullock, immolated for the sins of the high priest and his family, then with the blood of a goat, immolated for the sins of the people. Another goat, called the scapegoat, symbolically laden with the sins of all through a laying-on of hands, was led into the desert, sent back to Azazel.[8] This great and solemn sacrifice with its accompanying rites, full of meaning, held an important place in the liturgy of the Temple and the relationship of the people with God. This ritual was a confession of sin and of the mercy of the Lord, whose renewed forgiveness gave back life and joy to his people. In order to fathom the unheard of meaning of the unique sacrifice of Christ, we must keep in mind the deep significance of the solemn liturgy of the Day of

Atonement and, like the author of Hebrews, evoke it with all the respect due it.[9]

The yearly celebration of the sacrifice of atonement says in itself that no definitive pardon could be expected from it. This liturgy, like all those we celebrate, was conducted by sinful persons and in a temple that, although sacred, was not the dwelling of the Most High (see Acts 7:48); for "the God who made the world and all that is in it, the Lord of heaven and earth, does not dwell in sanctuaries made by human hands" (Acts 17:24). They are only copies of the true sanctuary, heaven, dwelling of God. Now, it is there—in this true sanctuary inaccessible to humankind—that Christ entered "that he might now appear before God in our behalf. Not that he might offer himself repeatedly, as the high priest enters each year into the sanctuary with blood that is not his own," by immolating a new victim each year. Otherwise, Christ, high priest and victim offered as sacrifice, "would have had to suffer repeatedly from the foundation of the world." For this to be possible, Christ would have had to suffer his passion and enter heaven only in a symbolic manner. Finally, such a conception would be a negation of the incarnation of the Son of God.

In truth, Jesus knew the fate of all humans: like them, he died but once. But, whereas humans will appear later to be judged, Christ in his resurrection enters in glory into God's sanctuary. He will appear a second time, not in order to complete the rite of purification, as the high priest of old, but "to bring salvation to those who eagerly await him," whom he will introduce into the heavenly sanctuary. "Behold, God's dwelling is with the human race. He will dwell with them and they will be his people and God himself will always be with them" (Rev 21:3).

> In the power of his purity of heart, his veracity of spirit, and the infinite love of his act, he faces God as high priest of the world. And though his sacrifice was made in time, in the historical hour of his death, it is celebrated eternally, in the endless present. Ages pass, immeasurable for human conception, but Christ remains standing, holding his sacrifice before the divine Presence until the end of all time. In the eyes of God, the millennia pass away and vanish as a day, but the sacrifice of Golgotha remains.[10]

False Devotion and Authentic Piety

Having entered Jerusalem, Jesus often taught in the Temple during the days before his passion. In this high place of worship and devotion, he was able to observe the behavior of all who attended. Like everybody, he particularly noticed the scribes, who assiduously frequented the Temple, their home, as it were. They went back and forth within the sacred precincts and surroundings, just as certain people do today in great sanctuaries, and who are readily recognized from their garb or their looks as "official persons" to whom one bows, to whom one gives the right of way, and whom one approaches only with reverence. Their gathering in a single place can give rise to various feelings: some people are impressed by this display and are delighted to have the opportunity to attend such a show; others seem to regard them with curiosity and amusement; still others consider them vainglorious. These diverse reactions can very well go hand in hand not only with a complete understanding—"This is bound to happen in this kind of place"—but also with a deep respect.[11] In these same places, it happens that one's attention is drawn, for instance, to a man or woman who seems to leap to the eye, a child or an old person with an impressive look in the eyes. Nothing of all this escaped Jesus, who so often gave proof of acute sensitivity and finesse of spirit in his observations.[12] But in contrast to us, he knew what was within each heart and could judge the secret intentions and motivations of the actions and attitudes of those who were walking about in the Temple, the possible discrepancy between what was and what appeared to be. Also, he discerned the significance of a furtive gesture that escaped others' notice. From his observations, he derived the teaching that the Gospel relates today (Mark 12:38-44).[13]

> Beware of the scribes, who like to go around in long robes and accept greet ings in the marketplaces, seats of honor in synagogues, and places of honor at banquets. They devour the houses of widows and, as a pretext, recite lengthy prayers. They will receive a very severe condemnation.

The invective is cutting, and no commentary can blunt its vehemence. On the other hand, the generalization must be correctly understood; it is part of a literary genre that does not bother with distinctions. Jesus does not say that all scribes fit this picture, verging on caricature. He has not forgotten that he has just seen a scribe to whom he said, "You are not far from the kingdom of God" (12:34).[14] Neither does he curse all scribes and say that all scribes have all these defects and behave in an equally shocking and scandalous manner. For another thing, Mark's first readers no longer had anything to do with the scribes Jesus spoke of. The evangelist does not record all these warnings to arouse our indignation toward people long dead, which could lead us to say, "Thanks be to God, we are not like them. But we certainly know people to whom these reproaches apply." Such use of Jesus' words related in the Gospel would be a dishonest one. It is to ourselves and not to others that we must hold up the mirror of the Gospel, to the community we belong to, and not just to some of its members.

It is true that the position one occupies in the Church community entails risks of all kinds of temptations. The search for honors, often a ridiculous one anyway, falsifies the relationships of the brothers and sisters with those who exercise ministry in the community. Besides, it is a counter-testimony to the gospel by the very persons who have been instituted to preach it by their acts as much—at least—as by their words. We must be aware of possible deviations in the exercise of authority from which no one is completely protected. Therefore, we must pray for those who by virtue of their ministry are exposed to all sorts of dangers. But we must also help them by not flattering them, as is too often the case. Finally, it is important that all of us in the community understand that Jesus' warning is also personally directed to us. To present oneself before God rather than before human beings: such a warning is addressed to all.

> He sat down opposite the treasury and observed how the crowd put money into the treasury. Many rich people put in large sums. A poor widow also came and put in two small coins worth a few cents. Calling his disciples to himself, he said to them, "Amen, I say to you, this poor widow put in more than all the other contributors to the treasury. For they have all contributed from their surplus wealth, but she, from her poverty, has contributed all she had, her whole livelihood.
> (Mark 12:41-44)

The money deposited in the treasury was not destined for the poor but for the upkeep of the Temple worship. It was, therefore, in some way, an offering directly made to God. Here again, we must correctly understand what is said. Jesus does not declare without value the offering of rich people—"large sums." The contrast is drawn between the surplus the rich contribute from and the very "livelihood" that the widow gives, between parting with only a portion of one's abundance and the total giving of one's very life, so to speak. The rich honor God; but the poor woman consecrates herself entirely to God. The rich, while dedicating only a part of their possessions to God, nonetheless rely on their money for their living; the widow wholly entrusts herself to God. In the last analysis, what is discussed here is not big money and small coins.[15] In the widow's offering, Jesus sees the evocation of the total gift of himself he is about to make.

I had gone, begging from door to door, on the road to the village, when your gold chariot appeared in the distance, and I was wondering who was thus king of all kings! My hopes rose and I was thinking, "The bad days are over"; and I was already expecting spontaneous alms and riches scattered all over in the dust.

The chariot stopped where I stood. Your eyes rested on me and you got down with a smile. Suddenly, you extended your right hand and said, "What do you have to give me?" Ah! What royal game was this, to beg from the beggar! I was at a loss and perplexed; finally, I slowly took from my bag a very small kernel of wheat and gave it to you.

But how great was my surprise when, at day's end, emptying my bag on the ground, I found a very small grain of gold in the middle of the heap of poor grains of wheat. I bitterly wept and thought, "Would that I had had the courage to give everything I had!"[16]

In the time of the prophet Elijah, when a severe famine afflicted the country, a poor widow—a pagan—did not hesitate to part with her remaining meager provisions for the benefit of a stranger. One day, Jesus saw a poor woman, also a widow, who was giving an offering of two small coins, "her whole livelihood," while rich people, leaving large sums in the box, only made a dent in their surplus. To these examples we could add others, no less admirable, whether personally witnessed or heard from others. The generosity of the poor toward those poorer than themselves is a daily occurrence. Every time a vast fund drive is organized to come to the aid of the victims of a catastrophe, for instance, one can cite the case of poor persons whose modest alms, sent with apologies for not doing more, move the organizers and arouse the admiration of the public. But these stories, even though read in the Scriptures, risk remaining episodes of the Golden Legend. Reading them briefly provokes an edifying feeling, eventually a gesture of generosity, and that is that. Whether one has the possibility of easily dipping into reserves or not, one willingly speaks of the prudence that must moderate generosity. Is it not in this spirit that Paul encouraged the Corinthian Christians to show generosity in their help to their brothers and sisters in Jerusalem? It is "not that others should have relief while you are burdened, but that as a matter of equality your surplus at the present time should supply their needs, so that their surplus may also supply your needs, that there may be equality" (2 Cor 8:13-14).[17] This language is more apt to motivate us than the admirable examples related in today's liturgy. At any rate, this is the sort of language that is customarily used to initiate a large movement of generosity and solidarity: the appeal is made to the true meaning and duty of sharing.

Moreover, the Gospel records Jesus' warnings, severely blaming the affected piety of certain religious people who pursue honors and even take advantage of their authority and the prestige attached to their position to exploit defenseless persons. Beyond these scandalous and peculiarly odious persons, Jesus' warning concerns not only those who abuse their authority to commit evil acts but all those who are preoccupied with appearance rather than substance. However, the depiction is so exaggerated that we would find it difficult to feel personally concerned. We more willingly see there a caricature that certain persons would be well advised to heed in order to amend their ways. In our own case, we should begin to consider whether we behave in a certain way just to maintain our status in society, and question whether we sometimes throw our weight around a little, perhaps arrogantly.

Should we remain at this level in our reading, we risk forgetting that here we are dealing with the words of Jesus and passages from Scripture, whose aims are of an order other than that of human wisdom, and that they are proclaimed during the celebration of the mystery of God and Christ. God sent his Son into the world for the salvation of all. In order to realize this mission, the Lord Jesus, our high priest, has, of his own free will, offered the sacrifice of his life to his Father.

> Though he was in the form of God,
> [he] did not regard equality with God
>   something to be grasped.
>   Rather, he emptied himself,
> taking the form of a slave,
> coming in human likeness;
> and found human in appearance. . . .
> (Phil 2:6-7)

> For you know the gracious act of our Lord Jesus Christ, that for your sake he became poor although he was rich, so that by his poverty you might become rich.
> (2 Cor 8:9)

> Whoever wishes to be first among you will be the slave of all.
> (Mark 10:44)[18]

The sometimes heroic generosity of the poor, the admirable humility one encounters not only among the little ones but even among the powerful of this world direct—especially during the liturgy—the eyes of Christians toward the Lord, the only true Poor One, the Master "meek and humble of heart" (Matt 11:20), who gave everything for sinners, including his own life. The Beatitude of the poor applies to him in its fullness,

and because he recognizes in the poor and humble an image of his Son,
the Father's eyes rest on them with such benevolence and joy.

> The poor woman approached unknown,
> without renown,
> a humble face among other faces;
> in her hand two little coins.
> The Son of Man looked,
> he saw the heart that gave everything.

> *The eyes of the Lord on the poor.*

> Blessed are you, God our Father!
> you reveal to the humble
> the mysteries of the kingdom.

> Blessed are you, God our Father!
> you choose those who have nothing,
> here they are, rich in faith.

> Blessed are you, God our Father!
> you lower proud looks,
> you save the lowly.[19]

The Thirty-third Sunday in Ordinary Time

Each celebration of the Eucharist recalls the end toward which salvation history is directed, a history that unfolds from its origins, which Christ accomplished, and whose full realization we are awaiting.

> Dying you destroyed our death,
> rising you restored our life.
> Lord Jesus, come in glory."[1]

The certainty that everything is oriented toward an end is at the heart of Christian faith and hope.[2] Every year, on the Thirty-third and penultimate Sunday in Ordinary Time, the Church offers us a celebration explicitly centered on the mystery of the end-time. This celebration corresponds to that which begins the liturgical year, the First Sunday of Advent.

> When the liturgical year celebrates facts, successions of historical gestures and deeds, it does not attend to these as such, but to the eternal contents they explain and hold. These contents are the great work of God for the benefit of humanity, the redemption by Christ, who wants to snatch humanity from the narrowness of time in order to introduce it into endless eternity.[3]

The liturgy thus invites Christians to consider all things under the aspect of eternity by grounding themselves in the certainties guaranteed by faith: creation, which God made beautiful and good, will be transfigured by the Spirit; Christ will come again; those who prepared themselves to receive him will live with him forever; this future is decided in the present. It matters little to know when and how the new world will appear: at the end of a slow germination, invisible to human eyes, or with the dazzling suddenness of a flash of lightning? The images that evoke it must not mislead us. The day and the hour remain the secret of God alone.

> To arrive where you are, to get from where you are not,
>   You must go by a way wherein there is no ecstasy.
> In order to arrive at what you do not know
>   You must go by a way which is the way of ignorance.
> In order to possess what you do not possess
>   You must go by the way of dispossession.

In order to arrive at what you are not
   You must go through the way in which you are not.
And what you do not know is the only thing you know
And what you own is what you do not own
And where you are is where you are not.[4]

We must note that on this Thirty-third Sunday in Ordinary Time, we end the reading of Mark's Gospel. On the following Sunday, the Solemnity of Christ the King, we shall read a passage from John.

Thirty-third Sunday

"Heaven and Earth Will Pass Away, but My Words Will Not Pass Away"

The Salvation of the People of God Will Come "in those days"
The Book of Daniel is one of a literary genre so peculiar that ancient Bibles—Hebrew, Greek, Latin—classify it in different categories: either among the Hagiographa (Writings) or the Prophets. The same is true of modern Bibles.[1] As in some prophetic books, we find visions in Daniel, but never any specific oracles pronounced in the Lord's name. Like the hagiographers, the author of the Book of Daniel reports facts, events. The details in some of these stories are remarkable and are consistent with what we know from other sources; they probably correspond to the period when the book was written.[2] Other narratives resemble edifying stories composed from memories of the past and embroidered to the point of improbability.[3] They aim at encouraging the readers to remain steadfast in their faith and assiduous in their observance of the Lord's laws in spite of external pressures, persecutions, and the bad example of those who have faltered.[4] They want to show that God always has the last word and that faithfulness to his laws is always rewarded. Finally, the author envisions the end of salvation history, which he calls the end-time. On this Sunday, we read a few verses of this "apocalypse" (Dan 12:1-3).[5]

History appears as an unceasing and always to be renewed struggle between good and evil, a sort of hydra—or dragon (Rev 12:3)—with seven heads, that rises with more vigor than ever each time one thinks one has mastered it. This experience threatens with discouragement those who heroically undertake this battle. Memory of past victories can give them heart for a moment. But how can one forget that today's or tomorrow's successes will certainly be challenged, like all the others, by new and increasingly aggressive assaults of evil? At this point, we see the apocalyptic writers revealing to us that at the end of history we shall see, after a last and especially violent confrontation, the dazzling and definitive victory of good. Although set at the horizon of history, this denouement is not far away.[6] In order for it to happen, the decisive intervention of an up to then hidden force will be necessary.

> At that time there shall arise
>   Michael, the great prince,
>   guardian of your people. . . .
> (Dan 12:1)

"Sent to serve, for the sake of those who are to inherit salvation" (Heb 1:14), angels, in the Bible, are messengers and executors of God's will.[7] They play an important role in the apocalyptic literature that describes the last day. But the Book of Daniel is the first to mention Michael.[8] His name—"who is like God"—designates him as the closest auxiliary and servant of God. If he "arise[s]"—stands erect—now, it is because the hour is dangerous and because God wants, once and for all, to put an end to evil. The struggle promises to be hard.

> It shall be a time unsurpassed in distress
>   since nations began until that time.
> At that time your people shall escape,
>   everyone who is found written in the book

in which the good works of everyone are recorded,[9] and not just his or her nationality. For the names of those saved from among all nations will be found in it (Isa 2:1).

One question presents itself: What will happen to those who perished in the struggles that preceded the final one? Their sacrifice certainly prevented a total victory of evil and allowed others to come forward in order to continue the struggle. Their martyrdom and heroism will be remembered with gratitude. Nevertheless, they died without having had the joy, however well deserved, of seeing the day of victory. Similarly, their tormentors, those who hideously tortured them, having died in the belief that their cause would prevail, are not going to witness the defeat. In brief, on whatever side they were, all, finally, will have the same fate. No, the author of Daniel answers. There will be many who rise after sleeping in the dust.

> Some shall live forever,
>   others shall be an everlasting horror and disgrace.

The fact that the just shared in the common fate of humanity will obtain for them a place in the kingdom to come. They will not undergo what John's Revelation calls "the second death."[10]

But the wise shall shine brightly
  like the splendor of the firmament,
And those who lead the many to justice
  shall be like the stars forever.

The condition of the risen is beyond imagination and can be evoked only through images as incorporeal as possible.[11] That of light is among them; it says that those who rise from "the dust of the earth" and the shadow of death[12] will have a share in the nature of God, who is light (see 1 John 1:5),[13] in a new world characterized by the radiance coming from God.[14]

Then the Lord will lift my head, and before his glance my veils will be
  snatched by fire,
And I shall remain there as a mirror that unveils before the worlds.
And the stars will recognize in me their light of praise,
  and the ages will recognize in me what is eternal in them,
  and the souls will recognize in me what is divine in them,
And God will recognize in me his love.
And no veil will fall over my head except the dazzling face of my judge.
Then the world will disappear.
And to see him will be called Grace, and Grace will be called the Infinite.
And the Infinite will be called Bliss. *Amen.*[15]

Throughout good days and disastrous ones, history is walking toward "that time" of light and salvation. The whole creation longs with all its strength to see this revelation. It "was made subject to futility" but hopes to "be set free from slavery to corruption and share in the glorious freedom of the children of God." "All creation is groaning in labor pains even until now" in expectation of the deliverance whose day is unknown but that cannot tarry (Rom 8:19-23).

Keep me safe, O God;
you are my hope.

O Lord, my allotted portion and my cup,
  you it is who hold fast my lot.

———

I set the LORD ever before me;
  with him at my right hand I shall not be disturbed.
Therefore my heart is glad and my soul rejoices,
  my body, too, abides in confidence;
Because you will not abandon my soul to the nether world,
  nor will you suffer your faithful one to undergo corruption.

You will show me the path to life,
  fullness of joys in your presence,
  the delights at your right hand forever.
(Ps 16:5, 8-11)

Sitting at the Right Hand of God, Christ Waits for Us

The five verses of this Sunday's second reading are taken from the conclusion of the long development in the Letter to the Hebrews on the priesthood of Christ, our high priest. They recapitulate what has already been said in different ways: the efficacy of Christ's sacrifice comes from the fact that only he is Priest in the full sense of the term (Heb 10:11-14, 18).[16]

One last time, the author of Hebrews draws a parallel between the priests of the old covenant and Jesus Christ: "Every priest stands daily at his ministry, offering frequently those same sacrifices that can never take away sins." The image is clear and symbolic. One could say that it visually evokes the intense liturgical activity of priests who daily, and still more on certain feast days, had innumerable sacrifices to offer in the sanctuary. Their multiplicity and their unceasing repetition showed that while granting to the sacrifices a special and very expressive value of intercession,[17] people were clearly aware of their limited efficacy: it depended upon the depth of feeling of those who asked for these sacrifices to be offered in their names. Christ, for his part, offered a perfect sacrifice, once and for all. He returned to the Father to offer it to him, and he does not need to repeat it. This is why he is not standing at his ministry; he has completed his priestly ministry—his service—with his passover; from now on he is no longer standing in the attitude befitting a servant, but seated "at the right hand of God."

> Do not believe that, because he is a priest, he always discharges his function; he was content to fulfill his ministry once, and then he sat down. For we must not imagine that he stands in heaven and ministers there; that is for those who serve. In the same way as he was servant, he also was priest and minister; but he remained neither servant nor minister; it is not for a minister to be seated, he must remain standing. The grandeur of the sacrifice is indicated by the very fact that it was offered only once and that this oblation was sufficient to effect what all other sacrifices had not been able to do.[18]

> To stand in the presence of God is the sign that one is his minister; but to sit near him proves that, like him, one receives the sacrifice.[19]

Christ, the only seated priest, is therefore different from all those who preceded him. But this image, which shows the incomparable superiority of Christ's priesthood over that of the old covenant, also shows that, in the new covenant, there is only one true Priest, Christ sitting at God's right hand. Henceforth, it is his sacrifice that the Church offers. The numerous Eucharists do not really replicate it, but make it present under the signs of bread and wine and give us the opportunity to receive its fruits. The celebrants of this paschal mystery are "standing priests," servants of the one High Priest. They do not replace him; they are "sacraments"—that is, visible and efficacious signs—of his presence. Their priestly ministry refers itself to the only Priest.[20]

They are ordained, mandated, sent to communicate to all the call of Christ, who invites us to receive the fruits of his unique sacrifice. Having taken "his seat forever at the right hand of God[,] now he waits until his enemies are made his footstool" (see Ps 110:2). On the side of God and Christ, all is completed, "made perfect forever"; by his perfect sacrifice, our High Priest has obtained from his Father the pardon of sins for all humankind. But humans live "in time," and although the victory is already won in heaven, on earth the struggle goes on. The sovereign efficacy of Christ's pasch reaches humans "in time" and progressively transforms their lives. Near God, Christ waits to take them into his glory, on the other side of the veil, in the heavenly sanctuary.

Return of the Son of Man, Gathering of the Elect

Under diverse and varied forms, the prophets foretold, under the term "Day of the Lord," a decisive intervention of God in the course of human history and salvation. "In those days" extraordinary events will occur. They will shake heaven and earth in the manner of a cosmic catastrophe of unimaginable magnitude. People will be terrified. But at the end of this harrowing period, the dawn of salvation will rise; this is why we speak of a "Day of the Lord" that the faithful must await in trust.[21] In the apocalypses,[22] this Day is that of the End, described with a wealth of images and symbols. Their precise meaning remains obscure and has given rise to all sorts of interpretations. By taking them together, we get a very vivid, impressive, and terrifying scene. In times of crises and upheavals—natural catastrophes, plagues, wars—apocalypses of whatever origin, often mixed together, find a renewal of popularity. Interpretations are circulated that claim to know the meaning of each image, each symbol, and, on that basis, pretend to announce with certainty and in great detail what is going to happen and to give precise dates to the foretold events.[23]

Of course, Jesus knew the prophecies and other biblical predictions concerning the Day of the Lord, particularly those of the Book of Daniel about the coming of the Son of Man,[24] a rather mysterious title that he applied to himself.[25] Besides, his teaching essentially bears upon the good news of the kingdom of God, the coming of which is at hand with the advent of the Son of Man.[26] The three Synoptics have kept the memory of a discourse of Jesus more explicitly devoted to this prediction of the end. Each of them narrated it in reference to the concrete circumstances of his time and to the situation of the Church in which he lived. But the three of them inserted it just before the account of the passion.[27] On this Sunday, we read the excerpt from Mark's Gospel dealing with the appearance of the Son of Man at the end of a period of undetermined duration, and especially troubled (Mark 13:24-32).[28]

> "But in those days after that tribulation
> the sun will be darkened,
>   and the moon will not give its light,
> and the stars will be falling from the sky,
>   and the powers in the heavens will be shaken."

This is the classical language of apocalypse.[29] We must not yield to the temptation of imagining the cosmic upheavals alluded to and still less of picturing them.[30] On the other hand, it is instructive to bring this description side by side with the story of creation. Then, God began by creating light, separating it from darkness,[31] afterwards making lights—sun, moon, stars—to illumine the earth and "mark the fixed times, the days and the years."[32] "In those days" humans will not have at their disposal their usual points of reference, trustworthy up till then. But this is not to say that creation will be destroyed and chaos will return as before, when "the earth was a formless wasteland" and "darkness covered the abyss." These disturbances will act as a prelude to the coming of the Son of Man. He will be seen "coming in the clouds with great power and glory." It is inconceivable that such a glorious appearance should happen in a desolate world, that it should have for its setting an indescribable heap of wreckage and ruins, that it should unfold on a stage filled with debris and other rubbish accumulated by the gigantic collapse of a world suddenly crashing to pieces. Rather, the image evokes a new creation, where the sun will be darkened, the moon will lose its light, and the stars will fall before the splendor of the Son of Man (see Rev 21:23).

"Then he will send out the angels and gather [his] elect from the four winds, from the end of the earth to the end of the sky." Mark fixes his readers' attention not so much on the "tribulation" that precedes the end as on the luminous and glorious manifestation of the Son of Man who comes to gather the elect. What is presented here is an encouraging perspective, the good news, or rather the ultimate fulfilling of the good news, "the gospel of Jesus Christ [the Son of God]," that began to be proclaimed after John the Baptist was cast into prison.[33] Indeed, there was no need to depict for the Christians to whom the evangelist was addressing himself the "tribulation" that they must confront before the coming of the Son of Man; they suffered from its harshness; it severely tested their hope and their courage. Grave events, recent or foreseeable, were felt as the announcement of an unparalleled catastrophe. Some Christians were violently expelled from Rome in 51-52. After the fire of Rome in July 68, Nero had set in motion a fierce persecution against Christians, accused of arson and delivered to popular vengefulness. Peter and Paul had been executed. Even though the destruction of the Temple by Titus' armies (in 70) had not yet taken place, the stranglehold on Jerusalem was worsening; rumors of war boded ill. There were plenty of reasons to feel pessimistic and to fear.[34] But the gospel says to Christians, in effect: "Do not panic, do not lose heart; it is not yet the end. Do not forget that the Son of Man will come to inaugurate a new creation and gather all the elect around himself."[35]

Still, a question remains that occurs again and again with new urgency, "Tell us, when will this happen, and what sign will there be when all these things are about to come to an end" (Mark 13:4). Jesus' answer is apt to disconcert us; in any case, it does not satisfy our curiosity. To know the day and the hour has no true importance for salvation. On the other hand, we must absolutely know how to act when faced with the prospect of the coming of the Son of Man "in those days" that remain and will remain undetermined. This is the teaching of the little parable of the fig tree.[36] "When its branch becomes tender and sprouts leaves, you know that summer is near. In the same way, when you see these things happening, know that he is near, at the gates." Appearances of false prophets, famines, wars, persecutions, catastrophes of all kinds (see Mark 13:5-13) are harbingers of the coming of the Son of God, as the onset of labor pains announces imminent birth (see 13:8). We must endeavor to decipher them, which is not without risk. The first Christians, in their impatience for the return of the Lord, had persuaded themselves that the event would occur during their lifetimes. They repeated Jesus' words, "Amen, I say to you, this generation will not pass away until all these things have taken place.'' But what meaning was to be given to the expression "this generation"?

> I observe, then, that though Christians might be mistaken in what they took to be signs of Christ's coming, yet they were not wrong in their state of mind, they were not mistaken in looking out, and that for Christ. Whether credulous or not, they only acted as one acts toward some person beloved, or revered, or admired on earth. . . .
>
> I had rather be he, who, from love of Christ and want of science, thinks some strange sight in the sky, comet or meteor, to be the sign of his coming, than the man, who from more knowledge and from lack of love, laughs at the mistake.[37]

To scrutinize without anxiety, but with attention to the signs of the manifestation of the Son of Man, reveals a faith that is awake and a holy haste to see his Day (see 13:33-37). If, on the contrary, this watchfulness and expectation slacken, we become ensnared in the here-below. Christian communities and the Church at large see their inner dynamism decrease, their missionary ardor cool. Sullenness sets in, blocking all apostolic boldness; even liturgy and prayer mutter along. "Heaven and earth will pass away, but my words will not pass away.'' The Son of Man is near, standing at the door, knocking. In order to hear him and open, so that he may enter and sit at our table, we must lend the ear of our heart (see Rev 3:20). "It is better to be wrong in our watching, than not to watch at all"[38] precisely because "of that day or hour, [that] no one knows, neither the angels in heaven, nor the Son, but only the Father.''

That the Son does not know must not surprise us: he has put on human nature in its entirety—except for sin—and therefore also its limits. We are thus decisively shown that questions of date and time in our earthly way of reckoning are not taken into account in matters of salvation. It is sufficient for us to know with certainty that the Day of the Lord will come, and to commit ourselves to the Father with a deep attitude of faith and trust.

In the sanctuary of heaven into which he entered after finishing his work, Christ, our high priest, seated at the right hand of God, waits for all things on earth to come to their conclusion. And we also are waiting, but standing, for the Day to come. To live in this attitude of watchfulness and study the signs of the coming of the Lord, allow us to discern, in the little or great events of our personal lives, of the life of the Church, and of the life of the world, the comings of Christ, unceasing, discreet, but decisive as he beckons to us and calls us to follow him day after day.

How many more centuries of pain
Before the full daylight, Lord?

You are patiently molding us, we are going toward the end,
But your body of humanity is slow to complete.

Not enough nights to welcome you,
Not enough heads to bow before you!

We announce you in the sufferings of the world,
We speak before being born.

In the shadow that covers us and where we are waiting for you,
We already sing your light.

How many more centuries before it may dazzle us,
How many remembrances of Christmas?

The Father of all love has entrusted his hope to us,
We stretch our hopes toward him.

In you, our hopes are all one;
Your hope quivers, it overcomes our pain.[39]

Thirty-fourth Sunday

Christ, King of the Universe

Since Vatican II,[1] the liturgical year has concluded with the feast of Christ the King, celebrated on the Thirty-fourth Sunday in Ordinary Time.[2] One minor peculiarity marks Year B. The Gospel reading of the feast is not taken from Mark, who has been our guide throughout the Sunday celebrations of the Day of the Lord that is devoted to the weekly memorial of Christ's pasch.[3] Mark's Gospel is set aside after the Thirty-third Sunday and a text from John's Gospel is chosen for the feast of Christ the King.[4]

Royal Enthronement of the Son of Man

> He received dominion, glory, and kingship;
>> nations and peoples of every language serve him.
> His dominion is an everlasting dominion
>> that shall not be taken away,
>> his kingship shall not be destroyed.
> (Dan 7:14)

Christians hear this proclamation and spontaneously understand it as a reminder of the royal enthronement of the risen Christ, welcomed in heaven by the Father. This perception corresponds exactly to the intention of the liturgy that employs this text from Daniel for the feast of Christ the King. Nevertheless, it is useful and fruitful to ponder these two biblical verses for a few moments (Dan 7:13-14).[5]

The sacred author relates what appears to him in the course of "visions during the night," in dreams. We would be mistaken if we understood that he really enjoys a vision in the strict sense of the term: this is not what he means; he simply has recourse to a literary genre quite popular in his time.[6] The very fact that the scene described is the fruit of the imagination reveals the deep thought of the author. When poets describe a landscape, a face in a way that does not correspond to objective reality or in a frankly surrealistic manner, it is because they see things in their imaginations, in their dreams. Besides, the text of the Book of Daniel shows a remarkable appropriation and development of images sketched in previous biblical writings. In other dreams, the author sees the fall of empires that collapsed, even though they were believed to be unshakable: Babylon, Media, Persia, the one founded by Alexander (see Dan 1:7-8).[7] He lives in an especially harsh time because the country is under the domination of Antiochus Epiphanes, who persecutes Jews and is bent on forcing them to abandon their religion. He, too, will fall, like all the others.[8] But this assurance does not come from an analysis of the political and military situation, which would allow an astute observer to foresee that the tables will be turned. The conviction of the author of the Book of Daniel rests on his faith in God, to whom alone belong power and dominion over the earth, as over heaven. God does not have a savior in reserve; he has already enthroned him at his side and has conferred on him "dominion, glory and kingship" that he might reign over all peoples and nations. Whatever the present trials may be, we must not be disheartened. In spite of appearances to the contrary, the order willed by God is going to be established. The "visions during the night" cannot lie.

But who is this mysterious Son of Man enthroned in solemnity at the side of him who sits on the throne?[9] Originally, the phrase son of man simply meant a human being. Owing to various influences that are difficult, if not impossible, to trace with any certainty, the Book of Daniel thus designates a person who, while remaining human, belongs to the heavenly world, the leader and representative of the holy ones of the Almighty. This term lost its original meaning and came to designate a specific person, a transition representing a remarkable advance in thinking. Salvation cannot come from just any human being, however prestigious, but only from the Son of Man: a human being, yes, but one who has an absolutely unique relationship with God, who is entrusted with an incomparable mission and unequalled power. Because the meaning of this title is at once mysterious and open, Jesus applied it to himself. This title described him as the Man who was more than a mere human being, and whose true identity could be discovered only through faith.[10] Therefore, when we read this title in the Gospels, we must remember the "visions during the night" recorded in the Book of Daniel. This text, which at first sight may seem nothing more than a beautiful image, shows how biblical thought progressed, eventually making use of material coming from other milieux. A banal locution designating "anyone," evokes the primordial human being who represents the whole species. From there, one ascends to the idea of a Son of Man who would be completely apart—one does not yet know how—nearer to God than anyone else, without, however, ceasing to belong to our human race. A dream? No, rather he whom God prepared and who came, Jesus Christ, the Son of Man, the Son of God become human.

The Book of Daniel also shows this piercing look "during the night," which is called hope based on faith.

> We are sometimes inclined to think that the same things are monotonously repeated over and over again in the history of creation. That is because the season is too long by comparison with the brevity of our individual lives, and the transformation too vast and too inward by comparison with our superficial and restricted outlook, for us to see the progress of what is tirelessly taking place in and through all matter and all spirit. Let us believe in Revelation, once again our faithful support in our most human forebodings. Under the commonplace envelope of things and of all our purified and salvaged efforts, a New Earth is being slowly engendered.[11]

"Beginning with Moses and all the prophets, [Jesus] interpreted to them what referred to him in all the scriptures" (Luke 24.27). The vision of the Book of Daniel opens us to the understanding of the mystery of Christ, King of the Universe, whom we proclaim in faith.

> *The Lord is king;*
> *he is robed in majesty.*
>
> The LORD is king, in splendor robed;
>   robed is the LORD and girt about with strength;
> And he has made the world firm,
>   not to be moved.
> Your throne stands firm from of old;
>   from everlasting you are, O LORD.
>
> ———
>
> Your decrees are worthy of trust indeed:
>   holiness befits your house,
>   O LORD, for length of days.
> (Ps 93:1-2, 5)

He Comes on the Clouds; All Will See Him

The last of the New Testament writings, the Revelation of John, presents itself from the opening verses on, as an unveiling of "what must happen soon": the return of Jesus, the object of the ardent hope and fervent prayer of the Church.[12] Today, we read an excerpt from the prologue of the book; it expresses well the author's intention, and gives a first glimpse of the spiritual and doctrinal density of his work, of his fiery style. This text, liturgical in character, fits in a remarkable way with the feast of Christ the King (Rev 1:5-8).[13]

"Grace to you and peace . . . from Jesus Christ, the faithful witness, the firstborn of the dead and ruler of the kings of the earth." What a fullness in this salutation, so well balanced that it seems borrowed from the liturgy! "Grace and peace" are the perfect gifts that contain all others, those to which Christians aspire with all their strength, which they ask of God, and which they never cease to wish one another. They are given by God and received with profound thankfulness. They come to us "from Jesus Christ." "Faithful witness" of the thoughts, the intentions, and the will of the Father, he made these known, as he had been instructed to do. Thus, he can testify to the good news that we have received.[14] God gives us "grace and peace" because in his Son, Jesus Christ, "the firstborn of the dead," he sees the new humanity, of which he has become the head, risen with him from the tomb. His exaltation at the right hand of God makes him the "ruler of the Kings of the earth"; for in him the universe has been redeemed. We can imagine John himself addressing this admirable salutation to the Christian assembly nourished by the same teaching we find reflected in his writing.

But the liturgy goes on. One of the elders of the community intones a thanksgiving—anamnesis:[15] "To him who loves us and has freed us from our sins by his blood, who has made us into a kingdom, priests for his God and Father, to him be glory and power forever [and ever]. Amen." In a few words, everything is recalled. "God is love" (1 John 4:8, 16). "In this way the love of God was revealed to us: God sent his only Son into the world so that we might have life through him. In this is love: not that we have loved God, but that he loved us and sent his Son as expiation for our sins" (1 John 4:9-10). "See what love the Father has bestowed on us that we may be called the children of God. Yet so we are" (1 John 3:1). Jesus manifested this by giving his life for us (see 1 John 3:16). We are called to reign in heaven near him, to take part "through him, with him, in him" in the eternal praise of the Father. As the Christian assembly still does today after the great doxology of the Eucharistic Prayer, John's assembly responds with one voice, "Amen! Amen!" in a great burst of faith and thankfulness.

Another of the persons surrounding John proclaims in turn:

> Behold, he is coming amid the clouds,
>   and every eye will see him,
>   even those who pierced him.
> All the peoples of the earth will lament him.
>   Yes. *Amen.*

Every liturgy, especially the Eucharistic liturgy, is both an anamnesis and an announcement of what is going to happen; it focuses on the fulfillment of all things. "Lord Jesus, come in glory."[16] The evocation of Christ's return borrows from the Book of Daniel (7:13)[17] and from the prophet Zechariah, who wrote, "They shall look on him whom they have thrust through, and they shall mourn for him as one mourns for an only son, and they shall grieve over him as one grieves over a firstborn" (12:10). The beginning of this same text is quoted in John's Gospel and refers to the soldier who thrust his spear into Jesus' side, from which "immediately blood and water flowed out" (see John 19:33-37). This episode has a special importance for John: he sees in it a sign of the gift of the Spirit and eternal life.[18] Henceforth, looking at the pierced heart of Christ is essential if one is to benefit from the salvation acquired by the blood poured out on Calvary. Those who, in faith, "look upon" (John 19:37) Christ on the cross know that he is coming back in glory: "Yes, in truth! Amen!"

The Lord himself concludes this gathering, liturgical in structure, by a solemn statement, perhaps pronounced by the president of the assembly, his spokesperson.[19] "I am the Alpha and the Omega . . . the one who is and who was and who is to come, the almighty." "I [am] the Alpha and the Omega, the beginning and the end": God speaks thus of himself (Rev 21:6); Christ also (see Rev 22:13), because he can say, like God, "I am" (Exod 3:14).[20]

Like God, who is always present and acting in the world of humankind, today as yesterday, and will continue tomorrow as today, Jesus says, "I am . . . the one who is and who was and who is to come." God is "the almighty." But Jesus, the Son of God, the Word who "was with God" and through whom "the world came to be" (John 1:1-3, 10), is also almighty. This faith is remarkably expressed, and rightly so, in the representations of Christ in glory—Pantocrator, "Master of Everything," "Sovereign Master"—that adorn the tympana or apses of many churches.

It is always with their eyes fixed on this icon that the Christian assembly celebrates the mystery of God and of Christ's pasch—dead, risen, glorified—who is, was, and comes to save his people. But the same icon must remain before our eyes and in our hearts, as Christians, every day of our lives, and chiefly when we find ourselves confronted by trials.

> I arise today
> through God's strength to pilot me:
> God's might to uphold me,

God's wisdom to guide me,
God's eye to look before me,
God's ear to hear me. . . .

———

Christ with me, Christ before me, Christ behind me,
Christ in me, Christ beneath me, Christ above me,
Christ on my right, Christ on my left,
Christ where I lie, Christ where I sit, Christ where I arise,
Christ in the heart of every [person] who thinks of me,
Christ in the mouth of every [person] who speaks of me,
Christ in every eye that sees me,
Christ in every ear that hears me.[21]

"My Kingdom Does Not Belong to this World"

The arraignment of Jesus before Pilate, the Roman procurator, occupies an important place in John's Gospel, whereas the examination by the high priest Caiaphas is hardly mentioned.[22] Whatever the general reasons that led the evangelist to deal at length with that phase of Jesus' prosecution,[23] this is the first and only time that Jesus finds himself face to face with a representative of political power. In trying the case of the man brought before him, Pilate, as is natural, seeks to learn what subversive activity this man is guilty of, that he should deserve death. In fact, it is the Roman functionary who inquires, before all else, about a possible claim of Jesus to kingship. If this accusation is proved true, it will suffice to bring the death penalty without any need for debate, since every proved rebellion against Caesar's authority is punishable by death ipso facto. But now we hear a dialogue between Pilate and Jesus on the subject of Jesus' pretension to kingship. This Gospel passage decisively illuminates the meaning and scope of the title of King given to Christ (John 18:33b-37).[24]

"Are you the King of the Jews?" This is a clever question, put by Pilate, who immediately perceives that the situation is delicate and full of traps. What do these men who have sent Jesus before his tribunal want? Are they conspiring to hear him take sides in some dark quarrel among themselves concerning the authority of one of their own? Does he have to deal with one of these rabble-rousers who appear at regular intervals in this country? Why have they delivered him into his hands to have him condemned to capital punishment? Pilate senses that there are hidden elements that escape him and that risk putting him in a dangerous position. Jesus' answer might give him a clue or at least allow him to proceed in his questioning. But Jesus does not answer; he himself asks a question, "Do you say this on your own or have others told you about me?" Jesus is not hedging; he wants Pilate to specify in what sense he is speaking of kingship. The procurator's reply betrays irritation and a haughty contempt for rabbinical subtleties, but it has the merit of clarity. Pilate speaks like everyone else, that is, like Romans: there is no place for quibbling about the meaning of the word "king." Let Jesus answer the question put to him! Jesus does so, and the pertinence of his response endures to this day. It, indeed, clarifies questions that continue to be asked and that the celebration of today's feast reactivates. Are all the ways of understanding his kingship and speaking about it correct? What does the title King of the Universe mean? Risks of ambiguities and errors are not negligible. This Gospel passage cannot be eliminated, and we must heed and ponder the Lord's words with even more attention because the subject is critical.

"My kingdom does not belong to this world. If my kingdom did belong to this world, my attendants [would] be fighting to keep me from being handed over to the Jews." The Gospels show that Jesus did not use any kind of force to impose his teaching upon anyone. Physical force is always obvious, but Jesus had no recourse to it. Nor did he employ other insidious means of coercion, such as exploiting people's dreams of an earthly paradise, or remaining silent about just how difficult it would be to practice his teachings.

He had sent those who surrounded him to preach in the ways and by-ways with "no food, no sack, no money in their belts" (Mark 6:8), telling them, "Whatever place does not welcome you or listen to you, leave there and shake the dust off your feet in testimony against them" (Mark 6:11). James and John were roundly rebuked on the day when, in their indignation at seeing the Samaritans unwilling to receive Jesus in their village, they suggested that they bring down fire from heaven upon the Samaritans (Luke 9:52). He taught that in order to be great in his kingdom, one must be the slave of all, as he himself was, who came "not to be served but to serve and to give his life as a ransom for many" (Mark 10:44-45). No, indeed, his kingdom does not belong to this world. And yet, Jesus is king, as he declares before Pilate.[25]

"For this I was born and for this I came into the world: to testify to the truth." Jesus has not been vested with power by humans; he comes from above. Already in this sense, his kingdom does not belong to this world. Moreover, he came "to testify to the truth." But "what is truth?" To understand what Jesus means, we must refer to the meaning that the Bible, not philosophy or common usage, gives to this word. In biblical language, truth is a road one can follow with complete trust in order to have life. It is contained in God's law because truth is something "to be done"; one must "be and walk in truth" by conforming one's actions and one's whole life to the will, to the word of God, "[a] lamp to [our] feet . . . / a light to [our] path" (Ps 119:105).[26] Jesus was sent by the Father and invested by him with the mission of testifying to that kind of truth. He taught it by words, by actions, and lastly by his death. He even is, personally, "the way and the truth and the life" (John 14:6).[27] All persons who belong to the truth, who are imbued with it, who keep in their hearts God's law, will, promises (see Ps 119:10-11),[28] recognize, with wonder, God's voice in Jesus', and consequently listen to it and welcome it.

> Listen, therefore, Jews and Gentiles, listen, all you kingdoms of the earth! I am not competing with your dominion in this world. "My kingdom does not belong to this world." Let go of this vain fear that caused Herod the Great to tremble when he learned of the birth of Christ, this fear that pushed him into killing so many children in hope of reaching Jesus, this fear that, more than his anger, made him cruel. "My kingdom does not belong to this world." What more do you want? Come to this kingdom that does not belong to this world, come to it in faith and do not grow cruel through fear.
>
> Indeed, what is his kingdom, if not those who believe in him and to whom he said, "[You] do not belong to the world any more than I belong to the world" (John 17:16). However, he wanted them to remain in the world, and this is why he says to his Father about them, "I do not ask that you take them out of the world but that you keep them from the evil one" (John 17:15). Consequently, he does not say here either, "My kingdom is not in this world," but "My kingdom does not belong to the world."
>
> For his kingdom is here below until the end of the world. Up to the harvest, it is mixed with weeds. And the harvest is the end of the world, when the harvesters, that is, the angels, come to take out of his kingdom all scandals, a thing that would be impossible if his kingdom were not here below: it is in the world as if on the road.[29]

To proclaim and celebrate Christ, King of the Universe, is to recognize with thanksgiving to God—"to him be glory, and power forever [and ever]"—that Jesus, enthroned at the right hand of the Father, is the Alpha and Omega, the beginning and the end of all things, the unique Savior of all human beings to whom he brings grace and peace, heavenly gifts.

His kingdom does not belong to this world, for it uses means that have nothing in common with those of the world. Jesus came "proclaiming the gospel of God: 'This is the time of fulfillment. . . . Repent, and believe in the gospel' '' (Mark 1:14-15). He showed by his testimony in words and deeds the way of truth and life that leads to the "kingdom of God . . . at hand.'' He has entrusted his Church and each one of his disciples, according to each one's vocation, with the mission of proclaiming this gospel throughout the whole world by using the same means he himself used: testimony even to death, if necessary. The Church and every Christian community must be, according to their possibilities, an image of this kingdom where, in order to become great, one joyfully becomes the servant of all, beginning with the weakest, the most destitute, the lowliest.

To follow Christ, King of the Universe, by going against the ways of the world, brings many difficulties. Jesus said it: "There is no one who has given up house or brothers or sisters or mother or father or children or lands for my sake and for the sake of the gospel who will not receive a hundred times more now in this present age . . . with persecutions, and eternal life in the age to come'' (Mark 10:29-30).[30] Indeed, "the kings of the earth rise up, / and the princes conspire together / against the LORD and against his anointed. . .'' (Ps 2:2). But God gave to the one he made king "the nations for an inheritance / and the ends of the earth for [his] possession'' (Ps 2:8b-c). We trustfully raise our eyes toward him who, his heart opened on the cross, draws everyone to himself (see John 12:32) to lead them with him into his kingdom (see Luke 23:43).

> Jesus, Lord, you are king of kings,
> Light of light, you!
> Light of light.
>
> O Word, before fulfilling the Law,
> You made heaven and earth, You!
> You made heaven and earth.
>
> You are the Alpha, You are the Omega,
> The core of the Mystery, You!
> The core of the Mystery.
>
> You took flesh, Truth of faith,
> Only Son of the Father, You!
> Only Son of the Father.
>
> Savior, O Christ, a human dead on the cross,
> God himself liberates us, You!
> God himself liberates us.[31]

Postscript

Every liturgical year celebrates the mystery of salvation prepared by God from the beginning, realized in Christ, and unfolding in time until its fulfillment at the second coming of the Lord. It recalls past events and turns our eyes toward expected events. But the here-and-now of the world, of the Church, of diverse Christian communities, and of every individual is integrated, in a dynamic way, into the history of salvation that never stops developing without interruption. This is what all passages from Scripture—both the Old and New Testaments—proclaim day in day out. But the liturgical year is not just a memorial of the past and a prophetic announcement of the future. Being a celebration, it takes the "today" of each believer and each community of the Church and the world and purifies and transforms it, so that it might be integrated into the building up of the holy city of "tomorrow." The light of God will illuminate this city when, after the struggles and trials here below, the immense crowd of all the redeemed will at last be gathered around Christ.[1]

Since the reform prescribed by Vatican II, the liturgical year is characterized by the reading of one of the three Synoptic Gospels. Thus the twofold dimension, divine and human, of salvation history is made clearer. Because, "in these last days" (Heb 1:2), the Son of God himself, born in our flesh, entered human history, whose slowness and heaviness, resistances and trials he knew, including the supreme trial of the death of a just person rejected by the world.

But who is this Jesus? He proclaimed he was coming to establish the kingdom of God. Why is his coming delayed for so long? To these and many other questions believers never cease asking themselves, each evangelist brings elements of an answer, and especially of reflection, quite real, because they are inserted into history. Each of them addressed a specific Christian community that was in a particular situation, with its difficulties, its problems, its questions, and its riches. Now, the liturgy allows us to receive, together with the testimonies of Matthew, Luke, and John, the testimony of Mark, which proves especially precious in our day.[2]

Mark speaks to Christians distressed by the living conditions of their

318

time. They are but a handful. The entire Church is persecuted, and the Lord appears to be insensitive to the storms that batter the world and the Church. Evangelization is advancing but slowly and meets with painful failures. Profound tremors disturb and even endanger the usual balance of the world; the future appears uncertain. What has happened to the power of the Lord's resurrection and the kingdom of God that he said was "at hand"? What is the use of renouncing everything for Christ?

To these Christians—with whom we feel a kinship—Mark says, "Why be astonished and scandalized by all this? Would you forget that the cross is the obligatory way to bring about the kingdom of God? Yes, we often face choices that demand heroism. But look at the Lord Jesus." Son of God, he was, the evangelist stresses, the most human of all humans with their weaknesses, their ignorance; he, too, met with harsh failures in the course of his ministry—to begin with, the lack of understanding and the slowness to believe exhibited by those he had chosen and even by his own family. The authority of his word was held in check by the lack of faith shown by many. But, indeed, the mystery of his person is not easily or totally penetrated. "But who is this Jesus of Nazareth?" The question is asked all through Mark's Gospel. Paradoxically, it is a pagan who, witnessing his death, recognizes in him "the Son of God" (15:39). From that time on, the time of hidden revelations granted to a few as a secret is over. Now the gospel must be proclaimed to all nations.

Nevertheless, Jesus remains elusive in many respects: it is impossible to enclose him within any limits. He seems to endlessly evade us. In fact, he draws us farther and farther onto unknown paths. He is ahead of us, so we always see him from the back, illuminated on the horizon where the dawn of the new day he announces is imminent. The liturgical climate of Mark's Gospel accentuates even more its relevance to our times. The Lord is here, but his presence is chiefly perceptible through signs, above all the Bread of Life which the fourth Gospel recorded and which is read during this liturgical year. Intimate moments with the Lord are always brief, like the stops of travelers who still have a long way to go: "Let us go elsewhere!" "Go in the peace of Christ!"

The rhythm at which, under Mark's guidance, we go through the liturgical year, reminds us that time is passing. We must not remain as a blind or a deaf and mute person, sitting alone by the roadside, when Jesus goes by more or less secretly. It is the opportunity for us to rise without hesitation, to leap up and join those who have met him before us and walk following him resolutely at a brisk pace. His day is about to dawn.

Day of the Living One
For our earth!
The fruit
That God blesses
Ripens into light:
Sun tearing night apart!

Day of the Living One
On our history!
The body
Bruised yesterday
Radiates his glory:
Love has broken death!

Day of the Living One
On our exodus!
From water
And the Spirit
All humans are reborn:
Each one bears a new name!

Day of the Living One
So far, so near!
Wine has been served to us
Announcing the nuptials:
The joy of the kingdom is coming![3]

NOTES

Ordinary Time B—Pages 1-2

1. Year B: 1994, 1997, 2000, 2003, etc.
2. This continuous reading is not integral. From the block 1:14–13:32, a little more than half is read: 248 verses out of 489. However, in Year B, we read Mark 1:1-8 on the Second Sunday of Advent, 1:7-11 on Epiphany, 1:12-15 on the First Sunday of Lent, 14:1–15:47 on Passion Sunday, 16:1-8 at the Paschal Vigil, 16:15-20 on Ascension Thursday. In all, in the course of Year B we thus read 420 verses of the 679 in Mark's Gospel. It must be added that we read the whole of Mark 1:14–12:44 every year from Monday of the First Week in Ordinary Time to Saturday of the Ninth Week.
3. A little more than a third in comparison to the one, a little less in comparison to the other.
4. There are no texts for the First Sunday in Ordinary Time because of the celebration of the Baptism of the Lord. But the First Week begins on the Monday that follows this feast or Epiphany when the latter occurs on 7 or 8 January.
5. Reading the whole of Mark's Gospel takes no more than one and a half to two hours. It would be worthwhile to do so at the beginning of Ordinary Time in order to take better advantage of the readings spread over twenty-seven Sundays.
6. This chapter is also read during Paschal Time, from Friday of the Second Week to Saturday of the Third Week.
7. The extreme dates between 1991 and 2007 are July 24 and August 29.

Practical Plan for the Gospel of Mark—Pages 3-8

1. See *Days of the Lord*, vols. 4:15; 6:2.
2. They are numerous and precise enough to allow us to place Jesus' life, ministry, and death within history as known from other sources.
3. See *Days of the Lord*, 6:2-6.
4. Ibid., 4:15-16.
5. The end of Mark's Gospel, which speaks of the risen Christ's appearances, belongs to the "inspired Scriptures." But this does not mean that it was written by Mark himself. See *Days of the Lord*, 3:28 (n. 16).
6. See B. Standaert, *L'Evangile selon Marc: Composition et genre littéraire* (Bruges: 1978) (doctoral thesis in theology at the Catholic University of Nijmegen); *L'Evangile selon Marc: Commentaire*, Lire la Bible 61 (Paris: Cerf, 1983) 10–34; J. Auneau, "L'Evangile de Marc," *Evangiles synoptiques et Actes des Apôtres*, in *Petite bibliothèque des sciences bibliques*, Nouveau Testament 4 (Paris: Desclée, 1981) 62–68.

7. Two parts objectively stand out: Mark 1:1-13 (preaching of John the Baptist, baptism of Jesus, brief mention of Jesus' stay in the desert) and Mark 14:1–16:20 (passion and resurrection of Jesus). For the remainder of the Gospel, the *Bible de Jérusalem*, editio major (Paris: Cerf, rev. 1973) provides a simple division which also is open to discussion: "Galilean Ministry" (1:14-7:23), "Journeys Outside Galilee" (7:24–10:52), and "Jerusalem Ministry" (11:1–14:37).

8. Thus, recently, B. Standaert, *L'Evangile selon Marc* and J. Auneau, "L'Evangile de Marc."

The Second and Third Sunday in Ordinary Time—Pages 9-10

1. In Year A, we read John 1:29-34 (the testimony given by John the Baptist concerning the one he has baptized); in Year C, John 2:1-11 (the sign at Cana).

2. See above, The Division of Sundays into "Sequences," and *Days of the Lord*, 4:18.

3. 1 Cor 6:13b-15a, 17-20 (Second Sunday); 7:29-31 (Third Sunday); 7:32-35 (Fourth Sunday); 9:16-19, 22-23 (Fifth Sunday); 10:31–11:1 (Sixth Sunday).

4. See the introduction to the First Letter to the Corinthians in *La traduction Oecuménique de la Bible, édition intégrale* (Paris: Brepols, 1987) 2741-2743.

5. Ibid., 2743.

Second Sunday—Pages 11-21

1. The story of his birth is also beautiful. Elkanah, a man from Rama-thaim in the hill country of Ephraim, had two wives. Hannah, whom he preferred, was childless. Every year, she went to the sanctuary in Shiloh. One day, she prayed with tears that the Lord give her a child. Her prayer was heard. She gave birth to a son, Samuel, whom she dedicated to the service of the sanctuary in which God had heard her (1 Sam 1:1-23). Samuel is the last of the judges, those charismatic leaders who governed Israel during the period preceding the institution of the monarchy. He is also the one who anointed the first two kings, Saul and David. Moreover, he is presented as a prophet and compared to Moses (Ps 99:6; Jer 15:1).

See "Juge" and "Samuel" in *Dictionnaire encyclopédique de la Bible* (Paris: Brepols, 1987) 703, 1165; A. Neher, *L'essence du prophétisme* (Paris: Presses universitaires de France, 1955).

2. He is thus depicted on many a souvenir card for first Communion.

3. Moses (Exod 3:1-22); Gideon (Judg 6:11-24); Samson (Judg 13:17-24); Amos (Amos 7:15); Jeremiah (Jer 1:4-10); Mary (Luke 1:26-38); Paul (Acts 9:3-9).

4. Catechumenate, novitiate, years in the seminary, engagement before marriage answer this need for unhurried discernment. Retreats have the same purpose.

5. See also, among other texts, Judg 6:15 (Gideon); 1 Sam 16:10-13 (David); Ezek 2:6-7.

6. "Infant" comes from the Latin *infans*, which means "unable to speak."

7. Wis 18:14-15 (entrance antiphon of the Second Sunday after Christmas).

8. The New American Bible translates Zeph 3:17 "He will renew you in his love." Other translations have "He is silent in his love."

9. Sur Jeanne d'Arc, *Un coeur qui écoute* (Paris: Cerf, 1966) 17.

10. Ch. Péguy, *Le mystère des saints Innocents*, in *Oeuvres poétiques complètes*, La Pléiade 60 (Paris: Gallimard, 1957) 787. In this text, Péguy does not specifically speak of Samuel, but of children in general.

11. See Isa 8:11; Jer 20:7-9, 15-16; Ezek 2:3; Amos 3:3-8.

12. Destroyed and depopulated by the Romans in 146 B.C., Corinth was reestablished by Caesar one hundred years later. The two ports on either side of the isthmus allowed ships to avoid rounding the Peloponnesus. As early as the seventh century, a trail made of wooden rollers on which to tow the boats had been installed; and in the nineteenth century, a canal was dug.

13. There was in Corinth a sanctuary dedicated to Aphrodite which employed one thousand hierodules (slaves attached to a temple). See "Corinthe" in *Dictionnaire encyclopédique de la Bible*, 301.

14. Acts 18:1-21.

15. Let us consider only the difficulties of living a Christian life in certain neighborhoods in any large city, of the influence of their climate, especially on children and young persons. Moreover, these are the people least able to choose their place of residence and to move elsewhere beyond the unhealthy area.

16. See M. Carrez, "La Première épître aux Corinthiens," *Cahiers Evangile* 66 (1988). Most commentators divide chapters 5 and 6 into three sections dealing with the gravest disorders in the community of Corinth: a case of incest (5:1-13), the recourse to pagan tribunals to settle differences between Christians (6:1-11), and a case of fornication (6:12-20). See also, the introduction to the First Letter to the Corinthians in the *Traduction Oecuménique de la Bible*, 2741-2743.

17. We must remember that Paul does not identify the body with what he calls "flesh," which designates the human being, body and spirit, under the sway of sin and its allurements.

18. This rediscovery and this rehabilitation are often a reaction against an attitude that led some to consider the body as the prison of the soul, as an object of shame. But the danger of this reaction consists in exalting the body to the point of making an idol of it.

19. The liturgical reading omits v. 16, which, repeating Genesis (2:24), underscores the gravity of licentiousness. "[D]o you not know that anyone who joins himself to a prostitute becomes one body with her? For 'the two' it says 'will become one flesh.'" The liturgists feared that, for lack of sufficient attention to the text, people might understand union with Christ in too gross a manner (v. 15), whereas Paul writes, "But whoever is joined to the Lord becomes one *Spirit* with him" (v. 17).

20. Here, Paul does not explicitly speak of the Church as body of Christ. But this doctrine, which is central in the First Letter to the Corinthians and in the whole of Paul's work, is underlying: 1 Cor 10:17; 12:12-27; 15:23; Eph 4:4, 15-16; 5:23; Acts 9:4-5; etc.

21. 1 Cor 3:16-17; 2 Cor 6:16; Eph 2:20-22; 1 Thess 4:8.

22. This catechesis is outlined in the First Letter to the Thessalonians (4:3-8), which is not only the first of Paul's letters but also the earliest of the New Testament writings. It must have been written in the beginning of 51, that is, only about a score of years after Jesus' death.

23. The body has its role in the liturgy. Standing, kneeling, prostrate, lifting one's hands are not commonplace gestures, attitudes, postures, but ways of expressing through the body—by the liturgy of the body—prayer, thanksgiving, attentive listening, openness of heart, etc., which cannot remain purely internal. Do we not rightly say that a liturgy is alive inasmuch as the participation is both internal and external?

24. "Do you not know?" Paul says twice.

25. St. Ephrem (ca. 306–373), *Hymnes sur le paradis*, VIII, 8, in *Sources chrétiennes* 137 (Paris: Cerf, 1968) 116.

26. Matt 3:11-15; Mark 1:7-8; Luke 3:15-18; John 1:10-28; 3:27-30; see also John 1:15. This insistence is perhaps for the benefit of lingering disciples of the Baptist who continued for a long time to wonder whether he was not the Messiah: Acts 13:25; 19:1-7; John 1:19-20; 3:28.

27. John 1:19–2:12 constitutes, after the Prologue (John 1:2-28), the true introduction to the fourth Gospel. Everything takes place within the framework of one week (John 1:29, 35, 43; 2:1).

28. We must not confuse this place with the other Bethany, near Jerusalem, the town where Lazarus and his sisters, Martha and Mary, lived.

29. In the Book of Revelation, "Lamb of God" is used twenty-nine times as a proper name to designate the Lord exalted in the heavens because he was immolated: 5:6, 8, 12, 13; 6:1, 16; 7:9, 10, 14, 17; 8:1; 12:11; 13:8; 14:1, 4 (twice), 10; 15:3; 17:14 (twice); 19:7, 9; 21:9, 14, 22, 23, 27; 21:1, 3. See also John 19:31-37.

30. Isa 53:7; Gen 22:8; Exod 12:21-23; Ps 34:21. See A. Jaubert, *Approches de l'Evangile de Jean*, in Parole de Dieu (Paris: Seuil, 1976) 135–139; "Agneau de Dieu" in *Vocabulaire de théologie biblique* (Paris: Cerf, 1970) cols. 26–28, and in *Dictionnaire encyclopédique de la Bible*, 22–23.

31. See above, Practical Plan, p. 3.

32. St. John Chrysostom (ca. 350–407), *Homélie XVIII sur saint Jean*, 1–2, in Oeuvres complètes, vol 7 (Paris: Vivès, 1869) 195–196.

33. Abraham Joshua Heschel, *God in Search of Man* (New York: Harper & Row, 1966) 136–137.

34. St. Bernard (1090–1153), *Sermon 84 sur le Cantique des Cantiques*, 3, in *Invités aux noces*, trans. and ed. P.-Y. Emery (Paris: Desclée, 1979) 162. This whole text consists of variations on the verb "to seek."

35. See "Voir" in *Vocabulaire de théologie biblique*, cols. 1377–1380.

36. John 15:4-7; 1 John 3:24; 4:16; etc. In John's Gospel and Epistles, "to remain" occurs 68 times (118 times in the whole of the New Testament). See "Demeurer" in *Vocabulaire de théologie biblique*, cols. 254–257, and in *Dictionnaire encyclopédique de la Bible*, 340.

37. P. Emmanuel, *Tu* (Paris: Seuil, 1978) 288.

38. This comment suggests that, at the time John writes, "Christ" has become a proper name whose original meaning is lost. We can say the same thing, a little father along, about "Kephas" which means "Peter."

39. John does not elaborate on this change of name. At the time he writes, Christians already know what mission Peter received from the Lord and exercised (John 21:15-20).

40. See John 6:70; 15:16; 1 Cor 8:2-3; 13:12; Gal 4:9.

41. P. Emmanuel, *Tu*, 293 (n. 36).

42. Commission Francophone Cistercienne, text and music J. Gelineau, *Hymnaire de la Liturgie des Heures* (Paris: Cerf-Chalet-Levain, 1990) 277. (Fiche U 114).

Third Sunday—Pages 22–32

1. Three chapters of 16, 11, and 11 verses for a total of 38.

2. The Book of Jonah is read on Monday (1:1–2:1, 11), Tuesday (3:1-10), and Wednesday (4:1-11) of the Twenty-seventh Week, odd years. Jonah 3:1-10 is also read on Wednesday of the first week in Lent and at the Mass of reconciliation; Jonah 3:10–4:11 is among the readings of the Mass for the evangelization of peoples.

3. Jesus speaks of the "sign of Jonah" and of his preaching (Matt 12:39-41; Luke 11:29-32). See the introductions of the *Bible de Jérusalem*, 1091, and of the *Traduction Oecuménique de la Bible*, 1173–1174; V. Mora, "Jonas," *Cahiers Evangile* 68 (1981); A. and P.-E. Lacocque, *Le complexe de Jonas*, in Initiations (Paris: Cerf, 1989); A. Maillot, *Jonas ou les forces de Dieu: Sophonie ou l'erreur de Dieu* (Neuchâtel: Delachaux et Niestlé, 1977); R. Basilier, "Jonas lu

pour aujourd'hui," *Revue réformée* 32 (1981–1982) 49–86; the articles "Jonas," "Jonas, livre," "Jonas, Signe" in *Dictionnaire encyclopédique de la Bible*, 676–678.

4. Without any doubt, Nineveh was a big city. Its perimeter totaled 19 miles and enclosed a surface of 1,600 acres. It had several public squares (Gen 10:12). But it did not take three days to cross it or go around it: three is a sacred number. The figures given connote gigantic proportions. "[A] hundred and twenty.thousand persons" (Jonah 4:11) means an innumerable population; the figure will be repeated in the Book of Judith (2:5) to describe the immense army of Nebuchadnezzar commanded by Holofernes. Forty is the number of the days of the flood (Gen 7:12), of the years of the wandering in the desert (Exod 16:35), of the days Elijah walked to reach Mount Horeb (1Kgs 19:8).

See the article "Ninive" in *Dictionnaire encyclopédique de la Bible*, 900–902.

5. The omission of verses 6 to 9 does not truncate the narrative. These only give details on how the inhabitants "great and small" react to Jonah's preaching. The king himself shares this movement of repentance: "[H]e rose from his throne, laid aside his robe, covered himself with sackcloth, and sat in the ashes" (v. 6). Furthermore, he decrees and proclaims throughout the city a fast, while enjoining all to "turn from [their] evil way and from the violence [they have] in hand" (vv. 7–9).

6. The Bible often says that God "repents": 2 Sam 24:16; 1 Chr 21:15; Jer 8:8; 26:3, 13, 19.

7 The *Jerusalem Bible* has" The death of the devout / costs Yahweh dear."

8. The contrast with what happened to Jeremiah is striking. Obeying God's order, Jeremiah wrote on a scroll the words addressed to Israel, Judah, and all nations: a call to conversion in order to avoid divine punishment. King Jehoiakim ordered the scroll seized, and he cut it into pieces and threw them into the fire. "Hearing all these words did not frighten the king and his ministers or cause them to rend their garments" (Jer 36:1-32). The contrast is the more striking since Jonah's narrative is strewn with expressions dear to Jeremiah.

9. St. Augustine (354–430), *Confessions*, bk. 10:27, trans. F. J. Sheed (Sheed & Ward, 1943).

10. See second reading of Second Sunday.

11. Thus "Everything is lawful for me" (1 Cor 6:12), probably Paul's expression, whose meaning the Corinthians distorted.

12. It is the distinction between chronological time (*chronos*), and the favorable time (*kairos*). See "Temps" in *Vocabulaire de théologie biblique*, cols. 1273–1284, and in *Dictionnaire encyclopédique de la Bible*, 1249.

13. "Time is running out": the Greek verb, in the passive form, suggests that divine action has shortened time by sending and raising the Son.

14. The Greek *musterion* (mystery) has as a Latin equivalent the word *sacramentum* (sacrament).

15. By no means does this mean living in the married state and abstaining from sexual relations: "Do not deprive each other, except perhaps by mutual consent for a time, to be free for prayer, but then return to one another, so that Satan may not tempt you through your lack of self-control. This is said by way of concession, however, not as a command" (1 Cor 7:5-6).

16. Without doubt, nothing shows this better than the central place love—of God and of others—holds in their lives. Love is the deep source of the greatest joys and of the most painful torments. Could it be otherwise with the disciples of him who, by his life and his death, revealed to us that God is love?

17. It is true that one cites the case of certain communities, called primitive, which do—or did—not know even barter, as everyone took advantage of the resources found in the common territory. This strictly closed economy can be maintained only as long as the group lives in isolation.

18. St. Benedict, for instance, wishes that everything necessary be found within the enclosure of the monastery: water, mill, garden, shops. The reason for this is to prevent the

monks from having to go out. However, he also speaks of the sale of monastery products. St. Benedict (ca. 480–543), *The Rule of St. Benedict*, eds. Timothy Fry, O.S.B., et al. (Collegeville, Minn.: The Liturgical Press, 1981), chs. 66, 57.

19. See *Days of the Lord*, 3:116–23.

20. P. Evdokimov, *Les âges de la vie spirituelle*, in Théophanie (Paris: Desclée de Brouwer, 1980) 58.

21. Literally, "after John had been handed over." "Handed over" is the term used to express the fate in store for Jesus and, later, his disciples: Mark 3:19; 9:31; 10:33; 13:9, 11-12; 14:10-11, 18, 21, 41-42; 15:1, 10, 15; Acts 2:23; 3:13; 21:11; 28:17. This same term is found in the other Gospels and Paul's letters to the Romans, the Corinthians, the Galatians, the Ephesians, the Colossians, and Titus. The locution "on the night he was betrayed" is familiar to us.

22. From the beginning of the Church, the link between the Precursor's ministry and Jesus' manifestation has been pointed out: Acts 1:22; 10:37.

23. These oracles from the Book of Consolation (Isa 40:1–55:13) are addressed to the exiles in Babylon, whose deliverance is approaching with the coming of Cyrus, God's instrument.

24. See Luke 5:1-11.

25. At what point along the shore of the lake, whose surface exceeds 77 square miles? This detail does not interest Mark.

26. Immediately after the expulsion of a demon in the synagogue at Nazareth (Mark 1:21-28), we read of the cure of Simon's mother-in-law (1:29-31), of numerous healings of people sick with various diseases (1:32-34), of the cleansing of a leper (1:40-45), of a paralytic (2:1-12), of the call of Levi (2:13-17).

27. The Rule of St. Benedict is a good example of prudence. It prescribes reluctance in opening the door to postulants. It even enjoins reserve toward them, to the point of rejection, in order to test the seriousness of their request. If postulants persevere, they are admitted first to the guest house, then to the novitiate, where the Rule is taught them and their vocation is tested (ch. 58). The same procedure is followed in all religious institutes.

Likewise, the seminary years aim not only at forming candidates for the priesthood but also at verifying the authenticity of their vocation. Then comes the decisive call of the Church, expressed by the bishop's authority.

28. The case of the vocation of Saul—who became Paul—is typical. The Lord himself told him, "Now get up and go into the city and you will be told what you must do." Then Ananias played his part (Acts 9:6-18; 22:10-16).

29. St. Augustine, *Confessions*, bk. 13:1.

30. Examples in the Bible are numerous: for instance, Moses while he was shepherding the flocks of his father-in-law, Jethro (Exod 3:1); Samuel in the sanctuary where he served (1 Sam 3:1-14); David in the pasture (1 Sam 16:6-13); Matthew at his post as tax collector (Matt 9:9-13; Mark 2:13-17; Luke 5:27-32).

31. In the Bible the image of the net is often used to speak of the snare set for human beings, especially the just: Pss 9:16; 10:9; 25:15; 31:5; 35:7-8; 57:7. God catches his adversaries in a net and masters them: Ezek 12:13; 17:20; 19:8; 32:2; Hos 7:12; Lam 1:23.

32. The episode of the rich man who wants to "inherit eternal life" is particularly significant. He leaves because Jesus tells him that he must sell all his goods (Mark 10:17-22).

33. This is explained by the fact that the Israelites are not a sea-going people. See "Mer" in *Vocabulaire de théologie biblique*, cols. 740–742, and *Dictionnaire encyclopédique de la Bible*, 809.

34. In all lists of apostles, Peter is always named first: Matt 10:2-4; Mark 3:16-19; Luke 6:14-16; Acts 1:13. See also Matt 17:1; 26:37; Mark 5:35.

35. P. Emmanuel, "Suis-moi," *Tu*, 289.

Fourth to Sixth Sunday—Page 33

1. The Jewish day goes from sunset to sunset. We would say that the sabbath begins on Friday night and ends on Saturday at the same hour. After sunset (on Saturday), the Sabbath rest ends. Then, but not before, is it permissible to bring sick persons to Jesus (Mark 1:32). The first day, as we reckon days, at Capernaum ends with these cures.

Fourth Sunday—Pages 34–42

2. Moses is named seventy-nine times in the New Testament. It speaks of him as a man of faith (Heb 11:23-29), as a mediator of the Law, which Jesus did not come to abolish but to fulfill (Matt 5:7, 21-48), a prophet who announces Jesus (Luke 24:27, 44); John 5:39, 46; Acts 26:22-23); and it gives testimony to him with Elijah at the Transfiguration (Matt 17:1-8; Mark 9:2-9; Luke 9:28-36). Jesus is the prophet similar (Acts 3:22; 7:37) but superior to him (John 1:17; Heb 3:1-6); he inaugurates a new covenant toward which the Law given to Moses was leading, as a pedagogue does a child (Gal 3:23-26). See "Moïse" in *Vocabulaire de théologie biblique*, cols. 778–781, and in *Dictionnaire encyclopédique de la Bible*, 851–52; H. Cazelles, *A la recherche de Moïse* (Paris: Cerf, 1979); R. Michaud, *Moïse: Histoire et théologie*, in Lire la Bible 49 (Paris: Cerf, 1979).

3. See J. Asurmendi, *Le prophétisme* (Paris: Nouvelle cité, 1985); L. Monloubou, "Les prophètes de l'Ancien Testament," *Cahier Evangile* 43 (1983); A. Neher, *L'essence du prophétisme;* "Prophète" in *Vocabulaire de théologie biblique*, cols. 1046–1057, and in *Dictionnaire encyclopédique de la Bible*, 1053–1056.

4. See Deut 5:23-27.

5. Deut 12:1-26:19 recapitulates the Lord's laws. In this "Deuteronomic Code," what concerns the prophets (18:9-22) immediately follows the prescriptions pertaining to Levites.

6. On Deuteronomy see J. Kennes, *Le Deutéronome* (Geneva: Labor et fides, 1967); P. Buis, *Le Deutéronome*, in Verbum salutis (Paris: Beauchesne, 1968); F. Garcia-Lopez, "Le Deutéronome," *Cahier Evangile* 63 (1988).

7. Matt 11:14; 17:10-12; Mark 9:11-13.

8. John 1:21, 25.

9. Matt 16:14; Mark 6:15; 8:20; Luke 9:19.

10. Matt 11:27; Luke 10:22; John 5:19-47; 7:28-29; 8:15-19, 43, 55; 10:30, 36-38; 14:1-14; 16:3, 15, 29-30; 17.

11. The Gospels attest to the fact the apostles themselves understood some of Jesus' words only after Easter and the coming of the Spirit: Mark 6:52; 9:32; Luke 9:45; 18:34; John 2:22; 8:27; 12:16; 13:7, 28; 14:26; 15:26.

12. J. Asurmendi, *Le Prophétisme*, 166–167.

13. 1 Cor 12:20; 11:5; 14:1, 3.

14. 1 Cor 7:1. Paul himself probably said this once. But we must understand his thought and not indiscriminately draw from it rules of behavior.

15. Second reading of Third Sunday.

16. X. Léon-Dufour, "Signification théologique du mariage et du célibat consacré," *Mariage et célibat: IVe Congrès de l'Association catholique internationale d'études médico-psychologiques*, Cogitatio Fidei 14 (Paris: Cerf, 1965) 25–38.

17. Paul's thought is still not completely formed. Ten years later, he will show how the mystery of marriage is to be understood in relation to Christ's union with the Church (Eph 5:23-32).

We must note that at the time of this writing (probably in the spring of 56), no gospel had yet been composed, even though some collections of the Lord's sayings were being circulated. Mark's Gospel is usually dated to the years 65–70; Matthew's and Luke's are later by ten or fifteen years. Concerning celibacy, we know this word of Jesus, on which Paul might have based his opinion, "Some are incapable of marriage . . . because they have renounced marriage for the sake of the kingdom of heaven" (Matt 19:12).

18. Paul does not give any details on what these "things of the Lord" are. By alluding to his own choice (1 Cor 7:7), he suggests that he is speaking of the apostolate or, more generally, the service of the churches.

19. In subsequent ages, all have not demonstrated as sane a vision of things. Thus, there have been many moralists and casuists in whose eyes sexual relations between spouses, considered as more or less sinful in themselves, found their only legitimacy in having procreation as their aim.

20. There are conclusions and applications not to be drawn from Paul's remarks on celibates' availability for "the things of the Lord." For instance, we cannot say that married ministers—priests of Eastern Churches, Protestant ministers—necessarily consider their pastoral and missionary zeal to be hampered by their familial responsibilities. Neither can we say that celibacy and undivided devotion to the tasks for which one has eschewed marriage are of necessity walking hand in hand. Whatever our station in life, we all have to struggle in order to remain generously faithful to our vocations. Perhaps some must struggle not to neglect what they owe their families; others know similar difficulties: union leaders, politicians, men and women whose professional activity is especially demanding, etc. Others must also reactivate their zeal again and again, not to yield to the temptation of a life turned back on itself, insipid and egotistic.

21. See Mal 2:14-16; Prov: 5:15-20; 18:22; 31:10-31; Qoh 9:9. Jesus invokes the teaching of Genesis (1:27; 2:24; 5:2) when people ask him about divorce (Matt 19:3-9; Mark 2:12).

22. Young brides received wishes for numerous children (Gen 24:60); fathers were congratulated on their numerous progeny (Ps 127:3-5; 128:3); grandparents were praised for the "crown" of grandchildren surrounding them (Prov 17:6). See also 1 Sam 4:20; 2 Sam 18:18; Ruth 4:13-14.

23. Gen 15:3-6; 16:4; 30:1; Ps 113:9; 1 Sam 2:5. See "Stérilité" in Vocabulaire de théologie biblique, cols. 1255–1258.

24. 1 Sam 4:20; 2 Sam 18:18; Ruth 4:13-14. The law of the "levirate" prescribed marriage between brother-in-law and sister-in-law when the latter was widowed before having a child. Thus the continuance of the line was insured (Deut 25:5-10). The story of the daughter of Jephthah (Judg 11:29-40) is typical of the importance given to marriage and motherhood. Jephthah makes the vow to immolate the first person who comes to meet him after the battle. It is his daughter. She does not refuse the sacrifice but mourns her virginity because she is going to die unmarried and childless.

25. Today, the reasons for which the value of celibacy is sometimes underestimated are not the same as formerly—to have children—but they stem rather from the exaltation of full-blown sexuality. This attitude can even lead one to undervalue or even despise those men and women who, for various reasons, live in a solitude which has not been really chosen. Often suspicion hangs over celibates. Women in particular are easily accused of being abnormal, repressed; they must struggle to find their place and gain respect in society.

26. Pope John Paul II, "La complémentarité du mariage et de la continence" (general audience of 4 April 1982), in La documentation catholique 79 (1982) 449.

27. Mark 1:14-15 (Gospel of Third Sunday).

28. See Practical Plan, p. 3.

29. The account of the second part of that typical day will be read next Sunday. It will end with the invitation to follow Jesus "throughout the whole of Galilee" (Mark 1:29-39).

The dynamic structure of Mark's Gospel is such that, once we begin to read it, we are easily led to continue to the end. It is worthwhile to take that risk in the beginning of this year's Ordinary Time. We need not fear the proclamation of the Sunday gospels will be felt as a mere and somewhat useless repetition. On the contrary, we shall derive greater profit from their solemn proclamation in the assembly.

30. After the chanting of the *Shema* ("Hear, O Israel!") (Deut 6:4-5) and other prayers, a text from the *Torah* ("Law") was read, followed by a passage from the prophets, then by a homily. This could be given by a member of the assembly who asked for leave to speak or was invited to do so. Jesus, and the apostles after him, took advantage of this opportunity to address the Jews on the sabbath: Matt 4:23; Luke 4:16-19, 44; Acts 13:5, 15; 14:1; 16:13; etc. The service concluded with a blessing, "The Lord bless you and keep you! . . ." (Num 6:24-26: Mass of 1 January). Organized in the fourth and third centuries B.C., this structure has remained substantially the same to the present.

See Ph. Rouillard, "La lecture de l'Ecriture dans la tradition juive," *Paroisse et liturgie* 51 (1969) 483-487.

31. The Hebrew Bible is divided into three parts: the Law or *Torah* (Genesis, Exodus, Leviticus, Numbers, Deuteronomy), the Prophets or *Nabim* (Isaiah, Jeremiah, Ezekiel, the other twelve prophets (Daniel is not included), and Josuah, Judges, 1, 2 Samuel, and 1, 2 Kings); the Hagiographers (Writings) or *Ketoubim* (Psalms, Wisdom books, etc.)

32. St. Jerome (ca. 347-420), in *Marc commenté par Jérôme et Jean Chrysostome*, in Les Pères dan la foi (Paris: Desclée de Brouwer, 1986) 45-46.

33. There are many examples of this: the paralytic whose mat was lowered by four men through an opening in the roof of the house in Capernaum (Mark 2:1-12); Jairus, who implored his daughter's cure, and the woman sick for twelve years (Mark 5:21-43); the folk at Gennesaret (Mark 6:53-56); the Syrophoenician woman and the deaf man (Mark 7:24-37); the blind man at Bethsaida (Mark 8:22-26); the father of a boy with a demon (Mark 9:14-29); the blind Bartimeus at Jericho (Mark 10:46-52).

34. In another case of exorcism reported by Mark, the devil also challenges Jesus in identical terms: "What have you to do with me, Jesus, Son of the Most High God? I adjure you by God, do not torment me!" (Mark 5:6). See also Mark 3:11-12.

35. In the world-view of the Bible, to know someone's name means to have power over that person.

36. This is why Jesus forbids the sick he has cured to give an ill-considered publicity to the miracles they have been favored with. It could cause a mistaken conception of the meaning and origin of his power (Mark 5:43; 7:36). Mark's Gospel shows elsewhere that the declarations, even the most accurate, made by the disciples remain imperfect, ambiguous, precisely in the measure in which they do not include the acceptance of the Son of God crucified: Mark 8:29-33; 9:9, 31-32; 10:32-45.

Concerning what is called "the messianic secret" in Mark's Gospel, we may note the following: the initiation into faith and the catechesis must be progressive; a premature request for an explicit profession of faith contains the risk of disappointment, should the believers realize that there remains an ambiguity in their minds, despite the literal exactitude of the creed. "For you, who really is Jesus Christ? Do we recognize him, do you recognize him as the Savior, the Son of God dead and risen?" It takes time for people to be able to say truthfully, "Yes, such is my faith."

See G. Minette de Tillesse, *Le secret messiaique dans l'Evangile de Marc*, in Lectio divina 47 (Paris: Cerf, 1968).

37. On this symbolism see "Mer" in *Vocabulaire de théologie biblique*, cols. 740-742, and in *Dictionnaire encyclopédique de la Bible*, 809.

38. Commission Francophone Cistercienne, *Tropaires des dimanches*, Le Livre d'Heures d'En-Calcat (Dourgne, 1980) 56.

Fifth Sunday—Pages 43–51

1. A composite piece of writing, the Book of Job is made up of two prose parts corresponding to one another, the prologue (1:1–2:13 and the epilogue (42:7-17), flanking a poetic central part (2:14–42:6). We probably have in the prologue and epilogue an old story from the
oral tradition of the Near East on the exemplary patience of a rich man who lost everything. As it was recorded in the Bible the book, in its current form, must have been written
between the sixth and fifth centuries B.C. This was the time of the great Greek writers
Aeschylus (ca. 525–456), Sophocles (ca. 496–406), Euripides (ca. 480–406), and Plato (ca.
428–348).

See the introductions in the *Bible de Jérusalem,* 649–651, and the *Traduction Oecuménique
de la Bible,* 1463–1471; *Dictionnaire encyclopédique de la Bible,* 637–675; J. Lévêque, ''Job, le
livre et le message,'' *Cahier Evangile* 53 (1985); S. Terrien, *Job,* in Commentaire de l'Ancien
Testament (Neuchâtel: Delachaux, 1963; Genève: Labor et fides, 1963); J. Steimann, *Job,
témoin de la souffrance humaine,* in Foi vivante 120 (Paris: Cerf, 1969); J. Lévêque, *Job et son
Dieu,* in Etudes bibliques (Paris: Gabalda, 1970); R. de Pury, *Job ou l'homme révolté* (Genève:
Labor et fides, 1982); ''Job et le silence de Dieu,'' *Concilium* 189 (1983).

2. This is the reason why the Book of Job is little used in the liturgy. Besides this Sunday's text and Job 38:1, 8-11 (God's mastery over the forces of the sea), a text chosen because of the Gospel reading of the calming of the storm at sea (Mark 4:35-41), read on the
Twelfth Sunday, we have the following excerpts: six passages from Monday to Saturday
of the Twentieth Week, even years; four passages among the texts selected for the anointing of the sick and viaticum; one among the texts of the Mass for the business of the city;
and a last text, especially beautiful and appropriate, for the Mass of the Dead.

> Oh, would that my words were written down!
> Would that they were inscribed in a record:
> That with an iron chisel and with lead
>   they were cut in the rock forever!
> But as for me, I know that my Vindicator lives,
>   and that he will at last stand forth upon the dust;
> Whom I myself shall see:
>   my own eyes, not another's, shall behold him,
> And from my flesh I shall see God;
>   my inmost being is consumed with longing (Job 19:23-27).

3. See A. Neher, *L'exil de la parole: Du silence biblique au silence d'Auschwitz* (Paris: Seuil,
1970).

4. Job 5:7, 27; 8:22; 11:13-20; etc.

5. These words were quoted by Bishop Lallier in the homily given at the funeral of the
Archbishop of Paris (1966–1968) on 17 February 1968, see *La documentation catholique* 65 (1968)
col. 432.

6. Fyodor Dostoevsky, *The Brothers Karamazov,* trans. Constance Garnett, rev. and ed.
Ralph E. Matlaw (New York: W. W. Norton, 1976) 225–227.

7. The Son of God, with arms extended,
   Has taken up everything in his offering,
   The human toil and work,
   The lost weight of suffering.
Commission Francophone Cistercienne, *La nuit, le jour* (Paris: Desclée-Cerf, 1973) 40; (Fiche
de chant P 105-1 et P LH 171) in *Hymnaire de la Liturgie des Heures,* 12.

8. 1 Cor 6:12; 10:23 (''Everything is lawful for me''); 6:12-20 (concerning sexual relations: Second Sunday); 8:1-13; 10:23-33 (concerning meat sacrificed to idols).

9. 1 Cor 7:29-35; see Third and Fourth Sundays.

10. This does not exclude the necessity of verifying the authenticity of vocations nor does it minimize the decisive role of the call of the Church.

11. See n. 17 for the Fourth Sunday.

12. In most unions or similar organizations, the full-time representatives are dispensed from working. Sometimes for their living expenses they receive the equivalent of the salary they earned before they began devoting their whole time to their new duties. It is understandable that Christians should see to the upkeep of those who labor for the gospel's sake and, if necessary, be reminded of this duty. But that it should be necessary to insist, to campaign . . .

13. Acts 18:3; 1 Cor 4:12.

14. See *Days of the Lord*, 3:210-15.

15. A. Valensin, *La joie dans la foi* (Paris:Aubier, 1955) 50.

16. M. Zundel, *Avec Dieu dans le quotidien* (Saint-Maurice: Editions Saint-Augustin, 1988) 17.

17. Mark 1:1; see Third Sunday, p. 28.
Perhaps we are not fully conscious of the meaning of the invitation, which the deacon or the priest pronounces, and the answer of the assembly. It is not the book that is acclaimed; it is offered to the veneration of the gathering because it is the sacrament of God's Word and not because it is a collection of words said by the Lord. We must remember how Jews treat the scroll of the Law, place it in a precious chest—a sort of tabernacle—where they take it from and put it back with reverence. In the same spirit, the Christian tradition has created beautiful Gospel books, considered precious objects used in worship. What shall we say of certain ways of acting: a nondescript book, similar to a paperback; a Lectionary put down anywhere, as if it were a mere accessory? Eventually it is even replaced for convenience by a simple sheet of paper with a copy of the text to be read. Similarly, to say, "This—the words I just read—is the word of God" does not exactly do justice to the announcement "The Gospel of Jesus Christ."

18. See Practical Plan, n. 5.

19. If we consider only Mark, we find the verb used in 6:14, 16; 12:26; 14:28; 16.6. The other evangelists concur in the meaning given to the word. Moreover, we notice that this verb occurs several times in the accounts of healing: Mark 2:9, 11, 12 (forgiveness and healing of the paralytic in Capernaum); 5:41 (raising of Jairus' daughter); 9:27 (healing of a boy with a demon).

20. See the *Traduction Oecuménique de la Bible*, 2830, n. w: "A variant, upheld by several Fathers, has: 'Rise from among the dead and you will touch Christ' or else 'and Christ will touch you.' We read, in the account of the raising of Jairus' daughter, 'He took the child by the hand and said to her, ''. . . Little girl, I say to you, arise!'' ' In the same way, concerning the child possessed by a demon, 'But Jesus took him by the hand, raised him, and he stood up' (Mark 9:27)."

21. *Missel romain*, Ordinaire de la messe, Préparation pénitentielle, III.

22. Mark 1:25; 3:12.

23. St. Ambrose (339–397), *Traité sur l'Evangile de saint Luc* I, in Sources Chrétiennes 45bis (Paris: Cerf, 1957) 174–175.

24. Luke's Gospel proves this: Jesus' prayer is always linked to a new phase or to an important circumstance of his mission. See *Days of the Lord*, 2:258, n. 53.

25. P. Evdokimov, *La prière de l'Eglise d'Orient* (Mulhouse: Salvator, 1966) 222.

26. The *Bible de Jérusalem* has *sortit*, "went out," both here and in the parable of the sower (Matt 13:3) cited below in the text. The Greek in both Gospels is *exelthen*, "went out." The New American Bible uses a different verb in each case.

27. St. Augustine, *Confessions*, bk. 10, XLIII.

28. Commission Francophone Cistercienne, *Tropaires des dimanches*, 59.

Sixth Sunday—Pages 52–59

1. It would be unfair to say that such a fear is due to an exaggeration of the danger of contagion. If one has visited a leprosarium, one understands the impression made by the sight of lepers and one is filled with admiration for those who devote their lives to caring for them. Even today, we speak of leprosy in the figurative sense to designate everything that gnaws away, every ill that spreads around. Later on, the plague would inspire a similar panic.

2. Exod 20:12; Lev 20:9; Deut 5:16; Prov 3:7-8; 10:27.

3. Prov 2:16-19; 5:1-5; 7:24-27; Sir 6:2-4; 31:10; 38:10.

4. This is the topic of the Book of Job.

5. We are not speaking here only of upsets or even catastrophes imputable to human actions as, for instance, those which affect the balance of nature, all manner of accidents resulting from culpable neglect, from contempt for others' lives, security, and rights. We are speaking also of calamities like war, genocide, the enslavement of entire populations or of large portions of populations.

6. On the contrary, casuistry looks only at particular "cases of conscience," which are by definition unique, individual. Inasmuch as we are not exactly in the same situation, we feel that the solution of this case does little or nothing at all for us. This is why casuistry leads to nearly interminable discussions and distinctions. (Yes, but . . . And if . . .) At best, it is based on a jurisprudence subject to diverse opinions.

7. By the way, we must note that Paul does not say that these meats are allowed or authorized. He speaks of their use. Whereas there is no problem for those with a well-formed conscience, those who, even wrongly, think they are participating in idol worship by eating food coming from a pagan sanctuary incur guilt by eating it. We often tend to forget that conscience—which we must strive to form well—is the immediate criterion of the moral value of an act, that good and evil do not reside in things but in the human heart and in the use we make of these things.

8. The Greek word *skandalon*, which gave *scandalum* in Latin and *scandal* in English, means "obstacle," "stone against which one stumbles."

9. P. Talec, *Un grand désir: Prières dan le secret, prières en commun*, (Paris: Centurion-Cerf, 1973) 181.

10. *Webster's New Universal Unabridged Dictionary*, 2nd ed. (New York: Simon and Schuster, 1979).

11. In support of this connotation, here is a quotation from Gide's *Roi Candaule II*: "One does not have friendship, one has pity for a poor person."

12. See "Miséricorde" in *Vocabulaire de théologie biblique*, cols. 766-771, and in *Dictionnaire encyclopédique de la Bible*, 847.

13. Fr. Varillon, *La parole est mon Royaume*, (Paris: Centurion, 1986) 69-70.

14. The cure of the deaf man (Mark 7:31-37) has been especially important in this connection. James' Letter attests that very early the manner in which Jesus proceeded to cure the sick influenced the rites: "Is anyone among you sick? He should summon the presbyters of the church, and they should pray over him and anoint [him] with oil in the name of the Lord, and the prayer of faith will save the sick person, and the Lord will raise him up. If he has committed any sins, he will be forgiven" (Jas 5:14-15).

15. St. John Chrysostom, *Homélie 25 sur saint Matthieu*, in *Le Livre d'Heures d'En-Calcat* (Dourgne, 1952) 125.

16. The Lectionary considerably waters down violence of Jesus' words. The *Bible de Jérusalem* has "le rudoyant Jésus le chassa aussitôt" (Jesus shook him and immediately chased him away). The Vulgate says, *"comminatus est ei,"* which literally means, "He menaced him as with the point of a sword" (by pointing a finger at him?).

17. Mark 5:43; 7:36; 8:26. See G. Minette de Tillesse, *Le secret messianique dans l'Evangile de Marc;* Fourth Sunday, n. 36.

18. P. de la Tour du Pin, *Une somme de poésie III, Le jeu de l'homme devant Dieu* (Paris: Gallimard, 1983) 289.

Seventh to Tenth Sunday—Page 60

1. See the introduction to the Second Letter to the Corinthians in the *Traduction Oecuménique de la Bible*, 2773–2778; M. Quesnel, ''Les épîtres aux Corinthiens,'' *Cahiers Evangile* 22 (1977); M. Carrez, ''La deuxième épître aux Corinthiens,'' *Cahiers Evangile*, 51 (1985); *La deuxième épître aux Corinthiens*, Commentaire du Nouveau Testament VIII (Genève: Labor et fides, 1986).

Seventh Sunday—Pages 61–69

1. The date of the Exodus from Egypt remains the object of discussion, but today it is generally agreed that it took place in the thirteenth century B.C. under the nineteenth Egyptian dynasty, that of Seti I and Ramses II (obelisk at the Place de la Concorde, Paris).

2. Although placed at the beginning of the Bible, the Book of Genesis is not—by far—the most ancient. It is calculated that its first chapter, in its present form dates back to the time of the Babylonian exile (sixth century B.C.) This is the time of Ezekiel the prophet. Jeremiah (seventh century), Isaiah, Amos, and Hosea (eighth century) are therefore clearly anterior. But these first pages of Genesis—especially the second and third chapters—have been set down in writing by using much older oral, and perhaps written, traditions.

See the introduction to the Book of Genesis in the *Bible de Jérusalem* and the *Traduction Oecuménique de la Bible.*

3. A part of this text (Isa 43:16-21) is read on the Fifth Sunday in Lent, Year C. See *Days of the Lord*, 2:179.

4. Isa 50:8; 51:5; 46:13; 56:6.

5. St. John Chrysostom, *Quatrième catéchèse baptismale*, 14–16, in Sources chrétiennes 50 (Paris: Cerf, 1957) 190–191.

6. E. Mounier, *Personnalisme et christianisme*, in *Oeuvres*, vol. 1 (Paris: Seuil, 1961) 741.

''This drop of blood that I have poured out for you'' is Mounier's paraphrase of number 553, ''Le Mystère de Jésus,'' from Pascal's *Pensées.*

7. Commission Francophone Cistercienne, *La nuit, le jour.* (Fiche de chant M LH 106-1).

8. After these whispers will come challenges to the disciples, then to Jesus himself, who finally will put an embarrassing question to his opponents (Mark 3:23). See B. Standaert, *L'Evangile selon Marc*, 48.

9. Cubic in shape, often consisting of one single, windowless room, the Palestinian house was topped by a flat roof made of a few beams and entwined branches covered with dirt. One had access to it by an outside staircase. It was not difficult to make an opening in this sort of roof. Concerning these details, see J. Dupont, ''Le paralytique pardonné (Mc 9,1-9),'' in *Assemblées du Seigneur*, première série, 73 (Bruges: Publications de Saint-André, 1962) 35.

Luke (5:19), who writes for readers unfamiliar with Palestinian houses, speaks of tiles removed to make a hole in the roof.

10. In Scripture, the terms ''faith'' and ''trust'' are closely related because they designate an attitude toward a person: to have faith in a person is to trust that person. Faith

does not have for its object only a truth to which one assents. Anyway, in the Christian perspective "truths to be believed" are not abstract propositions to which one must give intellectual assent, even without understanding them. For instance, to say "I believe in . . . the forgiveness of sins, the resurrection of the body" means "I believe in God, who forgives sins . . . , who raises the dead" and, at the same time, "I trust God and count on his mercy; I trust God because he is the God of the living and gives life."

11. G. Bessiere, *Jésus insaisissable*, in Epiphanie (Paris: Cerf, 1974) 44.

12. Jesus speaks thus to the woman who has been sick for twelve years (Mark 5:34). In similar terms, Jesus says to the blind man at Jericho, "Go your way; your faith has saved you" (Mark 10:52).

13. Specialists in the sacred texts, scribes played an important role from the Exile on. Deprived of liturgy, the people had no other point of reference than the text of the Law, which was the foundation of the exiles' cultural and religious identity. The efforts at restoration after the return to the land were based on a renewed knowledge of the Law and the traditions, which were the scribes' specialty. This is the reason they exercised the functions of counsels in court and of teachers. They held the opinion that competence in religious matters was acquired through assiduous study of the Scriptures (Matt 12:2; 19:4; 21:16; Mark 12:26; Luke 6:3; 10:26; 20:17; John 5:39). See "Scribes" in *Dictionnaire encyclopédique de la Bible*, 1178–1179.

14. Isa 43:18-19, 21-22, 24c-25 (first reading). See also Jer 31:34; Ezek 16:63; Hos 14:5; Mic 7:18-19.

15. In fact, when one thinks of it, one is stupefied to hear a human being, and even more to hear one's self pronounce, ". . . I absolve you from your sins, in the Name of the Father, and of the Son, and of the Holy Spirit."

16. On the title "Son of Man," see "Fils de l'homme" in *Vocabulaire de théologie biblique*, cols. 470–475, and in *Dictionnaire encyclopédique de la Bible*, 480–482.

17. Cl. Bernard, *Le temps du coeur nouveau: Chants, Prières*, Vivante liturgie 100 (Paris: Publications de Saint-André—Centurion, 1983) 166 (Fiche de chant L 197).

Eighth Sunday—Pages 70–78

1. See J. Asurmendi, "Amos et Osée," *Cahier Evangile* 64 (1988).

2. We must read the Book of Hosea and its pathetic evocation of the infidelities of the people of God, likened to a drama personally lived by the prophet himself. He has married a prostitute, Gomer; her children are illegitimate.

3. We should note the triple repetition of "I will espouse you."

4. "[Y]ou shall know the LORD." In the Bible, the verb "to know" implies an intimate union.

5. Engagement demanded that a gift be offered to the bride's parents. Here the gifts are offered to the bride-to-be. After the Exile, the Lord's part in this reunion is emphasized as most important. The people are exhorted to come back to the Lord, but he takes the first steps (Jer 31:21-22) and buys back his wife (Ezek 16:60-63) by covering her with the mantle of justice and the robe of salvation (Isa 61:10).

6. Mark 2:19-20; Matt 9:15; 22:1-14; John 3:29; Rev 19:7; 21:9-10; 22:17; 2 Cor 11:2; Eph 5:22-30. Vatican Council II, Dogmatic Constitution on the Church (*Lumen Gentium*), *The Conciliar and Post Conciliar Documents*, ed. Austin Flannery, OP (Collegeville, Minn.: The Liturgical Press, 1975) no. 7.

7. Bossuet, "Lettre IV à une demoiselle de Metz," in *Oeuvres complètes*, ed. F. Lachat (Paris, 1875) 27:310.

8. The sages of Israel understood that God was the author—the creator—of all that exists by their experience of what God had done for his people. See Seventh Sunday, n. 2.

9. In this same letter, Paul speaks of "false brothers" (2 Cor 11:13).

10. Especially in the beginning, some were distrustful of this man who only recently was violently persecuting the Church. See *Days of the Lord*, 3:162, "Difficult Beginnings of the Convert Saul's Apostolate."

11. An example of this is the formula "Everything is lawful for me" (1 Cor 6:12; 10:23).

12. See also Ezek 11:19-20; 36:26-28.

13. P. de La Tour du Pin, *Une somme de poésie*, I: *Le jeu de l'homme en lui-même* (Paris: Gallimard, 1981) 401.

14. Among the five controversies recorded in Mark's Gospel as taking place in Galilee, three concern the sabbath (Mark 2:1-12; 2:23-27; 3:1-6), one the meal with "sinners and tax collectors" (Mark 2:15-17), and one the practice of fasting (Mark 2:18-22).

Commentators have often stressed the parallelism between these controversies in Galilee and those which Mark locates in Jerusalem, before the passion (Mark 11:1–12:44).

See P. Renaud, "Le jeûne 'déplacé,'" in *Assemblées du Seigneur*, deuxième série, No. 39 (Paris: Publications de Saint-André—Cerf, 1972) 44-54.

15. Lev 16:29-31; Num 29:7. See Acts 27:9.

16. 1 Sam 7:6; Joel 1:14; 2:15; 2 Sam 1:12; 3:35; 31:13; Jdt 8:5-6.

17. Zech 7:3, 5; 8:19.

18. Matt 9:19; Luke 5:33; 18:12.

19. Amos 5:21; Jer 14:12; Isa 58:2-11; Zech 7:5. See "Jeûne" in *Vocabulaire de théologie biblique*, cols. 608–610, and in *Dictionnaire encyclopédique de la Bible*, 670–671.

20. These are the Gospel readings of the preceding four Sundays.

21. Jesus severely reproves the behavior of those who assume a dejected appearance and put on a long face when they are fasting (Matt 6:16-17). At the time, Jesus was finding fault with ostentatiousness in pious practices. But the dejected appearance and the long face which would be due to inner sadness should lead to questioning either the suitability of these practices for the person who adopts them or the manner in which the person understands them or both. Peace and joy have always rightly been considered the criteria of decisive discernments.

22. Eucharistic Prayer I for Masses of Reconciliation.

23. The Second Council of Braga, in 561, explicitly condemned the heretics who fasted on the day of the birth of the Lord and on Sundays because they denied the incarnation (H. Denzinger, *Enchiridion symbolorum*, No. 235). This condemnation was particularly directed to the disciples of a certain Priscillianus, who had founded in Spain, ca. 370, a sect whose doctrine is little known due to the secrecy surrounding it. "From the outset, it was a movement of excessive asceticism and of disturbing prophetism founded on apocrypha" ("Priscillien," *Dictionnaire de la foi chrétienne: Tome I, Les mots* [Paris: Cerf, 1968] 615).

24. Commission Francophone Cistercienne, *La nuit, le jour*, 31. (Fiche de chant M LH 122).

Ninth Sunday—Pages 79–89

1. The origin of the word and, as a consequence, its semantic meaning, remain obscure. There are many uncertainties concerning the origins of the sabbath, which has no equivalent in the world of antiquity. See "Sabbat" in *Vocabulaire de théologie biblique*, cols. 1151–1153, and in *Dictionnaire encyclopédique de la Bible*, 1140–1142.

2. As Sunday later on, the sabbath had its martyrs for whom a violation of the sabbath would have been apostasy (1 Mac 2:32-38).

3. The sabbath is roughly for the Jews what Sunday Mass is for us. People say, "Jews observe the sabbath," as they say, "Catholics attend Sunday Mass."

4. This is particularly impressive in the Jewish quarters of Jerusalem. On Friday night, when the sabbath begins, all activity akin to work suddenly stops; city bus service ends; and in certain clearly defined sectors, automobile traffic is forbidden. And on Saturday, equally suddenly, these activities are resumed. We can observe the same thing in the Jewish quarters of the big cities of the diaspora: not a single shop is open on Saturday, whereas, in adjacent streets, business is going on at full tilt.

5. Again, the same thing happened to the Christian Sunday, whose spiritual meaning developed and became richer in the course of centuries, even though, for many practicing Catholics, Sunday has been reduced to the legal obligation of attending Mass.

6. Exod 20:11; 31:17; etc.

7. Exod 23:12; 34:21; Deut 15:15; 16:12; 24:18, 22.

8. Concerning this text, see P. Buis, "C'est sabbat en l'honneur du Seigneur ton Dieu," *Assemblées du Seigneur*, deuxième série, No 40 (Paris: Publications de Saint-André—Cerf, 1972) 30–36.

The choice of this reading answers the needs of the liturgy: to proclaim an Old Testament text in harmony with the day's Gospel. But a better knowledge of the sabbath—its meanings, motivations, and reach—is interesting for Christians because, in spite of all differences, Sunday owes much to the sabbath from many points of view, in particular that of the theology and spirituality of weekly rest.

9. On the feast of the new moon, the first day of the month, business transactions were forbidden as on the sabbath (Lev 23:24; Exod 20:8).

10. This is the reproach addressed to Jesus' disciples (Mark 2:23-25).

11. We could give many similar examples taken from the still recent history of the Church. Let us think only of the precautions supposed necessary in order not to break the Eucharistic fast: one could not swallow a little water, even inadvertently while washing; one had to wait until after Communion to take any medication; etc. At the opposite pole, on Friday it was deemed permissible to eat a most plentiful meal without the least scruple, provided there was no meat on the menu, etc.

Casuistry legislated with the utmost seriousness the minimum time required to satisfy the obligation of Sunday Mass: it was enough to arrive at the Offertory and to wait until the end of Communion before leaving. . . .

Furthermore, Hosea's invectives could be addressed to Christians if we substitute Sunday for sabbath. Today, many Christians, freed from the social restraints which used to impose, among other things, the observance of Sunday, have not the slightest scruple in dispensing with attendance at Mass and with rest. Besides demonstrating a misunderstanding of the meaning and the importance of the Sunday assembly and the Day of the Lord, is not this the paradoxical result of the legalism and the juridical spirit which led many Christians to consider these observances as mere laws devoid of any significance for our faith and of influence on our lives?

12. On the composition of Deuteronomy, see F. Garcia-Lopez, "Le Deutéronome." In its present form, the book is patterned on models—"codes of laws" "documents of covenant"—used at that time in the Near East. They usually contain a preamble, laws, and often an epilogue in the form of a warning to those who would break the covenant and its obligations. This is the case for Deut 5-11; 12-26; 28.

The book, as it now stands, would have known a first redaction, the work of Levites coming from the north after the fall of Samaria in 721 B.C. King Hezekiah (715-687 B.C.) would have used this document to foster his reform in Isaiah's time, in particular to restore Jerusalem as the center of worship. The book fell into oblivion under the reign of the impious King Manasseh (ca. 687-642 B.C.), then was "discovered" in the Temple by true believers who had not forgotten it. It formed the basis of the reform undertaken by the saintly King Josiah in 622 B.C. (2 Kgs 22:1–23:30; 2 Chr 34:3-7).

13. We must not forget that the rights for everyone to one weekly rest day, yearly vacation, retirement benefits, guaranteed minimum wage, and limitation of the number of hours of work in a week are, in our Western countries, a recent acquisition. Despite this, many men and women are still subjected to conditions of work, lodging, etc. which in fact make them modern slaves, without the name. And all are far from being protected against exploitation which imposes on them real forced labor.

14. It goes without saying that this effort toward freedom must be pursued not only individually but collectively. Failing this, there will always be slaves and free persons.

15. A. J. Heschel, *Les bâtisseurs du temps*, Aleph (Paris: Les éditions de minuit, 1957) 113.

16. Ibid., 116.

17. M. Blondel, *L'action: Essai d'une critique de la vie et d'une science de la pratique* (Paris: Félix Alcan, 1893), rpt. (Paris: Presses universitaires de France, 1950) 381.

18. This art is a difficult one. If one wants to cover all possible cases, one risks a great deal. On the one hand, the keeping of the Law becomes, especially to the simple-minded, such a headache that they renounce it. On the other hand, as it is difficult to foresee all the possible and imaginable cases, the door is open to endless discussions which contribute nothing positive and even run counter to the intended objective. Faced with a swarm of different—if not contradictory—opinions, one may well conclude that anything is permissible. Finally, we must guard against multiplying particulars—even if we must resist those who request them—because many people unduly expect others to assume responsibilities which are the province of each one's enlightened conscience.

19. A. J. Heschel, *Les bâtisseurs du temps*, 129.

20. This catalogue listed thirty-nine forbidden tasks, among which were, naturally, plowing, sowing, and harvesting.

21. The "commandments of the Church" spoke of refraining from "all unnecessary servile work." The adjective in itself indicates that what is meant is daily work during the week. But then casuistry entered the scene. There were discussions about whether it was permissible to relax by puttering in one's shop or garden, by pruning a hedge, etc. But everyone found it normal and legitimate to exact, on Sunday, the usual services from those called today "home employees" whose task on that day could be even heavier in certain families whose members unashamedly enjoyed the Sunday leisure. Is it so certain that this attitude has totally disappeared and that today it does not influence the judgments, the reactions, and the actions of anyone?

22. The account of this episode in David's history is in 1 Sam 21:2-7. The prescriptions relative to the bread of oblation are in Lev 24:8-9.

23. This sort of specious argumentation is often that of certain fundamentalists who take biblical texts literally, ignoring literary genre, context, authors' intention.

24. The legitimacy of this principle is founded on the fact that the whole Bible has God for its principal author; it is expressed through the mediation of persons who wrote under his inspiration.

25. See above, "A Day of Sacred Rest in God's Honor," p. 79.

26. Romano Guardini, *The Lord*, trans. Elinor Castendyk Briefs (Chicago: Henry Regnery Company, 1954) 171.

27. In the synagogue at Capernaum, also on the sabbath, Jesus had freed a man from a demon. That cure had aroused only astonishment, because of the authority it manifested (Mark 1:21-28, Fourth Sunday). Now Jesus is coming to grips with certain persons' hostility.

28. Amos (8:5) vehemently stigmatizes those who dare to bemoan in their thoughts that the sabbath law hinders them from engaging in their usual business, always profitable, possibly dishonest. But no one would have had the audacity to do evil on that day. See above, p. 79–83.

29. Not to assist a person who is in danger makes one criminally culpable under the law.

30. Is this a truism? Certainly. But there are evident truths that bear repetition from time to time and whose field of application to daily life should be regularly checked. Would it be farfetched to say that on Sunday, even more than on other days, one should, for example, conduct oneself with particular prudence behind the wheel of one's car, to avoid any harm to others?

31. This term of hardening of hearts recurs several times in Mark's Gospel (6:52; 8:17) as well as the mention of the look which Jesus casts on all around him (3:34; 5:32; 10:23).

32. Attentive readers notice in this narrative a series of expressions found elsewhere in the Bible, where they have a definite sense. "Come up here before us" (literally "come stand") is a typical verb of the resurrection vocabulary. "Stretch out your hand" is the same as the order given to Moses when he was to witness to the Lord's power at the time of the crossing of the Red Sea (Exod 14:16-21; 26:27). "[H]is hand was restored" as Israel will be, according to the prophets, after the Exile (Isa 23:17-18; Jer 15:19; Ezek 16:55; See Acts 1:6). However we cannot affirm that Mark used these expressions on purpose and with reference to their biblical use.

33. On these questions, see M. Pelletier, *Les Pharisiens: Histoire d'un parti méconnu,* Lire la Bible 86 (Paris: Cerf, 1990).

The Pharisees did not constitute a monolithic party. Despite all the important things they held in common, the Jerusalem Pharisees differed from those who lived elsewhere, and the latter differed from city to city and region to region. All of them did not always have, at the same moment, the same attitude toward Jesus. When the Gospels speak of "the Pharisees," we must understand "some of the Pharisees" or else "some Pharisees from such and such a place." "The party of the Pharisees was a gathering of autonomous confraternities with a strong local character. There were no slogans or mottos coined in high places" (M. Pelletier, *Les Pharisiens,* 269).

34. Ibid., 295-311.

35. A.-M. Dubarle, "Signification du dimanche dans la Bible," *Le Dimanche,* Lex orandi 39 (Paris: Cerf, 1965), 59.

36. Commission Francophone Cistercienne, *Guetteur de l'aube* (Paris: Desclée, 1976) 11. (Fiche de chant A 173).

Tenth Sunday—Pages 90–97

1. On the Book of Genesis, see G. von Rad, *La Genèse* (Genève: Labor et fides, 1968); G. Auzou, *Au commencement Dieu créa le mond: L'histoire et la foi,* Lire la Bible 36 (Paris: Cerf, 1973); F. Castel, *Commencements* (Paris: Centurion, 1985); P. Gibert, *Bible, mythes et récits de commencement,* Parole de Dieu (Paris: Seuil, 1986); introductions to the *Bible de Jérusalem,* 23–30, and to the *Traduction Oecuménique de la Bible,* 35–43 (Pentateuque), 45–49 (Genèse).

The text read on this Sunday must have been written in Solomon's time (ca. 970–931 B.C.) with ancient traditions as its source.

2. This Portuguese proverb (*Deus escreve dreito por linhas tortas*) is quoted by Paul Claudel as an epigraph to his book *Le soulier de satin,* version intégrale (Paris: Gallimard) 9.

3. This account does not explicitly identify the serpent with the devil, as the Book of Wisdom (2:24) and the ulterior tradition do.

4. *Nouveau Livre de la foi: La foi commune des chrétiens,* eds. J. Keiner and L. Vischer; French edition, ed. Ch. Ehlinger (Paris: Centurion, 1976) 313. "Proclamation of Easter" (*Exultet*) on Easter night.

5. The Septuagint version (Greek translation of the Old Testament made by Jewish rabbis in Alexandria between the third and second centuries B.C.) confirms this interpretation. Whereas the word that means "progeny" is a neuter word (*sperma*), the subject of the verb

is in the masculine (*autos*), which gives the following: "He will strike your head." The ancient Latin versions follow suit. But in the Latin translation called the Vulgate, the work of St. Jerome (ca. 340?–420), which was the most widespread and the official version of the Latin Church, it is the woman who subdues the serpent. Hence the well-known Marian interpretation attested to by iconography showing Mary crushing the serpent's head. This is a result of the ambiguity of the Hebrew, from which St. Jerome worked. There is no feminine gender and the neuter is usually employed. The choice, therefore, is between "woman" and "progeny" as a subject of the verb.

6. Gen 49:10; Num 24:19.

7. Gen 11:29–23:19; see Rom 4:19; 9:7-9.

8. Gen 24–27.

9. Gen 29:6–35:24.

10. Isa 7:14 (Fourth Sunday of Advent, Year A).

11. Mic 5:1-3 (Fourth Sunday of Advent, Year C).

12. Therefore, concerning this anteriority of woman in sin, it is completely preposterous, not to say more, to make comments such as "Woman is more vulnerable to sin than man," or "Woman was, from the beginning, and therefore remains, man's temptress, the one through whom sin happens." The narrative of the Book of Genesis provides no grounds for such remarks, even if made by way of a joke. On the contrary, the narrative places woman in the foreground from the beginning of the scene in order that she may remain there until the final word, when God addresses the serpent, "You will be cursed . . . ," then refers to the woman, "Her progeny shall strike at your head."

13. Second reading of last Sunday. See above, "Power of the Risen Lord and Weakness of Humankind."

14. G. von le Fort, "Pâques," *Hymnes à l'Eglise (Hymnen an die Kirche)*, German text and trans. A. Duzan (Pau: Imprimerie Marrimpouey, 1982) 83–84; alternate edition, trans. P. Petit, Preface by P. Claudel (Tournai: Casterman, 1951).

15. Matt 13:57; Mark 6:4; Luke 4:24; John 4:44.

16. In like manner, the parents of the man born blind, whom Jesus cured, did not want to know anything of what happened to their son (John 9:16-23).

17. John also (7:5) evokes this lack of comprehension and the fact that Jesus' relatives did not believe in him. But his language is not as biting.

18. Scribes, not Pharisees. See Ninth Sunday, n. 34.

19. The origin and the meaning of the name Beelzebul, no doubt an insulting one, remains uncertain. See the notes in the *Bible de Jérusalem* and the *Traduction Oecuménique de la Bible*; "Béelzéboul" in the *Dictionnaire encyclopédique de la Bible*, 192.

20. Without calling them cases of possession, history has recorded many such examples. The Church authorities, up to our own times, have often been obliged to intervene, to discern truth from falsehood, and to protect the faithful from being misled in good faith by innocent victims of illusions or hallucinations—for instance, alleged appearances—or even by racketeers in the supernatural and miraculous, who exploit the unwary.

21. See Matt 7:16; 12:33; Luke 6:44; John 10:12; Acts 20:29.

22. Commission Francophone Cistercienne, *Tropaires des dimanches*, 74. (Fiches de chant U LH 73).

Eleventh Sunday—Pages 99–107

1. In the Book of Ezekiel, we read two allegories. First, that of the eagle who, having taken the top from a cedar and carried it away, brings back from this faraway place the

seed of a vine which it plants in the original land (Ezek 17:1-10). The explanations that follow (Ezek 17:12-21) give the key for the interpretation of the allegory. It concerns the events that followed the capture of Jerusalem by Nebuchadnezzar in 587 B.C. and the deportation of the elite of the people; the replacement of King Zedekiah, exiled in 497 B.C. to become afterwards the conqueror's humble vassal. Therefore, the allegory speaks of the renewal of the people, God himself taking the initiative and establishing another king, a young branch. This expression in the form of the Immanuel prophecies in Isaiah (11:1) is applied to one of David's descendants. He will be like a magnificent cedar, according to the image by which the Bible often designates the king (2 Kgs 14:9; Ezek 31:3-13; Dan 4:20-22). But the identity of this person is open to question.

2. Despite his profound disappointment caused by the kings' behavior and his loss of trust in the royal institution itself (Ezek 19:1-14), Ezekiel, in his vision of Israel's restoration, still has a place for a descendant of David (Ezek 34:23-24; 37:24-25).

3. This waiting was mixed with certain feelings of anxiety and impatience, in the measure in which they expected the Lord's imminent return.

4. See, for instance 2 Cor 4:6-11 (Ninth Sunday) and 4:13-5:1 (Tenth Sunday).

5. 1 Thess 4:17; Phil 1:23; Col 3:3.

6. Rom 6:11.

7. 1 Cor 7:29-35 (Third and Fourth Sunday).

8. St. Augustine, *Prier Dieu: Les psaumes*, ed. A.-M. Besnard, trans. J. Perret, in Chrétiens de tous les temps 3 (Paris: Cerf, 1964) 145–146.

9. Usually Paul distinguishes three steps: baptism (Gal 3:26-27; 4:6; 6:15; Rom 6:11; 2 Cor 5:17); heavenly life at the end (Rom 6:4-8; Col 2:12-13; 3:1-4); the between-time during which we prepare ourselves for the encounter with the Lord (Rom 13:14; 8:29-34; Gal 5:16-25; Col 3:9-10; Eph 4:22-24; 2 Cor 3:18).

10. See 1 Thess 3:13; 5:23; 1 Cor 1:8; Phil 1:10.

11. Ch. de Foucauld, "Vocation, méditation 194 sur les Evangiles," *Oeuvres spirituelles: Anthologie* (Paris: Seuil, 1959) 214–215.

12. Mark's Gospel records only two discourses of Jesus, both of similar length: the discourse in parables (Mark 4:1-34) and the discourse on the end time (Mark 13:1-37).

13. There are five parables in this first discourse: the Sower (4:1-9) and its explanation (4:10-20), the lamp (4:21-24), the measure (4:24-25), the seed which grows by itself (4:26-29), the mustard seed (4:30-32). The discourse concludes with Jesus giving the reason for his teaching in parables (4:33-34). On today's Gospel, see J. Dupont, "Deux paraboles du Royaume," *Assemblées du Seigneur*, deuxième série, No 42 (Paris: Publications de Saint-André—Cerf, 1970) 50–59; B. Standaert, *L'Evangile selon Marc*, 52–55.

14. The well-known parable of the sower is found in the three Synoptic Gospels. Matthew's version (13:1-23) is read on the Fifteenth Sunday in Ordinary Time, Year A; Mark's version (4:1-20) on Wednesday of the Third Week; Luke's version (8:4-15) on Saturday of the Twenty-fourth Week.

15. Mark is the only evangelist who reports this parable. But certain elements can be found in the parable of the weeds and the good grain which we read in Matthew (13:24-30).

16. Joel 4:13; Rev 14:14-15.

17. Ch. Péguy, "Le porche de la deuxième vertu, *Oeuvres poétiques complètes*, La Pléiade (Paris: Gallimard, 1957) 658.

18. K. Rahner, *Mission et grâce: Le XXᵉ siècle, siècle de grâce?* (Paris: Mame, 1962) 38–39.

19. See G. Minette de Tillesse, *Le secret messianique dans l'Evangile de Marc*, 57.

20. Symeon the New Theologian (949-1002), "Hymne 17," *Prière mystique*, Foi vivante 195 (Paris: Cerf, 1979) 88.

Twelfth Sunday—Pages 108-16

1. See above, Fifth Sunday, nn. 1 and 2.

2. See P. Auvray, "La toute-puissance de Dieu," *Assemblées du Seigneur*, deuxième série, No 43 (Paris: Publications de Saint-André—Cerf) 30-34.
This excerpt is taken outside its literary context because of its intrinsic interest and its relation to today's Gospel. Therefore, it is not necessary to recall here the dramatic life of Job crushed by adversities.

3. Exod 19:16-19; Judg 5:4-5; 1 Kgs 19:11-12; Pss 18:8-16; 49:3; Ezek 1:4; Nah 1:3.

4. Acts mentions these dangers and the adventures to which one exposed oneself at sea in the detailed record of the prisoner Paul's journey to Rome (Acts 27:1–28:13).

5. P. Valéry, "Le cimetière marin," *Poésies* (Paris: Gallimard, 1958) 100.

6. Pss 18:16; 65:8; 66:6; 74:13; 77:20; 78:13, 53; 89:10; 93:4; 95:5; 104:25-26; 106:9; 114:3, 5; 135:6; 146:6.

7. See "Mer" in *Vocabulaire de théologie biblique*, cols. 740-742, and in *Dictionnaire encyclopédique de la Bible*, 809.

8. This choice that forces itself upon a person is not to be confused with the "obligation" to make what is called "the profession of faith" at the end of the requisite number of years of catechesis. Such a celebration aims at giving adolescents the opportunity to personally and publicly profess their faith in the presence of the Christian community and the witnesses of their baptism; hence, its importance in the churches in which it has been established. It remains that the profession of faith is not limited to this sole celebration; it must be expressed throughout one's whole life. Moreover, every participation in a sacrament is a profession of faith both personal and ecclesial in virtue of one's baptism: the Eucharist, reconciliation, the anointing of the sick, of course, but equally, marriage—though perhaps few advert to the fact.

9. St. Benedict, *Rule*, ch. 4.

10. Even those who knew Jesus when he was on earth had to go beyond the merely human way of knowing him. The proof for this is that many saw only a man in him and others were slow to believe, as the Gospels often note.

11. See the first reading.

12. 1 Pet 3:13-22; 2 Pet 2:1-3; 3:3-7.

13. In patristic literature, the boat became the classical image either of the Church or of the Christian soul. See J. Quasten, *Initiation aux Pères de l'Eglise*, II (Paris: Cerf, 1957) 242.

14. St. Augustine, *Sermons*, 81:8, in *Oeuvres complètes*, vol. 16 (Paris: Vivès, 1871) 581.

15. We must not forget the effort of inculturation that went into the translation into Greek of the gospel preached in Aramaic by Jesus and its announcement in the Greco-Roman world, whose culture was completely foreign to the cultural and religious universe of the Bible, in spite of the scattering of Jewish communities throughout the Empire. The time of the barbarian invasions required a similar effort, of which we are little aware because we remember especially—if not exclusively—that only, or almost only, Latin, still used by the Church, has left its mark in the documents and writings which have come down to us.

16. "Do not be afraid." This is what Pope John Paul II said in his homily during the Mass of enthronement on 22 October 1978. *La Documentation catholique*, 75 (1978) 915.

17. D. Rimaud, *Les arbres dans la mer* (Paris: Desclée, 1975) 124. (Fiche de chant H 123).

Thirteenth Sunday—Pages 118-26

1. See, D. Colombo, "Méditation d'un sage sur la mort," *Assemblées du Seigneur*, deuxième série, No 44, Supplément (Paris: Publications de Saint-André—Cerf, 1969) 1-8.

2. Job 7:17; Pss 39:5-7; 144:4; Isa 2:22; Qoh 2.

3. It is a human couple—"male and female"—that God created "in his image."

4. Gen 2:16; Wis 3:4; Rom 8:29-30.

5. Wis 1:13-14; 2:23.

6. See, L. Ligier, *Péché d'Adam et péché du monde: I. L'Ancien Testament*, Théologie 43 (Paris: Aubier, 1960).

7. A.-M. Dubarle, *Les sages d'Israël*, Lectio divina 1 (Paris: Cerf, 1946) 192.

8. 1 Cor 11:7; 2 Cor 3:18; 4:4; Col 1:15.

9. Rom 5:12-17.

10. Origen (185?-?254), *Homélies sur la Genèse*, 1:13, Sources chrétiennes 7 (Paris: Cerf—Lyon: Editions de l'Abeille, 1943) 83. Elsewhere (ibid., 13:4, p. 224), he says, "God's image remains always in you, even though you should superimpose on it the image of earthly man."

11. The way he speaks of this collection—its organization so that all may generously participate in it according to their means, the actual collection of funds and their conveyance—shows how much the Apostle of the Gentiles has taken to heart the commitment to help the Mother Church. At the same time, one has here a living testimony to the solidarity of Churches which already in apostolic times were concerned about relieving the needs of the poorest among them. See, Acts 12:27-30; Gal 2:10; 1 Cor 16:1-3; 2 Cor 9:1-15.

12. Paul frequently uses the preposition "for" when he speaks of Christ's work and passion. Rom 5:6, 8; 8:11, 32; 14:15; 1 Cor 8:11; 2 Cor 5:14-15; Gal 2:20; Eph 5:2, 25. See, J. Dupont, "Pour vous, le Christ s'est fait pauvre," *Assemblées du Seigneur*, deuxième série, No 44 (Paris: Publications de Saint-André—Cerf, 1969) 35.

13. B.-M. Chevignard, *La doctrine spirituelle de l'Evangile*, Foi vivante 4 (Paris: Cerf, 1966) 126-127.

14. Acts 2:42, 44-45; 4:32, 34-35. See, J. Dupont, *Etudes sur les Actes des Apôtres*, Lectio divina 45 (Paris: Cerf, 1967) 516-518.

15. This exchange, which has always been honored in the Church, is more institutionalized in our day, to our delight. The communities which remain timidly and jealously closed in upon themselves end up, sooner or later, by withering away and becoming impoverished, whereas they had wanted to save their assets. Too much "prudence" is harmful because it often is, at bottom, a lack of trust in God and a short-sighted egoism.

16. The general intercessions are a grace, first for us who participate in them because these intercessions take into account others' needs and furnish us an opportunity to ask for them God's help which they need. But these petitions must be really universal and we must not think we have fulfilled our duty simply by entrusting others' troubles to God.

Besides, it is comforting to think that in other liturgical assemblies, near or far, similar prayers express the union which binds all Christian communities to each other.

17. Mark 3:21-35; 6:7-33; 11:12-26; 14:1-11.

18. See, J. Potin, "Guérison d'une hémorroïse et résurrection de la fille de Jaïre," *Assemblées du Seigneur, deuxième série*, No 44 (Paris: Publications de Saint-André—Cerf, 1969) 47; J. Delorme, "Deux miracles imbriqués," *Cahiers Evangile*, ½ (1972) 47-52.

19. The title of "synagogue official" may designate the person responsible for the synagogue or a prominent member of the community; in both cases, he is a highly visible person and known to all.

20. Her infirmity made her legally "unclean" and the Law forbade her to approach others (Lev 15:25).

21. We have here the only case in the Gospels where a cure is, so to speak, confirmed by Jesus instead of being the result of the word he pronounces. From that viewpoint, we can compare this singular episode with what Acts reports (5:15), "Thus they even carried the sick out into the streets and laid them on cots and mats so that when Peter came by, at least his shadow might fall on one or another of them."

22. St. Peter Chrysologus (380?–?450), "Sermons 33," *Patrologie latine*, 52, ed. J.-P. Migne, cols. 295–296.

23. Peter, James, and John will be the witnesses of the Lord's transfiguration (Mark 9:2-10), then of his agony in Gethsemane (Mark 14:33-42). The question has been raised: Did Jesus, after having chosen twelve from among his disciples "that they might be with him and he might send them forth to preach and to have authority to drive out demons" (Mark 3:13-19), distinguish these three, later considered "pillars" of the Church (Gal 2:9), to play a leading role? The *Rule of Qumran*, followed by the Jewish community settled on the northwestern shore of the Dead Sea, about seven and a half miles from today's Jericho, mentions, in VIII: 1-5, an organization in twelve and three.

24. Isa 29:19; Dan 12:2; Matt 11:4-5; Mark 12:18-27; Luke 7:22.

25. The verb "to sleep" is associated with the idea of resurrection only here and in the Letter to the Ephesians (5:14). But this idea is expressed elsewhere by similar verbs: "to fall asleep" in the Lord (1 Cor 15:18; 1 Thess 4:14), "to be asleep" (John 11:11). Before Jesus recalls Lazarus to life, he tells Martha, "Your brother will rise"; and Martha answers, "I know he will rise . . ." (John 11:23-24). For what concerns Jesus' resurrection, see, Matt 17:9-23; Mark 9:9-31; Luke 9:22; 18:33; John 20:9.

26. See, John 11:25 (the resurrection of Lazarus: Fifth Sunday of Lent, Year A).

27. Lazarus, too, began to walk at Jesus' command, "Lazarus, come out!" With his incredulous disciples when he manifests himself to them after the resurrection, Jesus eats a piece of grilled fish they have given him (Luke 24:41-43).

28. Un moine de l'Eglise d'Orient, *Présence du Christ*, (Chevetogne, 1961) 102–103.

29. St. Augustine, "Sermon sur le Ps 102: 7, 5, 11," *Les plus belles homélies de saint Augustin sur les psaumes*, ed. G. Humeau (Paris: Beauchesne, 1947) 318–319.

Fourteenth Sunday—Pages 127–35

1. J. Asurmendi, "Le prophète Ezéchiel, *Cahiers Evangile* 38 (1961); P. Auvray, "La vocation d'Ezéchiel: Ez 2,1–3,9," *Bible et vie chrétienne* 43 (1962) 18–26; Fr. Smyth-Florentin, "Un prophète au milieu d'eux: Ez 2, 2-5," *Assemblées du Seigneur*, deuxième série, No 45 (Paris: Publications de Saint-André—Cerf, 1975) 28–32.

2. Ezekiel was active between 597 and 570 B.C. See, *Dictionnaire encyclopédique de la Bible*, 463–464.

The immediate predecessors of Ezekiel were somewhat reticent to establish their authority on a sort of invasion of their being by the spirit of prophecy. They did not want to be mistakenly likened to those bands of visionaries and ecstatic individuals who were roaming about in Canaan (Hos 9:7). Ezekiel, for his part, often behaves as one subject to fits of ecstasy: he claims to be invaded by a mysterious force which impels him to act, often in an unusual manner (Ezek 3:14; 8:3; 11:24). God's creative power is at work through him as an intermediary (Ezek 37:1-15, the vision of the dry bones).

3. The expression occurs eighty-seven times in the Book of Ezekiel. It does not yet have the messianic implication that the Book of Daniel will give it: there, "son of man" will designate an unusual person upon whom God confers a sovereign authority (Dan 7).

4. P. Grostefan, *Dieu pour locataire* (Paris: Desclée, 1973) 60.

5. Gal 1:11-12. He then explains (Gal 1:17-24) that after his conversion he went to Arabia without going up to Jerusalem to see those who were apostles before him. Only three years later did he meet Peter, with whom he stayed for two weeks.

6. A similar recalling of the great things done by God is frequent in the Old Testament (Deut 33:29; 1 Chr 16:27; Pss 5:12; 31:11; 88:17; Jer 9:22-23; 17:14). In the New Testament, Paul is the only one who picks up this theme (2 Cor 11:12, 16, 17, 21, 30; 12:1-6).

7. The Greek word he uses to designate this trial—*scolops*—literally means "thorn," "pointed stake," or "cross."

8. Second reading, Ninth Sunday.

9. St. Thomas More (1478–1535), executed under Henry VIII for refusing to take the oath of supremacy, "Lettre 12 à sa fille Margaret," *Ecrits de prison,* trans. P. Leyris (Paris: Seuil, 1953), quoted in *Fiches d'Orval,* No 81.

10. Paul always shows a remarkable dignity and even a legitimate pride. He never tolerates a magistrate's not giving him the respect owed him. He does not accept that a subordinate guard be sent to lead him out of the prison into which he has been thrown without judgment; he demands that those responsible for his illegal incarceration come themselves. When a tribune wants to have him flogged, he proudly addresses the centurion in charge of carrying out the order, "Is it lawful for you to scourge a man who is a Roman citizen and has not been tried?" (Acts 22:25). Proud to be a citizen by birth, Paul demands to be respected as such. He will stand on his rights when he appeals to the tribunal of the emperor (Acts 25:10-11).

11. St. Paulinus of Nole (343–431), *Lettres,* 38:6, *Patrologie latine,* ed. J.-P. Migne, col. 360.

12. It is well known that the titles of "brothers" and "sisters" have a very wide meaning. As to Joseph, Mary's husband, he was considered Jesus' father.

13. Mark 1:22-27, Fourth Sunday.

14. Un moine de l'Eglise d'Orient, *Jésus: Simples regards sur le Christ,* (Chevetogne, 1962) 41–42.

15. P. Emmanuel, *Tu,* 321–322.

Fifteenth and Sixteenth Sunday in Ordinary Time
Page 136

1. See above, Ordinary Time, Year B.

2. Together with the Letters to the Philippians, the Colossians, and Philemon, the Letter to the Ephesians belongs to the group called the "Captivity Epistles." See, J. Cambier, *Vie chrétienne en Eglise: L'Epître aux Ephésiens lue aux chrétiens d'aujourd'hui* (Paris: Desclée, 1966); M. Zerwick, *La Lettre aux Ephésiens,* Parole et prière (Paris: Desclée, 1967); R. Baules, *L'insondable richesse du Christ: Etude des thèmes de l'Epître aux Ephésiens,* Lectio divina 66 (Paris: Cerf, 1971); E. Cothenet, *Paroles sur le chemin: Commentaires exégétiques du Lectionnaire dominical, année B* (Tournai: Centre diocésain de documentation, 1978) 234-239; the introductions to Ephesians in the *Bible de Jérusalem,* 1622, and in the *Traduction Oecuménique de la Bible,* 2815-2819; "Amos" in the *Dictionnaire encyclopédique de la Bible,* 50-51. The reading of Ephesians is continued through the Twenty-first Sunday.

Fifteenth Sunday—Pages 137–46

1. In 931 B.C., ten tribes seceded and formed the northern kingdom—Israel—whose capital was Samaria. Bethel became its religious center, and its sanctuary was a rival of the Temple of Jerusalem, the religious center of the southern kingdom, Judah (1 Kgs 11:28–12:33). This schism lasted until the ruin of Samaria in 721 B.C. At that time, Jerusalem became again the rallying point for the twelve tribes. But a nucleus of irreducible subjects of the northern kingdom continued to exist; they were the Samaritans mentioned in the

Gospels. Concentrated around the sanctuary built on Mount Gerizim, they were regarded as impious people with whom pious Jews were forbidden to associate.

2. The announced misfortunes and punishments are terrible. But the style and the vocabulary used to denounce the impiety, luxury, and injustice of the inhabitants are of a singular coarseness. See, for instance 4:1-3 (against the women of Samaria, called "cows of Bashan," a region across the Jordan, famous for its pastures and its herds of cows); 5:21-27 (against worship devoid of justice); 6:1-7 (against the false security of the high-born, who live in shameful luxury), read on the Twenty-sixth Sunday, Year C; 8:4-8 (against those who defraud and exploit the people), read on the Twenty-fifth Sunday, Year C; 9:1-4 (announcement of the destruction of the sanctuary). However, we should not conclude that Amos was a boor. His language, together with Isaiah's, is among the most beautiful of the Bible.

3. About 790-750 B.C.: 2 Kgs 14:23-29.

4. Although the Lectionary says "visionary," other translations, such as the *Jerusalem Bible* and the *Traduction Oecumenique de la Bible*, imply a strong suggestion of scorn.

5. "[I]t is the king's sanctuary and a royal temple." So saying, Amaziah implicitly recognizes his servility and the real function of the sacred place, of which he is in charge.

6. B. Pascal, *Pensées*, 617, Oeuvres (Paris: La Pléiade, 1939) 1030.

7. P. de La Tour Du Pin, *Une somme de poésie: III*, 312-313.

8. When he writes this letter, Paul feels that his end is near. At the time of embarking in Miletus to go to Jerusalem (he was arrested there and, at his request, sent to the Emperor's tribunal), he called together the ancients of the Church of Ephesus, where he had spent three years of fruitful apostolate, in order to bid them farewell (Acts 20:17-38).

9. It suggests a circular letter destined for several communities.

10. Taking other texts into account, in particular Eph 2:18, 22, we can understand "spiritual blessing" as "blessing of the Spirit" or "blessing in the Spirit." See, M. Coune, "A la louange de sa gloire: Ep 1, 3-14," *Assemblées du Seigneur*, deuxième série, No 46 (Paris: Publications de Saint-André —Cerf, 1974) 39.

C. Vagaggini, "La liturgie et la dialectique christologique et trinitaire du salut: *A Patre per Christum in Spiritu ad Patrem*," *Initiation théologique à la liturgie*, vol. 1, trans. Ph Rouillard (Bruges: Apostolat liturgique; Paris: Société liturgique, 1959) 135-174.

11. See. Gen 18:18; 22:18; 26:4; 28:14; Acts 3:25; Gal 3:8.

12. St. Irenaeus (135?-?202), *Contre les hérésies*, III, 18:1-2, Sources chrétiennes 211 (Paris: Cerf, 1974) 343-345.

In the Greek Fathers and in theology, "economy" designates the plan of salvation as God realizes and unfolds it.

13. Blessing of the baptismal water.

14. Confirmation.

15. Ordination of a priest.

16. Eucharistic Prayer No. 3.

17. Eucharistic Prayer No. 4.

18. The apostles are named "two by two" in the lists which give us their names. The mission "two by two" refers to a custom already observed by the disciples of John the Baptist and later found in Christian communities (Luke 7:18; Acts 8:14; 13:2; 15:36-40; 1 Cor 9:6). For testimony to be credible, it had to be given by at least two witnesses, as the Law prescribed (Deut 19:15).

19. Mark mentions one case when the disciples were unable to drive out a demon (Mark 9:14-29). Jesus' answer—"This kind can only come out through prayer"—remains enigmatic. The episode is surrounded by a rather ambiguous climate. The father of the possessed child first says to Jesus, "[I]f you can do anything. . ." Only afterwards does he say, "I do believe, help my unbelief!" Caught in the crowd in which controversies were rife, did the disciples themselves doubt? In any case, what is clear in this narrative is that

the driving out of a demon is due to God's intervention asked for with faith and trust, and not to a power one would possess by one's self.

20. J. Delorme, "Lecture de l'Evangile selon saint Marc, *Cahiers Evangile,* 1/2 (1972) 55-56.

21. Sandals and staff call to mind the equipment of the Hebrews on the evening of the Passover (Exod 12:11).

22. 1 Thess 1:6; 1 Pet 4:12-14.

23. Preface 5 of Sundays.

24. Preface 1 of weekdays.

25. Preface 2 of Apostles.

26. In Mark's Gospel, there are three scenes which concern the Twelve: the call of the first four on the lakeshore (1:16-20), the choosing of the Twelve "that they might be with him and he might send them forth to preach" (3:14-15), their first mission (6:7-13, this Sunday's Gospel). Now, each time, the episode is preceded by a recalling of Jesus' activity: in Galilee (1:14-15), for the benefit of the crowd (3:7-12), through the villages of the region (6:6).

27. It is rather curious to note that people often speak of the Church in and for the world as if it were a modern discovery.

28. Commission Francophone Cistercienne, *Tropaires des dimanches,* 89. (Fiche de Chant U LH 74).

Sixteenth Sunday—Pages 147-54

1. Shepherds had to seek pastures and watering places and defend the flock against wild beasts and thieves. Consequently, they were usually armed with crook and slingshot. They also were obliged to indemnify the flock's owner for lost animals, etc.

2. Moses had been a nomadic shepherd (Exod 3:1). At the time of the Exodus from Egypt, the Lord seemed like a shepherd leading his people: he protected them against dangers, supplied food, and guided them from spring to spring, whose locations in the desert were familiar to him (Exod 15:13; Ps 22). See, "Pasteur et Troupeau" in *Vocabulaire de théologie biblique,* cols. 917–921, and "Berger, Pasteur" in *Dictionnaire encyclopédique de la Bible,* 198–199.

3. On the Book of Jeremiah, see, H. Cazelles, "La production du Livre de Jérémie dans l'histoire ancienne d'Israël," *Masses ouvières* 343 (1978) 9–32; J. Briend, "Le livre de Jérémie," *Cahiers Evangile* 40 (1982); A. Ridouard, *Jérémie, l'épreuve de la foi,* Lire la Bible 62 (Paris: Cerf, 1983); *Jérémie, un prophète en temps de crise,* Essais bibliques (Genève: Labor et fides, 1985).

4. In the Bible, the expression "the sheep of your pasture" is frequently used to designate the people of God (Pss 74:1; 95:7; 100:3).

5. We must not forget that in arid regions, flocks keep moving to find pastures and water: the lost sheep is unable to find these; moreover, it is abandoned, without defense, to the attacks of all kinds of predators. A scattered flock is, in effect, a lost flock. This is why, even if one single animal has wandered off, the good shepherd looks for it through the desert (Matt 18:12-14; Luke 15:4-6). If we overlook these concrete data, we cannot properly appreciate the tragic condition of the lost sheep, of the scattered flock.

6. The Bible is the history of salvation, which unfolds in this world and will receive its fulfillment in the heavenly homeland towards which we are already walking. This is why it is always God who is involved and acts in the dispersion caused by sin and the gathering following conversion.

7. See, Fifteenth Sunday, n. 1.

8. 2 Sam 7:12; Isa 9:6.

9. With the first capture of Jerusalem in 598 B.C., Nebuchadnezzar installed, in Jehoiakim's place, a king he called Zedekiah, which means "God is justice (or salvation)." This king soon disappointed Jeremiah; however, he willingly listened to the prophet (Jer 37:3-21). During a new siege of Jerusalem, in 587 B.C., he was captured while he was attempting to flee, and Nebuchadnezzar blinded him (2 Kgs 24-25). See, "Sédécias" in the *Dictionnaire encyclopédique de la Bible*, 1181.

10. Matt 18:12-14; 15:24; Luke 15:4-7; 19:10; John 10:1-18; Heb 13:20; 1 Pet 2:25.

11. Although the word is found only a dozen times in his letters, reconciliation is an important concept in Paul's thought (Rom 5:9-11; 11:15; 2 Cor 5:18-21; Eph 2:13-18; Col 7:10-11). See, J. Dupont, *La réconciliation dans la théologie de saint Paul*, Analecta lovaniensia biblica et orientalia, ser. II, fasc. 32 (Louvain: Publications universitaires; Bruges-Paris: Desclée De Brouwer, 1953).

12. This excerpt from Paul's Letter to the Ephesians has the look of a hymn. Whether it is the reminiscence of a liturgical text or an original composition of Paul, it is a beautiful expression of faith.

13. It is not said that in the meantime Jesus remains alone, waiting for them to return. The Twelve have been sent "two by two," but not necessarily all at the same time.

14. In the plan and composition of Mark's Gospel, this narrative is the beginning of a long and important development commonly called "the section of breads," because the word "bread" occurs seventeen times in eighty-six verses (Mark 6:34-8:26). See, L. Monloubou, *Lire, prêcher l'Evangile de Marc: Homélies pour l'année B* (Mulhouse:Salvator, 1978) 88-106.

15. If we follow Luke, who is very clear on this point, "apostles" is a title reserved for the Twelve (Luke 6:13; 9:10-12; 11:49; 17:5; 22:14; 24:10; Acts 1:2; 2:37; etc.) In fact, the distinction is less absolute. In the primitive Church, others than the Twelve are called apostles—to begin with Paul, who loudly claims this title (1 Cor 9:1; 15:7-9; Gal 1:1. See also, Acts 14:14, Rom 16:7; 1 Cor 12:28; Eph 2:20; 3:5). On this question, see, J. Dupont, "Le nom d'Apôtres a-t-il été donné aux Douze par Jésus?" *Etudes sur les Evangiles synoptiques*, II, (Leuven:University Press—Peeters, 1985) 976-1018.

16. See, "Apôtre" in *Dictionnaire encyclopédique de la Bible*, 121: "In Christian language, it would be possible, without stretching the meaning too far, to translate 'envoy' by 'missionary.'"

17. The recalling of this first mission highlights the continuity between the teaching of Jesus and that of the Church. But it is also a warning directed to missionaries of the gospel.

18. To be able to fulfill their mission, those who are sent must accept to be taught by the Lord and his gospel, as did the apostles. It can also happen that they are sometimes, like them, overwhelmed by events and do not know what to do. Thus the apostles facing the crowds having nothing to eat (Mark 6:35-44).

19. The mention of the impossibility to eat and the departure for a deserted place prepare for—on the plane of composition—the narrative of the multiplication of the loaves to feed the hungry crowd (Mark 6:35-44).

20. Gospel of the Eleventh Sunday.

21. Gospel of the Fifth Sunday.

22. Un Moine de l'Eglise d'Orient, *Présence du Christ*, 54-56. This meditation does not pretend to exhaust the topic of rest—its value, its legitimacy on the human and spiritual planes—nor the topic of the necessary alternation between rest and work. It remains that everything, even rest, must be considered first of all from the point of view of God the Creator and of Christ, in God and in Christ. The same can be said of human liberty, a gift of God, who created human beings in his image.

23. It would be out of place to draw conclusions, such as: "Those who devote themselves unstintingly to the activities of the ministry and the apostolate cannot find time for prayer.

This is the business of those who, free from these duties, living in solitude, have leisure. They are called contemplatives to distinguish them from the active ones."

24. Thus in numerous psalms. See, Matt 18:27 (parable of the two servants); Luke 15:20 (parable of the father of two sons).

25. Matt 20:34; Mark 1:41; 9:22; Luke 7:13; 10:33.

26. Deut 8:3; Neh 9:13-15; Wis 16:28, 26. In its 176 verses, Psalm 119 sings God's word, spring of life, wisdom, "[a] lamp to [the] feet" of those who listen and obey it.

27. Mark 6:30-44; 8:1-9; Luke 24:25-32; Acts 2:42; 20:7. See, Y.-M. Congar, "Les deux formes du pain de vie dans l'Evangile et la Tradition," *Parole de Dieu et sacerdoce: Etudes présentées à S. Exc. Mgr Weber* (Paris: Desclée, 1962) 21-58.

28. Fundamentally, the bishop and the priest are ministers of the Eucharist because they are ministers of the Word, and vice versa. It is more clearly seen today: the one who presides at the gathering and the Eucharistic table must also, normally, deliver the homily.

29. J.-B. Dumortier, "Pasteurs à l'image du Christ," *Assemblées du Seigneur,* deuxième série, No 47 (Paris: Publications de Saint-André—Cerf, 1970) 61.

30. Throughout Mark's Gospel, the crowds appear eager to be near Jesus, who exerts on them an extraordinary attraction. At the time of the trial, they go away from him because they are manipulated (Mark 1:28, 35; 2:2, 13; 3:7-9, 20; 5:21, 24; 6:54-56; 9:15; 10:1, 46; 15:11).

31. Henri J. M. Nouwen, *The Way of the Heart: Desert Spirituality and Contemporary Ministry* (New York: The Seabury Press, 1981) 39-40.

32. Commission Francophone Cistercienne, *Tropaires des dimanches,* 92. (Fiche de chant U LH 54).

Seventeenth to Twenty-first Sunday—Pages 155-57

1. This discourse contains forty-six verses, from which forty are read. See, A. Jaubert, "Lecture de l'Evangile selon saint Jean," *Cahiers Evangile* 17 (1976), 46-51.

2. *Ordo lectionum missae,* 2ᵉ édition, 105, 1 (Libreria editrice vaticana, 1981) p. XLV. Indeed, immediately after the story of the disciples' return from their first mission (Mark 6:30-34, Sixteenth Sunday), Mark reports the first multiplication of loaves.

3. See, A. Feuillet, "Les thèmes majeurs du Discours sur le pain de vie: Contribution à l'étude des sources de la pensée johannique," *Nouvelle revue théologique* 82 (1960) 803-822, 1040-1062.

4. There are, beforehand, fourteen Sundays on which we read Mark's Gospel and twelve afterwards. On the Second and Thirty-fourth Sunday, the gospel readings are taken from John.

5. The same type of composition prevails in the other great discourses in John's Gospel, in particular those of chapters 14 to 17.

6. Luke 4:21.

7. "The homily is part of the liturgy, and it is strongly recommended that one be given because it is necessary to nurture Christian life. It must explain one aspect of the scriptural readings or of another text from the ordinary or the proper of that day's Mass, taking into account either the mystery which is celebrated or the hearers' particular needs" (*Présentation générale du Missel romain,* No 41). See, R. Gantoy, "Homélie, témoignage, partage," *Communautés et liturgies* 60 (1978) 387-404.

8. This is one of the objectives of *Days of the Lord.*

Seventeenth Sunday—Pages 158-64

1. The cycle of Elisha collects very old traditions, anterior, for a large part, to the eighth century B.C. (2 Kgs 4:1-8:15; 9:1-13; 13:14-25). These stories intend to show that Elisha was in no way inferior to his master, the great prophet Elijah.

Then ELISHA, filled with a twofold portion of his spirit,
    wrought many marvels by his mere word.
During his lifetime he feared no one,
    nor was any man able to intimidate his will.
Nothing was beyond his power;
    beneath him flesh was brought back into life.
In life he performed wonders,
    and after death, marvelous deeds (Sir 48:12-14).

See, "Elisée," in *Dictionnaire encyclopédique de la Bible*, 403.

2. The narrative of the cure of Naaman, stricken with leprosy, is read on the Twenty-eighth Sunday, Year C, (2 Kgs 5:14-17), and on Monday in the Third Week of Lent (2 Kgs 5:1-15a).

3. In contrast with Elijah, who was a solitary, Elisha has connections with the guild prophets of his time (2 Kgs 4:38-44; 6:1-7).

4. A. de Saint-Exupéry, *Pilote de guerre* (Paris: Gallimard, 1942) 200.

5. See, "Pain" in *Vocabulaire de théologie biblique*, cols. 875–878, and in *Dictionnaire encyclopédique de la Bible* (n. 1), 949–950; E. Lipinski, "La parole et le pain," *Assemblées du Seigneur*, première série, No 60 (Bruges: Publications de Saint-André, 1963) 40–62; D. Sésboüé, "Pain et vin," *Assemblées du Seigneur,* première série (Bruges: Publications de Saint-André, 1966) 54–74.

6. Num 5:15; Ezek 45:13.

7. Moreover, this man has chosen to accomplish the rite of offering by bringing his gifts to Elisha rather than to the Gilgal sanctuary, as he ought normally to have done, because at that time, the sacred place of Israel was in the hands of Baal's prophets. His gesture, therefore, means that he absolutely refuses to participate in idolatrous worship and that he remains firmly attached to the true God.

8. Recapitulation of the whole universe in Christ (Eph:1:10); union of Jews and Gentiles, the last phase of salvation (Eph 1:11-14); salvation already fundamentally gained (Eph 2:6); peace accomplished in the blood of Christ (Eph 2:11-22); the "mystery" of unity hidden for a long time and revealed today (Eph 3:6).

9. Paul is the herald of unity. Rom 12:4-5; 1 Cor 1:10; 8:6; 12:12, 27; 2 Cor 13:11; Phil 2:1-4.

10. Gal 5:19-21; Rom 1:28-32; 3:9; Eph 2:3.

11. Eph 2:15-18; Col 3:15.

12. There are five narratives in the Synoptic Gospels: Matt 14:13-21 (Eighteenth Sunday, Year A); Matt 15:32-37 (Wednesday, First Week of Advent); Mark 6:35-44 (Tuesday after Epiphany); Mark 8:1-10 (Saturday, Fifth Week in Ordinary Time); Luke 9:10-17 (The Body and Blood of Christ, Year C).

13. What appeals uniquely or principally to reason, requires a proportionate intellectual capacity in order to be understood. The "simple ones" may say, "This is too complicated for us; we do not succeed in following your learned reasonings." On the other hand, there is nothing discursive in a sign. We might not unfailingly and immediately comprehend its meaning, but whoever has an open mind and heart feels that this gesture, this action, has a meaning well worth seeking after. We could invoke many examples drawn from everyday life.

14. See, Second Sunday in Ordinary Time, Year C, *Days of the Lord*, 6.

15. See, Third Sunday of Advent, Year A, *Days of the Lord*, 1.

16. Matt 4:24–5:1.

17. Exod 24:1-18.

18. One can also observe other similarities between chapter six in John's Gospel and chapter eleven in the Book of Numbers: John 6:41-43 (Num 11:11); John 6:31 (Num 11:7-9); John 6:51-52 (Num 11:13).

19. When we slowly read the fourth Gospel, we often feel—and this is probably no illusion—that between sentences, there are, as it were, blanks to make room for reflections, comments, questions, etc. which arose when John was preaching. Any attempt to find or guess what is not said is very hazardous. But the written text is rich in implicit allusions, reminiscences, telling locutions. It was transmitted in this form in order that we may strive, with prayer, to discover its meaning, through prolonged and assiduous meditation in the secret of our room or in a group, helped by the tradition, the teaching, and the practice of the Church.

20. Andrew's remark recalls Moses' when he said to God, ''The people around me include six hundred thousand soldiers; yet you say, 'I will give them meat to eat for a whole month.' Can enough sheep and cattle be slaughtered for them? If all the fish of the sea were caught for them, would they have enough?''

21. See above, first reading.

22. The mention of this detail in a narrative that has little use for the picturesque touch and does not present this meal as a picnic improvised on the spot, thanks to the miraculous liberality of Jesus, surprises us a little. The general climate and the multiplicity of the allusions make us think rather of a place cleared of the ''thorns and thistles'' the soil produced after Adam's sin (Gen 3:18).

23. Matt 26:26; Mark 14:22; Luke 22:19; 1 Cor 11:23-24.

24. Luke 24:35; Acts 2:42.

25. Matt 26:29; Luke 22:16.

Here is a testimony, among others: In the cemetery of Priscilla, in Rome, a fresco represents a Eucharistic meal with the baskets of the multiplication of the loaves. One of the participants wears a hairpiece which, for a short time, was made fashionable by Faustina, the wife of Emperor Antoninus Pius (died 141).

26. Fauste (abbot of Lérins ca. 433, bishop of Riez in Provence in 462), ''Homélie sur le corps du Christ,'' *La messe: Liturgies anciennes et texts patristiques*, choisis et présentés par A. Hamman, Lettres chrétiennes 9 (Paris: Grasset, 1964) 257.

27. See, *Days of the Lord*, 2, *Lent*, 155–56; 3, *Easter and the Easter Season*, 30–31.

28. P. Emmanuel, *Evangéliaire*, Livre de vie 93 (Paris: Seuil, 1969) 99.

Eighteenth Sunday—Pages 165–72

1. See, ''Exil'' and ''Exode'' in *Vocabulaire de théologie biblique*, cols. 419–425, and in *Dictionnaire encyclopédique de la Bible*, 453–458.

2. See, ''Manne'' in *Vocabulaire de théologie biblique*, cols. 708–719.

3. The Bible often recalls these complaints and the temptation to return to Egypt: Num 11:4-23; 14:1-4; 17:6; 20:2-5; 21:5.

4. The unexpected arrival of this providential flock of quail, pushed by the wind and fallen in the camp, is recorded elsewhere in another context in which everything seems more natural (Num 11:31-32).

5. See, ''Manne,'' in *Vocabulaire de théologie biblique*, col. 708, n.1; and in *Dictionnaire encyclopédique de la Bible*, p. 781.

6. The word "bread," as for us today, has here the meaning of food in general.

7. On the sixth day, however, they were allowed to gather a double ration and, on the morrow, the sabbath, they found the supply for this day intact. Those who, lacking trust and disregarding the sabbath rest, went out, found nothing.

8. E. Fleg, *Moïse raconté par les Sages* (Paris: Albin Michel, 1956), 67, quoted in *Assemblées du Seigneur*, deuxième série, No 49 (Paris: Publications de Saint-André—Cerf, 1971) 40.

9. Freedom is not the faculty to choose anything, but to choose with certainty, knowing what one chooses. To choose false or evil things is not to demonstrate freedom but a weakness of intellect, which is the foundation of liberty. God is supremely free because he always wills what he clearly judges to be good. The more one hesitates to see what is good and just and to take a decision, the less one is free. We daily experience this when we say, "I don't know what to choose, what to do," and when we admire—and envy—those who choose aright without hesitation.

10. This is the truer and more necessary when one has been a Christian from infancy. Even then, some day, one must make the personal choice to be a Christian, to live as a baptized person must live. In certain cases, this personal choice is a true conversion.

11. R. Marle, *La singularité chrétienne* (Paris: Casterman, 1970).

12. Paul VI, "Discours à l'O.N.U.," 4 octobre 1965, *La documentation catholique*, 62 (1965) cols. 1737–1738.

13. To pass from the economy of the first Adam to that inaugurated by the second: Rom 5:18-19; 1 Cor 15:21-22; 45-49; 2 Cor 4:16.

14. Paul treats of newness when speaking of unleavened bread (1 Cor 5:6-8); of the Eucharist, new Covenant (1 Cor 11:25); of the apostolic ministry (2 Cor 3:5-6); of the circumcision of the heart and of our being a new creation (Gal 6:14-15); of the new life given at baptism (Rom 6:3-4); of Christian service in the newness of the Spirit (Rom 7:6).

15. Acts 2:42.

16. The lack of time is not always and for everyone an easy excuse or a false pretext for justifying oneself. When we read a gospel passage, we must not think of others but of ourselves and ask, "Is not this word meant for me?"

17. The "imprint"—the "seal"—makes us think of Jesus' baptism and of God's power which allows humans to work "signs" (Matt 12:28; Acts 10:38; Eph 1:13; 4:30; 2 Cor 1:22). It is also a term which belongs to the vocabulary of baptismal theology (Eph 1:13; 4:30; Rev 7:3-4).

18. Matt 17:5; Mark 9:7; Luke 9:35.

19. In the Law, there was a repertory of 613 precepts or interdicts. This inventory corresponds to an ever-present preoccupation: that of knowing what we must do to put ourselves right with the law and not be subject to fines, whether in the religious or in any other domain.

20. Deut 8:2-3; Wis 16:26. The manna was a trial of faith (Exod 16:4); the murmurings against Jesus recall those of the people in the wilderness (Exod 16:2); the unbelief of the people in the desert constitutes the background of the Discourse on the Bread of Life, whose central theme is faith, a theme developed elsewhere in the New Testament (1 Cor 10:1-11; Heb 3:7-19).

See, A. Jaubert, *Approches de l'Evangile de Jean*, 101.

21. Wisdom, too, invites the hungry and thirsty to come to her, saying,

Come to me, all you that year for me,
    and be filled with my fruits . . .
He who eats of me will hunger still,
    he who drinks of me will thirst for more . . . (Sir 24:18, 20).

22. Commission Francophone Cistercienne, *Tropaires des dimanches*, 95.

Nineteenth Sunday—Pages 173–80

1. 1 Kgs 17:1–19:21; 2 Kgs 1:1–2:18. See, "Elie," in *Vocabulaire de théologie biblique,* cols. 344–346, and in *Dictionnaire encyclopédique de la Bible,* 401–402; L. Monloubou, *Prophète, qui es-tu?,* Lire la Bible 14 (Paris: Cerf, 1968).

2. Elijah's return (Mal 3:23-24) must be a sign announcing the "Day of the Lord" at the end of time (Sir 48:1-11) and the coming of the Messiah (Matt 17:20-21; Mark 9:11-13). This expectation was great in New Testament times. John the Baptist's mission (Matt 17:11-14; Luke 1:17; John 1:21-25), then the manifestation of Jesus are put in relation with Elijah (Matt 16:14; Mark 6:15; Luke 9:19). Along with Moses, Elijah was at Jesus' side at the transfiguration (Matt 17:3-4; Mark 9:4-5; Luke 9:30, 33).

Elijah, one of the most popular prophetic figures in the Jewish tradition, is often mentioned in the liturgy.

Elijah is the model of the prayer of the just which obtains miracles (Jas 5:17-18). The scene of his ascension (2 Kgs 2:1-18), finally, is the origin of a whole spiritual and mystical tradition, especially among Carmelites, on the elevation of the soul to God.

3. Exod 19:5; Deut 4:20; 14:2; 32:8-9; Judg 5:3, 5, 11; 1 Kgs 8:53.

4. Baal was not the name of a god, but a term meaning Lord. As a consequence, people mentioned the Baal of such and such a place. Thus, there was in or near Jerusalem a temple of Baal (2 Kgs 11:18; 2 Chr 23:17). See, "Baal," in *Dictionnaire encyclopédique de la Bible,* 172–173. The priests in charge of one of these temples were convoked by Elijah on Mount Carmel for the famous sacrifice which cost the priests of the false lords their lives (1 Kgs 18:20-40).

5. These reigns are recorded in the Books of Kings (1 Kgs 14:21–19:21; 2 Kgs 33). After this period of religious decadence, came the reign of Joash, who had escaped the massacre of the members of his family (2 Kgs 11:1–12:13). His accession is the subject of Racine's last tragedy, *Athalie* (1691).

6. The mountain called Sinai in certain traditions is called Horeb in others. Whatever its name, a mountain is the symbolic place of the revelations of and the encounter with God. Thus in the Gospels, we have the mountain of the Discourse of the Beatitudes (Matt 5:1), of the multiplication of the loaves (John 6:3), of the transfiguration (Matt 17:1; Mark 9:2; Luke 9:28); the mountain upon which Jesus used to retire in silence and solitude in order to pray (Matt 14:23; Mark 6:48; Luke 6:12; 9:28); finally the mountain on which Jesus gathers his apostles to send them into the whole world (Matt 28:16). See, "Montagne," in *Vocabulaire de théologie biblique,* cols. 791–795.

7. Num 11:10-15; Ps 106:32-33.

8. Jer 15:10-11; 20:14-18.

9. K. Rahner, *Sur l'Eucharistie,* trans. Ch. Muller (Paris: Epi, 1966) 74–75.

10. Exod 16:35; Amos 2:10; Ps 95:10.

11. Exod 24:18; 34:28.

12. Matt 4:2, 11; Mark 1:12-13.

13. St. Bernard (1090–1153), *Sermon 83, sur le Cantique des cantiques 83:2-4,* quoted in *Lectures pour chaque jour de l'année. Prière du temp présent,* coédition, 1974, 760–761, after the translation (revised) of A. Béguin in, St. Bernard, *Oeuvres mystiques* (Paris: Seuil, 1953), 847–849.

14. L. Cerfaux, "Le thème parabolique dans l'Evangile de saint Jean," *Recueil Lucien Cerfaux,* II (Gembloux: Duculot, 1954) 23. One finds again the same method, for instance in chapter 14, with the questions of Thomas, Philip, or Judas (not Iscariot) which each time give Jesus the opportunity of clarifying his thought and making further revelations.

15. For the first time in the Discourse on the Bread of Life, John uses the term "Jews" to designate those who contradict Jesus. We must correctly understand this word. It in no way designates the whole of the people, but some religious authorities who have come

from Jerusalem and are hostile to Jesus. We must, therefore, understand "people from Judea." Beyond this original sense, the term applies to all unbelievers, whatever their origin and the times in which they live.

16. St. Augustine (354–430), *Traité sur saint Jean*, in H. Tissot, *Les Pères vous parlent de l'Evangile*, vol. 1 (Bruges: Apostolat liturgique / Paris: Société liturgique, 1953) 620–621. The text of the "poet" is from Virgil, *Eglogue*, 2.

17. A certain way of saying that we feel sorry for unbelievers—and to make them understand that this is the way we feel toward them—can be a form of contempt which constitutes a further obstacle unjustly put in their way.

18. Isa 54:13; Jer 31:33-34; Hos 2:21-22.

19. John 1:18; Matt 11:27.

20. This certitude does not authorize anybody to judge those who believe in God without going as far as believing in Christ. We can say only this: God wants all human beings to be saved; Christ died for all.

21. P. de La Tour Du Pin, *Concert eucharistique*, (Paris: Desclée, 1972) 45.

Twentieth Sunday—Pages 181–88

1. The Lectionary uses this book only two other times for Sunday liturgies: Prov 8:22-31 (Trinity Sunday, Year C) and Prov 31:10-13, 19-20, 30-31 (Third Sunday, Year A); and three times on weekdays: Prov 3:27-34; 21:1-6, 10-13; 30:5-9 (Monday, Tuesday, and Wednesday of the Twenty-fifth Week, even years).

2. As it has been transmitted to us, the Book of Proverbs gathers several collections or booklets (nine, according to the usual count) which must have had, beforehand, independent existences.

3. Effectively, the groupings are not the same in the Hebrew and Greek Bibles.

4. 1:8–9:18: after a title and a foreword (1.2-7) that is the introduction to the book.

5. Prov 1:20-33; 2:13-20; 4:1-9; 8:1-36.

6. Prov 2:16-20; 5:1-14; 6:20-35.

7. This is perhaps in Jerusalem, and this palace could be an allusion to that of Solomon, the Sage par excellence, under whose name the proverbs were written (Prov 1:20; Sir 24:10; Prov 8:15-16).

8. The dispatching of maidservants suggests the importance and the solemnity of this invitation; for, on other occasions, Wisdom intervenes in person (Prov 1:20-21; 8:1-3).

9. Prov 1:4, 10, 22, 24-33; 7:7.

10. St. Colomban (543–615), *Instructions spirituelles*, 13:2, in *Lectures chrétiennes pour notre temps*, K 4 (Abbaye d'Orval, 1972), quoted in *La Liturgie des Heures*, vol. 3, 459–460.

11. Luke 2:40, 52; 7:35; 11:31; 21:15.

12. At the end of the psalmody of Office of Lessons, lesson of the Morning Office.

13. Eph 1:10 (Fifteenth Sunday).

14. Eph 4:24 (Eighteenth Sunday).

15. John 15:18-20; Rom 13:11; Gal 3:19; Eph 6:11-13; Col 2:15-19; Phil 2:15.

16. St. Clement of Alexandria (ca. 150–215), *Le Protreptique*, I, 5, 3, Sources chrétiennes 2 (Paris: Cerf, 1949) 58.

17. Sundays in Ordinary Time, Preface 3.

18. John 3:13; see also, 6:27; 9:35; 12:34. In the Synoptic Gospels, on the contrary, the term applies to Christ in his role of Judge at the end of time.

19. John 3:14; 8:28.

20. John 5:25.

21. John 6:62; 12:23; 13:31.

22. On the link between the incarnation of God's Son and Jesus' Pasch, see, "From Bethlehem to Emmaus," *Days of the Lord: 3, Easter and the Easter Season.*

23. Matt 26:26-28; Mark 14:22-24; Luke 22:17-20; 1 Cor 11:23-25. See, J. Jérémias, *Le message central du Nouveau Testament,* Lire la Bible 8 (Paris: Cerf, 1966).

24. Up to now, John has used the Greek verb *phagein,* which simply means "to eat." From verse 54 on, he uses another, stronger verb—*trogein*—which means "to chew," "to munch," as a note (p. 2561, a) in the *Traduction Oecuménique de la Bible* indicates.

25. Certain people said, indeed, that God's Son had only assumed a human appearance, had only put on a bodily appearance. As a consequence, on the cross, he had suffered only in appearance. The proponents of this doctrine are called Docetists, from the Greek verb *dokein,* "to appear," "to seem." The origins of Docetism remain obscure, but it seems that John often aims at this erroneous doctrine, as already seen in his very strong phrase, "[a]nd the Word became flesh" (John 1:14). See the notes of the *Bible de Jérusalem* (p. 1530, a) and of the *Traduction Oecuménique de la Bible* (p. 2546, r).

26. Liturgy of the Mass, prayer at the fraction of the host.

27. In John's language, "given" means "delivered up."

28. St. Hilary, Bishop of Poitiers, (ca. 315–367), *De Trinitate,* VIII, 14, in J.-P. Migne, *Patrologie latine,* vol. 10, col. 246, trans. A. Hamman, *La messe: Liturgies anciennes et textes patristiques,* Lectures chrétiennes 9 (Paris: Grasset, 1964) 216.

29. D. Rimaud, *Des grillons et des anges* (Paris: Desclée, 1978), 106. (Fiche de chant T 126-1).

Twenty-first Sunday—Pages 189–99

1. See, "Josué" and "Sichem," in *Dictionnaire encyclopédique de la Bible,* 684–687, 1202–1203; G. Auzou, *Le don d'une conquête* (Paris:Orante, 1964). In the Hebrew Bible, the Book of Joshua—who is not its author but its hero—is classified with the second group of prophetic books, because it is a reflection on history seen as a dialogue between God and the people whom his word has created and whom he is leading to their destiny.

Shechem was the second capital of Solomon's kingdom (ca. 970–931 B.C.), then, after the schism of Jeroboam (ca. 931–910), that of the northern kingdom. After the Exile (597–538), it became the metropolis of the Samaritans, at the entrance of the defile between Mounts Ebal and Gerizim.

2. Among these objectives, there are those of quickening the awareness of one's belonging to one and the same people and of tightening the bonds which, at bottom, unite among themselves its members scattered by the necessities of daily life. This is the primary goal of all conventions of a movement, a party, etc.

3. See, R. Gantoy, "L'assemblée dans l'économie du salut," *Assemblées du Seigneur,* première série, No 1 (Bruges: Publications de Saint-André, 1962) 55–80.

4. The assembly is the primary and fundamental reality, regardless of the importance of what happens within it, in particular the Eucharist. This is why it is essential that there be Sunday assemblies, even in the absence of a priest.

5. The celebration of a sacrament is also a renewal of our faithfulness to God and our belonging to his people.

6. Origen, quoted in J. Daniélou, "Sacramentum fidei: Les figures du Christ dans l'Ancien Testament," *Etudes de théologie historique* (Paris: Beauchesne, 1958) 57.

7. Second reading of the Twentieth Sunday.

8. See Col 3:18-25, where St. Paul also speaks of the new relationships between husband and wife, children and parents, slaves and masters.

9. This is the title of a book on the evolution of the relationships between women and men, from earliest times to the present: E. Badinter, *L'un est l'autre: Des relations entre hommes et femmes* (Paris: Odile Jacob, 1986).

10. Similarly, what spiritual authors say of the obedience religious owe their superiors must be read and understood in correlation with what they enjoin upon the superiors. From this point of view, the *Rule of St. Benedict* is illuminating. Whereas chapter 5, on the obedience incumbent on monks, has 48 lines, chapters 2 and 64, devoted to the abbot, have, respectively, 118 and 56. But what is especially remarkable is Benedict's insistence on the responsibility of the superior, accountable at God's judgment for the lack of obedience of the monks entrusted to him. He must show them the good road by example more than by words. Furthermore, the whole of chapter 64 unceasingly refers to Christ, Shepherd of his flock. There is also chapter 71, dealing with the obedience monks owe one another.

11. This is the subject treated by E. Badinter, *L'un est l'autre* (n. 10).

12. P. de La Tour Du Pin, *Une somme de poésie, III,* 291-292.

13. J. Sulivan, *Le plus petit abîme* (Paris: Gallimard, 1965) 15.

14. Eucharistic prayer, invocation—epiclesis—of the Holy Spirit on the bread and wine.

15. St. Cyril of Jerusalem (315?-386), *Catéchèses mystagogiques,* IV, 3, 6, 9, *Sources chrétiennes* 126 (Paris: Cerf, 1966) 137, 139, 145.

16. John Henry Newman, "The Eucharistic Presence," *Parochial and Plain Sermons,* vol. 6, no. 11 (London: Longmans, Green, and Co., 1899) 151.

17. Vatican Council II, Dogmatic Constitution on the Church (Lumen Gentium), No. 11, *The Conciliar and Post Conciliar Documents,* ed. Austin Flannery, O.P. (Collegeville, Minn.: The Liturgical Press, 1975).

18. Vatican Council II, *Gaudium et Spes,* No. 15.

19. Vatican Council II, Gaudium et Spes, No. 38.

20. D. Rimaud, *Des grillons et des anges,* 58. (Fiche de chant T 42).

Twenty-second and Twenty-third Sunday—Page 200

1. On the Thirty-fourth Sunday, the celebration of Christ, King of the Universe, the Gospel reading is taken from John (18:33b-37).

2. See, "La Lettre de Jacques: Lecture socio-linguistique," *Cahiers Evangile* 61 (1987); L. Simon, *Une éthique de la sagesse: Commentaire de l'Epître de Jacques* (Genève: Labor et Fides, 1961).

In this letter, we see how a Christian catechesis has taken from the Old Testament elements chosen because of their permanent value. Rather than a first announcement of the gospel, we have here a rough outline of Christian morality, the Sermon on the Mount and the Beatitudes, and, more generally, the teaching of Matthew's Gospel, which insists upon the link between faith and action.

This letter was late in being incorporated into the canon of Scripture. See the introduction to the Letter of James in the *Traduction Oecuménique de la Bible,* 639-640.

It attracts our attention today particularly because of its firm teaching on right conduct in a society dominated by the split between rich and poor. See, J. Blondel, "Le fondement théologique de la parénèse dans l'Epître de Jacques," *Revue de théologie et de philosophie* 29 (1979) 141-152.

Twenty-second Sunday—Pages 201–08

1. The intention is taken into account as an aggravating circumstance (this is the case of premeditation) or an extenuating circumstance, but not if it has not been translated into action.

2. Deuteronomy is a rereading of the events and legislation at the time of the Exodus. It is an interiorization of the Covenant. Its theology is most rich, its style direct and warm. Its aim is to encourage the people to enter in earnest into the Covenant with all their heart and energy. See, the introduction to the Book of Deuteronomy in the *Traduction Oecuménique de la Bible*, 345–352, and "Deutéronome" in *Dictionnaire encyclopédique de la Bible*, 345–347.

3. Psalm 95, with this verse, is normally sung every day at the beginning of the first office of the day. However, it is provided that, if advantageous, it may be replaced by Psalm 100, 67, or 23.

4. This is the word of a sage of the Jewish diaspora in E. Wiesel, *Célébration hassidique: Portraits et légends* (Paris: Seuil, 1972) 139.

5. "The greatness of the Torah resides in the fact that it changes everyday. This is why humans find in it everyday an ever-new satisfaction." Ibid.

6. Ibid., 141–142. The *Talmud* is a vast juridical and moral compilation which includes and comments on the *Mishna*, which is a collection of laws and rules formulated by rabbis to apply and adapt biblical legislation. The *Mishna* was written down in the second and third centuries. There are two distinct *Talmuds*: the *Talmud of Babylon*, set down in writing at Sura in Mesopotamia, and the *Palestinian Talmud* (or *Talmud of Jerusalem*), written in Tiberias.

7. See, R. Draï, *La sortie d'Egypte: L'invention de la liberté* (Paris: Fayard, 1990). We would be gravely mistaken if we made fun of Jews and others whose lives are punctuated by observances bearing on details: men and women religious, for instance. We would thus fail to understand the deep meaning of this daily observance which expresses a continual faithfulness to God and which, besides, gives a structure to the self. We would thus forget that, in all relationships between persons, what counts above all, what is really significant, is the delicacy and attentiveness of every instant.

8. Prayer called "Aleynu," which concludes the synagogue worship, in S. Ben Chorim, *Le judaïsme en prière: La liturgie de la Synagogue*, Patrimoines (Paris: Cerf, 1984) 87–88.

9. Ibid., 48.

10. See, "Sagesse" in *Vocabulaire de théologie biblique*, cols. 1170–1178, and in *Dictionnaire encyclopédique de la Bible*, 1153–1155.

11. The two Greek words—*dôsis* (gift) and *dôrèma* (present)—are used only one other time in the New Testament (Phil 4:15 and Rom 5:16). For Paul, this gift is redemption: "[J]ust as through one transgression condemnation came upon all, so through one righteous act acquittal and life came to all . . . so that, as sin reigned in death, grace also might reign through justification for eternal life through Jesus Christ our Lord" (see Rom 5:12-21).

12. Eph 1:13; Col 1:5; 2 Tim 2:15.

13. John 1:14, 17; 8:45.

14. The beginning of verse 21 is not part of the liturgical reading. This exhortation is addressed to baptized persons. 1 Pet 2:1; Rom 13:12; Eph 4:22, 25. To reject evil and welcome salvation go hand in hand.

15. Acts 13:26; Rom 1:16; 1 Cor 1:18; 15:2; Eph 1:13; 1 Thess 2:13, 16; 2 Tim 3:15; Heb 4:12.

16. Matt 13:3-23, 31-32; Mark 4:26-29. The apostles are charged with scattering the word by the handful: Luke 1:2; Acts 6:2-4; 2 Cor 4:1-2; Col 1:25.

17. See, J. Dupont, "L'Evangile de saint Matthieu: Quelques clés de lecture," *Communautés et liturgies* 57 (1975) 21–32 ("Un enseignement à mettre en pratique").

18. Jas 1:26; 2:10, 14.

19. Acts 15:1-31. See, *Days of the Lord*, vol. 3, *Easter and the Easter Season*, pp. 192-95.

20. Some people remained firmly attached to this interdict, whereas others thought that to eat these meats had no religious significance. Paul shares the latter opinion, but he also thinks that we must avoid scandalizing the weak: 1 Cor 8:1-13.

21. Vatican II dealt with this question, in particular in the Pastoral Constitution on the Church in the Modern World (Gaudium et Spes), nos. 6, 56, 92, and in the Decree on the Church's Missionary Activity (Ad Gentes), nos. 11, 16, 18, 21, 22, 25, 26, 40. The most dramatic manifestation of this concern not to impose on all a particular tradition has been the introduction of living languages into the liturgy.

22. See Ninth Sunday, n. 34.

23. The question is formulated in a typical manner, "Why do your disciples not walk (halach) according to the way (halachah) of the elders?"

24. These washings, however, had one disadvantage. They meant that impurity was everywhere: in certain persons because of their condition—pagans with whom, even unknowingly, one might have had contact—or their state—people with diseases or hidden infirmities—or else their neglect of some prescriptions of legal purity. Paul, one day, sharply reproved Peter for refusing to eat with pagans (Gal 2:11-14).

Here again, we must guard against any summary and haughty judgment on this way of acting. The sign of the cross we make when going into a church after dipping our fingers in holy water is a significant gesture of purification, but only inasmuch as it is accompanied by corresponding sentiments.

25. This is the case of sacraments.

26. We must not confuse acting "according to conscience" and "with sincerity." In the former case, we conform our actions to the moral judgment of which our conscience is the bearer, even though sick. In the latter, we act without bothering to seek whether the act is good or bad.

This duty to act according to conscience seems to be excessive to certain persons. We would rather be able to refer to a list in which things are classified into two categories—"good," "bad"—so that we have no question to ask ourselves concerning their use. This desire makes light of human liberty and responsibility. On the other hand, the slightest amount of reflection will convince us that the best of things can be put to the worst of uses. Jesus gives a striking example of this: to dedicate one's goods to the Lord is excellent; but to put this consecration forward as a reason for refusing to help one's parents in need is odious (Mark 7:11-13).

27. P.-Y. Emery, "La réforme toujours nécessaire dans l'Eglise," Assemblées du Seigneur, deuxième série, No. 53 (Paris: Publications de Saint-André—Cerf, 1970) 61-62.

28. The mere intention to do good to someone never relieved a destitute person.

29. To reveal one's immoral desire can be an evil when this constitutes a temptation for other persons, for example by weakening them in the struggle they are engaged in, for their part, against a similar thought. This is why spiritual tradition teaches that we must not reveal the sins of our hearts except to persons "who know how to heal their own wounds as well as those of others." Rule of Benedict, ch. 46.

30. Origen, Commentaire sur l'Evangile selon Matthieu, XI, 15, Sources chrétiennes 166 (Paris: Cerf, 1970) 349-353.

31. Commission Francophone Cistercienne, Tropaires des dimanches, 107. (Fiche de chant A 185-1).

Twenty-third Sunday—Pages 209-16

1. Most editions of the Bible classify the Old Testament books in four groups: The Pen-

tateuch, the prophetic books, the wisdom books, the historical books. But the Hebrew Bible does not use this last category; these books are termed "first prophets."

2. The inspired sages and prophets are at a level and have a viewpoint different from that of political futurologists.

3. We would singularly minimize the prophets' role if we looked upon them simply and chiefly as inspired foretellers who have predicted the future, in particular Christ and his mission. In this case, we would have recourse to their oracles with a primarily apologetic intent to show that Jesus fulfilled these prophecies.

4. What is spoken of here is the exile to Mesopotamia of a number of the inhabitants of the kingdom of Judah, carried off by Nebuchadnezzar between 597 and 581 B.C. This exile would last until 538.

5. The prophet understands that with the successes of Cyrus, king of Persia, who continually is extending his power, the situation is bound to change. In fact, only a year after the capture of Babylon (538), he takes the first measures in favor of the Judeans. Not only does he insure the return of the exiles (Ezra 1:1-6), but he restitutes the gold and silver utensils taken by Nebuchadnezzar from the Temple (Ezra 1:7-11; 5:14-15), whose reconstruction he decrees.

6. Isa 40:1-2; 42:18-23; 43:8-10; 48:10.

7. The book of Isaiah has seen in Cyrus the one "anointed" by the Lord, chosen to accomplish his plans: Isa 41:1-2, 25; 44:28; 45:1, 13. See, "Cyrus" and "Exil" in *Dictionnaire encyclopédique de la Bible*, 319–320, 453–454. When the Bible says, "Your sins have caused your adversities. Nebuchadnezzar—or whoever else—was only the instrument of God," it does not say that this executor of divine sentences prevailed by virtue of his religious or moral superiority: a powerful person who dominates others through brute force remains an impious person. Certain modern preachers have not always spoken thus in similar circumstances. Their way of explaining the disasters striking a nation for its sins led one to understand that the others owed their victory to the merit of their lives.

8. On this topic, it is interesting to refer to rabbinical commentaries written after the New Testament accounts but echoing much older traditions. See, S. E. Rosenberg, *Le judaïsme: connaître le monde juif*, Bordas poche 25 (Paris: Bordas, 1972).

Commenting on the events of Exodus: "There were no deaf persons since all heard the Lord's word (Exod 20:18); no mute persons either since the whole people answered Moses (Exod 19:8)."

Concerning Isaiah's oracle: "All those who were suffering from bodily infirmities will be cured in the Messiah's world to come." Also, "Sins have been the cause, in this world, of the Israelites becoming blind to the Law . . . Then, they are deaf since they do not learn the Torah, and their eyes are shut since they do not see the Presence. This is why Isaiah cries,

> You who are deaf, listen,
>
> you who are blind, look and see! (Isa 42:18)

. . . What will God do in messianic times? First he will lift them to their feet, and then he will open their eyes and ears as it is written (Isa 35:5). Then they will hear the word of the Lord as it is written (Isa 30:21)." See, H. Strack and P. Billerbeck, *Kommentar z. N. T. aus Talmud und Midrasch*, (Munich, 1926) 1: 19, 593–594.

See also, R. Swaeles, "Celui qui vient pour nous guérir," *Assemblées du Seigneur*, première série, No 4 (Bruges: Publications de Saint-André, 1961) 51–64.

9. Matt 11:2-6; Luke 7:18-23.

10. This does not mean that the persons afflicted with these physical infirmities are guiltier than healthy persons. Jesus denounces such an interpretation (John 9:3).

11. Jas 1:27 (second reading, Twenty-second Sunday).

12. *Le petit Robert* defines "paternalism" as "a tendency to impose control, domination, under pretense of protection." P. Robert, *Dictionnaire alphabétique et analogique de la langue*

française, ed. A. Rey (Paris: Société du Nouveau Littré, 1976). We must recognize that the boundary line between the expression of a noble fatherly (or brotherly) sentiment and paternalism (in the pejorative sense) is not always very clear. As a consequence, one can pass from one attitude to the other unaware and without the sincerity of the truly fatherly (or brotherly) sentiment being affected. The same problem can be met among parents in relation to their children. They sincerely love their children; they are after their good with admirable devotion and total selflessness. And yet, in fact—that is, unconsciously—they exhibit a possessive, paternalistic behavior, not only ill-tolerated by their children, but liable to have serious, if not grievous, consequences on their psychological welfare, their harmonious development, and, later on, their adult lives. Moreover, not only good will and generosity enter into play, but also the way in which comportments, even the best-intentioned ones, are perceived by others.

13. Lev 19:15.

14. Rom 2:11; Eph 6:9.

15. *Doctrine des Douze Apôtres,* 12, quoted by L. Deiss, *Aux sources de la liturgie,* Vivante tradition 3 (Paris: Fleurus, 1964) 103.

16. Vatican II, Constitution on the Sacred Liturgy (Sacrosanctum Concilium), no. 2.

17. Matt 5:2; Luke 6:20.

18. G. Papini, *Mammon* (Paris: Payot, 1922), quoted in *Lectures pour chaque jour de l'année: Prière du Temps présent,* coédition (Paris, 1974) 480.

19. We notice the same traits in the narrative of the cure of the blind man of Bethsaida (Mark 8:22-26). "They brought to him a blind man and begged him to touch him. He took the blind man by the hand and led him outside the village. Putting spittle on his eyes he laid his hands on him . . ."

20. It is reported that the Emperor Vespasian (69-79) cured a blind man by putting saliva on his eyes: J. Delorme, "Guérison d'un sourd-muet: Mc 7, 31-37," *Assemblées du Seigneur,* deuxième série, No 54 (Paris: Publications de Saint-André—Cerf, 1972) 35. See also, A. Duprez, "Guérisons païennes et guérisons chrétiennes," *Cahiers biblique: Foi et vie* 9 (1970) 3-28.

21. Mark is the only evangelist who records Jesus' Aramean words: 5:41 ("Talitha koum," "Little girl, I say to you, arise!"); 14:36 ("Abba, Father").

22. Mark 3:5; 4:11-12; 7:6; 8:17-18.

23. Matt 16:16-17; Mark 8:29; Luke 9:20.

24. Saint Ambrose, *Des sacrements,* I, 1-3, Sources chrétiennes 25bis (Paris: Cerf, 1961) 61-62.

25. Isa 6:9-10; Jer 5:21; Ezek 12:2. See also Gen 1:10-12, 18, 25, 31; Isa 29:18; 32:3-4; 36:5-6; 42:7, 16, 18-19; 43:8.

26. Saint Ephraem (ca. 306-373), "Sermon sur notre Seigneur," *Le Livre d'Heures d'En-Calcat* (Dourgne, 1952) 447.

27. Commission Francophone Cistercienne, *Tropaires des dimanches,* 110. (Fiche de chant U LH 75).

Twenty-fourth Sunday—Pages 219-28

1. The four of them are used in the Lectionary: Isa 42:1-7 (Baptism of the Lord, Year A; Monday in Holy Week); Isa 49:1-6 (Tuesday in Holy Week); Isa 50:4-9 (Passion Sunday; Wednesday in Holy Week; Twenty-fourth Sunday in Ordinary Time, Year B); Isa 52:13–53:12 (Good Friday).

Concerning these "Songs of the Suffering Servant," see, the *Bible de Jérusalem,* 107; P. Grelot, *Les poèmes du Serviteur: de la lecture critique à l'herméneutique,* Lectio divina 103 (Paris:

Cerf, 1981); B. Maggioni, "Le troisième chant du Serviteur de Yahvé: Is 50, 4-9a," *Assemblées du Seigneur,* deuxième série, No 19 (Paris: Publications de Saint-André—Cerf, 1971) 28–30.

2. Some people have wondered whether this ill-treatment had a metaphorical sense. But nothing justifies this interpretation. Even today, we see—alas—men and women shamefully subjected to all sorts of torture, inflicted with technical means unknown in the past, in order to cause physical pain and degradation—all this because these persons denounce injustice and side with the oppressed.

3. The Letter to the Hebrews (10:5) places this verse of Psalm 40—quoted from the Greek translation—on Christ's lips when he entered the world:
Sacrifice and offering you did not desire,
but a body you prepared for me;
holocausts and sin offerings you took no delight in.
Then I said, "As is written of me in the scroll,
Behold, I come to do your will, O God."

4. Rom 1:16–11:36, in fact the whole of the doctrinal part of this letter.

5. This text is read on the Friday following Ash Wednesday. See *Days of the Lord, Lent,* 2:24

6. Feast of Christ, King of the Universe, Year A: *Days of the Lord,* 4:256

7. Rom 2:7; 1 Cor 15:58; 13:2; 2 Cor 9:8; Gal 6:4; 1 Thess 1:3; 2 Thess 1:11; 2:17.

8. St. Teresa of Avila, *The Interior Castle:* The Fifth Dwelling Places, Chapter 3, §11, trans. Kieran Kavanaugh, OCD, and Otilio Rodriguez, OCD (New York: Paulist Press, 1979) 101–102.

9. St. Ignatius of Antioch (d. ca. 110), *Lettre aux Ephésiens,* XIV, 1–2, Sources chrétiennes 10 (Paris: Cerf, 1951) 83–85.

10. There are 280 verses before the account of this episode and 354 afterwards.

11. Mark 9:30.

12. Caesarea Philippi is situated in the territory of the Syrophoenicians, to the north of Galilee, at the foot of Mount Hermon, near one of the principal sources of the Jordan.

13. Elijah's return was linked to the manifestation of the Messiah on the basis of a text from Deuteronomy (18:18) and, even more, on the basis of a prophecy by Malachi (3:23-24). In New Testament times, expectation of Elijah was strongly rooted in the popular mind (Matt 11:14; 17:11-13; Mark 9:11-13; Luke 1:17; 4:9).

14. Even in Herod's entourage it was said that Jesus was John the Baptist risen from the dead, or Elijah, or another prophet. Herod was inclined to think Jesus was John redivivus (Mark 6:14-16).

15. P. Emmanuel, *Tu,* 306–307.

16. Peter's profession of faith recorded here is clearly less developed than that in Matthew (16:16), who has him say, "You are the Messiah, the Son of the living God" (Twenty-first Sunday, Year A: *Days of the Lord,* 4).

17. Mark 1:24, 34, 44; 3:11-12; 5:43; 7:36-37; 8:26.

18. Isa 50:5-9a, first reading.

19. "Turned back" can be understood in different ways, in particular "when you have turned back to God or turned away from your errors," that is "converted." See Note *y* in the *Traduction Oecuménique de la Bible,* 2524.

20. P. Emmanuel, *Tu,* 312–313.

21. Matt 16:24 (Twenty-second Sunday, Year A: *Days of the Lord,* 4:171); Luke 14:27 (Twenty-third Sunday, Year C: *Days of the Lord,* 6:198–205).

22. For Mark, the gospel is Christ himself.

23. St. Augustine, *Homélie sur l'Evangile de Marc,* in *Patrologie latine,* ed. J.-P. Migne, vol. 38: col. 588, trans. from *La Liturgie des Heures* 3 (Paris, 1980) 1480–1481.

24. St. Ephrem, *Commentaire de l'Evangile concordant* or *Diatessaron,* XXXI, 15, Sources chrétiennes 121 (Paris: Cerf, 1966) 382–383.

Twenty-fifth Sunday—Pages 229–35

1. See, C. Larcher, *Etudes sur le Livre de la Sagesse,* Etudes bibliques (Paris: Gabalda, 1969) 128.

2. J. Onimus, *Le Perturbateur: Regards sur Jésus* (Paris: Cerf, 1974) 45–46.

3. The day of prayer for peace that took place in Assisi on October 27, 1986, was a memorable manifestation of this meeting in dialogue and prayer. One hundred thirty religious leaders attended, some forty of them non-Christian. See, *La documentation catholique* 83 (1986) 1065–1085.

4. Blessed Paul Giustiniani (1476–1528), in J. Leclercq, *Seul avec Dieu: la vie érémitique d'après la doctrine du Bienheureux Paul Giustiniani* (Paris: Plon, 1955) 161.

5. Pope Paul VI, *Go in Peace* (address before the United Nations, October 14, 1965), trans. Vincent A. Yzermans (St. Paul, Minn.: North Central Publishing Co., 1965) 18–19.

6. In fact, when the event occurred, the disciples were surprised and confused. The explanations we read in the account of the travelers to Emmaus (Luke 24:13-25) aim at elucidating why "it was necessary" that these events should happen, in other words, what was their meaning. Jesus does not simply say, "Nothing astonishing in all this; it was foreseen."

7. The expression "three days after"—which is already in the Book of Hosea (6:2)—has this meaning. The more precise term "on the third day" will come from the experience of the resurrection event (Matt 27:64; Luke 24:7, 46; Acts 10.40, 1 Cor 15:4).

8. H. Urs von Balthasar, *La foi au Christ,* Foi vivante 76 (Paris: Aubier, 1969) 181.

9. "The house," without further qualification, is, in Mark's Gospel, the usual place where Jesus converses with his disciples (Mark 1:29; 2:1; 7:17; 9:28; 10:10).

10. The other two announcements of the passion are also followed by a lesson for the disciples (Mark 8:34; 10:42).

11. Mark 9:33-50 constitutes a sort of "ecclesial discourse"—that is, one that concerns the life of the Church—like Matt 18 and Luke 9:46-50. In the early Church, there were already leaders more concerned with honors than service, as Matthew's Gospel, in particular, shows. See, J. Dupont, "L'Evangile de saint Matthieu," 24–25.

12. St. Augustine, "Sermon 340," 1–2, *Oeuvres complètes,* vol 19 (Paris: Vivès, 1873) 120–121.

13. Isaac de l'Etoile († ca. 1167), *Sermons,* 12, 6, Sources chrétiennes 130 (Paris: Cerf, 1967) 255.

14. Commission Francophone Cistercienne, *Tropaires des dimanches,* 116. (Fiche de chant U LH 82).

Twenty-sixth Sunday—Pages 236–43

1. Exod 33:7-11; Num 11:16; 12:4; Deut 31:14.

2. This way of speaking of the Spirit as of a quasi-physical reality that is taken, shared, distributed (1 Sam 10:5-13; 19:20) must not shock us. It is a way of describing a gift received in abundance, whose beneficiary is not the owner. It may happen that God withdraws it.

3. This is the meaning of "When the spirit came on them, they prophesied, but not again" (Jerusalem Bible). Moses was a prophet permanently established in this function (Exod 15:20; Deut 34:10). He was filled with the spirit to lead the people day after day. The others had only a delegated responsibility.

4. Nerses Snorhali (1102–1173), *Jésus, Fils unique du Père,* Sources chrétiennes 203 (Paris: Cerf, 1973), 195–196.

5. Isa 5:8; Jer 5:27-28; 9:22; Pss 62:11; 73:4-9; Luke 6:24-26; 12:15-21.

6. See also Matt 6:19-20; Luke 12:33.

7. St. Basil (329–379), *Homélie 6 contre la richesse*, 7, in A. Hamman, *Riches et pauvres dans l'Eglise ancienne*, Lectures chrétiennes 6 (Paris: Grasset, 1962) 76.

8. *The Jerusalem Bible* (London: Darton, Longman, Todd, 1966).

9. Helder Camara, *Le désert est fertile* (Paris: Desclée De Brouwer, 1971) 33–34.

10. L. Bloy, *La femme pauvre* (Paris: Mercure de France, 1948) 179–180.

11. Gospel of the Fifteenth Sunday.

12. The same zeal was shown another time when John, along with his brother James, suggested to Jesus that they call down fire from heaven upon a village of Samaria whose inhabitants had refused to receive Jesus. On that day, the two were reprimanded (Luke 9:51-55).

13. This case is different from that reported in the Book of Acts. Those who wanted to use Jesus' name to drive out demons seem to have acted with the intent of competing with Paul (see Acts 19:15-17).

14. A.-M. Carré, *Par amour de ton nom: Dieu et les autres*, Epiphanie (Paris: Cerf, 1972) 157–158.

15. P. Emmanuel, *Evangéliaire*, Livre de vie 93 (Paris: Seuil, 1969) 112.

16. Such is Paul's teaching and he lived according to this rule: Rom 14:1-15:13; 1 Cor 8:1-9:23.

17. A.-M. Besnard, *Du neuf et de l'ancien* (Paris: Cerf, 1979) 96.

18. The Valley of Gehenna, to the south of Jerusalem, was a dump where refuse was discarded. Besides, it had a sinister reputation because of human sacrifices which had taken place there.

19. Gospel of the Twenty-second Sunday.

20. Besnard, *Du neuf et de l'ancien*, 93–94.

21. Mark's Gospel opens by presenting Jesus himself as the Good News (1:1).

22. Commission Francophone Cistercienne, *Tropaires des dimanches*, 119.

23. Easter Preface IV.

Twenty-seventh and Twenty-eighth Sunday—Pages 244–45

1. As it is put here, the question does not directly bear on this point. The case is different for the parallel text in Matthew, "Is it lawful for a man to divorce his wife *for any cause whatever?*" (19:3). In both cases, Jesus is careful not to be trapped into scholarly discussions and not to take sides in the subtle distinctions that delighted the lawyers.

2. It contains 309 verses; the Letter to the Romans, 433; the First Letter to the Corinthians, 185.

3. Besides the introductions of the *Bible de Jérusalem*, 1623–1624, and of the *Traduction Oecuménique de la Bible*, 2917-2925, see C. Spicq, *L'épître aux Hébreux*, Sources bibliques (Paris: Gabalda, 1977); A. Vanhove, "Le message de l'épître aux Hébreux," *Cahiers Evangile* 19 (1977); "Hébreux, Epître," *Dictionnaire encyclopédique de la Bible*, 568–570.

4. For a long time, the letter was attributed to Paul, but not without hesitation even in early days.

5. Two chronological points of reference: on the one hand, Clement of Rome (ca. 95) uses it; on the other hand, the author often mentions, as if it were still being celebrated, the liturgy of the Jerusalem Temple, destroyed in 70.

6. The traditional title Letter to the Hebrews is due to the fact that the author addresses readers familiar with Jewish practices and traditions. The addressees seem, indeed, to be Judeo-Christians, that is, Jewish converts.

7. Other excerpts from the Letter to the Hebrews (for a total of 186 verses) are read at the daily masses in Ordinary Time, odd years.

Twenty-seventh Sunday—Pages 246-55

1. See G. von Rad, *La Genèse*, (Geneva: Labor et fides, 1968); "Genèse: Nos origines," *Le monde de la Bible* 9 (1979); P. Grelot, "Homme qui es-tu? Genèse 1-11," *Cahiers Evangile* 4 (1973); *Le couple humain dans la Bible*, Lectio divina 31 (Paris: Cerf, 1962) 31-36; A. Gelin, *L'homme selon la Bible*, Foi vivante 75 (Paris: Ligel, 1968); A. Barucq, "Je vais lui faire une aide . . . (Gn 2, 18-24)," *Assemblées du Seigneur*, 2ème série, No 58 (Paris: Publications de Saint-André—Cerf, 1974) 26-32.

One unjustly indicts both the authors of the Book of Genesis when one brings up scientific explanations of the origins and the scientists when one challenges them with what faith tells us. The Bible teaches that God created everything. Science scrutinizes observable facts and seeks to determine the causal relations between phenomena perceived by our senses. The transcendent God is not among these. Faith does not impose any limit to scientific curiosity and research which, for their part, do not block the scientists' way to faith in a Creator-God.

2. The other narrative is found in Gen 1:1-24.

3. Man (*adam*) is made out of clay (*adamah*).

4. O. Clément, *Questions sur l'homme* (Paris: Stock, 1972) 53-54.

5. Christian tradition has delighted in comparing Adam's sleep with that of the dead Christ. In the same way as Eve, the "mother of the living," was formed during the first man's sleep, the Church, the new Eve who gives birth to new creatures, was born from the open side of the crucified Christ.

6. No translation can render the play on words and the idea it expresses. For "man"— ish—calls his companion *ishshah*.

7. The other narrative says the same thing in a less picturesque way:

God created man in his image;
> in the divine image he created him;
> male and female he created them.

It stresses, besides, that God entrusted them both with ruling over the world. Our present narrative omits the mention of this mission because it is oriented toward the story of the fall and expulsion from Paradise. Each of the two accounts corresponds to one tradition and represents one stage of reflection. The Book of Genesis took both in without attempting to harmonize them. The two texts must be read and meditated one after the other, as they are—as one reads the Gospels—each of which represents one tradition, one particular manner of announcing the unique good news.

8. P. Emmanuel, *Duel* (Paris: Seuil, 1979) 151.

9. It is the more surprising to find, even in the Bible, belittling, even contemptuous expressions regarding women. One is embarrassed to recognize that the vibrant eulogy to "the worthy woman" (*Traduction Oecuménique*) refers only to her abilities as a "perfect housewife" at the service of her husband and of the prosperity of his possessions (see Prov 31:10-31). Of course, one can say that these proverbs reflect the general viewpoint of the surrounding milieux. It remains that the Bible is not yet free from a certain male-female antagonism contrary to the teaching of the first chapters of the Book of Genesis.

10. Usually it is only bigamy that is practiced: Gen 22:20-24; 29:15-30; 30:1-9; 36:11-12; Deut 21:15, 1 Sam 1:2; 2 Chr 24:3.

11. 2 Sam 3:2-5; 5:13; 12:8; 15:16; 20:3; 1 Kgs 11:3; 20:3-7; 2 Kgs 24:15; 2 Chr 11:21-23; 24:3. It was most often the desire to have many children that led men to take a second wife (see Gen 1:28; 9:1; Ps 127:3-7) especially if the first wife was barren or bore only daughters. They had to reckon also with the many interdicts relative to conjugal intercourse and with the fact that married very young, soon exhausted by pregnancies and work, women had a rather short period of fecundity.

12. Prov 5:15-19; 12:4; 18:22; 19:14; 31:10-31: Qoh 9:9; Sir 26:1-4.

13. Isa 50:1; 54:6-7; 62:4-5; Jer 2:2; Ezek 16:8; Hos 2:4-6.

See "Mariage" in *Vocabulaire de théologie biblique*, cols. 710–713, and in *Dictionnaire encyclopédique de la Bible*, 790–792.

14. See above, "The Twenty-seventh and Twenty-eighth Sunday in Ordinary Time."

15. See note 3 above.

16. This text is read at the Mass of the Day on Christmas.

17. Cardinal E.-C. Suhard, "Le prêtre dans la cité," Pastoral Letter, April 14, 1949, *La documentation catholique* 46 (1949), col. 587. The quotation from St. Augustine comes from *Commentary on Psalm 109:3* [110:3].

18. The grouping, after the words on scandal (Mark 9:38-48, Twenty-sixth Sunday) of these two teachings and the episode of the rich man (Mark 10:17-30, Twenty-eighth Sunday) probably comes from early catechesis.

19. Deut 24:1-4. It was the case if a young woman or her father had not revealed that she was not a virgin. But any false accusation invalidated the divorce, and in the case of calumny compensation was due (see Deut 22:13-19; 28-29). Of course, we read in the Book of Sirach, "If she walks not by your side, / cut her away from you" (Sir 25:25). But we deal here with one of those maxims found in all cultures and milieux, not with a legislative text. See "Divorce" in *Dictionnaire encyclopédique de la Bible*, 359.

20. See "Femme," ibid., 472–473.

21. Gen 16:4; 29:31-30:24; Exod 20:12; 21:17; Lev 19:3; 20:9; Deut 21:18-21; 27:16; Prov 19:26; 20:20; 23:22; 30:17; Sir 3:1-16.

22. Miriam (Exod 15:20-21; Num 12:1-2; Mic 6:4), Deborah (Judg 4:4), Huldah (2 Kgs 22:14-15), Noadiah (Neh 6:14), still others whose names have not been preserved (Ezek 13:17).

23. Exod 20:14; Lev 20:10; Deut 5:18. See "Adultère" in *Vocabulaire de théologie biblique*, cols. 24–25, and in *Dictionnaire encyclopédique de la Bible*, 19–20.

24. This probably explains why John the Baptist reproved Herodias (Mark 6:17-18). Perhaps Jesus' questioners also wanted to know his opinion on this "new" rule.

25. At least among the Hellenized Jews, the wife could initiate the divorce. Thus, the Jewish historian Josephus (ca. 37–ca. 100) had been abandoned by his wife.

26. To accept this conception of marriage as sacred never was easy. Already in apostolic times, there were failures, as attested, it seems, by Matthew 19:9. The Church continues to strive to resolve these failures in a spirit of mercy without undermining the principle of the indissolubility of Christian marriage. In a society no longer Christian, she does not impose, with the same rigor as in former days, sacramental marriage on baptized persons who do not perceive its sacred character and do not understand the indissolubility willed by God. However, the Church does not forsake the couples united by a civil marriage; on the contrary, she tries to find appropriate pastoral approaches.

27. Asterius, bishop of Amasea in Asia Minor (d. after 400), *Cinquième homélie sur saint Matthieu 19,3*, Lectures chrétiennes pour chaque jour de l'année (Paris: A.E.L.F., 1974) 619.

28. On the use of the verb "prevent" in a baptismal context, see J. Jérémias, *Le baptême des enfants pendant les quatre premiers siècles* (Le Puy—Lyon: Xavier Mappus, 1967) 68-74.

29. Matt 11:25; Luke 10:21.

30. P. Talec, *Laissez-vous tenter par Dieu: Homélies à la télévision* (Paris: Centurion, 1977), 76–77.

31. "This is a great mystery, but I speak in reference to Christ and the church" (Eph 5:32).

32. D. Rimaud, "Au Dieu de toute Alliance," *Les arbres dans la mer* (Paris: Desclée, 1975) 57–58.

Twenty-eighth Sunday—Pages 256–64

1. The phenomenon is almost as old as humanity itself. It was observable in particular in opulent cities of antiquity, in which wealth and luxury were displayed under all forms. But today, it has increased extraordinarily because in all countries, even the poorest, publicity creates unceasingly new and more numerous needs, so that one would be more at a loss than ever if, among all the goods proposed as indispensable, one had to choose the most desirable.

2. Wis 6:1–7:21.

3. The author is a cultured Jew of the end of the first century B.C. The common opinion is that he wrote his book during the reign of the emperor Augustus (31–14). He seems to have lived in Alexandria. In 58 B.C., the city had 300,000 freemen and twice as many slaves and mercenaries. In 50 B.C., its library boasted 700,000 volumes. Destroyed by fire in 47 B.C., it was partly reconstituted by Mark Anthony, who had 200,000 volumes placed there. It was definitively lost in A.D. 389 under Theodosius, emperor of Byzantium. See "Alexandrie" in *Dictionnaire encyclopédique de la Bible,* 32–34.

4. See "Aux racines de la sagesse," *Cahiers Evangile* 28 (1979); "Sagesse" in *Vocabulaire de théologie biblique,* cols. 1170–1178, and in *Dictionnaire encyclopédique de la Bible,* 1153–1155.

Besides the Book of Wisdom, the Second and Third Books of Israel Martyrs were written in this circle in which the Greek translation of the Bible, called the Septuagint, also was written—between the third and first centuries B.C. And we cannot forget the imposing work—exegetical, theological, and apologetic—of the Jew Philo, born in Alexandria between 15 and 10 B.C.

5. We must attempt to realize the magnitude of the efforts necessary to understand the old text and to adapt the Hebrew Bible into a Greek translation: problems of vocabulary and syntax arising from two radically different languages, but also the necessity of having recourse to concepts belonging to another culture, and all this while remaining as closely faithful to the original as possible.

6. Today, thanks to our means of communication, we are confronted everywhere by the worldwide diversity of cultures.

7. 1 Kgs 3:9-13; 2 Chr 1:1-13.

8. We can appreciate the force of these statements if we remember they were formulated in a city renowned for its stonecutters, goldsmiths, and silversmiths.

9. Swami Paramananda, *Mon Credo: Poèmes mystiques* (Lausanne: Pierre Genillard, 1954), 29.

10. The author insists on this prayer: Wis 8:17-9:18. See also Sir 51:13-22.

11. This superiority is a frequent theme of wisdom literature: Prov 3:13-15; 8:11, 19; 16:16; Pss 19:11; 119:72, 127; Job 38:15-19; see Matt 13:44.

12. Symeon the New Theologian (949–1022), *Hymnes,* 16, Sources chrétiennes 174 (Paris: Cerf, 1971) 11–13.

13. See 1 Kgs 3:9-13; 2 Chr 1:1-13. See also Gen 2:9—the discernment of good and evil is a "reserved" privilege.

14. Num 11:17, 23; Ezra 7:25; Prov 16:10; 2 Sam 14:17, 20; 23:1; 1 Kgs 3:11, 28; Dan 1:17.

15. Heb 1:1-2, second reading of the Mass of Christmas Day.

16. The Holy Spirit impelled the authors to write (this is why we say that the Scriptures are "inspired") and kept them from all error within the limits of the literary genre of the

writings and the authors' intent (this quality of the Scriptures is called "inerrancy"). The writings the Church lists (the "canon") as inspired Scriptures are called "canonical." See *Days of the Lord*, 3:321, n.2.

17. "Bible" comes from "Byblos," a city of ancient Phoenicia—today called Jebeil, about twenty-five miles north of Beirut—that controlled the trade of papyrus on which people wrote as early as the sixth century B.C. Very early, the Greek word *biblos* came to designate that on which people wrote, but also what was written. The plural, *biblia*, of the diminutive *biblion* became the name of the book of Scriptures. In Late Latin the Greek plural was taken to be singular, *biblia*, hence *Bible*.

18. Therefore, it is important and significant that this word should be proclaimed in the liturgy, and not only read individually by each in his or her own book. This does not detract from the value of personal reading of the Bible, nor from the spiritual benefit derived from it.

19. Baudouin de Ford (d. 1190), *Traités* (ou *Sermons*), trans. Ph. Tisseau, Patrologie latine 204, ed. J.-P. Migne, cols 452–453, in *Lectures chrétiennes pour notre temps* (Abbaye d'Orval, 1970) fiche L 30.

20. Matt 4:4; John 5:24-25; Eph: 2:17; 1 Thess 2:13; Jas 1:18; 1 Pet 1:23, 25.

21. Matthew (19:16-30) and Luke (18:18-30) relate this episode and the teaching following in the same montage: after the question on divorce and Jesus' words on the kingdom and children.

22. For Mark, every title given to Jesus is marred by ambiguity as long as one has not recognized him on the cross as Son of God. See Fourth Sunday, n. 36.

23. Exod 20:12-16; Deut 5:16-20; 24:14. This answer brings to mind that of Abraham in the parable found in Luke's Gospel (16:19-31). With the Law and the prophets one knows how to behave in order to share in eternal life.

24. G. Bessière, *Le feu qui rafraîchit*, Epiphanie (Paris: Cerf, 1978) 43.

25. A.-M. Besnard, "Homélie radiodiffusée pour le 6e dimanche du Temps ordinaire," *Télérama* 1154 (1972), rpt. in *Lectures pour chaque jour de l'année* (Cerf—Desclée de Brouwer— Desclée et cie—Mame, 1974) 526.

26. St. Athanasius (ca. 293–373), *Vita Antonii*, Patrologie greque 26, ed. J.-P. Migne, col. 841 C; B. Lavaud, *Vie de saint Antoine: Antoine le Grand, Père des moines* (Fribourg: Librairie de l'Université, 1943) 8.

27. St. Antony's example was of crucial importance for St. Augustine (354–430); see, *Confessions*, bk. 8: 12, 29.

28. The case is different with Jesus' word, "Some . . . have renounced marriage for the sake of the kingdom of heaven" (Matt 19:12) or with what Paul writes to the Corinthians when he preconizes the choice of celibacy, not without explicitly specifying that this is his personal advice (1 Cor 7:25-26).

29. Mark 1:16-20; 2:13-14; Matt 8:19-22; Luke 9:60-62.

30. It is common to speak of the "young" rich man on account of what Matthew says (19:22). But our gospel does not give any indication of this sort.

31. St. John Chrysostom, *Homélie 63 sur saint Matthieu*, in M.-H. Stebe—M.-D. Goudet, *Marc commenté par Jérôme et Jean Chrysostome*, Les Pères dans la foi (Paris: Desclée de Brouwer, 1986) 103.

32. J. Delorme, "Lecture de l'Evangile selon saint Marc," *Cahiers Evangile* ½ (1972) 90.

33. Pss 44:4, 7-8; 33:16-19; 107:13, 19-28; 18:20; 116:6; etc. See "Salut" in *Vocabulaire de théologie biblique*, cols. 1187–1188.

34. Pss 51:16; 118:14; etc.

35. This question is treated at length in Paul's Letter to the Romans (1:16–11:3).

36. This is not to say that only this has value in Jesus' eyes. Indeed, he teaches that on judgment day, the Son of Man will recognize as done to himself whatever good has been

done to satisfy others' needs (see Matt 25:31-46). It remains that, in this case too, the value of everything is judged in its relationship to Christ.

37. Commission Francophone Cistercienne, *La nuit, le jour,* 127-128. (Fiches de chant R 43-1; D LH 110).

Twenty-ninth Sunday—Pages 267-73

1. There are four songs of the Suffering Servant, all of which are used in the Lectionary: Isa 42:1-4 (Baptism of the Lord, Year A, see *Days of the Lord,* 1:296-297); 49:1-6 (Second Sunday in Ordinary Time, Year A, see ibid., 4:22-23); 50:4-9 (Passion Sunday, see ibid., 2:221); last, 52:13-53:12 (read in part today and in its entirety on Good Friday, see ibid., 3:24-25). See, P. Grelot, *Les poèmes du Serviteur: de la lecture critique à l'herméneutique,* Lectio divina 103 (Paris: Cerf, 1981).

2. If we consider the very individual character of the Servant spoken of in these four poems, it does not seem plausible that we have here the eulogy either of the just in general or of the chosen people undergoing the sufferings of exile.

3. When Jesus says that he has come to give his life "as a ransom," and, when he institutes the Eucharist, he refers to this type of cultic sacrifice (see Mark 10:45; 14:24).

4. See Matt 8:17; Luke 22:37; Acts 8:32-35; 1 Pet 2:22-25.

5. See "Prêtre" in *Dictionnaire encyclopédique de la Bible,* 1043-1045.

6. Exod 28:43; 29:30; Num 18:1-7.

7. Lev 10:11; Deut 33:8-10; Mal 2:7.

8. Lev 1:4, 9.

9. Fulgentius of Ruspe (468-533), *Lettres,* 14:36-37, in *Lectures chrétiennes pour notre temps* (Abbaye d'Orval) 197, fiche L 43.

10. See "Royaume" in *Vocabulaire de théologie biblique,* cols. 1142-1150, and "Royaume de Dieu" in *Dictionnaire encyclopédique de la Bible,* 1133-1136.

11. Hebrew recognized these nuances. Greek, and then Latin, used just one word: *basileia* (in Greek), *regnum* (in Latin). See these questions of vocabulary in "Royaume de Dieu" *Dictionnaire encyclopédique de la Bible,* 1133-1136.

12. Gospel of the Twenty-eighth Sunday.

13. Mark 5:37; 9:2; 13:3; 14:33-42. In his narrative, Matthew, probably wishing to spare the two apostles, has their mother approach Jesus with her request (see Matt 20:20).

14. A.-M. Besnard, *Du neuf et de l'ancien,* 33.

15. The cup of destiny, whether good or bad: Pss 11:6; 16:5; 75:9; Isa 51:17-23; Jer 25:15-26; Ezek 23:32-34. The immersion into water expresses an overwhelming misfortune: Pss 32:6; 42:8; 69:2, 16; 124:4; Job 22:11. The high priest took a bath of purification before entering the sanctuary: Lev 16:4.

16. Gospel of the Twentieth Sunday, Year C: *Days of the Lord,* 6:168-170.

17. Rom 6:3-11; Phil 3:10-11; Col 2:12.

18. St. Augustine, *Commentaire du Psaume 86,5,* in *Lectures pour chaque jour de l'année: Prière du Temps présent* (Paris: Cerf—Desclée de Brouwer—Desclée et Cie—Mame, 1974) 521.

19. Luke inserted this teaching within the framework of the Last Supper (see 22:24-27).

20. G. Bessière, *Dieu est bien jeune,* Epiphanie (Paris: Cerf, 1976) 87-88.

21. The characteristic terms of the gospel—"to serve," "to give [one's] life as a ransom for many"—are in effect found in the Songs of the Suffering Servant (see Isa 52:13; 53:10-11).

22. Commission Francophone Cistercienne, *Tropaires des dimanches,* 128. (Fiche de chant U LH 83).

Thirtieth Sunday—Pages 274–80

1. Jeremiah was sent by God "to root up and to tear down, / to destroy and to demolish," but also "to build and to plant" (Jer 1:10). This double mission made of him a man torn between his attachment to his people and the obligation to announce the disasters caused by their unfaithfulness. Besides, his oracles of threats won him, throughout his mission, numerous persecutions: several times, people wanted to do away with this person regarded as an intolerable prophet of doom and as an enemy of his own people. See: H. Cazelles, "La production du livre de Jérémie," *Masses ouvrières* 343 (1978), 9–31; J. Briend, "Le livre de Jérémie," *Cahiers Evangile* 40 (1982); "Jérémie, la passion du prophète," *Lumière et vie* 165 (1983); A. Ridouard, *Jérémie, l'épreuve de la foi*, Lire la Bible 62 (Paris: Cerf, 1983); *Jérémie, un prophète en temps de crise*, Essais bibliques (Geneva: Labor et fides, 1985); "Jérémie," "Jérémie, Lettre," and "Jérémie, Livre" in *Dictionnaire encyclopédique de la Bible*, 653–656.

2. Deut 7:6-8; 26:18-19. See John 15:16; 1 Cor 1:26-27; 1 John 4:10, 19.

3. Deut 8:5; Ezek 5:6-7; Amos 3:2. See Heb 12:5.

4. The hard road in the desert where, near the waters of Meribah, the people revolted against God, left deep traces in the collective memory of Israel: see Exod 17:1-7; Num 20:1-13.

5. See Fifteenth Sunday, n. 1.

6. Old Buddhist text quoted in A. Gélin, *Les Pauvres de Yahvé* (Paris: Cerf, 1953) 168–169.

7. In Jeremiah's vocabulary, the verb "to come back" almost always designates a turning of the heart, a conversion. See *Days of the Lord*, 2:208–209.

8. Heb 4:14-16 (Twenty-ninth Sunday, second reading).

9. The steps that lead to a more or less radical refusal, often a progressive one, of the sacramental economy are too many for us to attempt to enumerate. The same is true of the reasons that steer people in that direction or that are offered to justify their attitude. Christ, man and God, is at the heart of the sacramental character of the human relation to God. The Church, too, which is often the first object of the rejection of any intermediary between God and humans.

10. God rejects those who pretend to seize the priesthood (see Num 16–17).

11. People have pondered the question of knowing when, according to the author of the Letter to the Hebrews, God declared to Christ that he was his Son. J. Bonsirven, "Le sacerdoce et le sacrifice de Jésus Christ d'après l'épître aux Hébreux," *Nouvelle revue théologique* 65 (1969) 65, thinks that the author here alludes to the eternal filiation of the Son. On the contrary, J. Dupont, "Filius meus es tu," *Recherches de science religieuse* 35 (1948) 522, is of the opinion that what the author speaks of is the entry of the Risen One into glory.

12. For Ps 2:2, see Matt 3:17; 17:5; Acts 13:33; Heb 1:5; 2 Pet 1:17. As for Ps 110, it is the most often quoted in the New Testament and interpreted in its entirety in a messianic sense. See M. Gourgues, "Les psaumes et Jésus—Jésus et les psaumes," *Cahiers Evangile* 25 (1978).

13. See the articles in *Vocabulaire de théologie biblique*, cols. 732–733, and in *Dictionnaire encyclopédique de la Bible*, 806–807.

14. Heb 5:6, 10; 6:20; 7:1-3, 10-11, 15-17.

15. Heb 7:27; 9:11, 25-28; 10:10, 12, 14.

16. Rabbinical exegesis routinely uses this type of argument as a fulcrum for very interesting commentaries.

17. J. Daniélou, *Le mystère de l'Avent* (Paris: Seuil, 1948) 56.

18. Isa 26:19; 29:18-19; 35:5-6; 61:1.

19. Luke 4:18; Matt 11:5.

20. Matt 9:27-31; 12:22; 20:30-34; Mark 8:22-26; Luke 18:35-43; John 9:1-41. Luke (7:21) says that Jesus "granted sight to many who were blind."

21. This is one of the narratives "of transition" that give Mark's Gospel its structure (1:40-45; 4:35-41; 8:22-26; 10:46-52; 12:41-44; 14:51-52; 15:42-47). Each of them serves as a conclusion to a section of the Gospel (in this case, that which began with the second prediction of the passion, 9:30-32) and introduces the next one (that concerning the events which will take place in Jerusalem and immediate surroundings, starting with 11:1). On this structure, see B. Standaert, L'Evangile selon Marc, 109–173; L'Evangile selon Marc: Commentaire, Lire la Bible 61.

22. St. Gregory the Great (pope 590–604), Deuxième homélie sur les évangiles, in H. Tissot, Les Pères vous parlent de l'Evangile, 1 (Bruges: Apostolat ligurgique, 1954) 190.

23. Commission Francophone Cistercienne, Tropaires des dimanches, 131. (Fiche de chant G 242-1, with some modifications in the text of the stanzas.)

Thirty-first and Thirty-second Sunday—Page 281

1. This Gospel is read on Passion Sunday (also called Palm Sunday).

2. Mark 11:11-33, read on Friday and Saturday of the Eighth Week in Ordinary Time; 12:1-34, read from Monday to Saturday of the Ninth Week in Ordinary Time.

Thirty-first Sunday—Pages 282-88

1. See the introduction to Deuteronomy in the Bible de Jérusalem, 24, and the Traduction Oecuménique de la Bible, 345–352; F. Garcia-Lopez, "Le Deutéronome."

2. Deut 4:45–6:1. For this manifestation of God and the giving of the Ten Commandments see Exod 19:1 20:21.

3. This formula recurs five times in the Book of Deuteronomy: 11:5; 26:9, 15: 27:3; 31:20.

4. For nomads in the desert or their descendants, a well-watered land, planted with many trees in which bees abound and graced with rich pastures, is well nigh paradisiac.

5. This commandment is repeated five times in the books of the Deuteronomic code: Deut 10:12; 11:1; 13:4; Josh 22:5; 23:11.

6. S. Ben Chorin, Le judaïsme en prière: La liturgie de la Synagogue, Patrimoines-Judaïsme (Paris: Cerf, 1984) 43. Commentary: 41–54.

7. Deut 4:23, 39; 6:12; 32:7; etc.

8. The texts we have read since the Twenty-ninth Sunday have stressed the similarities: like all priests, Christ was taken from among human beings; his personal experience of human weakness and suffering enables him to understand those of others and to knowingly intercede with God. But he exercises his priesthood in the heavenly sanctuary, and he was instituted by God himself.

9. In the first covenant, the priests had to belong to the tribe of Levi. Today, in the Church, the choice is made by the bishop who calls those candidates whom he ordains.

10. Therefore, in the Church's sacramental regime today, a multiplicity of successive ordinations.

11. It is commonly said that one is a priest forever. This means that ordination—like baptism and confirmation—imprints a seal, the "sacramental character" which the Council of Trent (seventh session, 1547, Canon 9) defined as "a certain spiritual and indelible mark which does not allow the repetition of the sacraments of baptism, confirmation and holy orders" (G. Dumeige, La foi catholique: Textes doctrinaux du Magistère de l'Eglise [Paris: Editions de l'Orante, 1961] 378). But this does not mean that, having been ordained, one continues to exercise one's ministry after death. At any rate, the sacramental economy is strictly

for this time and not for eternity. Then, indeed, we shall not be under the regime of faith and "signs," but under that of charity, face to face, with Christ as the only intermediary—mediator—between God and the elect. "I saw no temple in the city, for its temple is the Lord God almighty and the Lamb" (Rev 21:22, Sixth Sunday after Easter, Year C; see *Days of the Lord*, 3:195–197).

12. See Thirtieth Sunday, n. 1.

13. This text is used on the Thirty-first Sunday, Year A; see *Days of the Lord*, 4:236–238.

14. *The Roman Pontifical: Ordination of Deacons, Presbyters, and Bishops* (Washington: National Conference of Catholic Bishops, Bishops' Committee on the Liturgy, 1973) 45–46.

15. On his authority, see Mark 11:27-33; on the tax due to Caesar, see Mark 12:13-17; on the resurrection of the dead, see Mark 12:18-27.

16. The episode is also told by Matthew (22:34-40). But the climate is different, as well as the context and the spirit in which the question is asked. Mark is the only one who cites the first word of the *Shema*, "Hear, O Israel!" Matthew's text is read on the Thirtieth Sunday, Year A, *Days of the Lord*, 4:233–235.

17. Likewise, every Christian, even one who has lost the habit of praying, knows at least the beginning of the Our Father.

18. First reading.

19. This text is taken up in Deuteronomy (5:6-9), which is composed of documents from diverse times. See the introductions to this book (n. 1 above).

20. This is not a mere nuance. To call God "the One" is to profess a strict monotheism. When capitalized, One is no longer an adjective, but a proper name befitting God alone.

21. This text is read at the Mass of the Solemnity of the Sacred Heart, Year A.

22. Hos 2:4-16a; 8:1.

23. In particular Lev 19:15-18, 33-34.

24. Matt 5:43-46; Luke 6:27-35; 10:29-37 (parable of the Good Samaritan); etc.

25. Alas, we must recognize that today we are not often on that level, sometimes far from it. We have only to think of the relationships between citizens belonging to different circles or social classes, between Christians of different denominations. And what shall we say about foreigners, especially those who dwell with us?

26. St. Vincent de Paul (1576–1660), "Lettre à Louise de Marillac," *Oeuvres de saint Vincent de Paul*, ed. P. Coste (Paris: 1920-1925) 2:190.

27. Ibid., 2:40.

28. Gospel of the Twenty-eighth Sunday.

29. St. Ephrem (ca. 306–373), *Commentaire de l'Evangile concordant* or *Diatessaron*, XVI, 23, Sources chrétiennes 121 (Paris: Cerf, 1966) 296.

Thirty-second Sunday—Pages 289–97

1. 1 Kgs 17:1–2 Kgs 2:14. The division of the Book of Kings into two parts is artificial: the "Cycle of Elijah" begins in the first part (according to the present division, 1 Kgs) and continues in the beginning of the second part (2 Kgs).

See "Elie" in *Vocabulaire de théologie biblique*, cols. 344–346, and in *Dictionnaire encyclopédique de la Bible*, 401–402.

2. Ahab reigned over Israel and Samaria from 874 to 853 B.C. On this king and queen and on the meaning of the word "baal," see Nineteenth Sunday, nn. 4 and 5.

3. 1 Kgs 17:1-9.

4. Gen 38:14-19; 2 Sam 14:2; Jdt 10:1-4; 16:7.

5. Among other examples in biblical stories: the meeting of Rebekah with Abraham's servant commissioned to seek a wife for Isaac (Gen 24:18-67), and especially the encounter of Jesus with the Samaritan woman at Jacob's well (John 4:1-42).

6. P. Emmanuel, *L'Autre* (Paris: Seuil, 1980) No 135.

7. Lev 16; 23:27-30; 25:9; Num 29:7-11. See "Expiations, Jour des," *Dictionnaire encyclopédique de la Bible,* 461–462. Today, Yom Kippur, along with Passover, is still the great celebration of the Jewish community. See *Days of the Lord,* 3:350, nn. 4 and 5.

8. See Gen 6:4. Azazel was the name given to the "leader of the sons of heaven." "Sent to Azazel" (Lev 16:10) approximately means "sent to the devil."

9. The Letter to the Hebrews does not devalue the rites it alludes to and does not in any way deride them. On the contrary, the author manifestly thinks highly of them. Otherwise, his "demonstration" would not have any persuasive power. Therefore, we must listen to what he says and forget the eventual, baseless caricatures of those ancient rites, in particular the scapegoat, routinely used to designate a person to whom people attribute the wrongs done by others in order to easily free themselves from any responsibility.

10. Romano Guardini, *The Lord,* trans. Elinor Castendyk (Chicago: Henry Regnery Company) 465–466.

11. Thus, in Rome during the last Council, many went to St. Peter's Square when the general sessions let out. This was a unique opportunity to see a great number of bishops and important persons. One was proud to be able to identify one of them, especially when they were well known and, even better when, before all eyes, one was able to say hello to one of them, one's own bishop for instance.

12. The parables are studded with scenes and details borrowed from daily life.

13. Luke records the warning against scribes (20:45-47) and the episode of the widow's contribution (21:1-4) in the same terms as Mark. Matthew has a much longer text listing a series of invectives against scribes and Pharisees (23:1-36), but without any mention of the widow's offering.

14. Gospel of the Thirty-first Sunday.

15. Paul writes to the Corinthians concerning the money he is is collecting for the benefit of the Jerusalem Church. Evoking the generosity of the believers in Macedonia, he says that in their poverty they showed admirable liberality. And he adds that they gave themselves (2 Cor 8:1-5).

16. R. Tagore, *L'offrande lyrique,* No 50 (Paris: Gallimard, 1949).

17. This text is read on the Thirteenth Sunday.

18. Twenty-ninth Sunday, second reading.

19. Commission Francophone Cistercienne, *Tropaires des dimanches,* 137.

Thirty-third Sunday in Ordinary Time—Pages 298–99

1. Memorial Acclamation A.

2. "End" is *eschaton* in Greek; hence, "eschatology," the study of the end times.

3. Odo Casel, *Le mystère du culte dans le christianisme,* Lex orandi 6, (Paris: Cerf, 1946), 136.

4. T. S. Eliot, "East Coker," *Four Quartets,* in *The Complete Poems and Plays* (New York: Harcourt, Brace and Company, 1952) 127.

Thirty-third Sunday—Pages 300–08

1. In Catholic Bibles, the Book of Daniel is placed after Ezekiel (thus in the Jerusalem Bible). The Hebrew Bible and Protestant Bibles place it after the Book of Esther; the *Traduction Oecuménique de la Bible* follows this custom.

On the Book of Daniel see the introduction in the *Bible de Jérusalem*, 1083–1085, and in the *Traduction Oecuménique de la Bible*, 1965–1702; *Dictionnaire encyclopédique de la Bible*, 327–330; A. Lacoque, *Daniel et son temps* (Geneva: Labor et fides, 1983).

2. Placed under the name of a prophet contemporary with the exile to Babylon (597–538 B.C.), the Book of Daniel, whose author is unknown, must have been composed toward the end of the reign of Antiochus IV Epiphanes, King of Syria (175–164 B.C.).

3. Among the best known stories are those concerning young Daniel and his companions. Selected to be in the household of Nebuchadnezzar, they are given permission to respect the traditional taboos concerning food. Their wisdom causes them to be noticed by the king. Daniel interprets the king's dreams and even sees himself entrusted with important court responsibilities. When, against his will, Nebuchadnezzar has to condemn the companions to perish in the furnace and Daniel in the lions' pit, they come out of the ordeals unharmed and their tormentors are the ones who perish (Dan 1–7).

4. Antiochus, who practiced a politics of hellenization, wanted to oblige Jews to adopt all pagan customs—especially in matters of food—and even to worship the gods. He violently persecuted them, pillaged and profaned the Temple of Jerusalem (December 7, 167 B.C.). The resistance was fierce. Some had recourse to arms. After a few remarkable successes, their heroic revolt was brutally repressed (167–166). Within this context, the Book of Daniel represents a non-violent form of resistance. It is a subversive piece of writing. For it urgently incites readers to resolute disobedience to the king by proclaiming that God and the persevering faithfulness of believers will finally prevail over the tyrant. But, as always in such circumstances, this call to rebellion is expressed in veiled terms, with imagery and symbols, with reminders of what happened in the past, in the time of king Nebuchadnezzar for instance. In fact, in 164, under Antiochus V Eupator (164–162), the Temple was reconquered and purified.

5. Apocalypse, from the Greek *apocalyptein*—"to unveil"—means "revelation" (*apocalypsis* in Greek). John's Revelation is set within a context of crisis. It urges its readers to stand fast in trial and persecution, keeping their eyes on "what must happen soon" (Rev 1:1; 22:6).

6. This way of speaking corresponds to experience. At the time of a grave crisis, people easily come to disbelieve the possibility of a happy ending which, however, remains the object of an intense hope. During this dark period, some do not cease proclaiming, "Liberation will come soon." Their assurance rekindles courage in others and, at the same time, intensifies the expectation. But when the great day does arrive, people catch themselves saying, "It was awfully long in coming. However, you were right to announce it for the near future."

7. Their names correspond to the missions entrusted to them: Raphael, "God heals" (Tob 3:17; 12:15); Gabriel, "Hero of God" (Dan 8:16; 9:21).

8. See also 10:13-21. See "Anges" in *Vocabulaire de théologie biblique*, cols. 58–61, and *Dictionnaire encyclopédique de la Bible*, 59–61; "Michel" in *Dictionnaire encyclopédique de la Bible*, 827.

9. Isa 4:3; 65:6; Mal 3:16; Dan 12:1; Pss 56:9; 87:6; Luke 10:20; Rev 13:8; 20:12.

10. Rev 2:11; 20:6, 14; 21:8. It is here, in the Book of Daniel, that the promise of individual resurrection is clearly stated for the first time.

11. Indeed, a realistic representation cannot express the profound transformation of a risen being of flesh who, nonetheless, will keep his or her identity. Paul then speaks of a "spiritual body" (1 Cor 15:44), an expression that baffles the imagination.

12. Ps 107:10; Luke 1:79.

13. See also John 1:9; 8:12; 1 John 1:7.

14. Isa 30:26; 60:19-20; 65:17; Rev 21:23-24.

15. G. von Le Fort, *Hymnes à l'Eglise* (Tournai: Casterman, 1952) 104.

16. The omitted verses, 15-17, are a quotation from the Book of Jeremiah (31:33-34) in which the author sees a promise of the holiness gained for humanity by Christ's sacrifice.

> '' 'This is the covenant I will establish with
> them after those days,' says the Lord:
> 'I will put my laws in their hearts,
> and I will write them upon their minds,'
> he also says:
> 'Their sins and their evildoing
> I will remember no more.' ''

Jer 31:31-34 is read on the Fifth Sunday in Lent, Year B. See *Days of the Lord,* 2:152-154.

17. This sort of liturgy with animal sacrifices has become so foreign to our way of thinking, as well as to our conception and practice of worship, that we instinctively tend to deny any meaning or value to it and even to proudly despise such a religious expression. This is an ever-present danger when we are faced with models belonging to another culture and another sensibility. Hence come ridiculous misunderstandings and seriously erroneous judgments. In any case, the author of the Letter to the Hebrews, for his part, knew too well the Temple liturgy and its grandeur to fall into this defect and paint a caricature. See Thirty-second Sunday, n. 9.

18. St. John Chrysostom, *Homélies sur l'Epître aux Hébreux,* 13:3, *Oeuvres complètes de saint Jean Chrysostome,* trans. J. Bareille (Paris, Vivès, 1873) 10:448.

19. Ibid., 18:1, 471.

20. Certain ways of speaking of a priest as another Christ are, to say the least, ambiguous. Paul had a more exact notion of his mission and of the responsibility of the Apostles instituted by the Lord, ''We are ambassadors for Christ, as if God were appealing through us'' (2 Cor 5:20); ''Paul, servant of Christ Jesus.'' See Rom 15:8, 16; 2 Cor 6:4; 11:23; Eph 3:7; Col 1:7, 23, 25.

21. It is impossible to indicate all the scriptural texts in which we find this expression, the meaning of which is very complex anyway. The notion of ''Day of the Lord'' is comparable to that of ''parousia'' (a Greek word coming from *pareinai,* ''to be present'') which, in the religious sense, belongs chiefly to the New Testament. See ''Jour du Seigneur'' in *Vocabulaire de théologie biblique,* cols. 618–625; ''Jour de Yahvé'' and ''Parousie'' in *Dictionnaire encyclopédique de la Bible,* 688–690 and 990ff.

22. See n. 5 above.

23. This phenomenon occurs in any age. We can see it today. One is not a little surprised to observe it flourishing in a particular manner in circles ignorant of things religious, but imbued with the scientific spirit. In order to nourish and corroborate these ''visions,'' people indiscriminately draw from all possible sources including, of course, biblical apocalypses.

24. Isa 13:10; 34:4; Joel 2:10; 4:15; Dan 7:13-14.

25. To limit ourselves to Mark's Gospel, 2:10, 28; 8:31, 38; 9:9, 12, 31; 10:33, 45; 13:26; 14:21, 41, 62.

26. Again, in Mark's Gospel, 1:15; 4:11, 26, 30; 9:1, 47; 10:14-15, 23-25; 11:10; 12:34; 14:25; 15:43.

27. Matt 24:1-44; Mark 13:1-37; Luke 21:5-33. In all three, the point of departure is a remark made by the disciples on the splendor of the Temple, whose destruction Jesus announces.

28. Even if certain traits refer with some precision to specific events—the destruction of the Temple in particular—if there is a mention of a tide of persecutions, of the preaching of the Gospel throughout the entire word, it would be risky to seek to refer each element

to a precise historical event, risky to say the least and of scant interest: the purpose of this prediction lies elsewhere.

29. See n. 24 above.

30. Let us not picture these events in the way films of cosmic catastrophes or horror movies do it, for example. The most successful do frighten those who forget that they are seeing a film. But most do not take them absolutely seriously. We tell ourselves that reality will be completely different and that we shall not witness the End comfortably settled in our seats, which makes a huge difference.

31. Gen 1:2-5, the first day.

32. Gen 1:14-19, the fourth day. Psalms in particular often evoke the regularity of these "signs" that imperturbably follow their courses, fixed by God: Pss 8:4; 89:38; 104:19; 136:7-9.

33. Mark 1:1, 14.

34. In general, people think that Mark's Gospel was written between 65 and 75. Even if it did not take place before the writing, the ruin of the Temple in Jerusalem was a still recent event at the time the Gospel was distributed; for it certainly took several years in an era when the copies of a book had to be done by hand one after the other, which was time-consuming even for a small book.

35. See R. Swaeles, "Rassemblement et pèlerinage des dispersés," Assemblées du Seigneur, première série, No 78 (Bruges: Publications de Saint-André, 1965) 37-78.

36. J. Dupont, "La parabole du figuier qui bourgeonne (Mc 13,28-29 par.)," Etudes sur les Evangiles synoptiques, I, Bibliotheca Ephemeridum theologicarum lovaniensium LXX-A (Louvain: University Press—Peeters, 1985) 474-497.

37. John Henry Newman, "Sermon 17," Parochial and Plain Sermons (London—New York—Bombay: Longmans, Green, and Co., 1899) 6:243-244.

38. Ibid., 246.

39. P. de La Tour Du Pin, Psaumes (Paris: Gallimard, 1970) 315.

Thirty-fourth Sunday—Pages 309-17

1. Vatican II, opened by John XXIII on October 11, 1962, closed by Paul VI on December 8, 1965.

2. See Days of the Lord, 4:256-264, for the origins and evolution of this feast instituted in 1925 by Pius XI.

3. Mark is our guide in Year B, despite the fact that from the Seventeenth to the Twenty-first Sunday the reading of his Gospel is interrupted. Instead, we read Jesus' discourse after the multiplication of loaves in John's Gospel (6:1-69).

4. The reason is that Mark's Gospel contains no text that explicitly deals with this kingship of Christ, comparable to the great scene of the Judgment in Matthew (25:31-46, Year A) or to that of Luke (23:35-43, Year C) which reports Jesus' answer to the good thief's request, "Jesus, remember me when you come into your kingdom."

5. On the Book of Daniel, see Thirty-third Sunday, nn. 1 to 5.

6. This literary device structures the whole of Daniel. Scenes succeed one another according to the logic of imagination and are linked to one another according to their conventional meanings because each one is usually followed by its interpretation.

7. These four empires are seen as four monstrous beasts; their description is frankly surrealistic.

8. See Thirty-third Sunday, n. 4. The symbolic language which designates the tyrant without naming him—but everybody understands—perfectly fits this type of literature, which is a form of resistance to oppression and an encouragement addressed to those who refuse

to submit to it. When Nazi power seemed invincible, Cardinal Saliège of Toulouse, France, wrote: "There are mountains that slide. There are black clouds that burst. There is violence that wears out. There are houses that collapse. There are species that disappear. There are colossi that sink. There are earthquakes that swallow up. There are vexations which betray weakness. There are radio broadcasts that lie. There is one God, who never fails" (*Les menus propos du cardinal Saliège*, II: *Le Français* [Toulouse: Editions l'Equipe, 1947] 21–22). These maxims would have been innocent in another context. At the date of their publication, they were a bold and courageous denunciation. Nobody was named, but everybody knew who and what was in question. The final appeal to God's immutability proclaimed what was, under the circumstances, the true foundation of hope.

9. It is certain that the Ancient One designates God; this is why Bibles capitalize this title. Aged, he is ageless, which is a way of suggesting that he possesses life without beginning or end. There is nothing in this representation that evokes an easy-going God, in the bad sense of the term.

10. See "Fils de l'homme" in *Vocabulaire de théologie biblique*, cols. 470–475, and in *Dictionnaire encyclopédique de la Bible*, 480–482.

11. Pierre Teilhard de Chardin, *The Divine Milieu* (New York, Evanston, and London: Harper & Row, Publishers, 1960) 133.

12. Rev 1:1; 22:6-7, 20. Concerning this book, see the introductions in the *Bible de Jérusalem*, 1779–1781, and the *Traduction Oecuménique de la Bible*, 3023–3029; "Apocalypse, Livre" in *Dictionnaire encyclopédique de la Bible*, 87–89; A. Läpple, *L'Apocalypse de Jean*, Lire la Bible 24 (Paris: Cerf, 1970); P. Prigent, *"Et le ciel s'ouvrit"*: *L'Apocalypse de saint Jean*, Lire la Bible 51 (Paris: Cerf, 1980); D. Mollat, *Une lecture pour aujourd'hui: l'Apocalypse*, Lire la Bible 58 (Paris: Cerf, 1982).

The book could have been written during the reign of Domitian (81–96) or during that of Trajan (98–117).

13. Despite its title, John's book cannot be interpreted as one of the contemporary Jewish apocalypses. The prophetic "visions" certainly occupy the greatest part of the book (4:1–22:15), but they concern Christ and the full manifestation of his work of salvation. Besides, we cannot forget the important letters to the seven Churches (1:4–3:22).

14. John 3:11, 32, 34; 5:19; 7:16; 8:26, 28; 12:49; 14:10, 24.

15. "Anamnesis" means "memory," "evocation of the past." Every Eucharistic prayer contains the anamnesis of the work of Christ: his passion, death, resurrection, ascension.

16. Memorial Acclamation B.

17. First reading above.

18. Water—Spirit: John 3:5; 4:14; 7:38-39. Blood—Eternal Life: John 6:53-55.

19. This way of proclaiming the Lord's words is typical of the prophets' language and of the liturgy, a prophetic action. The Lord, whose words are reported, is not a faraway Lord. He himself speaks, here and now, through the prophet's mouth—"oracle, the word of the Lord"—in the same way he himself acts, here and now, through what his servant, the minister of liturgy and sacraments, does and says. The classical formula does explain this well, "Peter baptizes, Judas baptizes, it is always Christ who baptizes."

20. "Amen, amen, I say to you, before Abraham came to be, I AM" (John 8:58). But also, "I am" the shepherd, "the gate for the sheep" (John 10:7), the Way, the Truth, and the Life (John 14:6). See *Days of the Lord*, 3:143–144 (and n. 19), 158–159.

21. St. Patrick (ca. 389–461), "The Lorica," *The Works of St. Patrick*, trans. Ludwig Bieler, Ancient Christian Writers 17 (Westminister, Md.: The Newman Press; London: Longman, Green and Co., 1953).

22. John 18:24. The arraignment of Jesus before the religious authorities takes place before Annas, the father-in-law of the high priest (see 18:13-14, 19-24). The trial before Pilate is in 18:28-19:16 (29 vv.).

23. John's Gospel presents in an original way the suit brought against Jesus by his own people. This suit is at the heart of the discussions following the cure of the man born blind and of the questioning to which this man is subjected. By expelling him from the Synagogue, the authorities seek to harm Jesus (see 10:22-42). The decision to put him to death is taken after the raising of Lazarus (see 11:1-54): " 'It is better . . . that one man should die instead of the people, so that the whole nation may not perish.' He did not say this on his own, but since he was high priest for that year, he prophesied that Jesus was going to die for the nation" (11:50-51).

His dossier, already compiled by the religious authorities, is the occasion for his appearing before Pilate. Several times, the procurator leaves the tribunal where he is making his own inquiry in order to discuss the case with the leaders of the people (see 18:29, 33, 38; 19:4-5, 9).

24. See D. Mollat, "Jésus devant Pilate," *Bible et vie chrétienne* 39 (1961) 23-31; Cl. Boismard, "La royauté universelle du Christ," *Assemblées du Seigneur*, deuxième série, No 65 (Paris: Publications de Saint-André—Cerf, 1973), 36-46.

25. "It is you who say I am a king." This translation is found in the Lectionary and the *Traduction Oecuménique de la Bible* and renders Jesus' answer somewhat ambiguous. The translation of the Jerusalem Bible is more clearly affirmative, "It is you who say it . . . Yes, I am a king."

26. See "Vérité" in *Vocabulaire de théologie biblique*, cols. 1328-1335, and in *Dictionnaire encyclopédique de la Bible*, 1301-1302.

27. See *Days of the Lord*, 3:158-161.

28. One would have to quote the 176 verses of Ps 119.

29. St. Augustine, *Traité 115 sur l'Evangile de saint Jean*, in H. Tissot, *Les Pères vous parlent de l'Evangile* (Bruges: Apostolat liturgique, 1955) 2:466-467.

30. Gospel, Twenty-eighth Sunday.

31. J. Frié, in *Hymnaire de la Liturgie des Heures* (Paris: Cerf—Chalet—Levain, 1989) 213, and in *Missel noté de l'assemblée* (Paris: Brepols—Cerf—Chalet—Levain, 1990) 421. (Fiche de chant P 128).

Postscript—Pages 318-20

1. Rev 7:9-17; 14:1; 21:1-7, 9-27; 22:5.

2. Mark's Gospel was almost totally absent from the liturgy prior to Vatican II. Only eleven excerpts were read: 6:47-56 (Saturday after Ash Wednesday); 14:32–15:46 (Tuesday in Holy Week); 16:1-7 (Easter); 16:14-20 (Ascension); 8:1-9 (Sixth Sunday after Pentecost); 7:31-37 (Eleventh Sunday after Pentecost); 9:16-28 (Wednesday of Ember Days in September); 10:13-21 (February 27, feast of St. Gabriel of Our Lady of Sorrows); 6:17-29 (August 29, Beheading of St. John the Baptist); 11:22-24 (November 17, feast of St. Gregory the Wonderworker); 16:15-18 (December 3, feast of St. Francis Xavier). In sum, 169 verses of a Gospel that contains 679; only 30 verses were read on Sundays or a major feastday.

3. Commission Francophone Cistercienne, *Prières aux quatre temps: Des poèms et des chants*, Vivante liturgie 101 (Paris: Publications de Saint-André—Centurion, 1986) 67. (Fiche de chant I LH 172).